USER EXPERIENCE AS INNOVATIVE
ACADEMIC PRACTICE

Foundations and Innovations in Technical and Professional Communication

Series Editor: Lisa Melançon

Series Associate Editors: Kristin Marie Bivens and Sherena Huntsman

The Foundations and Innovations in Technical and Professional Communication series publishes work that is necessary as a base for the field of technical and professional communication (TPC), addresses areas of central importance within the field, and engages with innovative ideas and approaches to TPC. The series focuses on presenting the intersection of theory and application/practice within TPC and is intended to include both monographs and co-authored works, edited collections, digitally enhanced work, and innovative works that may not fit traditional formats (such as works that are longer than a journal article but shorter than a book).

The WAC Clearinghouse and University Press of Colorado are collaborating so that these books will be widely available through free digital distribution and low-cost print editions. The publishers and the series editors are committed to the principle that knowledge should freely circulate and have embraced the use of technology to support open access to scholarly work.

Other Books in the Series

Joanna Schreiber and Lisa Melançon (Eds.), *Assembling Critical Components: A Framework for Sustaining Technical and Professional Communication* (2022)

Michael J. Klein (Ed.), *Effective Teaching of Technical Communication: Theory, Practice, and Application* (2021).

USER EXPERIENCE AS INNOVATIVE ACADEMIC PRACTICE

Edited by Kate Crane and Kelli Cargile Cook

The WAC Clearinghouse
wac.colostate.edu
Fort Collins, Colorado

University Press of Colorado
upcolorado.com
Denver, Colorado

The WAC Clearinghouse, Fort Collins, Colorado 80523

University Press of Colorado, Denver, Colorado 80202

© 2022 by Kate Crane and Kelli Cargile Cook. This work is licensed under a Creative Commons Attribution-NonCommercial-NoDerivatives 4.0 International.

ISBN 978-1-64215-136-7 (PDF) | 978-1-64215-137-4 (ePub) | 978-1-64642-268-5 (pbk.)

DOI 10.37514/TPC-B.2022.1367

Library of Congress Cataloging-in-Publication Data

Names: Crane, Kate, editor. | Cargile Cook, Kelli, 1959- editor.
Title: User experience as innovative academic practice / edited by Kate Crane and Kelli Cargile Cook.
Description: Fort Collins, Colorado : The WAC Clearinghouse ; Boulder, Colorado : University Press of Colorado, 2022. | Series: Foundations and innovations in technical and professional communication | Includes bibliographical references.
Identifiers: LCCN 2022009833 (print) | LCCN 2022009834 (ebook) | ISBN 9781646422685 (paperback) | ISBN 9781642151367 (adobe pdf) | ISBN 9781642151374 (epub)
Subjects: LCSH: Instructional systems—Design—Case studies. | Curriculum planning—Case studies. | Student participation in curriculum planning—Case studies.
Classification: LCC LB1028.38 .U74 2022 (print) | LCC LB1028.38 (ebook) | DDC 371.3—dc23/eng/20220419
LC record available at https://lccn.loc.gov/2022009833
LC ebook record available at https://lccn.loc.gov/2022009834

Copyeditor: Meg Vezzu
Designer: Mike Palmquist
Series Editor: Lisa Melonçon
Series Associate Editors: Kristin Marie Bivens and Sherena Huntsman

The WAC Clearinghouse supports teachers of writing across the disciplines. Hosted by Colorado State University, it brings together scholarly journals and book series as well as resources for teachers who use writing in their courses. This book is available in digital formats for free download at wac.colostate.edu.

Founded in 1965, the University Press of Colorado is a nonprofit cooperative publishing enterprise supported, in part, by Adams State University, Colorado State University, Fort Lewis College, Metropolitan State University of Denver, University of Alaska Fairbanks, University of Colorado, University of Denver, University of Northern Colorado, University of Wyoming, Utah State University, and Western Colorado University. For more information, visit upcolorado.com.

Land Acknowledgment. The Colorado State University Land Acknowledgment can be found at https://landacknowledgment.colostate.edu.

Contents

Acknowledgments vii

1. Out of Industry, Into the Classroom: UX as Proactive Academic Practice. . . 3
   Kate Crane

2. Beyond Lore: UX as Data-Driven Practice 25
   Kelli Cargile Cook and Kate Crane

3. User Profiles as Pedagogical Tools in the Technical and Professional
   Communication Classroom 39
   Sarah Martin

4. User Experience and Transliteracies in Technical and Professional
   Communication 65
   Laura Gonzales and Josephine Walwema

5. Using Student-Experience Mapping in Academic Programs: Two
   Case Studies 87
   Tharon W. Howard

6. "A Nice Change of Pace": Involving Students-as-Course-Users Early
   and Often 109
   Beau Pihlaja

7. Learning from the Learners: Incorporating User Experience into the
   Development of an Oral Communication Lab. 137
   Lindsay Clark and Traci Austin

8. Ideating a New Program: Implementing Design Thinking Approaches
   to Develop Program Student Learning Outcomes. 161
   Luke Thominet

9. Using UX Methods to Gauge Degree Efficacy 197
   Kelli Cargile Cook

10. Real-World User Experience: Engaging Students and Industry
    Professionals Through a Mentor Program 219
    Lee-Ann Kastman Breuch, Ann Hill Duin, and Emily Gresbrink

11. User Experience Design and Double Binds in Course Design. 251
    Mark Zachry

12. User Experience in the Professional and Technical Writing Major:
    Pedagogical Approaches and Student Perspectives. 265
    *Jennifer Bay, Margaret Becker, Ashlie Clark, Emily Mast,
    Brendan Robb, and Korbyn Torres*

13. Program as Product: UX and Writing Program Design in Technical
and Professional Communication..............................285
  Christine Masters-Wheeler and Gracemarie Mike Fillenwarth

Contributors 315

Acknowledgments

Although this project began before the COVID-19 pandemic, it was written and revised in the midst of the lockdowns and the profound personal and professional changes that accompanied it. We could not have known when selecting these chapters what the future held for us. For this reason, especially, we are grateful to our authors who met deadlines and responded to reviews with grace and goodwill.

We are also grateful to the Foundations and Innovations in Technical and Professional Communication series editors, especially Kristin Bivens. Thank you, Kristin, for engaging Kate in a conversation that led us to producing this collection and for shepherding us through the process. You answered our questions patiently and advocated for us when editorial processes were new or opaque to us.

A group of nine reviewers offered recommendations for our chapters. Although it is not always easy to hear criticism and suggestions from reviewers, we acknowledge the time, energy, and thought that they contributed. They asked tough questions and made us dig deep in response, not always in ways we anticipated but certainly in ways that made these chapters stronger. We thank them for their efforts.

Kelli, specifically, would like to acknowledge and thank a special group of scholars whose research introduced her to user experience (UX) and engaged her in discussions of UX and pedagogical innovation: Drs. Nick Carrington, Nancy Barber-Chase, Kate Crane, Elizabeth Kafka, Sarah Martin, and Brian Still. She is also grateful to the directors and members of the Women Faculty Writing Program (WFWP) at Texas Tech for asking her to dedicate three hours weekly to research activities. She could not have completed this project without WFWP's support.

Kate would like to thank her colleagues who entertained the idea of using UX methods to revise the English studies degree at Eastern Washington University. In particular, Drs. Logan Greene, Chris Valeo, Matthew Binney, Tracey McHenry, Beth Torgerson, and Justin Young showed great patience as she led them through ideation activities during their many task force meetings. In many ways, the work of the English Studies task force became a playground for Kate to continue exploring how UX could inform programmatic change. Kate is most grateful to her co-editor and co-author, Kelli, for graciously sharing her experience and wisdom throughout the production of this collection. Kelli was the only person on Kate's list for potential collaborators, and it has been an honor to work with her—from beginning to end and through a pandemic—on this project.

As we wrap up this production, we thank our families, especially the furry ones who frequently remind us, and rightly so, where our priorities should lie.

Finally, to everyone who was involved: we laughed, we cried, we persevered, and, one day in the not-too-distant future, we will meet to celebrate this collection's completion. Bring your dancing shoes.

USER EXPERIENCE AS INNOVATIVE ACADEMIC PRACTICE

1. Out of Industry, Into the Classroom: UX as Proactive Academic Practice

Kate Crane
EASTERN WASHINGTON UNIVERSITY

Abstract: User experience (UX) is an established practice in industry and is taught as a necessary skill for future technical and professional communicators. However, its use in technical and professional communication (TPC) pedagogy and program development is notably absent in TPC literature. This chapter contextualizes and situates UX in TPC, documenting its evolution from user advocacy to usability, to user-centered design, and then to UX. UX is a broadly used term that, at its core, values design processes that are focused on the user experience (notably, user-centered design, human-centered design, participatory design, and design thinking). Further, UX promotes the collection of user data to understand how the user experiences products and processes in a way that promotes iterative design and assessment. UX is contextually bound, non-linear, and often not generalizable; yet, to build and assess programs and curricula, TPC needs to take a UX approach to our work to best serve our student users and our field.

Keywords: student users, user experience, pedagogy, technical and professional communication

Key Takeaways:

- User advocacy and UX is a cornerstone of all technical and professional communication work.
- Localized UX and small-scale studies best apply to pedagogical and programmatic design.
- Proactive UX work strengthens curricula and programs.
- UX and design processes (user-centered design, human-centered design, participatory design, and design thinking) are imperative for successful curricula and programs.

I began my user experience (UX) journey by accident. My personal statement to my future Ph.D. program stated that I wanted to learn how technology changed the ways students wrote and engaged with texts. I had never heard the terms "user experience," "user-centered design," or "usability." Technical and professional communication (TPC), even then, was on the periphery of my writing studies experience as I had mostly taught first-year composition up to that point. That was in 2010. Four years later, I was iteratively testing how students interacted with syllabi. I was also playing with eye-tracking technology as a metric for usability studies. Ten years later, I had co-written a book on user-centered design, collaborated with colleagues on designing research projects with UX methods, collaborated to design curriculum using UX methods, and was even approached to begin this book collection on how UX methods could be applied to curriculum design. I'm not bragging; rather, upon reflection, I see how UX has permeated my everyday work as an educator, program director, researcher, and designer.

It was my syllabus study, however, that really showed me the potential of UX for curriculum and program design. In 2014, I developed a usability study to determine if student users would use a PDF syllabus or a non-linear web syllabus more effectively. I observed 21 students per syllabus mode (42 total) perform five tasks each. The syllabus usability test findings were as follows:

1. The PDF's efficiency errors were often the result of users locating incorrect information for a task.
2. Users used print navigation cues (such as headings) to stop in locations where the correct information was not available to complete a task.
3. Term confusion led to using navigation cues that did not help users locate information.
4. Users' previous experience with syllabi led to generic expectations about how they would use new syllabi (Crane, 2015).

However, the more significant conclusion that I took from this usability study was that the usability test was not generalizable beyond the specific context of this particular syllabus evaluation. What I mean by this is that once I revised the syllabi to be more usable, or a new population of students was tested, or I moved to a new institution with different policies and procedures, or new technologies were better suited to deliver syllabi, the test conducted in 2014 would be insignificant beyond a historical perspective of usability using two texts and technologies in 2014. That is not to say that usability testing, or this study, is insignificant; rather, it's an acknowledgement of usability testing's limitations. Usability evaluates products in a very specific context that changes based on the stage of a design process, the users tested, and the environment where the product is being tested. Usability, therefore, should only be used iteratively to understand how a design works for users at any given time or environment. Second to this conclusion was my understanding that course documents are (or should be) student-user centered and that it is an instructor's responsibility as an information designer to understand the student-user experience while using these documents. In this chapter, I use the syllabus usability study to illustrate the complexity of curricular materials and the importance of UX as we approach designing these materials for students.

Now that I am a faculty member and program director, I tend to see most tasks through the lens of UX. Claire Lauer and Eva Brumberger (2016) analyzed job postings for technical communicators and found that "the core competencies" of user experience (UX) and information design were placed directly in the realm of technical communicators' work and skill sets (p. 262). Historically, TPC as a discipline has centered its identity around user advocacy, which evolved from usability to UX. Unfortunately, this user focus has mostly been discussed in TPC research as an application in industry rather than pedagogy or program design.

While user research has focused on industry applications, academic programs have evolved in UX education at institutions, such as the University of Washington's Human-Centered Design and Engineering, Michigan State's Experience Architecture, and the Milwaukee School of Engineering's User Experience degrees. Nevertheless, UX as a philosophical principle and methodological tool for the work we do in designing TPC programs and curriculum has been absent. Yet this work is imperative to designing innovative programs that attract students, prepare them for the field, and adapt to students' ever-changing needs. In other words, TPC program and curriculum designers ought to model the work their students will be expected to do post graduation. Offering UX instruction is different than programs developing curricula through UX. Based on the lack of published research on UX in program development, I claim that TPC program designers ought to demonstrate UX thinking while designing and assessing their programs and courses; this is an argument that the collection makes cumulatively throughout each chapter.

This collection derives its focus from this assumption: UX is a vital theory and principle that should guide TPC academic work. *To frame this assumption, this chapter contextualizes UX in TPC, and, in particular, attempts to tease out the differences between various design and research methods that are related, yet often conflated.* Further, it shows the interrelated nature of UX design methods and the various user research methods that inform UX designed products. Although by no means exhaustive in its discussion of design and research methods, this chapter attempts to show the hierarchy of UX and its relationship to design and research methods. At the same time, using illustrative examples from my own syllabus research, I discuss the various opportunities and challenges of UX work.

■ From Usability to User Experience in TPC

To understand TPC's emphasis on UX, a brief history of its evolution is necessary. UX is a fairly new concept in technical and professional communication studies. However, its emergence in design fields, especially in TPC, follows a longer path of TPC professionals trying to situate users in such a way that they are part of the design process for any system.

Before UX, and even usability studies, existed, designers focused on creating products through system-centered design (also referred to as the waterfall method). System-centered design focused more on the needs of the system to function as the designers intended. The problem with this approach is that systems, even well-built systems, are not always usable for the people those systems were designed for. Usability evaluation (through testing or heuristics) was used to ensure that end-users (or those who would use the designed product) could actually use the product to complete intended tasks. However, usability was applied at the end of a design process once a product was built and nearly ready for distribution (i.e., being implemented or sold). The problem with this model is that users were only part of the design process once the design was complete, and their usability data only applied when tweaking final designs before being sent to the workplace, marketplace, or classroom.

Usability first and foremost references how usable a product is for completing a task. The International Organization for Standardization (ISO, 2018) defines usability as the "extent to which a system, product, or service can be used by specified users to achieve specified goals with effectiveness, efficiency, and satisfaction" (sec. 3.1.1). Usability testing was often (and sometimes still is) conducted in an experimental fashion to locate bugs in the system or to identify other major concerns that would create problems for the user. Usability evaluations focused on narrowly defined tasks that users would complete while using the product. These experiments tested for usability, but their mission was to ensure products were used for the tasks designers anticipated and to ensure those tasks were completed in the simplest way. This focus did not inform designers how users were interacting with the product in their real-world environment (Mirel, 1991; Redish 1995). Usability, usually under human-computer interaction (HCI) fields, limited itself to traditional experimental methods that focused on comparing interfaces and users' interactions to "long lists of guidelines of good practice" (Dumas, 2007, p. 55). This experimental method limited the amount of data specific to users' environments; users were tested in labs under strict testing protocols rather than in their own working environments or while performing tasks pertaining to their actual work. Joe Dumas (1989) argued for usability professionals to act as change agents "to have a long-range impact on the way an organization develops products" (p. 37). He advocated for involving usability early in the design process to understand how users interact with products.

As Dumas (1989) advocated, usability evolved. The usability profession became a movement away from a systems-based approach that used experimental methods to evaluate the usability of products. Usability professionals' new approach ultimately led to a focus on smaller-scale studies that provided an easier, more cost-effective method for incorporating usability iteratively in a product's design process (Barnum, 2019; Krug, 2014; Nielsen 1993). Further, as Janice Redish (1995) notes, usability took on a more integral role as computing became more common, users began using computers for various tasks, and new features provided more opportunity but also more usability problems. TPC, in particular, brought new methods of research beyond quantitative experimental research and a new focus on user advocacy.

Though much of the work in usability studies has focused on software and hardware, TPC professionals applied usability methods to test documentation long before usability testing helped in the evaluation of computers and software (Redish, 2010). TPC practitioners saw themselves as user advocates, and usability testing was one method TPC practitioners used to ensure that documentation could effectively assist its end users in completing their tasks (Redish & Barnum,

2011). Further, Robert Johnson (1998) discussed the importance of listening to users, whom he calls "the better judges" of technology use (p. 11). As user advocates (Redish, 2010), TPC's role was to ensure that the user was at the center of designing content or products.

In 1993, Jakob Nielsen published *Usability Engineering*, in which he claimed that usability ought to be used throughout the design process by performing small tests iteratively between design stages. This strategy emphasized that, although usability professionals would only test a handful of users (he suggested five per iteration), these tests would inform the overall usability of the product for users. Using Nielsen's model, five users per iteration could potentially lead to dozens of users throughout the design's lifecycle. Further, this strategy suggests that users are agents within the design of the system, rather than novices experiencing the system only as end users. This aggregate user data and the design improvements upon incorporating user observations would ensure that the product's usability was well tested before the final distribution of the design.

Nielsen also proposed five dimensions of usability: learnability, efficiency, errors, memorability, and satisfaction. Building on Nielsen, Whitney Quesenbery (2003) provides a model for usability, the five E's: effective, efficient, engaging, error tolerant, and easy to learn. Table 1.1 outlines these two models.

Table 1.1. Nielsen's and Quesenbery's Usability Characteristics

Nielsen's Five Usability Attributes (1993)	Quesenbery's Five Usability Dimensions (2003)
Efficiency: The system should be efficient to use, so that once the user has learned the system, a high level of productivity is possible (p. 26).	Efficient: The speed (with accuracy) with which users can complete their tasks (p. 84).
Memorability: The system should be easy to remember, so that the casual user is able to return to the system after some period of not having used it, without having to learn everything all over again (p. 26).	Effective: The completeness and accuracy with which users achieved their goals (p. 83).
Satisfaction: The system should be pleasant to use, so that users are subjectively satisfied when using it; they like it (p. 26).	Engaging: The degree to which the tone and style of the interface makes the product pleasant or satisfying to use (p. 86).
Errors: The system should have a low error rate so that users make few errors during the use of the system, and so that if they do make errors, they can easily recover from them. Further, catastrophic errors must not occur (p. 26).	Error Tolerant: How well the design prevents errors, or helps with recovery from those that do occur (p. 87).
Learnability: The system should be easy to learn so that the user can rapidly start getting some work done with the system (p. 26).	Easy to Learn: How well the product supports both initial orientation and deepening understanding of its capabilities (p. 88).

Four of Nielsen's and Quesenbery's components for usability are very similar. For instance, users need to be able to complete tasks efficiently, learn a system in a reasonable amount of time, and recover from errors when they are made. Perhaps the first glimpse of user experience in usability was Nielsen's "satisfaction" and Quesenbery's "engaging" components. Both of these components indicate that users should feel good about using a product. These dimensions acknowledge that a workable product does not determine adoptability. Rather, emotional reactions to the product are also a factor for how users determine what product is best for completing a task (consider, for instance, how many people switch between PC and Mac platforms or iPhones and Androids). Users choose their preferences based on logic and emotion. The only differences in usability components between these frameworks are Nielsen's "memorability" dimension (the ability to remember the system enough to easily complete future tasks) and Quesenbery's "effective" aspect (which indicates that the users could successfully complete their goal). Both of these usability qualities deserve a place in our consideration of how usable a product or process should be. But, more importantly than comparing the differences in models, using models such as Nielsen's and Quesenbery's provided us with frameworks to understand data in relation to users' experiences with a system.

In the early 2000s, technical and professional communicators were still concerned with the usability of content, but they also took a turn in thinking about how their role as user advocates needed to begin even earlier and, on a more basic level, than what usability affords. In usability, there must be a product to test. Thus, the more dynamic the product, the more complex the problems that would arise. Barbara Mirel (2002) describes this problem as a lack of understanding usability in terms of "users' complex work-in-context" and notes that "if usefulness is to take center stage, a shift is needed in analyzing and designing for complex tasks" (p. 167). In other words, not only should we be concerned with how well users can complete tasks, but researchers should not assume that their (or a designer's) preconceived ideas about users' work is a fair representation of the complexity of users' work beyond a usability lab (or any testing situation).

Breaking down usability further, Michael Albers (2004) delineates three types of usability that are dependent on the product's level of complexity: simple, complicated, and complex. Simple usability employs a single path to complete a task, provides predefined answers to questions, predicts systematic changes and effects, and exists within a closed system. An example of simple usability is having students log in to a learning management system (LMS). My institution uses Canvas, and students only have one pathway for logging in to the LMS. First, they need to use a link (or correct URL) to navigate to Canvas. Students are then directed to the institution's single sign-on page, where they input their username and password. If their credentials are accepted, the Canvas dashboard appears. Thus, there is one pathway for signing in, and students know they have completed the task if they see their Canvas dashboard after they sign in.

Complicated usability is still part of a closed system, has predefined answers to questions, and a "description can be given," but there are multiple pathways for completing a task (Albers, 2004, p. 16). To distinguish between simple and complicated, consider how students use an LMS to turn in an assignment. There is one task to complete—submit the assignment. However, students may have multiple pathways to turn in that assignment. For instance, in Canvas, students have at least three ways to find the assignment page and submit their assignment files: 1) they can click on the assignment in their to-do list, which takes them to the assignment page; 2) they can go to the "Assignment" link on the course's Canvas menu; or 3) they can find the assignment link in the class modules. They can choose any of these options to turn in the assignment and, if navigated correctly, they should be able to submit the assignment correctly, and I can view their assignment in my grading queue. Thus, the user has more options for how to complete the task.

Complex usability, the final of the three types, does not have a clear description of its tasks, solutions, or questions. It is "part of an open system," and tasks may require leaving a system to be completed (Albers, 2004, p. 16). A complex system takes away more of the designer's control, and the user's actions are more unpredictable. The work done in program and curriculum design falls more directly under the realm of complex usability. When studying syllabus use, for example, it was impossible for me to predict how, where, when, and for what purpose students would use a syllabus. Student users could stay in Adobe Reader to complete tasks using the PDF syllabus, but they could also click on a hyperlink that led to a university code of conduct policy with additional navigation options. Thus, creating this system may seem simple (it's on the syllabus, right?), but the syllabus document relies not only on instructor design but also on the design of university webpages to inform its construction. As TPC instructors and program designers consider how student users will use course or program materials, we must all consider how the materials we create work in conjunction with other factors such as websites, learning management systems, or even email platforms students use.

As these descriptions illustrate, Mirel and Albers forecasted the shift to UX before they began using the language, but this move further distanced usability (as a concept and evaluation method) as the sole attribute needed to advocate for users. Relying on usability could be seen as one of the major flaws in my syllabus design. Though I designed a syllabus based on program and university needs, I didn't really know what students needed or how they used the syllabus. I had been encouraged, for years at many different institutions, to include as much information in my syllabus as possible; doing so would make it bulletproof and, therefore, effective. This, of course, was not the case. The syllabus worked for me and administrators, but not for students. A usability test was a start in understanding the nuances of student use but was not enough for understanding the students' user experience while trying to find and use information—such as the attendance policy or major assignment descriptions—on the syllabus. In other words, the priorities of instructors, programs, and the institution at large did not represent the priorities of students.

Users need to be considered before designs are drawn, programmed, or outlined. Michael Salvo (2001) noted that, though a popular method, usability focuses on the end product rather than on collaborative design where users are participants in design instead of just the observed. Since this time, models such as user-centered design, human-centered design, participatory design, and design thinking have influenced TPC's work. The need for a clear distinction between researching users' success with tasks and the need to design the experience of users became the exigency needed for user experience to emerge as an overarching theory where design processes and user research methods (including usability testing) contribute to understanding a users' holistic experience.

■ User Experience for TPC

After analyzing my syllabus usability test's results, I learned that usability testing alone could not answer the questions I posed for my study. The syllabus and the students who use it are part of a complex academic system with multiple factors, stakeholders, tasks, environments, and functions. Thus, looking at usability alone, though a good starting point, led to more questions than it could answer. In essence, syllabus designers need a UX approach to understand how students interact with a syllabus within the context of their myriad uses. This is one example of why TPC instructors and program designers need to understand how UX functions within an interconnected web of design processes (user-centered design [UCD], human-centered design [HCD], participatory design, and design thinking) and research methods (observation, self-reporting, affinity diagramming, usability testing, etc.).

User experience is a theory and practice that emphasizes the need for functional products that integrate the users' needs and experiences. The ISO (2018) defines user experience as "users' perceptions and responses that result from the use and/or anticipated use of a system, product, or service" (sec. 3.2.3). These perceptions may include "users' emotions, beliefs, preferences, perceptions, comfort, behaviors, and accomplishments that occur before, during, and after use" (sec. 3.2.3). Thus, user experience goes beyond asking *how well a user can complete a task* to *how the user feels as they prepare and actively interact with a product*.

Given its historical development, user experience is an ambiguous term often confused or conflated with various research methods and theories. Don Norman and Jakob Nielsen (n.d.) state that "'User Experience' encompasses all aspects of the end-user's interaction with the company, its services, and its products" (para. 1). For this reason, user experience focuses on a more holistic understanding of the user, the user's context of use, and the user's experience as they interact with a given product. It is a theory or philosophy, supported by design processes that put the human user in the center of design processes, whether these processes are labeled as user-centered design (UCD), human-centered design (HCD), participatory design, or design thinking; these design processes are then enacted through four iterative stages:

1. collecting information about human users (those most likely to use products upon design completion),
2. designing prototypes that can be used by these human users to collect additional data about their use,
3. redesigning products in response to the first two methods, and
4. testing and retesting products during and after distribution.

Whichever stage is enacted, UX researchers should be most concerned with their users' feelings about and interactions with the product, which are gauged through user research, collaborative activities or design, and even usability testing. But user experience is primarily concerned with how a product or process is built and maintained to support all its users. In other words, designers study and incorporate data about users' experiences with the design to continue adapting the product or process to best fit users' productive and emotional needs.

Another emerging theory related to UX is *experience architecture* (XA). XA, first used in customer relations, was introduced to technical and professional communication by Liza Potts. Discussing XA and its focus on collaborative teams, Potts (2014) explains that XA "focuses on architecting the end-to-end experiences of the participants" (p. 3). Further, XA focuses on how participants interact with systems as part of a larger ecosystem. In other words, participants do not work in a vacuum; they use systems that are influenced by multiple factors, including factors that are not work related. XA focuses on how the human experience is affected (for better or worse) by using technological systems (Potts & Salvo, 2017).

XA builds on the principles of UX, and its name certainly focuses on the idea of building (or architecting) the experience for and with participants. UX ought to take note of this metaphor, not only because it is a valuable theory from which to draw new, innovative ideas but also because UX designers are building experiences for other people. Whether they are navigating new software, an interactive museum exhibit, or an academic program, designers of these products have created the map for which users can navigate through their experience with the system. Thus, when undertaking a new design endeavor, designers should never underestimate the impact their building has on the people that use their product. Further, like UX, "experience architects need to hear from users, participants, researchers, designers, developers, business analysts and various other stakeholders" (Potts, 2014, p. 4).

XA considers UX as a design method that helps support the XA mission. However, in this collection, we use UX in a similar way to how Potts and Salvo (2014) use XA: as a theory and practice that aims to understand the holistic experience of users and design according to users' needs and feelings. I acknowledge and appreciate the use of different terms as TPC, user needs and interaction, and marketplaces evolve; however, I place particular value in work that supports users as they navigate through various resources (electronic technologies, print resources, and organizational processes) more than claiming a new name for this work. We use UX in this collection to acknowledge the history and emphasis of user advocacy in TPC. That emphasis has paved the way for scholars and practitioners to continue pushing the boundaries for how user advocacy is enacted as new problems arise in the development of technologies, processes, and services. In other words, UX and XA can coexist as related umbrella concepts which design theories and research methods fall under as long as they use design processes and research methods that center, support, and include users in constructing new products.

UX and XA are not tidy or simple theories to enact. Rather, they are non-linear, highly contextual, and often not generalizable. Their use throughout the design process often reveals new UX challenges through each iteration and over the entire lifecycle of the product. Whereas a design iteration may end, UX work never does. Though UX professionals may begin thinking about their product from a UX process before any prototype is created, this is not always the case. Sometimes, UX does not become a conscious act until designers are ready for their idea to be seen or used. Alternatively, designers may inherit a product or process that needs revamping to better serve users. This is one reason why evaluating the usefulness of a product may be the first step in researching user experience.

Further, UX research, whether applied in industry or the academy, has its limitations. One of these limitations is reaching a level of generalizability. Recent articles about research in TPC have stressed the importance of conducting and reporting on research that can be replicated to test the researchers' findings (Lauer, 2016; Meloncon & St.Amant, 2019). UX research is highly contextual, and solutions are often quickly deployed to create a better user experience. Thus, conducting UX research means using very specific methodologies that are appropriate for the local context of the users' needs, rather than aiming for generalizability. This does not mean that UX research eschews *empirical research*, which, according to Mary Sue MacNealy, "describes and/or measures observable phenomena in a systematic way that has been planned in advance of the observation" (as cited in Meloncon & St.Amant, 2019, p. 130). The value of systematic research in UX is clearly seen in the design and research models discussed here and in other TPC literature. However, localized research for curriculum, community projects, or industry interactions with customers may not be as easily replicated based on the specific context they inhabit.

The specific, localized context is one that UX scholars have already noted. The small-scale studies such as guerilla usability or discount usability are highly valued in agile processes, and they are valuable in these localized pedagogical contexts as well, as we see in this volume's chapters. UX studies, according to Brian Still (2010), "allow for experimentation, for proactive research that enables practitioners to stay a step ahead" (p. 104). Carol Barnum (2019) further advocates for the small-scale study in "development scenarios" that work "particularly well in Agile development methodologies" (p. 2). She emphasizes that "the goal of UX research is to identify or uncover *valid* findings, fix them, and iterate the process to discover more" (p. 3). Thus, the methods necessary to create rigorous UX research certainly fall within the parameters of TPC's empirical research focus. Moreover, the limited number of participants helps create solutions to UX problems by prioritizing iterative methods without depleting resources.

Though Still and Barnum both focus on small-scale studies for industry, this volume's authors claim that these small-scale studies are equally important to programmatic and curriculum design. TPC program designers can not only use scholar/instructor expertise or industry expertise to answer their questions. Another important stakeholder needs to be considered: students. For instance, one decision we all must come to when creating a program is how many course credits we should include in our major/minor/certificate. Will students want to spend one quarter of their college credits to get a degree in a TPC program, or will they feel this does not give them enough experience with TPC curricula? If we create a major that is one half of students' college credits, will they feel the content being taught is too repetitive between classes? Will they feel rushed to finish their degree on time? To answer these questions, we need to understand our student population, based on what they say their priorities and goals are. In this case, the UX process ought to start by talking to all stakeholders, including students. Then, based on the data collected, program designers can weigh the needs of all stakeholders to best design a program that ultimately can be marketed to students (see Cargile Cook and Masters-Wheeler & Fillenwarth in this collection).

■ UX Design Processes

UX is often conflated with other design processes because UX design was (and still is) used in place of user-centered design and human-centered design. This is a mistake. UX is the umbrella theory and principle—a methodology, if you will—that designers and researchers should adopt. But there are many means for achieving the UX end goal. *User-centered design* (UCD), *human-centered design* (HCD), *participatory design*, and *design thinking* can all be used to support a UX project. These four design methods have more in common than not. This is a strength for UX as a concept, practice, and field. UX is supported by design methods that integrate user research and feedback. Instead of designing for users, UX-focused designers build and assess products and processes with users and understand that each new user, new product or process, or new environment irrevocably changes the user-product system. Designing for UX is an act of humility and empathy. Choosing the best design process for a strong UX product is part of architecting that product. It is with this in mind that I describe four design methods that lend themselves to UX design. I limited my discussion to these four design processes because they have been the most widely discussed in TPC literature.

UCD focuses on designing products and processes in a way that, from planning to distribution, places users at the center of the design process. The goal of centering users is making sure that designers understand the system requirements needed for users to work effectively (Baek et al., 2008; Cosgrove, 2018; Still & Crane, 2016). UCD keeps users at the center of the design process, encouraging an iterative design model that incorporates user data and feedback throughout the design process.

However, some scholars believe we should move away from labeling people "users" as this term can dehumanize those who work with the systems designers create. For instance, Don Norman advocated for UCD in the 1980s, but by the time he released the revised and expanded version of *The Design of Everyday Things* in 2013, he changed his focus to HCD. He defines HCD as "an approach that puts human needs, capabilities, and behaviors first, then designs to accommodate those needs, capabilities, and ways of behaving" (2013, p. 8). One of the main differences between UCD and HCD, is the shift in nomenclature from "users" to "humans." This is not to minimize either process; rather, it acknowledges that some UX scholars and designers feel that the term "users" is not the best way to refer to people. The use of this term has been questioned for its perceived focus on efficiency (Opel & Rhodes, 2018). However, "human" clearly centers the work of HCD as a humane endeavor—one that ultimately is rooted in humanity and working for and with people while designing. Mark Zachry and Jan Spyridakis (2016) explain HCD as a perspective that "acknowledges the role of humans in actively constructing artifacts" (p. 394). Emma Rose (2016) furthers this distinction, stating that "human-centered design should look more broadly and provide a way to consider how design can support or constrain the needs of people whose lives are impacted by both the systems and policies that are created by a more digitized world" (p. 428). Thus, HCD emphasizes the important role designers play in creating systems that influence how people live, their ability to interact with and within these systems, and the consequences when designs do not enable people to interface with these systems effectively.

We all have our own guiding principles for choosing language, and that does not mean one method, UCD or HCD, is more or less valuable. In fact, they mimic each other in many ways. TPC literature often uses UCD and HCD interchangeably (sometimes even acknowledging the choice to use one or the other terms). What is important to note is that they each follow a process that begins with understanding users/humans and consulting with them throughout the lifecycle of the design (See Figure 1.1).

Participatory design, as compared to UCD and HCD, focuses on a more democratic process for creating new products (whether for the workplace or commercial purposes). Used as a design process, participatory design focuses on designing *with* people, rather than designing *for* people. They are, as Michael Muller (2009) explains, "full participants in activities" (p. 166). Participants become members of the design team rather than mere observers or subjects for data collection.

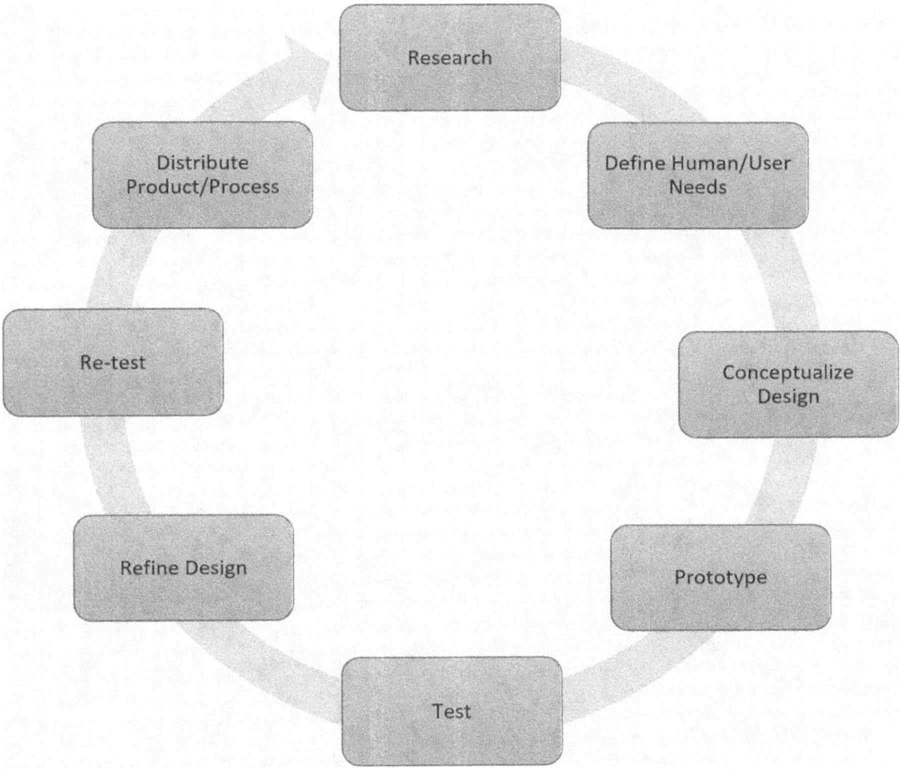

Figure 1.1. UCD/HCD process.

As seen in Figure 1.2, participatory design is about co-production rather than one designer making decisions in isolation and asking for user feedback at specific points in the process. The user is a *co-designer*, one that participates throughout the design. Co-designers are actively involved in the planning, research, design, delivery, and evaluation of a product (e.g., a syllabus) or process (e.g., developing a mentoring program for TPC majors—see Lee-Ann Kastman Breuch, Ann Hill Duin, and Emily Gresbrink's chapter in this collection). The participatory design process is as concerned with building relationships as it is with delivering appropriate, usable products to its users. This emphasis on a design's relationship with its participants is at the heart of participatory design. It is democratic in the way it approaches the participant as an expert and co-designer.

Design thinking, a relatively new theory introduced to TPC, distinguishes itself as a way of problem-solving that emphasizes empathizing with users, defining the problem, ideating solutions, prototyping designs, and testing the designs' effectiveness (Dam & Siang, n.d.; Pope-Ruark et al., 2019).

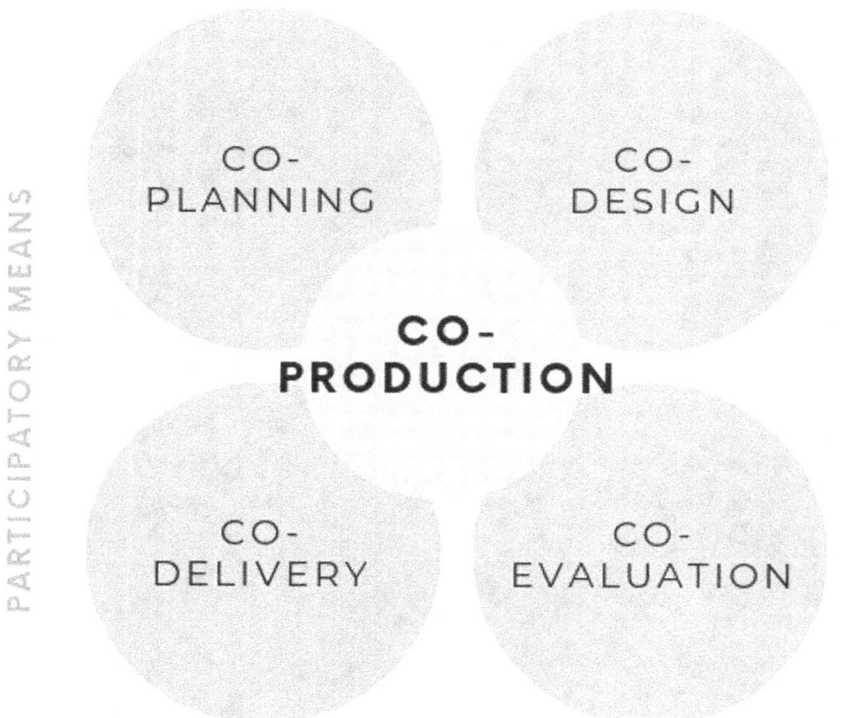

Figure 1.2. Co-production by Kelly Ann McKercher (as adapted by Stephens, 2019).

Design thinking's values (see Figure 1.3) mimic the processes and values of user-centered, human-centered, and participatory design. As Tharon Howard states, "Many UXers see design thinking as just a repackaging of what they've always done" (as cited in Pope-Ruark, 2019, p. 444). However, Howard and Melonçon acknowledge design theories' commitment to UX and TPC's user advocacy mission (Pope-Ruark, 2019).

These design methods provide a guide for how to develop new products and processes; more important, the design methods all include stages where user feedback is necessary. In fact, not one of these design methods is described as a linear process because when user research or feedback is collected and analyzed, designers may have to revert back to an earlier stage in the design. For instance, my syllabi were complete, but my research showed flaws in the design. Students wanted relevant information (such as grading and attendance policies) closer to the beginning of the syllabus, and my use of academic discourse made navigating to the correct

Out of Industry, Into the Classroom 17

information confusing for students. Reverting back to collecting user research and designing new prototypes with student users may be the best, next iteration for the syllabus study. When our designs don't work out, we need to go back to user research.

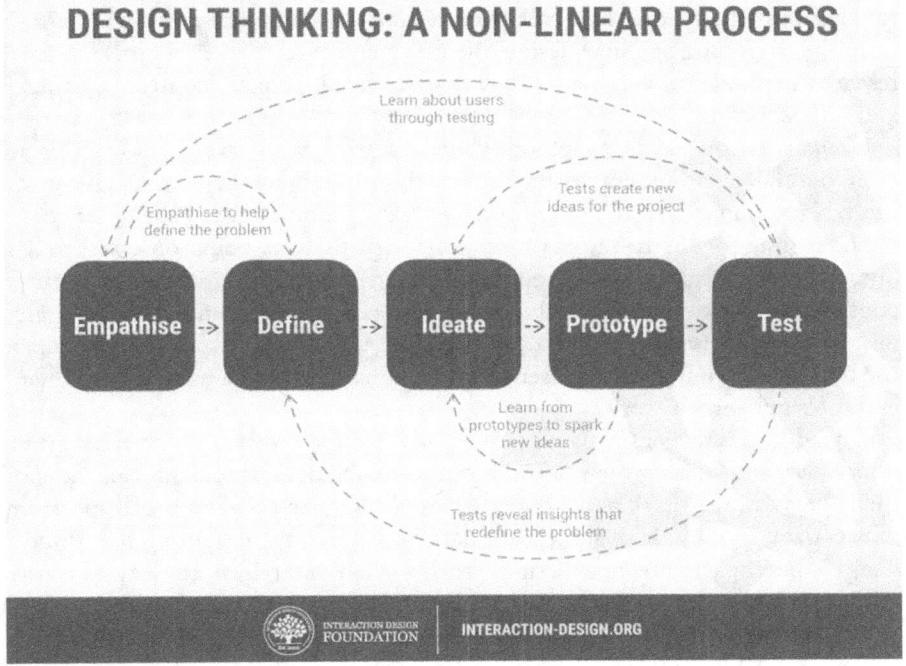

Figure 1.3. Design Thinking Process by Teo Yu Siang CC BY-NC-SA 3.0 (Dam & Siang, n.d).

To demonstrate how these design methods work within UX and XA, Table 1.2 summarizes the relationship between these theories, the design processes, and the methods that might be used in these processes. It illustrates a hierarchy of methods where design processes/methods support developing a positive user experience; the research methods inform designers throughout the design process. Worth noting, however, is that user research methods continue to evolve and expand; those methods listed in Table 1.2 are far from a complete list.

Table 1.2. UX/XA Processes and Methods

Theory	User experience and experience architecture			
Design Methods & Processes	User-centered design	Human-centered design	Participatory design	Design thinking
User Research Methods	Contextual inquiry	Self-reporting		Collaborative design studio
	Affinity diagramming	Prototype feedback		Usability testing

■ UX Research Methods

As Table 1.2 illustrates, UX research methods support the design process. These methods can be used in various design stages. The goal of the design method is to determine the type of data collection needed. If the design process is starting from the beginning of a new design, the first step is to understand users. The two research methods from Table 1.2 that align with this step are contextual inquiry and self-reporting.

Contextual inquiry is a method where researchers observe users working in their natural environment to understand how they complete tasks (Beyer & Holtzblatt, 1999; Still & Crane, 2016). Contextual inquiry (also called a *site visit*) includes time for the researcher to consult with the user being observed to ask questions about how tasks were completed, get clarification about why a user chose one action over another while completing their task(s), and, more generally, discuss how the user felt while completing the task. Contextual inquiry is one of the best ways to understand a user's context of use and how a user's environment and tools affect their work.

In addition to contextual inquiry, *self-reporting methods* (such as surveys, interviews, and focus groups) can help researchers understand the behaviors of their users toward a task or product. Self-reporting can collect a broad spectrum of user data (in the case of surveys) or data from a narrow user group that is most likely to be impacted by new designs (this is where interviews are very relevant). Although I had already studied syllabi and had a syllabus model ready to test, I still administered a survey to student users in the specific program I was studying (Crane, 2015). Doing this not only gave me important demographic data to determine who my representative user was, but it also provided me with information about what these students prioritized when using syllabi. I learned, for instance, that students were more interested in the information about what they had to do (such as assignments, absence policies, and grading policies) than they were in my teaching philosophy or university boiler plate language. I was then able to use this data to determine which tasks were "representative" for my user population. This preliminary data was imperative to understanding not only who my student users were but, more importantly, what their motivation and priorities were for using a syllabus.

When researchers have enough information about users that they understand user needs, priorities, and beliefs, they proceed to the next design stage: conceptualizing or ideating. Here is one place where the design process may affect methodological choices. For some designers, the data collected to understand the user would be enough to begin ideating, building, and prototyping a product. However, other design processes, such as participatory design, would advocate for ideating with users via a collaborative design studio or affinity diagramming exercise.

A *collaborative design studio* pairs designers and users together to collaborate on possible designs to address a problem. This collaboration ought to focus on making design a more democratic process and, ideally, lead to clear design directions, such as a list of features that are necessary to address users' needs or a rapid prototype (such as a paper prototype) of the new product (see Elizarova et al., 2017 for more participatory design methods). *Affinity diagramming* is another tool that involves designers collaborating with users to understand what attitudes and/or values are shared amongst the user and designer group. Often, this work is done on a whiteboard or by using sticky notes. For instance, if I were redesigning syllabi with students, I may use affinity diagramming to discover the most valuable information for students using the syllabus. In smaller groups, students would be asked, "What are the most important elements of the syllabus for you?" and then I would ask them to work through the following process:

1. Each person writes an attitude, value, or idea on a sticky note (one idea per sticky note).
2. All participants' sticky notes are examined for patterns.
3. Patterns are identified by clustering sticky notes.
4. Patterns are compared between groups.
5. All students discuss how/if these patterns should become part of the course syllabus.

Affinity diagramming provides all participants the opportunity to make their values and attitudes known without succumbing to group thinking. This practice can also lead to low-fidelity co-designed prototypes where users can construct their own syllabus, in this case, using the values discovered from affinity diagramming and program and university syllabus requirements to create their own student-as-user-centered syllabus. There are many other collaborative research methods—these two represent a couple methods that I have worked with. The point of this research grouping is that it invites users/participants/students to be part of the design process instead of being seen only as end users. This is also an exercise that introduces students to work with/as participants, and teaches instructors how to practice participatory design in the classroom. (See Beau Pihlaja's chapter in this collection for more examples of class co-design activities and Luke Thominet's chapter for information on affinity diagramming to create program student learning outcomes.)

The final two user research methods I will address here are opportunities for prototype feedback and usability testing. In many ways, prototype feedback and usability testing try to achieve similar ends: How will users engage with the product? *Prototyping feedback* may include asking users to complete a task using a prototype to gauge how well the prototype allows users to accomplish their goals, asking users to create a journey map as they are working with the prototype to understand how the users navigate a product and how they feel while doing so, or asking users to help construct or improve a prototype while they are working through a problem. Prototypes, especially those that are low-fidelity (using less technical means for construction, such as paper prototypes), provide a low-stakes opportunity to see a design used before more resources (such as money and time) are spent on perfecting a product.

I leave *usability testing* as the last method of discussion not because I believe usability testing should only be executed at the end of a design but because it is one of the most time-intensive methods. Usability testing involves researchers evaluating a product by observing representative users completing representative tasks. Researchers collect various quantitative data (time on task, types of errors, number of inputs—such as mouse clicks or keyboard entries—and dwell time between inputs) and qualitative data (observations, pre- and post-test surveys or interview, etc.). Examining these data together help researchers to decide how well the user can work with the product. Whereas many usability tests are still facilitated in usability labs, more usability testing options have emerged, such as remote testing using videoconferencing software (e.g., Zoom or other usability-specific tools), mobile usability equipment that can be used in users' environments, and even testing that can be done by outside administrators who then share the data with researchers (e.g., UserTesting).

What is important to understand about all of these methods is that they can be used in different ways than what I have presented above. Ultimately, we use research methods to help answer questions wherever we are in the design process. It is possible to have a complete, finished product that you want to evaluate by conducting a usability test first. This was the case of my syllabus test. My design was already complete and had been used for a long time. However, I was interested in understanding how well this design worked for students. Starting with usability testing was an important step in understanding the user experience of students—more so than understanding the deficiencies of my syllabus. It would be just as appropriate to observe students (through contextual inquiry) to see how, or if, they use a syllabus differently in a natural environment rather than a testing situation.

■ UX and This Collection

This collection emphasizes the importance of UX not only as an area of research in TPC, but as a necessary practice for our work as curriculum and program designers. Though the field acknowledges the importance of UX in industry, the work TPC instructors and program administrators perform while designing courses and programs (and the artifacts associated with each) is not acknowledged as UX work. It should be. This UX work is some of the most important work we do for our field because future UX and TPC professionals interact directly with this work. Therefore, UX needs to be part of our arsenal for conducting innovative academic work.

As UX professionals, TPC instructors and program administrators must choose from the UX toolkit as they create, assess, and revise their work. Again, I use Still's (2010) emphasis on using small-scale studies to be proactive, and TPC, as a discipline, ought to focus on being proactive in research and pedagogy. Being proactive means starting with small, localized studies that provide designers with enough information to start building, retrofitting, or rebuilding new courses and programs. Being proactive means collecting data to understand how students succeed with the artifacts or processes we build for them and how those artifacts or processes hinder their work. Being proactive means understanding students' ecosystems, which our classes and programs are only a small portion of, to design programs that work within those ecosystems. To be proactive, we need to work with the resources and participants that we have and strive to create better student experiences.

This collection claims, promotes, and demonstrates how UX is an academic practice in myriad ways. The authors of the following chapters describe various impetuses for employing UX work to answer questions about teaching and program development. Authors chose diverse methods to collect and analyze data to understand student users. Though authors may use similar methods, their reasons for using these methods are unique and specific to their particular research and design goals. They demonstrate how to use the small-scale study in ways that produce rigorous, yet localized data to continue iterating their course and program designs. These studies further demonstrate the versatility of UX, the design methods that support UX as a practice, and the research methods used to collect data. This collection is a starting point for discussing a UX pedagogy that we hope will continue far beyond the work we have done here.

This chapter is only the first of a two-part introduction. In Chapter 2, Kelli Cargile Cook and I continue to situate UX as an academic and pedagogical practice, one that fills an important role in TPC's mission to be student-user advocates. In doing so, we argue that UX methods help us go beyond anecdotes to inform classroom and program administration practices. Further, we provide several journey maps illustrating how this collection can be read. This is our humble attempt at making UX a proactive academic practice.

■ References

Albers, M. J. (2004). *Communication in complex information: User goals and information needs for dynamic web information*. Lawrence Erlbaum.

Baek, E., Cagiltay, K., Boling, E. & Frick, T. (2008). User-centered design and development. In J. M. Spector, M. D. Merrill, J. van Merriënboer & M. P. Driscoll (Eds.), *Handbook of research on educational communication and technology* (3rd ed., pp. 659–670). Lawrence Erlbaum.

Barnum, C. (2019). The state of UX research. *Journal of Usability Studies, 15*(1), 1–7.

Beyer, H. & Holtzblatt, K. (1999). Contextual design. *Interactions, 6*(1), 32–42. https://dl.acm.org/doi/10.1145/291224.291229.

Cosgrove, S. (2018). Exploring usability and user-centered design through emergency management websites: Advocating responsive web design. *Communication Design Quarterly, 6*(2), 93–102.

Crane, K. (2015). *The usability of the course syllabus: Testing syllabi modality and comprehension* [Doctoral dissertation, Texas Tech University]. Texas Tech University Libraries. https://ttu-ir.tdl.org/handle/2346/64572.

Dam, R. & Siang, T. (n.d.). *5 stages in the design thinking process*. Interaction Design Foundation. https://www.interaction-design.org/literature/article/5-stages-in-the-design-thinking-process.

Dumas, J. S. (1989). Stimulating change through usability testing. *SIGCHI Bulletin, 21*(1), 37–44.

Dumas, J. S. (2007). The great leap forward: The birth of the usability profession (1988–1993). *Journal of Usability Studies, 2*(2), 54–60.

Elizarova, O., Briselli, J. & Dowd, K. (2017, December). Participatory design in practice. *UX Magazine*. https://uxmag.com/articles/participatory-design-in-practice.

International Organization for Standardization. (2018). *Ergonomics of human-system interaction* (ISO 9241-11:2018). https://www.iso.org/standard/63500.html#:~:text=ISO%209241-11.

Johnson, R. R. (1998). *User-centered technology: A rhetorical theory for computers and other mundane artifacts*. SUNY Press.

Krug, S. (2014). *Don't make me think revisited* (3rd ed). New Riders.

Lauer, C. (2016). Re-considering research: Why we need to adopt a mixed-methods approach to our work. *Communication Design Quarterly, 4*(3), 46–50.

Lauer, C. & Brumberger, E. (2016). Technical communication as user experience in a broadening industry landscape. *Technical Communication, 52*(3), 248–264.

Meloncon, L. & St.Amant, K. (2019). Empirical research in technical and professional communication: A 5-year examination of research methods and a call for research sustainability. *Journal of Technical Writing and Communication, 49*(2), 128–155.

Mirel, B. (1991). Critical review of experimental research on the usability of hard copy documentation. *IEEE Transactions on Professional Communication, 34*(2), 109–122.

Mirel, B. (2002). Advancing a vision of usability. In B. Mirel & R. Spilka (Eds.), *Reshaping technical communication* (pp. 165–187). Lawrence Erlbaum.

Muller, M. J. (2009). Participatory design: The third space in HCI. In A. Sears & J. A. Sacko (Eds.), *Human-computer interaction* (pp. 165–185). CRC Press.

Nielsen, J. (1993). *Usability engineering*. Morgan Kauffman.

Norman, D. (2013). *The design of everyday things*. (Revised and expanded ed.). Basic Books.

Norman, D. & Nielsen, J. (n.d.). *The definition of user experience (UX)*. Nielsen Norman Group. https://www.nngroup.com/articles/definition-user-experience/.

Opel, D. & Rhodes, J. (2018). Beyond student as user: Rhetoric, multimodality, and user-centered design. *Computers and Composition, 49*, 71–81.

Pope-Ruark, R. (2019). Design thinking in Technical and Professional Communication: Four perspectives. *Journal of Business and Technical Communication, 33*(4), 437–455.

Pope-Ruark, R., Tham, J., Moses, J. & Conner, T. (2019). Introduction to special issue: Design-thinking approaches in Technical and Professional Communication. *Journal of Business and Technical Communication, 33*(4), 370–375.

Potts, L. (2014). *Social media and disaster response: How experience architects can build for participation*. Routledge.

Potts, L. & Salvo, M. J. (2017). Introduction. In L. Potts & M. J. Salvo (Eds.), *Rhetoric and experience architecture* (pp. 3–13). Parlor Press.

Quesenbery, W. (2003). The five dimensions of usability. In M. J. Albers & B. Mazur (Eds.), *Content and complexity: Information design in Technical Communication* (pp. 81–102). Lawrence Erlbaum.

Redish, J. (1995). Are we really entering a post-usability era? *ACM SIGDOC Asterisk Journal of Computer Documentation, 19*(1), 18–24.

Redish, J. (2010). Technical communication and usability: Intertwined strands and mutual influences commentary. *IEEE Transactions on Professional Communication, 53*(3), 191–201.

Redish, J. & Barnum, C. (2011). Overlap, influence, intertwining: The interplay of UX and technical communication. *Journal of Usability Studies, 6*(3), 90–101.

Rose, E. (2016). Design as advocacy: Using a human-centered approach to investigate the needs of vulnerable populations. *Journal of Technical Writing and Communication, 46*(4), 427–445.

Salvo, M. J. (2001). Ethics of engagement: User-centered design and rhetorical methodology. *Technical Communication Quarterly, 10*(3), 273–290.

Stephen, D. (2019, July 27). *What is co-design—Kelli Ann McKercher—Beyond Sticky Notes*. Duncan Stephen. https://duncanstephen.net/what-is-co-design-kelly-ann-mckercher-beyond-sticky-notes/.

Still, B. (2010). Mapping usability: An ecological framework for analyzing user experience. In M. Albers & B. Still (Eds.), *Usability of complex information: User goals and information needs for dynamic web information* (pp. 90–108). Lawrence Erlbaum.

Still, B. & Crane, K. (2016). *Fundamentals of user-centered design*. CRC Press.

Zachry, M. & Spyridakis, J. (2016). Human-centered design and the field of Technical Communication. *Journal of Technical Writing and Communication, 46*(4), 392–401.

2. Beyond Lore: UX as Data-Driven Practice

Kelli Cargile Cook
TEXAS TECH UNIVERSITY

Kate Crane
EASTERN WASHINGTON UNIVERSITY

Abstract: This chapter opens by connecting user experience (UX) and pedagogical practice. It then asks and addresses the central question of this collection: *How can we engage user experience approaches to better understand and engage students in order to strengthen technical and professional communication degrees, programs, courses, units within courses, and even lessons?* With this question in mind, the final section of this chapter offers four journey maps through the collection. Each map offers readers a distinctive route through the collection while introducing individual chapters and exploring how these chapters can be read as a whole.

Keywords: lore, pedagogy, user experience, student-centered, journey maps

Key Takeaways:

- UX as a pedagogical practice offers teachers a methodological alternative to lore.
- UX methodologies allow teachers to test what they think they know and provide insights about that which they do not clearly understand.
- Student-centered and user-centered are not pedagogically synonymous terms.
- UX terminology needs to be critically examined and carefully adopted as it refers to students as users.

Teachers have always been iterative information designers. Stephen North (1987) discussed how teacher-practitioners create their students' classroom experiences over 30 years ago in *The Making of Knowledge in Composition: Portrait of an Emerging Field*. He writes that "[Teacher] practitioners are always tinkering with things, seeing if they can't be made to work better" (p. 25). Through this tinkering, teacher-practitioners build a body of "*lore*," which North defines as "what has worked, is working, or might work in teaching, doing, or learning writing" (1987, p. 23). Compared to other methods of inquiry, North critiques lore for its lack of generalizability: it is a "self-contained" solution arising from experience that either works or doesn't work (p. 51). If the solution works, it may be passed on to others; if not, it is discarded and forgotten. In its place, another solution is tried, and so it goes. In concluding his chapter on practitioner lore, North acknowledges the following:

> The academic reflex to hold lore in low regard represents a serious problem in Composition, and Practitioners need to defend themselves—to argue for the value of what they know, and how they come to know it. For that very reason, though, they need to be more methodologically self-conscious than any other communities: to know the limits of authority the other modes of inquiry can claim, on the one hand; but to know the limits of their own, as well, and work within them. (1987, p. 55)

Although this collection focuses on technical and professional communication, not composition, we begin this chapter with a nod to North (1987) because the collection's focus on *user experience* (UX) has deep roots in both the concept of *practice* and the concept of *inquiry*: UX might be defined as a practice that improves human experiences through situated inquiry within a highly contextualized space. As Crane discusses in Chapter 1 of this collection, UX is a practice that evolved when the usability profession moved from experimental laboratory designs "to a focus on smaller-scale studies that provided an easier, more cost-effective method for incorporating usability iteratively in a product's design process." These small-scale iterative studies are somewhat like the daily, weekly, and semesterly revisions teacher-practitioners historically have made to their courses and curricula. To decide what needs to be changed, teacher-practitioners perform reflection-in-action, "the art by which practitioners sometimes deal with situations of uncertainty, instability, uniqueness, and value conflict" (Schon, 1984, p. 50). In other words, when teacher-practitioners encounter a comforting or discomforting situation affecting student success, they take note and, if necessary, adjust. The situations noted or adjusted do not occur in isolation: teachers encounter them with their students. Successful or failed situations *with* students lead teachers to reflect on ways to improve their practice.

While we honor the iterative knowledge-making of teacher-practitioners, we agree with North's concerns that teacher lore lacks methodological rigor. Decision-making and adjustments often rely on a guess or hunch about what would make classrooms a better experience. As veteran teachers ourselves, we recognize that our classroom experiences from one semester affect the classroom experiences we build the next. At the same time, UX research has made us aware that, although we watch our students in the classroom and monitor their successes, often we do not solicit or invite their participation when we make curricular decisions. For example, our students are rarely with us when we revise our course syllabi as a semester begins or work with other faculty to update or revise our programs. Even when we can solicit and implement student feedback, we may face challenges that prevent us from implementing student recommendations. (For an example of these challenges, see Mark Zachry's chapter in this collection.)

If we neglect to include students in curricular decisions, we are not alone. In fact, assessment practices in higher education rarely acknowledge student experience. While curricular design and assessment at the degree, program, course, and even unit/lesson levels are commonplace on university and college campuses, in most cases, content experts—teachers, program directors, and other administrators—decide what content is taught and how that content will be assessed. These decisions are then codified in plans that track students' demonstrable achievement of assessment measures. Students function as by-products of curricular design, and, as such, students and their achievements are measured, weighed, analyzed, and reported. Rarely do teachers, program directors, and other administrators engage students other than as functional by-products of curricula. In typical waterfall design, students' functionality is measured at the end of the instructional unit in terms of what they can and cannot do.

This collection examines a different approach to instructional design and assessment, one that moves students and their experiences to the center of academic practice and provides teacher-practitioners with numerous methods to support inquiry. It explores a central question: *How can we engage user experience approaches to better understand and engage students in order to strengthen technical and professional communication degrees, programs, courses, units within courses, and even lessons?*

In choosing chapters to include in this collection, we looked for three key qualities:

1. authors who exhibited reflection-in-action, a quality we admire in teacher-practitioners;
2. rigorous method(s) employed to identify educational needs and promote change; and
3. student engagement in identifying and implementing needed change.

As we worked with our authors, we learned that UX approaches can be applied successfully within educational settings, but, as Dawn Opel and Jacqueline Rhodes (2018) have noted, UX terminology is not comfortably overlaid when describing educational situations. Further, like teacher lore, findings from UX approaches are often local and ungeneralizable. We discuss these problems in the next section. In the latter sections of this chapter, we argue that, nevertheless, UX is an effective academic practice. Using a series of journey maps through chapters, we introduce the collection's authors who have shown us that UX can lead to methodologically sound, responsive iterative changes in our classrooms and degree programs.

■ Problems with UX as an Academic Practice

There are many examples of scholars employing user experience design and research methods to investigate important aspects of students' experiences.

Natasha Jones (2018) uses human-centered design to study how viewing students as end users of syllabi can create a stronger document for student use. By surveying students' attitudes about syllabi, Jones finds that "students are able to identify design elements that help them to locate and use information in a course syllabus" (p. 33). Further, she argues that "In positioning our students as expert end users, we can include them as co-creators for designing our course deliverables" (p. 34). Brian Still and Amy Koerber's (2010) usability study focusing on how students use instructor feedback on an assignment and Tharon Howard's (2008) study concluding that students use writing handbooks in ways that simple usability testing cannot accurately gauge are both examples of how UX methods can be used to test our preconceived ideas of how students do (or do not) use the resources instructors provide. These studies show that testing what we think we know can provide insights about that which we do not clearly understand.

However, any attempt to adapt UX design principles to academic practice bumps immediately into terminology and naming issues. UX evolved from industry practices and, with those practices, came terminology that many academics find unacceptable. UX is associated with terms like "user," "product," and "processes," terms that seem to strip away the humanity of the classroom. Opel and Rhodes (2018) argue, in reference to user-centered design (UCD), that "certain industry discourses have become so ubiquitous that design and use of technology is tied inextricably to accumulation of capital" (p. 74). Further, they claim that "an ethic of expediency and efficiency undergird the move" to using UCD in learning environments (Opel & Rhodes, 2018, p. 75). Collin Bjork (2018) provides a similar argument about the limitation of usability studies, claiming that they lack "attention to politics and ideology" (p. 7). Michael Greer and Heidi Harris (2018) further these claims, stating, "We cannot simply substitute 'students' or 'learners' for 'users'"; instead, they choose the term "student-user" to distinguish between a user who "seeks to achieve a single task or goal" and a student who "is a learner, with complex, long-term needs and goals" (p. 15). These authors are concerned that language and frameworks emerging from commercial endeavors (making better products for end users) are inadequate, especially when considering student needs. Instead, Opel and Rhodes and Bjork call for merging rhetoric with UCD/usability studies to remind us of the complexities inherent in the use of any product.

Similarly, we have been asked how or if "user-centered" and "student-centered" practices are synonymous. We see two problems with conflating the terms. First, student-centered, as we understand it, was a movement to decentralize the classroom: from lecture to student-centered activities that promote learning (Barker and Kemp, 1990). Writing studies already has a long history of promoting pedagogies moving away from a lecture-centric classroom toward a student-centered classroom (Opel and Rhodes, 2018). Donna Kain (2003) explains that "student-centered approaches derive from constructivist views of education, in which the construction of knowledge is shared and learning is achieved through students' engagement with activities in which they are invested" (p. 104). Viewing students as users is different from this movement. Student users are, instead, people who rely on resources created or chosen by an instructor or program administrator to facilitate their learning and complete their work.

A second problem is that authors who prefer "student-centered" instead of "user-centered" narrow the focus of user experience. As discussed in Chapter 1, the evolution from usability to user experience in technical and professional communication (TPC) has positioned itself as one of user advocacy. On the one hand, how UCD and usability are defined in industry does not need to be transferred verbatim to TPC classroom contexts or TPC research. However, user experience design and research methods can be used to generate user data and pedagogical products (such as syllabi, learning management system designs, iterative student profiles, program learning outcomes, etc.) in ways that consider student users innovatively. While we should never disregard the limitation of our research, user experience methods can help instructors and program directors iteratively design documents or test their own assumptions. It is, of course, the responsibility of TPC class and program designers to consider the rhetorical factors involved in creating course materials and spaces for learning. Whereas we understand the difficulty in conflating industry and academic practices, they are inextricably connected. To dismiss industry practices and terminology completely is to erase the history of our field.

While we acknowledge that these problems exist, in this collection we do not grapple with these terms extensively. Instead, we have allowed our authors to choose terms they are comfortable with, and they have not disappointed us. While some have chosen to use terms directly from UX, e.g., referring to students as "users" and curricula as "products," others have chosen to reference students with terms ranging from "student users" to "co-creators." As we wrapped up the collection, we considered asking for one final revision to make more terminology consistent throughout, but eventually we decided to let the differences stand. Our decision leaves the terms open for consideration and discussion, and we encourage readers of these chapters to arrive at their own conclusions.

■ UX as an Academic Practice and Solution

Awareness of the sometimes uneasy fit of UX terminology, we argue, does not weaken UX's potential as an academic practice. As we noted above, we prefer to think of UX (and experience architecture [XA], for that matter) in terms of the inquiry afforded. A UX toolkit offers teacher-practitioners many potential methods, as Crane describes in Chapter 1. These methodological tools, when applied in context-rich settings with student users, deliver data that confirm or deny hunches that gut instinct and lore have previously relied on. The chapters in this collection demonstrate how a UX toolkit can be employed to make innovative decisions about lessons/activities, courses, curricula, and extracurricular problems or other academic challenges. Because readers may come to these chapters with a variety of questions or challenges, we considered four different organizations for the collection, each one providing a different user/reader experience through the collection as a whole. In the subsections below, we introduce the chapters through four different journey maps and invite readers to choose their own journey through the collection.

Focus on Student-Users Journey Map

In this first journey map, the chapter organization illustrates how UX methods allow teacher-practitioners to work with students to design course activities, lessons, and entire curriculum. Chapters fall into four categories: Situating User Experience, Understanding Users, Designing with Users, and Redesigning with Users, and chapters are ordered as they are in the table of contents (Figure 2.1).

Figure 2.1. Focus on student-users journey map.

The first set of chapters following the introductory chapters—Understanding Users—provides examples of how surveys and journey maps can be used to collect data from students. Sarah Martin's chapter describes a series of surveys she uses throughout the semester to collect data from students on their expectations, majors, and interests in order to determine what workplaces to focus on when teaching a technical and professional communication service course. On the other end of the academic spectrum, Tharon Howard's chapter describes two case studies. The most detailed case presents an assignment his graduate students completed to collect user data in order to redesign a departmental website. Also working with graduate students, Laura Gonzales and Josephine Walwema's chapter explores a course design they developed with a transliteracy focus. In their chapter, four of their graduate students provide their own transliteracy narratives and describe the UX projects they implemented, ranging from a high school classroom to a non-governmental organization (NGO) website.

The next set of chapters—Designing with Users—explores how academic innovations can be identified and implemented by engaging with students who will use them. Beau Pihlaja's chapter describes how he used UX methods to teach students in a pilot course, Texts and Technologies that Changed the World. Through an examination of the course learning management system (LMS) and syllabus, he asked students to consider how their experiences might suggest changes to these documents to better suit their needs. Lindsay Clark and Traci Austin's chapter provides a description of how they used a variety of methods, ranging from surveys to observations, to prototype an oral communication lab in their department. Luke Thominet's and Kelli Cargile Cook's chapters both discuss how they used multiple UX methods to write student learning outcomes and gauge the efficacy of new certificate and degree programs. In the final chapter of this section, Lee-Ann Kastman Breuch, Ann Hill Duin, and Emily Gresbrink recount their use of UX methods to design a mentor program between graduate and undergraduate students and their program's advisory board.

The final set of chapters explores how students can support the redesign of academic course assignments, courses, and programs. Mark Zachry's chapter identifies double binds as a problem instructors may face when they use UX methods to adjust student assignments within a course. His chapter considers how students' needs and wants can conflict with other course or administrative requirements. Both Jennifer Bay et al.'s chapter and Christine Masters-Wheeler and Gracemarie Mike Fillenwarth's chapter take on the revision of programs, but with different approaches. Bay and her student co-authors describe how they engaged students and alumni to assess their program's effectiveness, while Masters-Wheeler and Fillenwarth's chapter considers how program data gathered from a common student survey can be employed in two different academic programs.

Focus on Goals Journey Map

Another approach to this collection asks readers to consider what questions they seek to answer through UX inquiry. To ask questions through a UX lens, we need to have clear goals for what the data and process are seeking to accomplish. Goals, of course, affect scope:

- Does an individual assignment in a course need revision to better communicate the assignment requirements to students?
- Does an existing course LMS shell need revamping for a new term so students can locate content more easily?
- Is a program trying to revise its course offerings to appeal to students looking for courses focusing on professionalization?

All of these questions have a goal, and UX methods can be useful to design or redesign any of these new "products." The goal of the project, its scope, and the context must shape the UX process. Not only is this necessary to ensure teacher-practitioners have developed a product or system that considers student experiences, but it is also necessary to create goals and develop a UX plan that matches the scope and context of the project. Doing so may lead to upending the linear process we typically follow in curricular design and assessment, but that process is not representative of the dynamic work UX professionals and researchers engage in every day. From a UX perspective, chapters in this collection can be organized into working with four curricular design/redesign goals: activity/lesson design, course design, curricular design, and extracurricular design. See Figure 2.2 for a journey map that illustrates this organization.

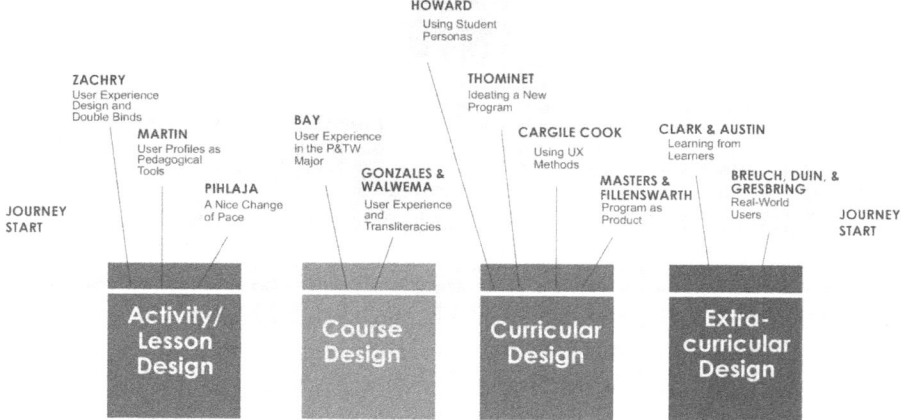

Figure 2.2. Focus on goals journey map.

Following this map allows readers to focus on specific areas of change, whether their interest is in making small adjustments to a class activity or adding new extracurricular activities between students and a successful advisory board. Chapters within each section can be read in any order.

Focus on Methods Journey Map

Although the third journey map has only three categories—understanding, looking, and making—it is more complex than the previous two. The journey map is based on Luma Institute's (2012) *Innovating for People: Human-Centered Design Planning Cards*, a card deck which categorizes the design process into three skill sets:

- **Looking**: Observing human experience
- **Understanding**: Analyzing challenges and opportunities
- **Making**: Envisioning future possibilities (n.p.)

Using Luma Institute's card deck, we sorted the chapters into these categories. Readers who decide to follow this journey map will find that some chapters appear in more than one category and under more than one method. For example, Tharon Howard's chapter includes two case studies; within those case studies, he explains how his studies included multiple methods, including user profiles and personas, task analyses, and operative imaging. On the other hand, some chapters use only one method, such as Masters-Wheeler and Fillenwarth's surveys. For this reason, some chapters appear only once on the map.

By including a map that focuses on methods, we emphasize the idea that user experience is a methodology, as Brian Still (personal communication, February 24, 2020) frequently reminds us. As a methodology, user experience is a set of methods we engage in this collection to design innovative academic activities, courses, curricula, and extracurricular activities. Among UX's methods are the six Crane introduces in Chapter 1 (contextual inquiry, self-reporting, collaborative design studio, affinity diagramming, prototype feedback, and usability testing) as well as 14 additional methods that we have grouped using Luma Institute's categories. Figure 2.3 provides a journey map you can follow if you are particularly interested in specific methods and their application in this collection's chapters.

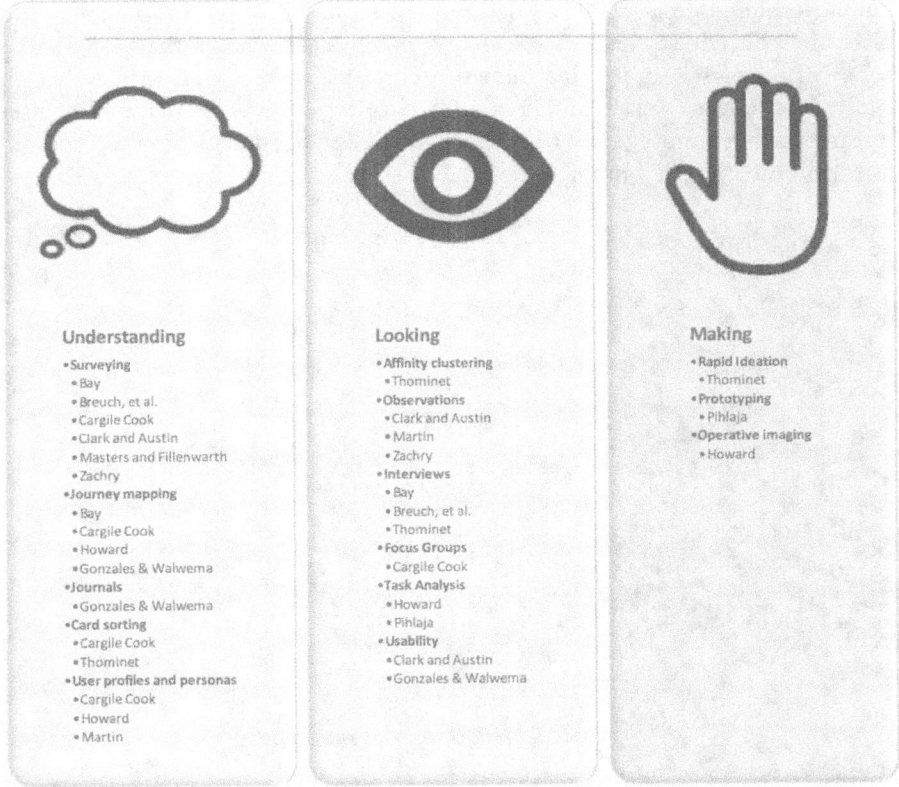

Figure 2.3. Methods journey map.

Focus on Design State Journey Map

A UX process can begin anywhere in the design process. Texts about UX tend to discuss UX from the beginning of a design process, focusing on human/user research and ideation. However, UX can begin anywhere in a design cycle. Sometimes, it is more useful to examine a current design, test that design, and redesign it to create better products or processes. In other cases, testing an existing design, learning about its weak points, collecting human/user research, and then redesigning is the best process for improving a design. This design state journey map's purpose is to meet our readers, or users, where they are. Based on where readers are in their design process, they can use the chapters associated with that design stage to help strategize their current and next moves in the design process. Some of these chapters overlap with previous stages' recommended chapters; however, as is the nature of user experience, we do not see these chapters needing to be followed linearly or sequentially. We invite readers to use these chapters where they best assist them in their design.

In this cyclical map (Figure 2.4), we use the user-centered design (UCD)/human-centered design (HCD) design process map presented in Chapter 1 to place the collection's chapters in relation to the design stage they use or discuss. For research and defining human/user needs, we recommend focusing on Martin's, Thominet's, and Cargile Cook's chapters for studies that collect user research and incorporate that research in the design of student profiles, program learning outcomes, and program design.

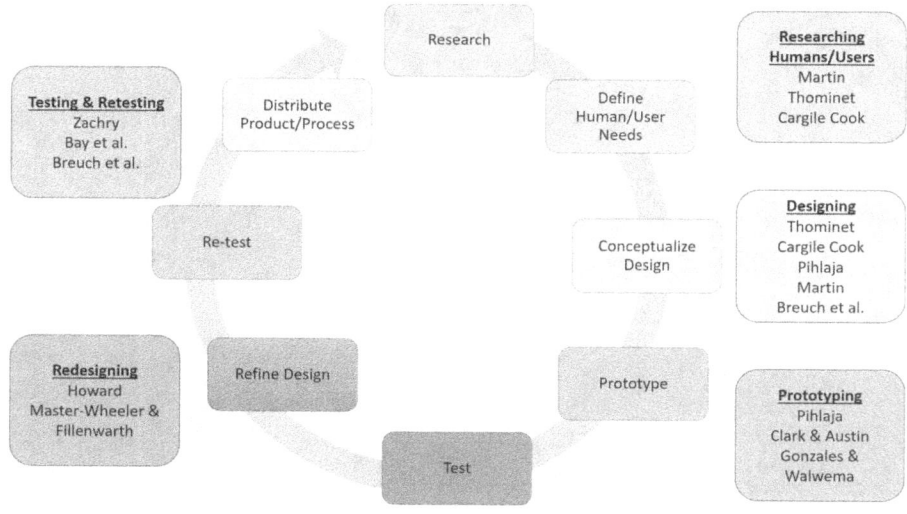

Figure 2.4. Design state journey map.

If the reader has researched and has analyzed that research to determine human/user needs, we recommend beginning with chapters that discuss designing curricular products: Cargile Cook, Thominet, Pihlaja, Martin, and Breuch et al. These chapters discuss the design of curricula, outcomes, course resources, student profiles, and a mentoring program respectively. In all these chapters, authors detail the process they used to decide how to take their research and ideations to create new, contextually appropriate products or processes for their students and programs.

The prototyping chapters discuss the use of prototyping to create sketches of ideas, sometimes with students (as in the case of Pihlaja and Gonzales and Walwema), or to test ideas (in the case of Clark and Austin). These chapters are particularly useful for readers who have conceptualized designs but are looking for a way to incorporate these designs into a working model that can be tested.

The next stage—redesigning—skips the testing stage, not because testing is unimportant or should move elsewhere in the cycle, but because we grouped test and retest categories together (this will be discussed next). Testing is still an important stage to gauge and reflect on prototypes or existing products you are trying to learn more about. Redesigning assumes that at least one round of testing has already taken place (through usability testing or heuristic evaluation). Howard's and Masters-Wheeler and Fillenwarth's chapters both discuss redesigning a product based on feedback given for previous products and curricula.

Finally, the testing and retesting stage discusses the use of UX methods to test an implemented program (such as a mentoring program, academic program, or course curricula) and reflections based on these tests. Zachry's, Bay et al.'s, and Breuch et al.'s chapters exemplify the reassessment of previous work to indicate the success of this work and where improvement may be needed.

With these four journey maps, we have attempted to provide readers with multiple tables of contents to make the user experience of this collection adaptable for different users and goals. Though there are certainly endless ways to reimagine the journeys readers will take with this book, these are the four patterns we thought most useful. We invite readers, however, to make their own journey map with this collection and use it to best meet their needs.

User Experience as a Tool for Innovative Academic Practice

Whichever journey map readers decide to follow through this collection, we expect that they will find innovative ideas for using UX as an academic practice. UX methods, as Martin explains in her chapter, produce new insights grounded in student data. Similarly, Nick Carrington (2020) explains that he uses UX methods to "validate what I thought to be true along the way" (n.p.). As these teacher-practitioners note, using UX methods helps to document lore and support hunches with data. Further, it moves technical and professional teacher-practitioners from just teaching about user experience methods to actually using them to improve their students' experiences. Even in situations like the double binds Zachry describes, taking a UX approach to academic innovation provides teacher-practitioners with a means to articulate the conflict that can exist between student needs or wants and instructor expertise and know-how.

As Janice Redish (2010) noted, "we are not our users, and users will always surprise you" (p. 193). Students are one user population in the technical and professional communication ecosystem. Other users are present too: faculty, staff, administrators, future employers, and accreditation agencies, among others. However, student know-how and expertise are too often silenced when faculty and administrators design course materials and build programs. When students feel they cannot complete an assignment or reasonably dedicate the time to complete program requirements, they know they have other options better aligned to their particular experience. Viewing students as users situates them in a place where we can truly study their needs and interactions with our courses and programs; in return, we can create content and design programs that students understand, and, through student feedback, we can improve them.

As we noted at this chapter's beginning, we believe instructors do UX every time they teach a class. Instructors use student feedback, observations from classes, and assessment to alter assignments or syllabi to better fit the needs of students and meet the outcomes of a course. While they may not be acknowledged formally as UX, certainly an element of UX exists in these practices. Engaging with UX design processes and methods takes the guesswork out of this common experience and replaces hunches with data. While UX practice is more time-consuming than relying on hunches, UX data provides unique situational insights about specific contexts in which we teach and learn, and, although UX methods naturally pair with the pedagogical work teacher practitioners do, we may not use them in a formalized, conscious way. We should.

■ References

Barker, T. T. & Kemp, F. O. (1990). Network theory: A postmodern pedagogy for the writing classroom. In C. Handa (Ed.), *Computers and community* (pp 1–27). Boynton/Cook.

Bjork, C. (2018). Integrating usability testing with digital rhetoric in OWI. *Computers and Composition, 49*, 4–13.

Carrington, N. (2020). *Using UX/UCD methods to create a content strategy* [Doctoral dissertation, Texas Tech University]. Texas Tech University Libraries. https://ttu-ir.tdl.org/handle/2346/85744.

Greer, M. & Harris, H. S. (2018). User-centered design as a foundation for effective online writing instruction. *Computers and Composition, 49*, 14–24.

Howard, T. (2008). Unexpected complexity in a traditional usability study. *Journal of Usability Studies, 3*(4), 189–205.

Jones, N. N. (2018). Human centered syllabus design: Positioning our students as expert end-users. *Computers and Composition, 49*, 25–35.

Kain, D. J. (2003). Teacher-centered versus student-centered: Balancing constraint and theory in the composition classroom. *Pedagogy, 3*(1), 104–108.

Luma Institute. (2012). *Innovating for people: Human-centered design planning cards.*

North, S. M. (1987). *The making of knowledge in composition: Portrait of an emerging field.* Boynton/Cook.

Opel, D. S. & Rhodes, J. (2018). Beyond student as user: Rhetoric, multimodality, and user-centered design. *Computers and Composition, 49,* 71–81.

Redish, J. (2010). Technical communication and usability: Intertwined strands and mutual influences. *IEEE Transactions on Professional Communication, 53*(3), 191–201.

Schon, D. A. (1984). *The reflective practitioner: How professionals think in action.* Basic Books.

Still, B. & Koerber, A. (2010). Listening to students: Usability evaluation of instructor commentary. *Journal of Business and Technical Communication, 24*(2), 206–233.

3. User Profiles as Pedagogical Tools in the Technical and Professional Communication Classroom

Sarah Martin
TEXAS TECH UNIVERSITY

Abstract: This chapter presents a 16-week exploratory study on developing student-user profiles in an introductory undergraduate technical and professional communication (TPC) course. It explores the following research question: *How can TPC instructors leverage student-user profiles to guide course and lesson design decisions in an introductory TPC course?* Presenting three iterations of a student-user profile, the chapter describes two key activities that TPC instructors can practice and refine for their own courses and lessons: (1) developing and iterating a student-user profile before, during, and after a course; and (2) understanding how information from a student-profile can inform course and lesson design decisions. It addresses the role of user-centered design (UCD) approaches in TPC activities such as course and lesson design, and encourages TPC instructors to conceptualize UCD as a philosophy and methodology (Johnson, 1998; Norman, 1986, 1999; Still & Crane, 2016) to apply UCD approaches in the TPC classroom. Benefits and challenges of developing a student-user profile are discussed.

Keywords: user profiles, user experience, user-centered design, technical communication pedagogy

Key Takeaways:

- Developing student-user profiles grounded in UCD methods offers a way for technical and professional communication instructors to apply UX approaches to their course and lesson design.
- Following UCD methods to develop a student-user profile can help TPC instructors and department chairs avoid self-referential design where they impose their own understanding or mental models of how students should interact with, understand, and apply course material.
- Development and use of a student-user profile as a pedagogical tool is not unique to TPC. A student-user profile can be used to understand the student experience in broad academic settings, but TPC instructors should lead this charge.

Developing user profiles is a central activity in user-centered design (UCD) projects that support user experience (UX) inquiries (Cooper, 2004; Garrett, 2011; Pratt & Nunes, 2012; Still & Crane, 2016). User profiles are visual and textual composites that codify actual observational, self-reported, or performance data about a user. They help guide decision-making during a design process by keeping stakeholders' needs at the forefront of a UX project. UX projects may address product, process, and program development, but course and lesson design has not always been considered a primary venue for UX or related UCD activities, such as user profile development (K. Crane & K. Cargile Cook, personal communication, 2019; Getto & Beecher, 2016; Lallemand et al., 2015). Approaching the curriculum design process from a UX perspective with associated UCD methods, however, can ground curriculum decisions in student-user data.

Students are not always framed as central stakeholders in course and lesson design (Still & Koerber, 2010). Course and lesson design decisions are often the result of expert knowledge; seasoned instructors, program directors, and department chairs regularly evaluate, brainstorm, and codify what will "work" best for users (students). Yet this expert-based design approach does not always result in user-centered outcomes (Garrett, 2011; Lowgren & Stolterman, 2007). In this way, developing user profiles—student-user profiles—grounded in UCD methods offers a way for technical and professional communication (TPC) instructors to apply UX approaches to their course and lesson design. A UX approach positions students as central stakeholders, rather than functional by-products (K. Crane & K. Cargile Cook, personal communication, 2019), as curriculum decisions are made. Accordingly, TPC instructors should apply UCD methods to the curriculum design process to better understand the student-user experience.

This chapter presents a 16-week exploratory study on developing student-user profiles in an introductory undergraduate TPC course. It offers a starting point to explore the following research question: *How can we leverage student-user profiles to guide course and lesson design decisions in an introductory TPC course?* This exploratory study describes two key activities that TPC instructors can practice and refine for their own courses and lessons:

1. developing and iterating a student-user profile before, during, and after a course
2. understanding how information from a student-user profile can inform course and lesson design decisions

First, I will discuss the role of UCD approaches in TPC activities such as course and lesson design. I will address what TPC instructors can gain by conceptualizing UCD as a philosophy and methodology to apply UCD approaches in the TPC classroom (Johnson, 1998; Norman, 1986, 1999; Still & Crane, 2016). Next, I will review how user profiles support UCD projects, noting how they are developed, iterated, and consulted to make design decisions (Baxter et al., 2015; Bias & Mayhew, 2005; Ceraso, 2013; Garrett, 2011; Ma & LeRouge, 2007; Still & Crane, 2016). I will then describe the methods I used to develop, alter, and apply my student-user profile during the exploratory study and include models of my draft student-user profile during the semester to its current state. I will present mock-ups of different phases of the student-user profile and address how I altered both the profile and course content based on profile development.

Lastly, I will outline the benefits of developing and applying a student-user profile during the course and offer suggestions to fellow TPC instructors who want to adopt similar profile development practices. I will also discuss why student profiles are useful in individual course and lesson development and how they might be applied in broader curricula decisions (e.g., department meetings, online vs. live class course design, designing for international students, etc.). In turn, this chapter showcases one approach to making curriculum design decisions at the course and lesson level more student-user-based rather than solely expert-based.

■ UCD as a Philosophy and Methodology in TPC Classrooms

For technical and professional communicators (TPCs), understanding *users*—students or other institutional stakeholders—is not just a pretense to ensure users "get" the content, follow directions, or comply with product or process requirements. TPCs bring a unique reverence for user advocacy when defining, addressing, and evaluating problems (Andersen et al., 2013; Anschultz & Rosenberg, 2002; Brumberger & Lauer, 2015; Cargile Cook, 2002; Carliner, 2001; Ceraso, 2013; Cleary & Flammia, 2012; Hart-Davison, 2013; Johnson, 1998, 2004a, 2004b; Mirel, 2013; Redish & Barnum, 2011; Rude, 2009; Schriver, 2013). This reverence for user advocacy can extend to pedagogical and curriculum design decisions.

Applying UCD methods such as user-profile development in the classroom is ultimately about identifying and honoring a user's "knowledge of know-how and use" (Johnson, 1998, p. 5) or honoring the knowledge that users bring to a communication interaction. Accordingly, drawing on UCD methods to honor student knowledge in the curriculum design process is a suitable step for TPC instructors.

For TPC instructors to successfully apply UCD methods to course and lesson design, they must conceptualize UCD as both a philosophy *and* methodology. As Brian Still and Kate Crane (2016) put it, UCD is "something to be believed but also practiced" (p. 44). Applying UCD methods when we make curriculum, course, or lesson design decisions allows TPC instructors and administrators to holistically value student users in these contexts. It is the valuing of user knowledge, of *metis*, in technical communication that creates a "rhetoricized space" (Johnson, 1998, p. 33) where users can "negotiate technology in use and development" (Johnson, 1998, p. 33) through a "dialogic relationship" (Salvo, 2001, p. 276). Honoring user knowledge to design meaningful systems is the work of UCD. UCD as a methodology, then, provides a vital framework for TPCs to place student users at the center of the course and lesson design process.

At the heart of sound UCD methodology is an iterative design process with representative users, representative tasks, and triangulated user research and usability testing methods (Barnum, 2011; Cooper, 2004; Dumas & Redish, 1999; Garrett, 2011; Hackos & Redish, 1998; Krug, 2014; Pratt & Nunes, 2012; Still & Crane, 2016). UCD as a methodology then follows "its own set of methods and principles that serve to execute the methodology's theoretical concepts" (Still & Crane, 2016, p. 44). There is no single path, or to Norman's (1986) concern, no single method or specific combinations of preferred methods to "do" UCD. There are hundreds of UCD methods (Hanington & Martin, 2012). More so, UCD draws on methods from many different fields. Contextual inquiry, for example, which is heavily regarded in UCD (Beyer & Holtzblatt, 1999), stems from ethnographic research (Lowgren & Stolterman, 2007). A UCD method is suitable or not based on the researcher's inquiry, the design situation (Lowgren & Stolterman, 2007), and the determination of how the information gleaned from a particular method informs the design process.

In short, UCD as a philosophy in TPC is necessary, but not sufficient. UCD as a philosophy and methodology offers principles and frameworks to champion user perspectives throughout the design process. UCD methods, such as user profiles, offer a fruitful means for TPC instructors to bring a UCD approach to course and lesson design.

■ User Profiles as a UCD Method

As a method, user profiles help UCD practitioners understand user goals, the use environment, and use context so that they can make informed design decisions. *User profiles* are documents that codify actual observational, self-reported, or performance data about a user. As Still and Crane (2016) put it, "A user profile is a set of defining characteristics, based on your research, that represents a particular group of users" (p. 101). They suggest that user profiles help distinguish different user groups and the "most significant representative characteristics" (p. 195) of these groups.

Accordingly, user profiles can include real demographic information; observational or self-reported data about user habits, goals, motivations, and pain points; and even direct user quotes that capture their perspectives (Baxter et al., 2015; Bias & Mayhew, 2005; Ceraso, 2013; Garrett, 2011; Ma & LeRouge, 2007; Still & Crane, 2016). Like a customer or empathy map (Cao, 2018; Knox, 2014), user profiles can help designers consider what a user thinks and says, sees, does, hears, and feels as they complete primary tasks and goals. In turn, user profile development strategies generate actionable user data that UCD practitioners can use to design products, systems, content, and processes that help users achieve their primary goals, or, as Janice Redish (2010) puts it, to help users simply do the work they need to do.

Personas differ from user profiles in that they are fictionalizations of user profiles. That is, once a user profile is generated based on user research, it can be repurposed into a persona to help design teams understand broader groups of general user needs. As Jesse Garrett (2011) notes, "A persona is a fictional character constructed to represent the needs of a whole range of real users" (p. 49). He explains that personas can serve as "example cases during user experience development" (p. 51). That is, while a user profile is built upon specific, individual user data, a persona offers a macro synthesis of these user insights. Alan Cooper (2004) explains this relationship:

> Personas are not real people, but they represent them throughout the design process. They are hypothetical archetypes of actual users. Although they are imaginary, they are defined with significant rigor and precision. . . . Personas reveal themselves through our research and analysis. (p. 101)

Creating user profiles is part of this UCD research and analysis that can be further developed into personas as the design process evolves.

In summary, profiles and personas differ in that they are actual vs. fictionalized representations, but they are both generated from user data and incorporated into UCD projects (Getto & St. Amant, 2015; Pratt & Nunes, 2012; Still & Crane, 2016; Unger & Chandler, 2012; Van Velsen et al., 2013). A user profile should therefore include relevant information that will help a designer anticipate user needs for the design outcome. In turn, TPC instructors can leverage student-user profiles to help guide course and lesson design decisions by considering student expectations and behaviors with the course content.

Methods: Developing Student-User Profiles for an Undergraduate TPC Course

My goal for this exploratory study was to see how creating a student-user profile might facilitate course and lesson design decisions in an introductory TPC course. At the time of data collection, I was teaching two 16-week synchronous online sections of an undergraduate TPC course at a large state university. The course fulfilled a general university degree requirement and included 25 students from a variety of majors and school years in each section.

I had previously taught the same course at the same institution but perceived a disconnect between the course material and student understanding about the material, learning management system, and course expectations. In response, I reframed my role as a TPC instructor facing student confusion to *a designer facing a design problem for users*. I had some general demographic data about my student users (i.e., year in school, major, residency) from institutional databases, but I only had a superficial, anecdotal recollection of their attitudes, expectations, challenges, motivations, and perspectives about the course material based on prior teaching experiences.

Accordingly, I drew on specific observational, self-report, and student performance information during the new semester to develop a student-user profile to better understand my students and their needs. I did not apply for or receive Institutional Review Board (IRB) approval for this study because I am reporting on the process I used to develop a student-user profile rather than directly reporting on student data. The user profiles I developed and present include composite characteristics that represent a particular user group (Still & Crane, 2016).

Recall that I focused on two key activities to explore how TPC instructors might leverage student-user profiles to guide course and lesson design decisions:

1. developing and iterating a student-user profile before, during, and after a course
2. understanding how information from a student-user profile can inform course and lesson design decisions

Table 3.1 describes the time period, data documentation, and analysis methods that I used to develop and refine different iterations of my student-user profile.

Table 3.1. Data Collection and Analysis Methods

Time Period	Data Documentation Method	Data Analysis Format
Before 1st class meeting	General Information Questionnaire	Google Forms, 14 questions, exported to Excel spreadsheet
Develop Student-User Profile		
Class meetings	Student questions, homework sharing, class discussion	Diary entry in course log
Assignment grading	Major assignments 1 and 2, major problems and success implementing TPC principles	Diary entry in course log
Mid-term	Midterm Questionnaire	Google Forms, ten questions, exported to Excel spreadsheet
Refine Student-User Profile		
Class meetings	Student questions, homework sharing, class discussion	Diary entry in course log
Assignment grading	Major assignments 3 and 4, major problems and success implementing TPC principles	Diary entry in course log
Refine Student-User Profile		
After course completion	Institutional Course Evaluation	TBD

First, I reviewed self-reporting data from a 14-question General Information Questionnaire (Appendix A) that I send to students as standard practice before the course begins. I issue the General Information Questionnaire to my students each semester to learn about who my students are and their general course and professional goals. The questionnaire is voluntary, and I have used past data to address student concerns regarding accessing online courses, for example, or to plan specific lessons regarding TPC artifacts (e.g., if I know many students are engineering majors, I will find TPC artifacts in the engineering field for specific lessons).

I emailed the General Information Questionnaire to both of my course sections one week before, three days before, and one day before our first class meeting. I received 35 responses (87% response rate) and exported the data into a new Profile Data Excel spreadsheet. I reviewed and isolated information that would help me distinguish the "most significant representative characteristics" (Still & Crane, 2016, p. 195) of my student users based on my design goal—to see what I could learn by developing a student-user profile. In my case, understanding (1) my students' motivations for taking the course, (2) their expectations for what the course was about, and (3) their current understanding of the course topic was valuable. Profile development practices stress a need to understand what users care about, their mental model when they engage in an experience, or similar perspectives that help characterize the user experience (Cooper, 2004; Garrett, 2011; Getto & St. Amant, 2015; Pratt & Nunes, 2012; Still & Crane, 2016; Unger & Chandler, 2012). Accordingly, I created an Excel spreadsheet that reflected student motivations, expectations, and their understanding of TPC. The spreadsheet had the following headings and corresponding information:

- Motivations: rationales for why students were taking the course, including what skills they hoped to achieve by taking the course, or what university requirement they hoped to fulfill
- Expectations: what students anticipated the course might be about, including specific subjects, strategies, or assignments, that may or may not be addressed
- TPC Understanding: what students indicated TPC was about, what TPC was not about, and how they defined different TPC terms

I also isolated general demographic data and included a summary of my students' majors and year in school in the spreadsheet.

Next, I reviewed the data under the Motivations, Expectations, and TPC Understanding categories for alignment with student habits, goals, motivations, and pain points about the course (Cooper, 2004; Garrett, 2011; Getto & St.Amant, 2015; Pratt & Nunes, 2012; Still & Crane, 2016; Unger & Chandler, 2012). I annotated this data on a piece of paper separated into six general user profile categories that were relevant for my study goal. This paper became the start of my student-user profile. (See *Results: Using Student Profiles to Inform Curriculum Design* for a description of profile categories and iterations).

During the semester, I reviewed additional questionnaire and observational data to refine my student-user profile. That is, I incorporated new questionnaire and observational information about student comments and performance in a diary log format (Rolfe, 2006; Tracy, 2013) to help triangulate the user data with user see-say-do information (Still & Crane, 2016) as a guide. I took notes during class discussions, assignment reviews, and on student questions regarding the course content. For example, if a student commented that TPC only seemed relevant to writing, I noted this in the "Thinks TPC is About" part of my user profile. I also noted problems and successes that students had applying TPC principles in the first and second major course assignments, and subsequently their third and fourth major assignments. I completed a similar process with the Midterm Questionnaire information. I emailed students and posted on the course Blackboard page a link to a second, 10-question Google Forms Midterm Questionnaire (Appendix B). (This questionnaire is also standard practice in my course.) I received 32 responses (80% response rate) and exported the data into an Excel spreadsheet to compare any new relevant information about students' experiences with my user profile.

As later discussed, the student-user profile categories expanded or shifted based on new insights from the observational, self-report, and student performance information during the semester. I then incorporated data from my formal institutional course evaluation for additional user insights.

Results: Using Student Profiles to Inform Curriculum Design

This exploratory study aimed to accomplish two key things: (1) demonstrate a way for TPC instructors to develop and iterate a student-user profile before, during, and after a course and (2) showcase how information from a student-user profile might inform course and lesson design decisions. Suitably, this section will review the study results by explaining the process I used to develop and refine my student-user profile. I will also offer specific examples of how insights from my student-user profile directly informed course and lesson design decisions.

Student-User Profile Iteration A

As previously mentioned, the initial draft of my student-user profile was based on general student demographic data and student responses to a 14-question General Information Questionnaire. Based on this information, I concentrated on six primary categories that describe the TPC student. I focused on these six categories because they helped me better understand my TPC student user: a personifying quotation, demographic information, student perceptions of TPC, concerns, needs, and wants. That is, these categories helped me account for student perceptions, expectations, and needs. While some of these category themes are common in user profile or persona development (Cooper, 2004; Garrett, 2011; Pratt & Nunes, 2012; Still & Crane, 2016), I did not create these specific categories before I began my data collection. Rather, I based these categories on data from the General Information Questionnaire and the course registration list.

I began with a basic pen and paper drawing for my first student-user profile. (Note: the drawings were refined to a higher fidelity in PowerPoint for publication and legibility.) Figure 3.1 illustrates the first iteration of my student-user profile. It includes one box for each information category, which I labeled with the category title. Next, I listed relevant information for each information category.

Personifying Quotation: In the first box, "Intro to TPC Student," I included a personifying quotation based on student questionnaire comments. The personifying quotation is a general synthesis—in my own characterization—of user information that I reviewed for the student-user profile. The quotation framed the general attitude of my students and their concerns before the first day of class.

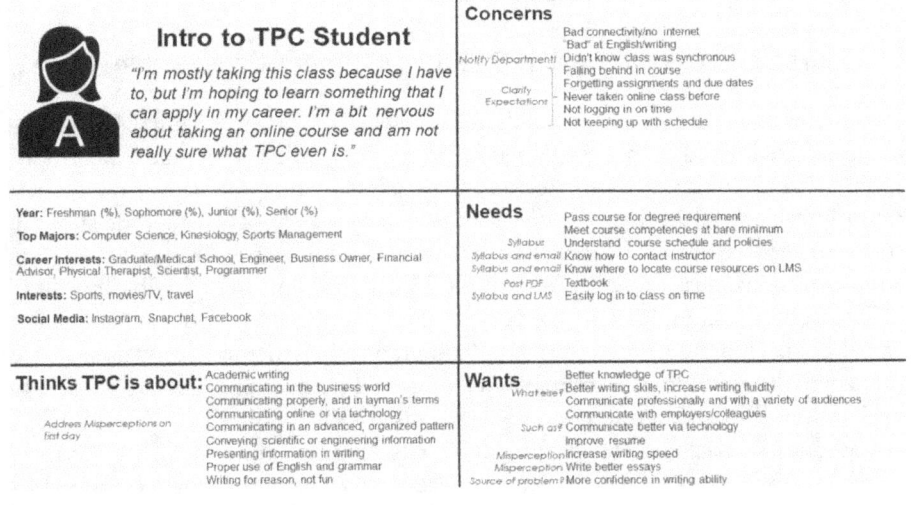

Figure 3.1. Student-user profile A.

Demographic Information: The second student-user profile category, general demographic information, indicated who my students were, their interests, and some basic TPC habits. I documented their year in school, major, career interests, leisure interests, and social media use. The most useful part of this data in terms of lesson and course design was student majors and career interests. As you will read in subsequent sections, I removed the general demographic information from my second and third iterations of the student-user profile. In these profiles, I focused more on documenting student perspectives about TPC content because it more meaningfully informed my lesson design.

Perspectives about TPC: The third category pinpointed what my students thought TPC was about. Recall that students made a variety of statements via the General Information Questionnaire or during class discussions about what TPC was. Their responses varied from simplistic to partial definitions, and sometimes they referenced specific genres and mediums involved.

Concerns: The fourth category identified three major student concerns about the course: students did not know the course met synchronously, they were uneasy about the online medium, and they were nervous they might do poorly in the course based on previous English class experiences.

Needs and Wants: The fifth and sixth categories of my student-user profile included student needs and wants. As an instructor (serving as a course designer), I had to anticipate and distinguish student needs and wants. For example, I based the information in the student needs category on student questionnaire responses, my previous instructor experience, and department and university initiatives. The information focused on passing the course, understanding the main concepts, and successfully functioning in the course. Student wants were directly informed by the introductory questionnaire responses.

Course and Lesson Design Changes (Student-User Profile A)

I was able to make five immediate course and lesson design changes before the course started based on my student-user profile draft. First, I included more definitional TPC work in the first lecture. Creating the user profile gave me insight into my students' attitudes towards the course: they were mostly apathetic about it, they were unsure what TPC was, but they were looking forward to at least making a resume. In response, I presented multiple TPC definitions to highlight how TPC differs from and complements communication practices and products in different career fields. (Note: I learned from the demographic information in my user profile that some of my students were public relations and marketing majors, so I chose to explain how TPC related to these fields because of this finding.)

Second, I selected TPC documents and scenarios common in my students' desired career fields to illustrate course concepts (e.g., patient discharge and medication instructions for aspiring medical professionals) rather than choosing random examples that might generate engagement. Using these documents resulted in rich discussion where students offered personal experience to support the concept. For example, one student shared their tattoo care instructions as an example of bad TPC.

Third, based on my work to understand student concerns for my profile, I was able to immediately notify the department about student registration confusion. As the student-user profile indicates, students were concerned that the course was synchronous because they did not understand that during registration; they had concerns about scheduling and sufficient internet access. Since these student concerns were captured in the profile, the department could accommodate students needing to change sections before the course began and could alter the registration process for subsequent semesters. Fourth, and related to my new knowledge about student confusion over the synchronous course, I refined the syllabus to emphasize important components of a synchronous online course. I did not realize that most of my students thought the course was asynchronous, so this was a meaningful content change.

Lastly, having a better understanding of student needs meant I could prepare responses to student questions or confusion ahead of a class meeting or plan to ask particular clarifying questions during a class meeting. For example, the student-user profile illustrated key student misperceptions—that we would focus heavily on writing speed or essays. In turn, I made a point to review what the course would particularly cover and *not* cover, rather than just sharing the general learning objectives (that might leave them still thinking we were writing essays!). Information in the student wants category, for example, guided me to ask clarifying questions of students; I could plan to ask in a lecture what they were specifically hoping to learn about "communicating via technology" (which they shared on the questionnaire).

Overall, preparing a student-user profile draft before the course started let me make actionable plans and changes to course content and lesson design. Figure 3.1 also illustrates the personal notes that I made in each category to facilitate this process.

Student-User Profile Iteration B and C

During the second and third student-user profile iterations, I refined the profile to better understand and clarify student perceptions about the course and its content. I reviewed student assignment performance, my diary log, and midterm questionnaire information (see Methods) and made three primary changes to the student-user profile in response.

First, I removed the demographic information. Students' school year, for example, did not indicate a key difference in student perceptions or experience based on class discussion or assignment performance. This change streamlined my profile to include more relevant observational data, with a "Think & Say" category to more pointedly capture student perceptions about the course content. *"Think & Say" statements* in a user profile capture what a user might state or contemplate when they interact with a product or process (Still & Crane, 2016).

Second, I included a "Do" category that captured relevant student practices such as their willingness to share examples during class discussion, their confusion over certain course concepts, and their failures or successes following assignment guidelines (see "Do," Figure 3.2). I also expanded the "Challenges" category to include problems students had with the course content. For example, I noted that while students were remembering certain concepts, they were also overgeneralizing their application (see "Challenges," Figure 3.2). I still included general student challenges from the first iteration of the student-user profile because they hindered student performance: falling behind in the course, missing due dates and assignments, not logging in on time, not keeping up with the schedule, and having technology problems during class.

Overall, in iteration B and C, I was able to include more detailed information about student challenges, needs, and wants (see Figure 3.2 and Figure 3.3) as I reflected on user see-say-do (Still & Crane, 2016) information. While some of the general student needs remained the same from iteration A to C (e.g., pass the course, meet minimum requirements), the biggest change was greater specificity in student needs and wants as I refined the student-user profile.

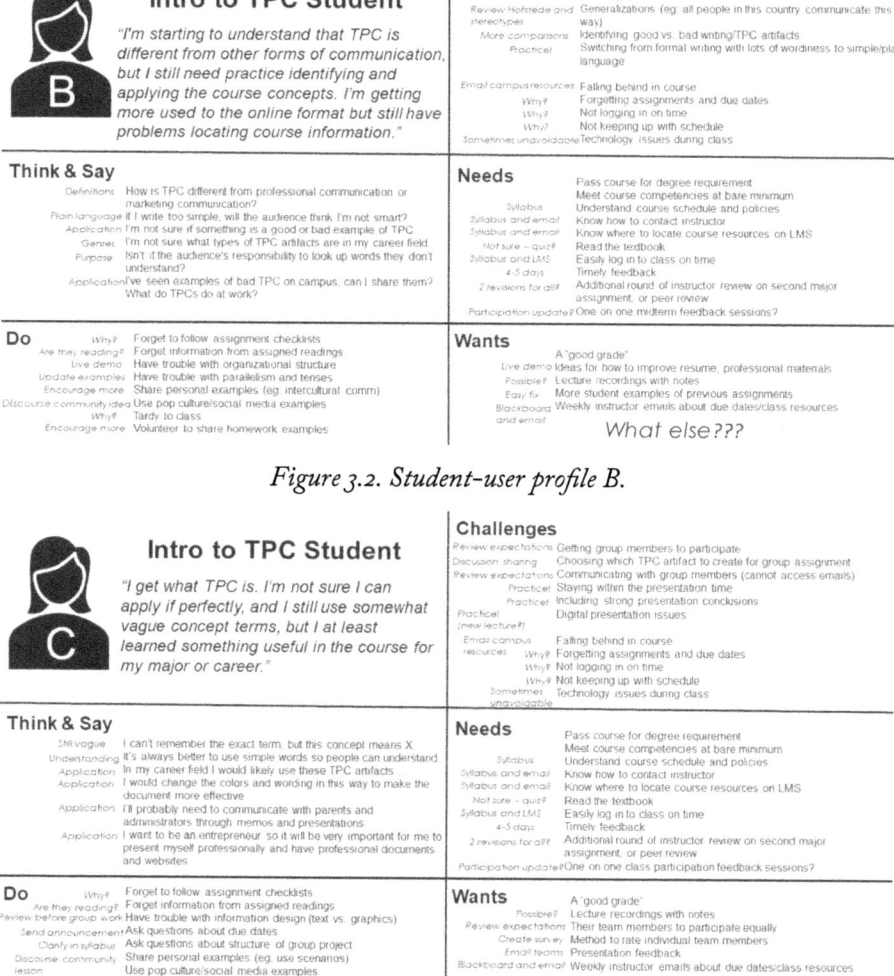

Figure 3.2. Student-user profile B.

Figure 3.3. Student-user profile C.

Last, I refined the personifying quotation. Recall that the *personifying quotation* is a general synthesis, and my own characterization, of user information that I reviewed for the student-user profile. The quotation in iteration B and C is my characterization of what I observed users see, say, or do during the course (Still & Crane, 2016). The personifying quotes in iteration A through C provide a distinctive view of the student experience as students progressed through the course:

> Iteration A: "I'm mostly taking this class because I have to, but I'm hoping to learn something that I can apply in my career. I'm a bit nervous about taking an online course and am not really sure what TPC even is."
>
> Iteration B: "I'm starting to understand how TPC is different from other forms of communication but still need practice identifying and applying the course concepts. I'm getting more used to the online format but still have problems locating course information."
>
> Iteration C: "I get what TPC is. I'm not sure I can apply it perfectly, and I still use somewhat vague concept terms, but I at least learned something useful in the course for my major or career."

Refining the personifying quotation in each iteration meant I could detect a change in student attitudes, experiences, and competencies at different points of the course.

Course and Lesson Design Changes (Student-User Profile B and C)

I made direct pedagogical changes during the course based on iteration B and C of the student-user profile. Some changes were simple and procedural:

- uploaded more student examples from previous assignments onto the LMS
- created a live video demo of me grading an assignment where I emphasized specific course concepts such as information design based on student challenges and needs in the student-user profile
- provided additional student examples and a grading video in response to the "Think & Say" profile B category (e.g., "I'm not sure if something is a good or bad example of TPC") and C category ("I can't remember the exact term, but this concept means X")
- emailed a class recap after each class that repeated due date information already available on the LMS, and included assignment due dates on all lecture slides, and other LMS locations besides the physical assignment, based on student challenges with forgetting or not locating due dates

A larger pedagogical change included a new discussion activity about genres. In iteration B, for example, I learned that students were grappling to understand what TPCs might do in the workplace or what TPC artifacts they might have to create or manage in the workplace if they do not become TPCs. In response, I altered my lesson on genres to include an exercise where students brainstormed potential TPC artifacts that they might be responsible for in their desired career field. I documented the genres for each career field in a notebook that was visible on the screen during class (see Figures 3.4 and 3.5). (Note: we started off with presentations and expanded to broader genres as the discussion evolved.) We discussed which genres overlapped and what TPC concepts might be important for each genre. I often used examples of the specific artifacts my students mentioned during this genre activity to illustrate concepts in other lectures.

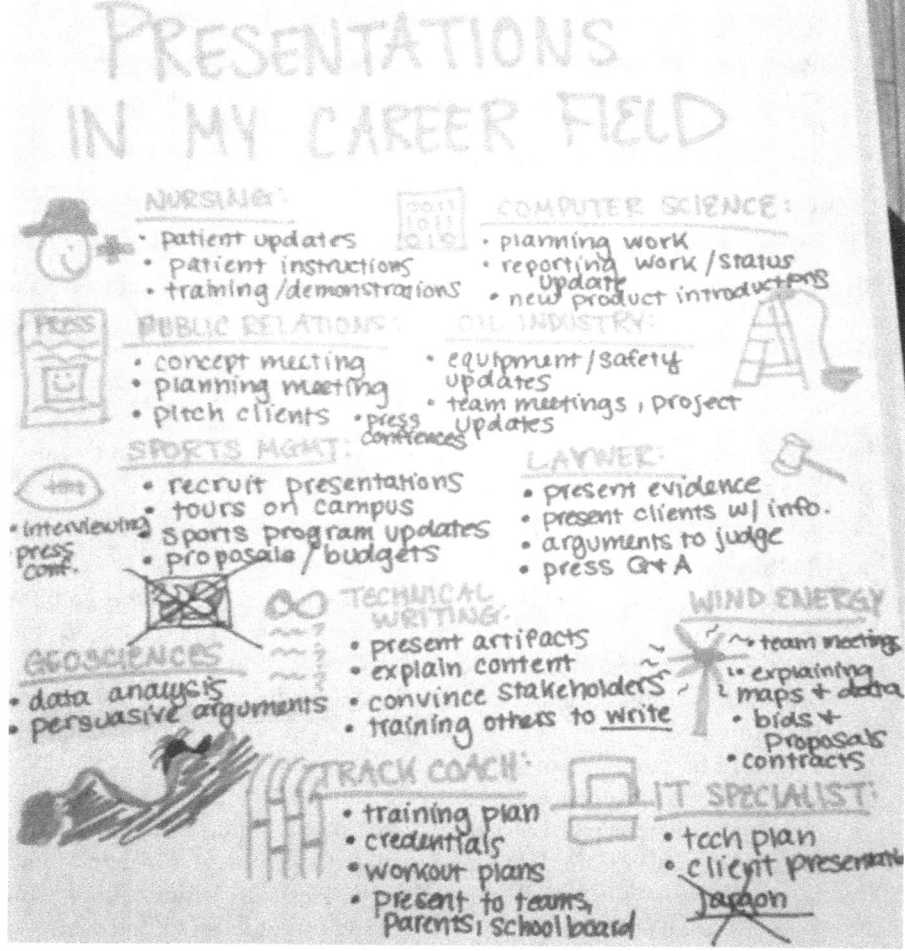

Figure 3.4. Potential TPC artifacts in student career fields.

User Profiles as Pedagogical Tools 53

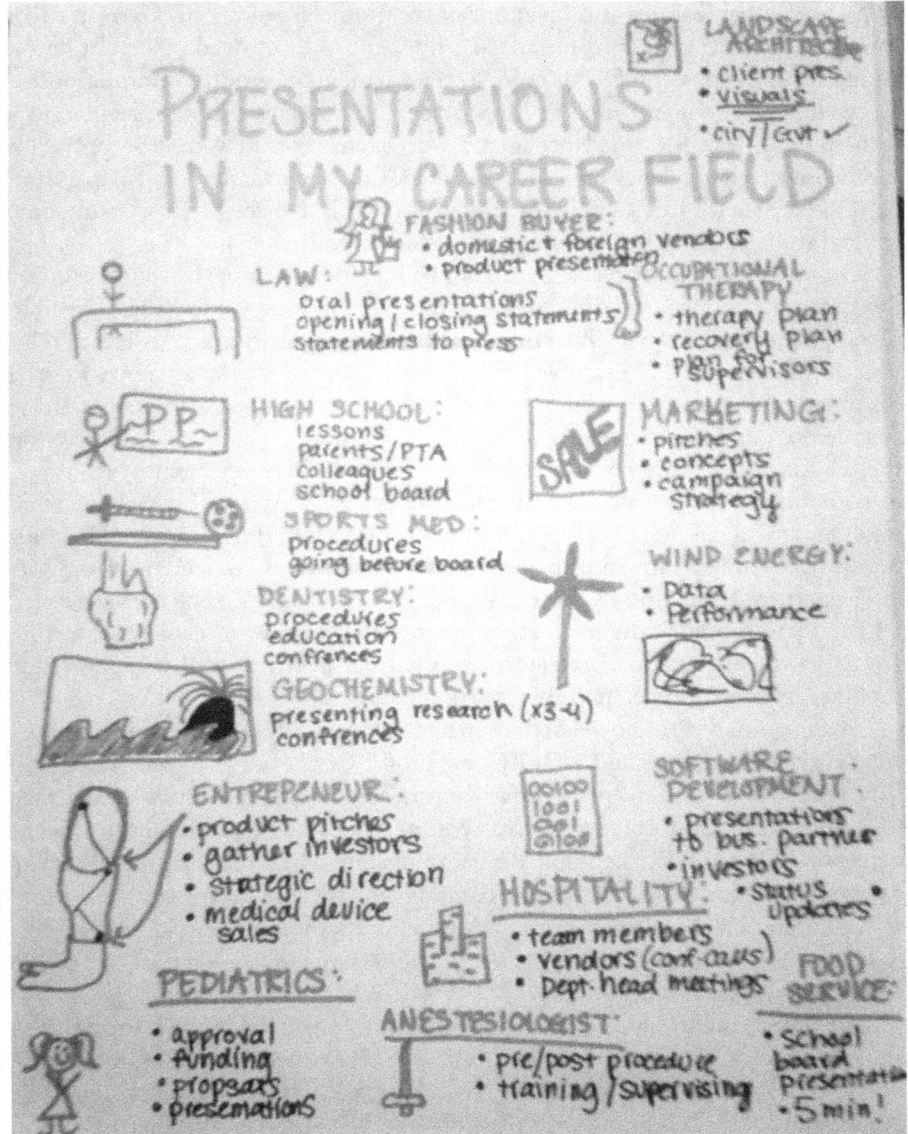

Figure 3.5. Additional potential TPC artifacts in student career fields.

Adopting Student-User Profile Development

I offer the following suggestions to fellow TPC instructors who want to adopt similar profile development practices. First, start small with low-fidelity activities where the actual features and functions of the profile are minimal (Garrett, 2011); paper, pencil, and a class roster are just fine. You do not need colorful photos, an interactive digital profile, or complete academic background information for every student. A student-user profile will ideally end up as a robust, detailed tool to help you make informed pedagogical decisions. You may have information about how your students conceptualize TPC, interpret assignments, and even navigate an LMS. But starting out, all you need is a piece of paper and some general student information from your registered student list.

On the paper, simply place the title of your student user in the center. Review the demographic information that you have about your students (i.e., year in school, major, hometown). Determine if there are any patterns that create relevant user categories. For example, are all your students TPC majors? Are they all freshman? Are they a mix of non-majors and different school years? Segmenting this demographic information can help you consider how to present TPC on the first day of class with a strategic level of technicality (e.g., "genre" vs. "types" of communication for majors and non-majors respectively). Think about what else you might know about your students to start building your student-user profile. Do you have any international students? Do you have students from different parts of the country? These distinctions may or may not be relevant based on what you subsequently learn about your users, but they offer simple starting points to consider as you brainstorm student perspectives until you can refine them with observational and self-reporting data.

Starting small with a low-fidelity version of your student-user profile also gives you flexibility to adjust and identify new profile categories that will strengthen your synthesis of student perspectives and needs. For example, you may decide that demographic information such as year in school is not as relevant to student perceptions about TPC content. By being flexible with your student-user data categories you can simply follow the data to identify more meaningful categories as you interact more with students. Table 3.2 lists sample student-user questions to focus on at the lesson, course, and curricular design level as you start to develop your student-user profile.

It's important to be open to trial and error as you create and iterate your student-user profile. Creating a user profile is a research activity; like all research, new questions and insights will emerge. Alter your student-user profile categories as needed. The point is to develop a student-user profile that helps you describe and understand the TPC student in relation to a specific lesson, course, or program.

In addition to starting small with a low-fidelity student-user profile, you should document assumptions and misperceptions—from both students *and* you. Were you sure that juniors and seniors would understand writing in a professional style and tone more easily than underclassmen because they have taken a composition prerequisite? Were you surprised that a freshman knew more about information design because they saw a student project about information design and poster presentations featured on your department web page? Understanding and documenting what our student users come into our courses knowing (or not knowing) and where they are learning about TPC outside our immediate classrooms can strengthen the student-user profile. More importantly, it can also help you make departmental suggestions about where students might be looking for information about TPC programs. Students might also vocalize assumptions about content and assignments (e.g., "I figured that everyone in the audience spoke English so I didn't see a reason for visuals," and "The assignment checklist didn't give examples of what a professional font was so I just used the font you used in the syllabus"), which can guide areas of clarification for instructors and limit the number of frustrated students who might be nervous about an assignment requirement.

Table 3.2. Sample student-user questions for lesson, course, and curriculum design

Lesson Design	What do students think TPC is?
	What do students think the difference between TPC and other communication or writing courses is?
	What types of TPC documents do students encounter in a typical day?
	What types of TPC documents do students encounter in their major?
	What types of TPC documents do students encounter on campus?
	What popular culture reference might students understand?
Course Design	What are students' frustrations about taking this course?
	What are students' misperceptions about taking this course?
	What do students think this course is about?
	What are students' goals for this course? (Besides an "A")
	What are students' career goals and how do the TPC course and assignments support them?
	What campus organizations are students involved in that they could support with TPC assignments?
Curriculum Design	Why do students select TPC as their major?
	Why do students drop TPC as their major?
	How do students think our TPC program differs from other writing or communication programs?
	Where are students learning about curriculum/major course offerings?
	What order do students expect courses to be offered in?
	What skills do students expect to learn as a TPC major?
	Where do students find information about the curriculum?
	Do students understand the major/minor requirements?

For instructors who decide to develop student-user profiles, further research regarding the profile development process, student engagement, and department collaboration is beneficial. Research about the profile development process can help determine, for example, how long one iteration of a student-user profile is relevant, or when instructors or departments should start from scratch. What system, artifact, or process you are trying to improve will determine whether an existing profile can be iterated or a new profile should be created. Specifically, your design inquiry, or what you are trying to learn about users to improve their experience, (e.g., how do TPC students use the LMS?) will determine how much a profile must be altered or discarded. In short, your design inquiry will guide your student-user profile development activities. Be open to altering or creating new profiles, but remain focused on understanding your representative users (Barnum, 2011; Cooper, 2004; Garrett, 2011).

Different profile development processes might also include more formal test session environments where instructors can ask more direct questions about student perceptions. For example, because I was logging student comments and actions during class sessions, I was not always able to stop and ask follow-up questions about related insights. If a student stated during class discussion that they expected to learn new technologies in the course while in the same breath mentioning they chose PowerPoint for the presentation they abruptly started to give, it was not an appropriate time for me to ask questions. I could not ask which technologies they were hoping to learn or what gave them the impression, from the course description or elsewhere, that we might do so.

Reporting on student engagement in the profile development process is also useful. TPC instructors might consider applying participatory design methods (Muller & Druin, 2009; Sanders, 2002; Schuler & Namioka, 1993), having students work in groups to create their own profile, or having students discuss whether an instructor-developed profile is an accurate reflection of their student experience. Engaging students in the profile development process may clarify student perspectives as users can put things into their own words and reduce instructor assumptions about the student experience. However, TPC instructors should triangulate their profile data with what they observe students do (Still & Crane, 2016).

Lastly, reporting on departmental collaboration in creating or evaluating student-user profiles can tell us how, and if, student-user profiles inform departmental decisions. Sharing user profiles, for example, means a department can gain a broader view of student perceptions and focus their profiles on specific course/department objectives and initiatives (e.g., where do students go to find our major requirements?). Also, creating student-user profiles as a department can foster dialog about the most important user perspectives instead of who in the department knows more about what students want or need based on a colleague's position or length of service. Discussions regarding user considerations can actually deescalate conflicts (Jurca et al., 2014). The focus of the discussion becomes more about sharing observational, performance, and behavioral data to reach relevant user insights rather than disagreeing about past experience with students or what students might want.

■ Conclusion

In this study, I created a student-user profile for an introductory TPC course. It helped me make meaningful course design decisions grounded in actual student-user data and practice reflection-in-action (Lowgren & Stolterman, 2007) during the course; I could adjust the course and lesson design based on insights from the student-user profile so the course remained user-centered. Importantly, the student-user profile was based on triangulation of user "see-say-do" information (Still & Crane, 2016) rather than sole self-report data such as course surveys or student evaluations. While those tools can support a student-user profile, on their own they cannot supplement the robust approach of creating a user profile based in UCD methods. Additionally, developing the student-user profile helped me reflect on my own pedagogical choices and style to improve my performance. It also encouraged me to keep learning more about my students' experiences.

While I received anecdotal feedback that students appreciated the design changes I made, I did not formally measure the relationship between the use of the student-user profile and student success. Recall that my study was exploratory in nature. Future studies could examine the efficacy of student-user profiles in a TPC course setting. There are challenges with implying causation and isolating student success indicators based on implementing a student-user profile. For example, justifying the results and adoption of UCD, or related UX approaches, can be nebulous (Bias & Mayhew, 2005; Jokela & Buie, 2012; Martin et al., 2017; Redish, 2012). TPC instructors then might isolate a particular student outcome and develop a student-user profile based on that outcome vs. student success in an entire course.

For example, a TPC instructor could create a student-user profile geared toward understanding a more acute use context, such as LMS interactions. The instructor could have specific student success parameters, such as reduction in questions about where to locate course information and student submission errors, or an increase in student visits to a particular LMS page, to measure success in response to design changes they make based on a student-user profile about the student LMS experience. The challenges of evaluating the efficacy of a UCD method such as a student-user profile, however, should not dissuade its study.

Additionally, the development and use of a student-user profile as a pedagogical tool is not unique to TPC. A student-user profile can be used to understand the student experience in broad academic settings. But TPC instructors are likely candidates to lead this charge. In the TPC classroom, a student's experience with the course content—lessons, assignments, reading material, instructor feedback, and the like—reflects a specific knowledge or experience within a use context

(Johnson, 1998; Spinuzzi, 2013; Wilson & Wolford, 2017) that TPC instructors have an obligation to honor. In turn, being part of the TPC field means we have an obligation to honor the knowledge, experience, perceptions, and goals that students bring to the TPC classroom when we design our courses. If we are to be design-oriented user advocates, as James Dubinsky (2015) suggests, it is time to practice UCD methods ourselves to best support the primary users—students— of the courses and lessons we design. UCD and overarching UX work is, after all, a "natural extension of the work that [TPCs] already do" (Lauer & Brumberger, 2016, p. 249), and there is a call for more UX-based approaches in TPC (Pope-Ruark et al., 2019). TPC instructors with prior TPC industry experience may also be well-versed in user profile or other UCD design methods. I encourage them to apply these methods to TPC course design and report on their work.

The nuance between making course design changes grounded in user data, such as insights gleaned from a student-user profile, to improve the student-user experience versus doing what we "think is best" as TPC instructors is paramount. Following UCD methods to develop a student-user profile can help TPC instructors and department chairs avoid self-referential design where we impose our own understanding—our own mental models—of how students should interact with, understand, and apply course material as we design our courses. This self-referential and "expert-based design" is a quick recipe for discouragement, disappointment, and confusion about why students did not understand content, did not follow directions, or could not even locate the syllabus. We can do our diligence to avoid self-referential design and creating elastic users (Ilama, 2015) in our mind that fit the mold of what an ideal TPC student should be. From a UCD and TPC perspective, *not* taking the time to methodically understand users, or worse, making assumptions about who your users are and what they care about, is a fast track to failure for any design process.

Ross Unger and Carolyn Chandler (2012) warn that personas, and I argue this is also applicable to user profiles, are "going to be a lot like Santa Claus: They'll only be valuable as long as people believe in them" (p. 125). Believing in student-user profiles helps us move from an instructor/chair (i.e., expert/designer) view to a student-user view of our course content and lessons to make meaningful course design changes. Developing a student-user profile may be a new technique for the most seasoned instructors—a technique potentially even viewed as elementary given its simplicity—but student-user profiles offer a strategic UCD-based approach to capture user perspectives across TPC departments that can streamline and prioritize an understanding of the student-user experience.

References

Andersen, R., Benavente, S., Clark, D., Hart-Davidson, W., Rude, C. & Hackos, J. (2013). Open research questions for academics and industry professionals: Results of a survey. *Communication Design Quarterly Review*, *1*(4), 42–49.

Anschultz, L. & Rosenberg, S. (2002). Expanding roles for technical communicators. In B. Mirel & R. Spilka (Eds.), *Reshaping technical communication: New directions and challenges for the 21st century* (pp. 149–163). Lawrence Erlbaum.

Barnum, C. (2011). *Usability testing essentials: Ready, set...test!* Morgan Kaufmann.

Bias, R. & Mayhew, D. (2005). *Cost-justifying usability: An update for the internet age.* Morgan Kaufmann.

Baxter, K., Courage, C. & Cain, K. (2015). *Understanding your users: A practical guide to user research methods.* Morgan Kauffman.

Beyer, H. & Holtzblatt, K. (1999). Contextual design. *Interactions, 6*(1), 32–42.

Brumberger, E. & Lauer, C. (2015). The evolution of technical communication: An analysis of industry job postings. *Technical Communication, 62*(4), 224–243.

Cargile Cook, K. (2002). Layered literacies: A theoretical frame for technical communication pedagogy. *Technical Communication Quarterly, 11*(1), 5–29.

Cao, J. (2018). *The practical guide to empathy maps: 10-minute user personas.* UXPin. https://www.uxpin.com/studio/blog/the-practical-guide-to-empathy-maps-creating-a-10-minute-persona/.

Carliner, S. (2001). Emerging skills in technical communication: The information designer's place in a new career path for technical communicators. *Technical Communication, 48*(2), 156–175.

Ceraso, A. (2013). How can technical communicators plan for users? In J. Johnson-Eilola & S. Selber (Eds.), *Solving problems in technical communication* (pp. 237–261). University of Chicago Press.

Cleary, Y. & Flammia, M. (2012). Preparing technical communication students to function as user advocates in a self-service society. *Journal of Technical Writing and Communication, 42*(3), 305–322.

Cooper, A. (2004). *The inmates are running the asylum.* Sams.

Dubinsky, J. (2015). Products and processes: Transition from "product documentation to . . . integrated technical content." *Technical Communication, 62*(2), 118–134.

Dumas, J. & Redish, J. (1999). *A practical guide to usability testing.* Intellect Books.

Garrett, J. (2011). *The elements of user experience: User-centered design for the web and beyond.* New Riders.

Getto, G. & Beecher, F. (2016). Toward a model of UX education: Training UX designers within the academy. *IEEE Transactions on Professional Communication, 59*(2), 153–164.

Getto, G. & St. Amant, K. (2015). Designing globally, working locally: Using personas to develop online communication products for international users. *Communication Design Quarterly Review, 3*(1), 24–46.

Hackos, J. & Redish, G. (1998). *User task analysis for interface design.* Wiley.

Hanington, B. & Martin, B. (2012). *Universal methods of design: 100 ways to research complex problems, develop innovative ideas, and design effective solutions.* Rockport.

Hart-Davidson, W. (2013). What are the work patterns of technical communication? In J. Johnson-Eilola and S. Selber (Eds.), *Solving problems in technical communication* (pp. 50–74). Chicago: University of Chicago Press.

Ilama, E. (2015, June 9). Creating personas. *UX Booth.* http://www.uxbooth.com/articles/creating-personas/.

Johnson, R. (1998). *User-centered technology: A rhetorical theory for computers and other mundane artifacts.* SUNY Press.

Johnson, R. (2004a). Audience involved: Toward a participatory model of writing. In J. Johnson-Eilola & S. Selber (Eds.), *Central works in technical communication* (pp. 91–103). Oxford University Press.

Johnson, R. (2004b). Complicating technology: Interdisciplinary method, the burden of comprehension, and the ethical space of the technical communicator. In J. Dubinsky (Ed.), *Teaching technical communication: Critical issues for the classroom* (pp. 24–44), Bedford/St. Martin's.

Jokela, T. & Buie, E. (2012). Getting UX into the contract. In E. Buie & D. Murray (Eds.), *Usability in government systems: User experience design for citizens and public servants* (pp. 251–265). Morgan Kauffman.

Jurca, G., Hellmann, T. & Maurer, F. (2014, July). Integrating Agile and user-centered design: A systematic mapping and review of evaluation and validation studies of Agile-UX. In *Agile Conference (AGILE), 2014* (pp. 24–32). IEEE.

Knox, N. (2014). How to use persona empathy mapping. *UX Magazine*. http://uxmag.com/articles/how-to-use-persona-empathy-mapping.

Krug, S. (2014). *Don't make me think, revisited: A common sense approach to web usability.* New Riders.

Lallemand, C., Gronier, G. & Koenig, V. (2015). User experience: A concept without consensus? Exploring practitioners' perspective through an international survey. *Computers in Human Behavior, 43*, 35–48.

Lauer, C., and Brumberger, E. (2016). Technical communication as user experience in a broadening industry landscape. *Technical Communication, 63*(3), 248–264.

Lowgren, J. & Stolterman, E. (2007). *Thoughtful interaction design: A design perspective on information technology*. MIT Press.

Ma, J. & LeRouge, C. (2007). Introducing user profiles and personas into information systems development. *AMCIS 2007 Proceedings*, 237.

Martin, S., Carrington, N. & Muncie, N. (2017). Promoting user advocacy to shift technical communication identity and value. *Technical Communication, 64*(4), 328–344.

Mirel, B. (2013). How can technical communicators evaluate the usability of artifacts? In J. Johnson-Eilola & S. Selber (Eds.), *Solving problems in technical communication* (pp. 285–309). University of Chicago Press.

Muller, M. & Druin, A. (2009). Participatory design: The third space in HCI. In A. Sears & J. Jacko (Eds.), *Human computer interaction: Development process* (pp. 166–181). CRC Press.

Norman, D. (1986). Cognitive engineering. In D. Norman & S. Draper (Eds.), *User centered system design: New perspectives on human-computer interaction* (pp. 31–61). Lawrence Erlbaum.

Norman, D. (1999). Affordance, conventions, and design. *Interactions Magazine, 6*(3), 38–43.

Pope-Ruark, R., Tham, J., Moses, J. & Conner, T. (2019). Introduction to Special Issue: Design-thinking approaches in technical and professional communication. *Journal of Business and Technical Communication, 33*(4), 370–375.

Pratt, A. & Nunes, J. (2012). *Inter-active design: An introduction to the theory and application of user-centered design*. Rockport.

Redish, G. (2010). Technical communication and usability: Intertwined strands and mutual influences. *IEEE Transactions on Professional Communication, 53*(3), 191–200.

Redish, G. (2012). *Letting go of the words: Writing web content that works*. Morgan Kaufmann.

Redish, G. & Barnum, C. (2011). Overlap, influence, intertwining: The interplay of UX and technical communication. *Journal of Usability Studies*, *6*(3), 90–101.

Rolfe, G. (2006). Validity, trustworthiness and rigor: Quality and the idea of qualitative research. *Journal of Advanced Nursing*, *53*, 304–310.

Rude, C. (2009). Mapping the research questions in technical communication. *Journal of Business and Technical Communication*, *23*(2), 174–215.

Salvo, M. (2001). Ethics of engagement: User-centered design and rhetorical methodology. *Technical Communication Quarterly*, *10*(3), 273–290.

Sanders, E. (2002). From user-centered to participatory design approaches. In J. Frascara (Ed.), *Design and the social sciences: Making connections* (pp. 1–8). CRC Press.

Schriver, K. (2013). What do technical communicators need to know about information design? In J. Johnson-Eilola & S. Selber (Eds.), *Solving problems in technical communication* (pp. 386–427). University of Chicago Press.

Schuler, D. & Namioka, A. (1993). *Participatory design: Principles and practices*. CRC Press.

Spinuzzi, C. (2013). How can technical communicators study work contexts? In J. Johnson-Eilola & S. Selber (Eds.), *Solving problems in technical communication* (pp. 262–284). University of Chicago Press.

Still, B. & Crane, K. (2016). *Fundamentals of user-centered design*. CRC Press.

Still, B. & Koerber, A. (2010). Listening to students: A usability evaluation of instructor commentary. *Journal of Business and Technical Communication*, *24*(2), 1–28.

Tracy, S. (2013). *Qualitative research methods: Collecting evidence, crafting analysis communicating impact*. Wiley-Blackwell.

Unger, R. & Chandler, C. (2012). *A project guide to UX design*. New Riders.

Van Velsen, L., Wentzel, J. & Van Gemert-Pijnen, J. (2013). Designing eHealth that matters via a multidisciplinary requirements development approach. *JMIR Research Protocols*, *2*(1), e21.

Wilson, G. & Wolford, R. (2017). The technical communicator as (post-postmodern) discourse worker. *Journal of Business and Technical Communication*, *31*(1), 3–29.

■ Appendix A: General Information Survey

Welcome! Please answer the following questions so that I can better understand your interests and course goals.

1. **Name (First and Last)**

2. **Major (or undecided)**

3. **Year** *Mark only one oval.*
   ○ Freshman
   ○ Sophomore
   ○ Junior
   ○ Senior

4. I am taking this course because . . . *Mark only one oval.*
   ○ I have to
   ○ I'm interested in the subject
   ○ Both

5. If I had to describe technical communication in 1 sentence it would be:

6. Career goals after (i.e., work as a Public Relations executive)

7. Favorite hobbies

8. Favorite foods

9. Beach or mountains? *Mark only one oval.*
   ○ Beach
   ○ Mountains

10. Dogs or cats? *Mark only one oval.*
    ○ Dogs (Woof, woof)
    ○ Cats
    ○ No thanks

11. Favorite shows or movies

12. Last social media account you used

13. Any concerns about taking an online course?

14. What you want to get out of this course?

15. Anything else you want me to know?

■ Appendix B: Midterm Survey

This survey is anonymous. Please be honest in your responses so I can improve the course.
* Required

1. Check all course lesson tools that you find helpful * *Check all that apply.*
   ○ PowerPoint Slides
   ○ Sketch Videos
   ○ Document Camera (when Instructor writes on paper during class)
   ○ Textbook
   ○ Blackboard Announcements on how to prepare for class
   ○ Other:

2. I can find the course content I need easily on the Blackboard site. *
   Mark only one oval.

         1   2   3   4   5
   Disagree   Agree

3. I like that we have live class meetings. * *Mark only one oval.*

           1   2   3   4   5
   Strongly disagree   Strongly agree

4. I feel completely comfortable asking the Professor questions during class. * *Mark only one oval.*

           1   2   3   4   5
   Strongly disagree   Strongly agree

5. The Professor values student time. * *Mark only one oval.*

           1   2   3   4   5
   Strongly disagree   Strongly agree

6. I am learning something that I can apply to my career in this course. *
   Mark only one oval.

           1   2   3   4   5
   Strongly disagree   Strongly agree

7. I'm glad ENGL 2311 is a required course. * *Mark only one oval.*

           1   2   3   4   5
   Strongly disagree   Strongly agree

8. What are two things you like about how the Professor teaches this course? *

9. What are two things you wish the Instructor did differently? *

10. Is there anything else you want to say about the course so far?

4. User Experience and Transliteracies in Technical and Professional Communication

Laura Gonzales
UNIVERSITY OF FLORIDA

Josephine Walwema
UNIVERSITY OF WASHINGTON

Contributors: Estefania Castillo (The University of Texas at El Paso) Mohammed Iddrisu (Arizona State University), Corina Lerma (The University of Texas at El Paso), and Jennifer Wilhite (The University of Texas at El Paso)

Abstract: Drawing on data from a user experience (UX) class facilitated at a university on the Mexico/U.S. border, this chapter connects concepts of transliteracy and UX, positioning these frameworks as useful models for introducing students to intercultural technical communication. Using student narratives and course assignments, the authors trace students' connections to intercultural communication, UX, and transliteracy, while also assessing students' experiences in a piloted UX class. Ultimately, the authors argue that by incorporating UX strategies and practices in curricula, and by providing students with opportunities to reflect on their own connections to UX course concepts and tools, technical and professional communication (TPC) programs can continue to "emphasize the complexities of culture" and the role of technical communicators as designers who create meaning among and across "texts, contexts, artifacts, and media" (Walwema, 2018, p. 335). The authors suggest that multidisciplinary approaches that pair UX and transliteracy can introduce new students to intercultural technical communication while also providing avenues for students to shape and localize course design and content through their own interests, backgrounds, and experiences.

Keywords: intercultural communication, localization, participatory design, borderland UX, journey mapping

Key Takeaways:

- Incorporating UX research methods, specifically affinity diagramming and journey mapping, into course design research can provide useful feedback for instructors and programs seeking to incorporate UX and technical communication courses in their curricula.
- Instead of waiting until the end of the semester to formally assess student data and make curricular changes in a transliteracy-focused UX course, a

- Transliteracy is a helpful framework for bridging connections between UX and intercultural technical communication.
- Combining transliteracy with iterative course design practices drawing from UX can bring empathy, efficiency, and emotional engagement by intentionally co-creating experiences with students.

While many technical and professional communication (TPC) and writing studies programs incorporate and acknowledge the value of user experience (UX) pedagogies and training for students, not all programs have established infrastructures for teaching UX. In these cases, faculty may have the challenge of developing UX courses for and with students and other faculty who may not have previous experience in this area. This was the case for Laura, who was faculty in a rhetoric and writing studies program that wanted to increase training for graduate students in technical communication and user experience. In the fall of 2017, Laura piloted a UX course as a special topics offering for M.A. and Ph.D. students. In this course, Laura used the concept of transliteracy as a way to connect her students' previous experiences and interests with concepts in UX. She also incorporated elements of UX research practices, such as affinity diagramming and journey mapping, into her course assignments to gain iterative feedback from students throughout the course. This approach helped illustrate how students in Laura's program, many of whom came from composition, literature, and philosophy backgrounds, oriented to and engaged with UX research practices and methodologies, particularly as they prepared for an increasingly competitive job market.

Rather than starting the course with a more traditional discussion of technical communication and UX, starting with the concept of transliteracy allowed Laura to begin her course by asking students to examine their own transliteracies (i.e., ability to read, write, and interact across a range of media) and interests as they intersect with various platforms, tools, and media, ranging from different social media platforms to material practices that they navigate in their everyday contexts. *Drawing on these experiences, as well as on Josephine's training and experiences in intercultural technical communication, this chapter threads concepts of transliteracy, UX, and intercultural technical communication.* In addition, we discuss how incorporating UX research methods, specifically affinity diagramming and journey mapping, into a piloted UX research course can provide useful feedback for instructors and programs seeking to introduce UX and technical communication courses in their curricula.

■ Defining Transliteracy

For students from interdisciplinary backgrounds, such as those introduced in this chapter, the concept of UX and the field of technical communication might initially seem disconnected from other fields traditionally found in English studies, including literature, creative writing, English education, and even rhetoric. Because UX has historically emphasized White/Western concepts and approaches, these areas of work may also be unwelcoming to students from various racial, ethnic, and linguistic backgrounds (Cardinal et al., 2020). For these reasons, we, as authors of this chapter, find the concept of transliteracy to be a useful entry point into UX and intercultural technical communication, particularly due to transliteracy's emphasis on digital making and cultural localization.

A dominant approach to intercultural communication in TPC draws from Geert Hofstede's (1980) six cultural dimensions that subsume people's values within cultural differences, Edward Hall's (1976) low- and high-context cultures, and Fons Trompenaars and Charles Hampden-Turner's (1993) distinction between universalism and particularism. These approaches, while instructive in understanding differences across national cultures, are also abstract theories that can perpetuate preconceived notions of people and their cultures. Critical challenges to these dominant theories of intercultural communication argue that these theories view culture as a stable construct (see Spyridakis & Fukuoka, 2002; Honold, 1999) and nations as indicative of cultural differences (Walwema, 2018). Our study addresses these challenges by grounding our analysis of technical communication and UX in the concept of transliteracies (Thomas et al., 2007). In particular, we find Stornaiuolo et al.'s (2016) transliteracies framework fitting for our project in that it "examines the situated, contingent, and ideologically rooted nature of meaning making across modes" (p. 72). This framework is instructive in its attention to the way people make meaning both socially and materially. It allows us to account for the increasingly global movement of people; advances in the technologies they use (Gonzales & Baca, 2017); and, in the era of global migration, the expanded cultural, ethnic, and national backgrounds through which communication occurs. Based on this framework, we can tease out the myriad of subcultures that exist within perceivably dominant cultures (Vertovec, 2017), while simultaneously helping students new to technical communication and UX to see themselves as important contributors to these fields of study due to their own interests and backgrounds.

The prefix *trans-* articulates literacy beyond its *a priori* understanding of individual competencies to transliterate acts "across a broad range of communication platforms" and practices constitutive of all human activity (Stornaiuolo et al., 2016, p. 71). *Transliteracy*, then, is a means to interrogate participatory narratives that emerge from transcultural and cross-cultural communication; to make meaningful connections across media, boundaries, and spaces; and to develop a more expansive understanding of a people. This broad reading of transliteracies conceives of texts as inclusive of media across platforms. It encompasses not just digital technologies but also the social, cultural, political, economic, and historical practices from which texts emerge. It challenges established biases towards print text as the definition of literacy and the ability to read, write, and make (linear) arguments, as opposed to other multimodal literacies in which meaning can be co-constructed through multiple media.

A transliteracies framework shifts the focus from individual ability to meaning making across technologies, platforms, and media. In essence, transliteracies are facilitated by humans' adaptations of technology to encompass "digital tools, multimodal representation, a global audience, and dynamic movement across physical, and virtual contexts" (Stornaiuolo et al., 2016). Consider, for example, thriving communities on social media such as Black Twitter and Black LinkedIn that convey the counterpublic voices of Black Americans. As Marc Hill (2018) notes, these spaces serve as "critical rejoinders" to, for example, Habermas' public square, which, in assuming dominant cultural norms, excludes the oppressed class. Through these media, Black Americans challenge dominant narratives about themselves and thus express their truth without the gatekeeping functions or boundaries imposed by White cultural dimensions. Similarly, Ashanti Martin (2020) observes that LinkedIn has, in the wake of the pandemic and the outpouring of grief over the killing of George Floyd, become Black America's "virtual water cooler" (para. 7), where Black Americans speak directly to business executives about workplace expectations of respectability and professionalism. The resulting texts generated in such forums, media, and platforms, be they audio or video, become sites and texts for critical interrogation and engagement. These texts act as knowledge sources invaluable to intercultural technical communication, as transliteracy practices are open to seeing cultures as dynamic and people's movements, interactions, languages, and artifacts as constitutive of texts worth critical examination. This fluidity among cultures and digital platforms is at the core of what we want to teach our students in UX—to develop methods for understanding culture not as a fixed entity, but as fluid, constantly emerging, and iterative. Transliteracy thus provides students with an entry point into broader conversations in UX regarding user research and ethical technology design. As we will illustrate in the next section, we use transliteracy and its connecting of culture and media as an overall orientation and approach to teaching UX and technical communication, particularly when introducing new students from diverse backgrounds into the practices, theories, and orientations of these fields.

▪ User Experience and Transliteracy

According to the International Organization for Standardization's (2019) definitions of ergonomics of human-system interaction, *user experience (UX)* encompasses a person's "perceptions and responses that result from the use and/or anticipated use of a system, product or service" (section 3.15). User experience researchers are concerned with understanding how a person feels when using a product, service, or interacting with an organization (Rose et al., 2017). As the contributions in this collection make clear, UX is increasingly gaining attention in technical communication curricula, although, as Janice Redish and Carol

Barnum (2011) argue, the two fields have always been closely related and intertwined. As these overlaps continue, we argue that UX, particularly when taught through a transliteracy approach, can provide an avenue for programs to prepare students to engage with increasingly global and diverse communities, understanding the fluidity embedded in communication practices across platforms and cultures. As Emma Rose et al. (2017) explain, "Technical communication has had an intertwined history with UX and the skills that technical communicators possess overlap with those required in UX positions" (p. 6).

Increasingly, just as with technical communication research and practice, UX researchers and practitioners acknowledge the presence, importance, and value of *user localization*, which Huatong Sun (2012) defines as "design situations of localizing a technology for assorted local cultures and those of designing a technology for collaborative use between users from different cultures at the same time" (p. xvi). UX, through its "shift from a systems-centered approach to a user-centered approach" (Rose et al., 2017, p. 3) can help emphasize the *humanistic perspective to technical communication*, which Natasha Jones (2016b) defines as the understanding "that technical communication is not neutral or objective. Instead, technical communication is imbued with values" (p. 4).

In "Social Justice in UX: Centering Marginalized Users," Rose et al. (2018) use UX frameworks, methodologies, and practices to "center groups that are often overlooked or marginalized to consider how design, methods, and practices might shift and change . . . through the lens of social justice that can reinvigorate design practice and its impact with an attention to oppression" (p. 1). In this piece, Rose et al. (2018) present several projects that leverage methods and practices in UX to enhance cultural awareness and sustainability, arguing that "a social justice perspective can reinvigorate ethical discussions of design" (p. 1).

As previous research demonstrates, UX is a valuable field that can help students to practice a cultural awareness across various platforms and media. As an innovative framework, UX can be deployed to tackle social issues that are constantly shifting and that resist single solutions. Although many programs and courses have argued for the value of UX training, particularly within technical communication curricula, the notion of technology design and UX research more broadly can be intimidating to students who do not have experience in this area, especially given the overwhelming whiteness of UX as a field and industry.

Transliteracy can be a starting place for innovating UX that traverses cultures and addresses stakeholder needs. It frees UX design from pre-conceived constraints; produces new paradigms; and allows UX to listen to cultures and people, preferably in their own words, spaces, and mediums, by providing channels through which this knowledge can be accessed. Like UX, transliteracy begins by developing and understanding insights about the people we intend to work with. Bringing a transliteracy perspective to UX practice allows students to work toward centering users' cultural traits in the design process; to avoid making assumptions of users; and to research culture more expansively beyond academic journals in order to design tools and technologies that are reflective of local users, avoid stereotypes, and differentiate stereotypes from cultural characteristics. The transliteracy model helps UX designers determine what the target culture communication patterns might be. By gaining a snapshot of the communication environment in a particular culture to discuss implications for intercultural UX, technical communicators can interpret what they have listened to, generate new ideas, and incorporate those ideas to create UX that emerges from the users' sociocultural contexts.

UX research practices can also provide valuable opportunities for instructors and program administrators to design courses that are localized to students' needs and interests. Designing curricula through a UX orientation can provide insights into how students understand course concepts and ideas, allowing students to become co-creators of their own pedagogy. As Ann Shivers-McNair et al. (2018) explain, "a collaborative approach to designing and redesigning for usability not only in the structure of a class, but also in the projects that happen in and beyond that class" can help instructors to "implement participatory, accountable user-centered design (UCD) principles and practices in their teaching and writing" (p. 36). Thus, as Laura piloted a UX course through a transliteracy approach, we (the authors of this chapter) also employed UX methods and strategies to assess students' experiences with course content.

Using UX Methods to Trace Students' Journeys in a UX Course

In this classroom case study, we demonstrate how transliteracy in UX functioned in a graduate course with students from various racial, linguistic, and disciplinary backgrounds. Since this is not an empirical study of classroom practice but is instead an experiential pilot study of a single course, in the following sections we provide details about the course content, readings, and assignments, before presenting narratives from four students who illustrate, in their own words, how they oriented to UX and transliteracy through their own projects. The purpose of sharing these narratives and examples is to continue expanding the frameworks through which UX is introduced and taught in interdisciplinary programs, particularly with students from non-traditional backgrounds.

Course Overview

The UX course piloted by Laura took place at a university situated on the Mexico/U.S. border. The course consisted of 12 graduate students, all of whom were enrolled in a rhetoric and writing studies program at either the M.A. or Ph.D. level. In the borderland context in which this course was situated, community members (including the students in the course itself) communicate across a wide range of media as they move across the Mexico and U.S. borders. For example, several of the students in this course (as well as the students in the university more broadly) live in Ciudad Juarez, Chihuahua, Mexico, and commute to El Paso, Texas, to attend school each day. Through these transitions, students engage in transliterate practice as they communicate in various languages (including Spanishes and Englishes) across digital platforms that have different functionalities on each side of the border. These platforms include international messaging apps like WhatsApp, social media platforms like Instagram and Snapchat, as well as learning management systems and cloud-based services like Blackboard or Google Drive. In this way, although students in this particular course did not identify previous experiences with UX before starting the course described in this chapter, students did have ample experience engaging with transliteracy. Thus, bringing UX and transliteracy concepts and practices together in the course allowed students to recognize their own expertise in these areas while also learning new methods for technology design.

Methods

In order to both get insights into how students from various disciplinary, linguistic, and cultural backgrounds oriented to UX and transliteracy and to get feedback from students in this pilot course, we incorporated assignments and activities that allowed students to trace their journeys through their course and report their findings. We also engaged in iterative analysis of student work, both as faculty and researchers in UX and in collaboration with the students themselves. Rather than being an empirical study of student work, this course was an experiential pilot study intended to facilitate pedagogical and curricular improvements. Instead of waiting until the end of the semester to formally assess student data and make curricular changes, the reflexive and iterative feedback loop between students and the instructor allowed us to make curricular changes throughout a single semester as we traced students' experiences alongside students themselves. All 12 students in the class completed the same assignments and participated in the same discussions, and we obtained Institutional Review Board (IRB) approval (identification number 1201128-1) to publish student work stemming from this course.

In this chapter, we draw on our own experiences working with students in this course while also including narratives from four students who expressed interest in publishing their journeys through this course in this particular collection. The four students are Estefania, a transfronteriza Chicana student who lives in Juarez, Chihuahua, Mexico, and commuted to school in El Paso, Texas; Mohammed, an international Ph.D. student from Ghana who previously studied English literature and philosophy; Corina, a Chicana student in her second year of her Ph.D. program in rhetoric and writing studies; and Jennifer, a White Ph.D. student in rhetoric and writing studies who also works as a K-12 teacher.

We eschew conducting formal analysis and coding of student projects in favor of incorporating unedited narratives from students into this chapter while discussing how these narratives and their surrounding discussions shaped the structure of the course itself as well as our own understandings of how UX and transliteracy came together throughout the class. Because students enrolled in the course were graduate students, we felt that it was important to include their perspectives on course material without positioning these perspectives as our own. Furthermore, drawing on important work on the value of narratives in technical communication and human-centered design (Jones, 2016a), we wanted to include complete student narratives to thoroughly illustrate students' experiences in their own words.

Collaboratively, the authors of this chapter and all students in the course practiced UX methods to assess and evaluate the course experience on a weekly basis, as well as to assess how students' definitions of UX were developing throughout the course. For example, every two weeks, the class used affinity diagramming to come up with themes and illustrations of course concepts. According to Kara Pernice (2018), *affinity diagramming* is a UX research method intended to "efficiently categorize then prioritize UX ideas, research findings, and any other rich topics" along with various stakeholders (n.p.). In the class, students would use sticky notes to define UX as they saw it at that point in the semester, and then they would theme the definitions based on similarities. For instance, in the affinity diagramming exercise that students completed as they were reading Indi Young's *Practical Empathy*, students defined UX on their sticky notes as "combining your heart and your brain," "learning to see the world through another's eyes and ears," "listening to user's stories and experiences," and "understanding that failures are part of the UX design process." Then, students grouped these definitions under the theme of "empathy," which they then discussed through the week's readings, through their presentations of current apps and platforms, and through their practicing of different UX research methods as described in Baxter et al.'s (2015) *Understanding Your Users: A Practical Guide to User Research Methods*. By tracing the development of students' definitions of UX throughout the semester, we could consistently assess the impact that course readings and activities had on student learning while also making adjustments to the readings and other course materials when necessary.

In addition to in-class activities, drawing on the concept of *journey mapping*, which Sarah Gibbons (2018) defines as "a visualization of the process that a person goes through in order to accomplish a goal" (n.p.), students provided weekly feedback that reshaped the course through their comments on a collaborative Google Doc that we called the Notebook of Relations. As stated on the course syllabus, the purpose of this Notebook of Relations was for students to "practice collaboration and content management, which are critical components of UX and tech comm research and practice." Each week, each student was expected to contribute approximately 500 words to the Google Doc, where they were to synthesize the readings for the week, make connections between each other's assessments and discussions, and reflect on what they were learning in the class as a whole. Instead of individual reading reflections, the Notebook of Relations was intended to be a space where students made purposeful connections not only across the course readings, but also between the course readings and outside content, their own interests, and each other's evaluations. In this way, the Notebook of Relations served as a space where students practiced transliteracy by making purposeful connections across disciplinary conversations while simultaneously working across platforms as they moved from taking their individual notes to organizing and curating notes in a collaborative document.

As a journey map that provided insight into both individual and collective student experiences, the Notebook of Relations also allowed both the instructor and students to make adjustments to course content based on iterative feedback throughout the semester. For example, as students made connections between the course readings and their own interests, one student commented in the Notebook of Relations that he was interested in learning more about content strategy, especially as it relates to the design of non-governmental organization (NGO) websites that depict African communities (communities that he is invested in as an international student from Ghana). Based on this comment, the student and two classmates searched for and selected readings on content strategy that the whole class read and that these three students in particular presented in class in lieu of their previous presentation plan. This flexibility and reflection throughout the course allowed students to more mindfully engage in their own learning, while also helping the course instructor and other interested stakeholders to trace the themes and issues that most resonated with students in this pilot class.

At the end of the semester, students were asked to condense their Notebook of Relations into written course reflections that also drew on journey mapping methods by asking students to discuss their journeys through the class and their growing understanding of UX and transliteracy in this context. Through these narrative reflections, the course instructor, as well as program administrators, gained insights into how students from diverse disciplinary, cultural, and linguistic backgrounds oriented to UX concepts and ideas. In this way, these journey maps served as reflections on a single course while also informing the development of future courses and program structures. By incorporating UX methods in the design of a course focused on transliteracy and UX, we were able to trace how students made connections between culture, literacy, usability, and ethics throughout a semester.

Course Goals

As stated in the course description, the UX course that we describe in this chapter was intentionally positioned as interdisciplinary, drawing from fields like rhetoric and writing studies, technical communication, and literacy studies. Leveraging students' diverse cultural, racial, linguistic, and disciplinary backgrounds, the course took on a transliteracy orientation by encouraging students to recognize the fluidity of languages, cultures, and media as they are enacted in their own transnational context on the Mexico/U.S. border. For example, students practiced UX methods in the course, including contextual inquiry, field studies, card sorting, participatory design, interviewing, focus groups, and usability testing. They practiced these methods by making connections to their own disciplinary interests and applying new skills and frameworks to established skills. For example, one student in this course identifies as a veteran with previous training in journalism. For his project, he brought together a group of veterans in his community and conducted focus groups about veterans' experiences at their university. Through several focus groups and interviews with veterans in the area, this student created a participatory design project intended to inform university stakeholders about the needs that veteran students may have on campus. This project required collaboration between the on-campus veteran services office, the disability services office, and the writing center. Throughout the course, the student involved in this project referenced his training in journalism as a skill that allowed him to condense the perspectives of various stakeholders and report them to different units on campus to facilitate communication in this participatory design project. A transliteracy approach, in this case, allowed this student (as well as others in the course) to identify how their interests and previous skills could merge with new course content.

Course texts included readings specifically on transliteracy and technical communication (i.e., Walwema's [2018] "Transliteracies in Intercultural Professional Communication), as well as readings that introduce transliteracy concepts in rhetoric (e.g., Horner et al.'s [2015] discussion of transmodality and translingualism, Shipka's [2016] discussion of transmodality, Gonzales' [2015] discussion of translingualism and rhetorical genre studies, as well as Alim and Pennycook's [2007] "Glocal Linguistic Flows"). In addition, students read Indi Young's (2015) *Practical Empathy*, Janine Butler's (2016) "Where Access Meets Multimodality," Sean Zdenek's (2015) *Reading Sounds*, Huatong Sun's (2012) *Cross-Cultural Technology Design*, and Whitney Quesenbery and Kevin Brooks' (2010) *Storytelling for User Experience*. To practice UX research methods throughout the course as they developed their own projects, students also read and took turns presenting on various chapters in Baxter et al.'s (2015) *Understanding Your Users: A Practical Guide to User Research Methods*.

The purpose of pairing interdisciplinary readings together in the course was to find points of connection between students' backgrounds and interests and what was a totally new field of study for them: technical communication and UX. Further, by incorporating readings across areas, students had the opportunity to not only read about but also practice transliteracy, as they made connections across discrete areas of study, platforms, and contexts, as well as cultures, through their course projects.

Course Assignments

In addition to the Notebook of Relations and the final narrative reflection, each week, one student presented a short (approximately 5-minute) discussion on a tool or technology that exhibited some of the conversations and practices that were discussed in class. For example, one student shared the Calor App, which is an Apple Watch-compatible app that is being designed to monitor body temperature and is intended to prevent heat strokes for farm workers who work in extreme temperatures on a daily basis (https://startsomegood.com/calorapp). Through their brief presentation, students were to not only discuss the features of an app but to also assess the implications and design of the app as it pertains to various populations. For example, the student discussing the Calor App not only analyzed the design of the proposed app platform but also brought up potential implications of this design, including the fact that having farmworkers wear an Apple Watch had implications of privacy issues, especially in relation to location tracking and documentation status. In this way, students considered not only the profits, design, or usability of a potential platform but also the implications that new designs may have for these particularly vulnerable workers and, more broadly, for historically marginalized communities.

The biggest project of the semester was a research project that asked students to "practice UX research methods discussed in class (e.g., community-based UX, focus groups, usability tests, cognitive walkthroughs, among others) to answer a specific research question of interest." Because all of the students in the class came from different linguistic, cultural, national, and disciplinary backgrounds, students approached these projects through different orientations, and they selected UX research methods that connected to their specific interests. As demonstrated by the student narratives that follow, students' orientations to UX were enhanced by an awareness of transliteracy and through constant discussion about the value of intercultural communication in technical fields.

Student Narratives

At the end of the course, students were asked to develop a UX research project that reflected both their definitions of and orientation to technology design. Students were to practice UX research methods in the project, and they were to then present their projects to the class at the end of the semester. In these presentations, students discussed the design of their projects as well as how they defined and redefined transliteracy and UX throughout the course. In these presentations, students also provided feedback related to the course structure and focus, explaining how their own interests in UX shifted as they read and discussed work across fields throughout the semester.

In keeping with the transliteracies framework, in the sections that follow, we introduce narratives written by four students in this course where they describe their journeys in coming to understand UX through their course experiences. In addition, students also discuss their own backgrounds, interests, and positionalities in relation to our course context and to their broader community within and beyond the university. Given that the purpose of this collection is to "practice user experience as a process for developing new frameworks, such as program design, curriculum, and technologies," we incorporate space for students to reflect on their own experiences with UX as both course content and process. We believe that the narratives that follow illustrate the importance and value of introducing UX through a transliteracy approach that highlights the importance of movement across languages and media simultaneously. The narratives also showcase how the iterative design of the course, which incorporated students' interests and feedback throughout the semester, allowed students to feel more connected to UX principles and practices that in turn motivated them to see themselves as part of this growing field.

Estefania

My name is Estefania and I am a *transfronteriza* student living in the Ciudad Juarez and El Paso border. Being from Ciudad Juarez and commuting to the United States to study all my life has really influenced the way that I identify myself and the work that I choose to do today. For the longest time, I felt torn between two opposing identities from both my home life and my academic and social life. I always felt like an outsider in the cultures which surrounded me, hanging somewhere in between Mexican and American cultures. It was only when I decided to define my own identity that I began to feel more comfortable in this culturally rich and diverse border community. Today I embrace my transfronteriza Chicanx identity in my personal life and in my work as a UX researcher.

Commuting every day and switching between cultures every single day has really made me aware of how these daily normal practices fit into UX. We cannot make products that are human-centered if we do not take into account that we have diverse audiences with various and unique needs that should be met. If we pay more attention to our users and understand where they come from and how this translates to different needs since the beginning, we will be able to create a product that can be used by many. While serving the needs of diverse communities, we will create more accessible content for all audiences.

For example, in my course project, I conducted usability tests of online graduate school applications for international students so that they can become more user friendly to these students. The graduate school application is already a complex and lengthy process, and this process is often even more complicated for international students because of the extra requirements and lack of information. Taking a closer look at application websites through a transliteracy approach, it is easy to see that there is a need for these websites to become more accessible and easier to use for international students. My goal is to take the needs of international students and to make sure that they are being addressed by the application websites. By meeting the needs of the different users, the end product will be more accessible and user friendly for everyone.

Mohammed

I am from Ghana, West Africa, and have varied proficiencies in six languages: English, Arabic, Hausa, Dagomba, Akan, and Ga. Culturally, I exhibit different ways of being and doing, but the most dominant ones are my Islamic culture and my Ghanaian culture.

I think UX promotes diversity and inclusivity in ways that give certain populations access to certain technologies. However, embedded within the expansion of access to some populations are ideological elements that point to issues of domination/superiority. For example, I bought my laptop in Saudi Arabia where Arabic is the dominant language. Although the laptop has both Arabic and English alphabets on the keyboard, the English letters and symbols are more prominent than the Arabic ones, and yet the target population for this laptop is people who barely speak any English. Undoubtedly, the bilingual keyboard gives access to Arabic speakers to use this laptop, but the Arabic alphabet is smaller in size than the English one, making it more difficult for Arabic users. The question is, why would the English alphabet be more prominent (or even be present) on a laptop targeted at Arabic speaking customers? I see some little tension between both languages any time I use my laptop.

My UX project focused on content strategy with particular emphasis on the (mis)representation of African communities on the websites of Non-Governmental Organizations (NGOs). Through a focused group discussion with four graduate students from four different African countries and usability testing on the websites of two NGOs, this project highlighted the user experience of first-time potential donors and discussed how non-profit organizations' misrepresentation of Africans may affect the former's attraction of donors within the African community. Although the participants were diverse culturally and technologically, one of the profound issues that was discussed across the board by the participants was the projection and homogenization of African communities as indigent populations in dire need of rescue. This homogenization was evident in the images and videos on the websites of the two NGOs that were used as a case study. Donors on the websites were mostly white, while beneficiaries were either Africans or some other non-white populations. The participants could not identify with donors portrayed on the websites, and they indicated that this could potentially affect their decision to donate. Consequently, at the end of the project, I made recommendations about technology design decisions that website developers can incorporate to reposition African communities as active contributors to and not merely beneficiaries of the operations of NGOs.

This is not only ethical, but it will also help NGOs to attract more donors from African communities through online platforms.

Corina

My hometown is El Paso, Texas, and it was not until recently that I understood the significance this small fact had in my life and hopefully my future. During my undergraduate years, I worked as a notetaker/scribe for the Center for Students with Disabilities. As a notetaker, I was assigned certain students facing different physical, sensory, or cognitive disabilities. I was then provided with a schedule of their classes (including math, science, English, and others), which I would attend on a regular basis. In spite of the high degrees of diversity embedded in this seemingly simple task, one aspect of taking notes was always unwavering and stagnant. All notes had to be taken strictly following the Cornell note-taking system, a method devised in the 1940s by Walter Pauk, an education professor at Cornell University. The notes were extremely structured, as they followed specific guidelines such as maintaining two columns for questions and synthesis and leaving five to seven lines at the bottom of the page for an overall summary. Reflecting back on this experience with a rhetorical lens and with a focus on transliteracy, I can clearly see a clashing of ideologies, technology design, identities, as well as a lack of user-centered design or user experience embedded within this note-taking method.

It is unlikely that Pauk's perception of a student when developing Cornell notes in the 1940s was a Hispanic eighteen-year-old student who is visually impaired but appreciates progressive metal and lives in the border town of El Paso in the 2000s. Not to mention the complicated power dynamic of having a twenty-year-old Latina student possibly majoring in Journalism with a different set of values and experiences shaping her definition of "good notes" take those notes and then make a copy and place them in a folder with the student's name in an office to avoid all contact or feedback. Despite the mission of the center to provide students with an equal opportunity to complete their educational goals, these methods for providing accessibility did not problematize common notions of usability based on normalizing behaviors that also positioned technology as a unidirectional process or tool.

Many of these past experiences understanding the important and often suppressed role identity plays in technology design encouraged me to take a risk in my UX and technology course at my current university. In this course, I presented on the article titled, "Beyond Compliance: Participatory Translation Safety Communication for Latino Construction Workers," by Carlos Evia and Ashley Patriarca (2012). The study focuses on the challenges and responsibilities that come with developing cross-cultural communication strategies to ensure Hispanic construction workers' safety. The authors mention that for one of the workshops for construction workers, lotería, a game like BINGO commonly played in Mexican households, was chosen as a learning activity. Since, from a participatory approach, games "are a way to create a common language, to discuss the existing reality, to investigate future visions" (Ehn & Sjorgen quoted in Evia and Patriarca, 2012, p. 354), the authors mention the lotería cards were successful in communicating technical information to Spanish-speaking audiences in part due to the deep roots the game holds with the Hispanic community. The idea presented in the article made me question the activity I would be presenting for class and gave me a sense of responsibility. This responsibility encouraged me to view lotería no longer as a game but as a pedagogical tool in technical communication, especially in an academic institution with a predominantly Hispanic population.

Lotería as a technology design strategy pushes towards multimedia pedagogical practices and moves past a technical and objective view of technology towards a culturally situated practice. Lotería ceases to be defined simply as a Mexican game for entertainment and helps students analyze the ways in which culturally-sustaining games can invoke community memory and performance. Therefore, I reviewed some of the readings for the class and chose some of the key concepts and terms and developed a class set of cards to play lotería in class. I created game boards that listed common concepts in the course, such as "UX," "usability," "affinity diagramming," "social justice," and "translation." During my presentation, each of my classmates had a gameboard with these words listed in a randomized order. To play the game, I read definitions in a randomized order, while my classmates looked on their gameboard to see if the definitions I read aloud correlated with the key terms on their game boards. Every time I read a definition that matched a key term on their boards, my classmates would put an "X" on their boards in the corresponding spot (similar to the rules of BINGO). The first person to get five "Xs" in a row would yell "lotería!" to signal that they had won the round. Through this game, my classmates had to know the definitions of all the keywords listed on their boards, in order to know when they should mark a spot with an "X." For many of my peers, the memory of having played lotería before became evident in their enthusiasm and engagement with the activity. It is necessary for students, technical communicators, and scholars to reflect on the ethical and social responsibilities embedded in language use and pedagogical choices allowing for practices that promote students' cultural expertise, diversity, and agency.

Jennifer

I am a full-time high school dual credit English teacher and full-time Rhetoric and Writing Ph.D. student.

Public school classrooms are designed for an able-bodied, English-speaking audience, as are the tools and technology provided to assist teachers. I have been gifted with a variety of students, all of whom come with their own idiosyncrasies, proclivities, and abilities. My border school is Spanish-speaking dominant and, as a gringa from Idaho, I always need to be cognizant of cultural differences and do my best to teach variety in language instead of colonizing my pupils with Standard English. This year, I had the honor of teaching a deaf student. After twenty minutes of our first class, I realized that her experience of my classroom would be vastly different from the experience of her peers.

Laura's user experience class taught me to initiate participation design that goes beyond allowing students to pick their own seats. As part of my research for my UX class project, I sat down with ASL [American Sign Language] interpreters at my school, my student, and a set of paper shapes that represented desks, projectors, the students, interpreters, and everything else that manifests in the classroom. We had a conversation about where everything was located in class throughout the course of a day and discussed how we could rearrange the classroom so that the student had a more in-depth experience of the class and so that the ASL interpreter was more comfortable and felt like part of the learning experience instead of an accessory. My student delineated places that she could not see me or had trouble keeping track of me (I'm an animated teacher) and the interpreter at the same time. She was able to, using the paper shapes, show me paths I could take around the classroom that would keep her involved because in every class experience there are the inside jokes that help the class bond and the side conversations that clarify and contribute to understanding content material.

We talked about the tools of the classroom and what technologies help build knowledge. ASL's grammar is different from English; thus, reading for her did not necessarily mean quick comprehension of written texts. Utilizing the principles of UX, we were able to design a classroom experience that included my student and taught me that the material world we live and learn in is imbued with ideologies that caters [sic] to the dominant norm. Utilizing UX helped me not only uncover unconscious assumptions about students that do great damage, but it also provided the tools to build a more inclusive classroom.

■ Implications

A transliteracy orientation to UX encouraged students to make connections between race, nationality, culture, language, and the technology of design. As the student narratives demonstrate, it is not enough for UX to consider diverse users; it has to take the next step of understanding users' sense of who they are in order to address their needs in a more targeted way. The narratives show that UX through a transliteracies framework encourages UX researchers to look more closely at the inequities that manifest in products and services. This is exemplified by Mohammed's narrative on the English subordinated laptop when its intended users are speakers of Arabic, the donor-recipient calculus on the nongovernmental agency website that depicts Africans homogeneously and as indigents, and the Cornell notetaking system described by Corina that was designed with a specific end-user in mind. Designing products this way may be a result of our interpretations of dominant theories of intercultural communication that typically flatten cultures of entire continents like Europe, and, in this case, Africa without accounting for the multiple peoples, their values, ideologies, and the circumstances in which the product will be used. The transliteracies framework to UX was useful in identifying and describing the relevant contexts within which the research took place as part of the findings.

Typically, UX research occurs in focused group discussions, interviews, surveys, etc., which are one-off events that commodify or extract (Cardinal et al., 2020) participants' insights, which are then interpreted by researchers as codes and lenses through which one can understand communities. But those short-term exchanges do not tell the entire story of a people. A transliteracy framework allows the researcher to contextualize a people beyond those one-off exchanges. As the narratives illustrate, pairing UX methods with various community identities (e.g., students with various dis/abilities, African communities, Latinx communities) yielded projects that speak to rather than about (or worse, around) communities. UX-inspired assignments such as journey mapping, the Notebook of Relations, and affinity diagramming activities allowed students to speak back to what they were reading while applying these readings to their own interests, experiences, and research. As we continue developing courses that thread UX and transliteracy, we hope to continue embracing this iterative course design while also maintaining an emphasis on interdisciplinarity and intercultural communication.

Because transliteracies are integrative of a wide range of media, when coupled with UX—which draws from scientific, technological, and artistic sources—a transliteracy framework allows students to see all media (see lotería above) as valuable in understanding the everyday lives of people and to critically examine it (media) for its perceived benefits (see Mohammed's and Corina's narratives). And as transliteracies accommodate a wide range of media, students were able to orient their research skills to practices that would otherwise be zones of exclusion for communities moving fluidly among platforms, borders, and sites.

UX and transliteracy help us learn insights about people, what they value, how they relate, why they accept or disregard certain things, and how/why they make unspoken things known, visible in a sort of grounded approach to learning. Jennifer's discussion of working with a deaf student, for example, exemplifies a perfect pairing of UX with transliteracy by taking the student's needs into account and refiguring an inclusive classroom for student and interpreter. We often forget that academia is a privileged space for those unaffiliated with its practices. And while it is true that academic institutions introduce learners to and expand their knowledge of the academy, it is also true that learners come to us with knowledges that they may deem unworthy of institutions, but which, in fact, offer crucial foundations for and entry points into what we have to teach them. This approach helps students tap into what they know, allowing them to see that as integral to what they are learning.

A transliteracies framework in UX can lead to empathy beyond walking in others' shoes to yield cognitive and emotional insights into the communication needs of others. As a framework, it allows students to envision themselves as technology designers who can build infrastructure that can lead to positive change. For example, students were able to uncover technological needs that would not have been easily voiced in surveys, focus groups, or through other more traditional UX methods. Through transliteracy and UX, students were able to extrapolate meaning from both concepts to reimagine content management, to make purposeful connections among what might otherwise be disparate subdisciplines, and to manifest their own expertise even when and where they were not aware they had it.

Operating both within the paradigm of scholarship, through close reading and analysis, and outside of it, students were able to chart new directions for UX in agentic and critical ways. We envision such forays both for the students and the communities they represent as helping to bring the academy and society closer. Furthermore, the iterative design of the course provided opportunities for students to see themselves as not only participants, but also as designers of the course who worked together with the instructor to reshape course content fluidly across projects, topics, and readings. A transliteracies framework in UX also assures that advocacy for users is done by both scholars and users. Rather than limit user responses to select quotes, a transliteracy framework values all user media, including audio or video stories, as legitimate sources of knowledge that together paint a panoramic picture of communities, and change minds and attitudes.

∎ Conclusion

We understand that the discussion we present in this chapter is limited to a small sample of students in a very specific location. Further, we realize that the course we discuss does not necessarily follow conventional themes, methods, or practices in more traditional UX courses that may be situated in traditional technical communication programs. Instead, what we present in this chapter is an illustration of an experimental UX course that took place with a group of students who did not have a background or training in technical communication or UX but who did embody many of the principles in transliteracy—mainly, a keen awareness of the connections between media and culture, an ability to move fluidly across cultural and technological boundaries to accomplish rhetorical tasks, and an understanding that tools and technologies are imbued with cultural ideologies. Through this course, we learned that incorporating UX practices in TPC programs can provide students with additional skills and experiences in learning cross-cultural and intercultural communication while also leading to the development of TPC programs that are user-centered and accessible. We saw constantly engaged students who held themselves accountable through transliteracy practices and in their "points of connection," thus manifesting the very attributes we want to impart.

The confidence accrued through course discussions and analysis of readings allowed students to reflect on the course content and to propose changes that were more aligned with what they were learning. Leveraging students' transliteracies helps bridge the gap between what students know and what content they need to learn. Granted, allowing for these kinds of shifts goes against some of our practices of planning the course ahead of time, but isn't the essence of UX iterative improvement based on user needs (Gonzales et al., 2017)?

Transliteracy in UX cultivates a kind of empathic understanding that spurs the imagination. It helps practitioners become attuned to the perspectives and intentions of communities they wish to impact. And in some sense, this pairing erases the binaries that are inherent in the very essence of UX and intercultural communication. Bringing UX and transliteracy together makes a compelling case for designing technologies and experiences that are attuned to people's sensibilities and way of being. Although we realize that the examples, narratives, and experiences that we share in this chapter are very localized to a specific course and context, we believe that the pairing of UX and transliteracy, as well as the attention to students' backgrounds and interests in designing UX curricula, can be incorporated into other programs and contexts seeking to introduce UX. The clear takeaway for UX and TPC is that combining transliteracy with iterative course design practices drawing from UX can bring empathy, efficiency, and emotional engagement by intentionally co-creating experiences with students to be better immersed in students' everyday lives.

■ References

Alim, S. H. & Pennycook, A. (2007). Glocal linguistic flows: Hip-hop culture(s), identities, and the politics of language education. *Journal of Language, Identity, and Education, 6*(2), 89–100.

Baxter, K., Courage, C. & Caine, K. (2015). *Understanding your users: A practical guide to user research methods*. Morgan Kaufmann.

Butler, J. (2016). Where access meets multimodality: The case of ASL music videos. *Kairos: A Journal of Rhetoric, Technology, and Pedagogy, 21*(1). http://kairos.technorhetoric.net/21.1/topoi/butler/index.html.

Cardinal, A., Gonzales, L. & Rose, E. J. (2020, October). Language as participation: Multilingual user experience design. In *Proceedings of the 38th ACM International Conference on Design of Communication* (pp. 1–7). ACM.

Evia, C. & Patriarca, A. (2012). Beyond compliance: Participatory translation of safety communication for Latino construction workers. *Journal of Business and Technical Communication, 26*(3), 340–367.

Gibbons, S. (2018b). *Journey mapping 101*. Nielsen Norman Group. https://www.nngroup.com/articles/journey-mapping-101/.

Gonzales, L. (2015). Multimodality, translingualism, and rhetorical genre studies. *Composition Forum, 31*, 85. https://compositionforum.com/issue/31/multimodality.php.

Gonzales, L. & Baca, I. (2017). Developing culturally and linguistically diverse online technical communication programs: Emerging frameworks at University of Texas at El Paso. *Technical Communication Quarterly, 26*(3), 273–286.

Gonzales, L., Potts, L., Turner, H. N. & Brentnell, L. (2017, August). Working with ladies that UX: Building academic/industry partnerships for user research projects. In *Proceedings of the 35th ACM International Conference on the Design of Communication* (p. 29). ACM.

Hall, E. T. (1976). *Beyond culture*. Doubleday.

Hill, M. L. (2018). "Thank you, Black Twitter": State violence, digital counterpublics, and pedagogies of resistance. *Urban Education, 53*(2), 286–302.

Hofstede, G. (1980). *Culture's consequences: International differences in work-related values*. Sage Publications.

Honold, P. (1999). Learning how to use a cellular phone: Comparison between German and Chinese users. *Technical Communication, 46*(2), 196–205.

Horner, B., Selfe, C. & Lockridge, T. (2015). Translinguality, transmodality, and difference: Exploring dispositions and change in language and learning. *Enculturation Intermezzo*. http://intermezzo.enculturation.net/01/ttd-horner-selfe-lockridge.pdf.

International Organization for Standardization. (2019). *Ergonomics of human-system interaction — Part 210: Human-centered design for interactive systems*. https://www.iso.org/obp/ui/#iso:std:iso:9241:-210:ed-2:v1:en.

Jones, N. N. (2016a). Narrative inquiry in human-centered design: Examining silence and voice to promote social justice in design scenarios. *Journal of Technical Writing and Communication, 46*(4), 471–492.

Jones, N. N. (2016b). The technical communicator as advocate: Integrating a social justice approach in technical communication. *Journal of Technical Writing and Communication, 46*(3), 342–361.

Martin, A. M. (2020, October 11). Black LinkedIn is thriving. Is LinkedIn OK with That? *The New York Times*. https://www.nytimes.com/2020/10/08/business/black-linkedin.html.

Pernice, K. (2018). *Affinity diagramming: Collaborate, sort, and prioritize UX ideas*. Nielsen Norman Group. https://www.nngroup.com/videos/affinity-diagramming/.

Quesenbery, W. & Brooks, K. (2010). *Storytelling for user experience: Crafting stories for better design*. Rosenfeld Media.

Redish, J. C. & Barnum, C. (2011). Overlap, influence, intertwining: The interplay of UX and technical communication: Invited essay. *Journal of Usability Studies, 6*(3), 92–101.

Rose, E. J., Edenfield, A., Walton, R., Gonzales, L., Shivers McNair, A., Zhvotovska, T., Jones, N., Garcia de Mueller, G. & Moore, K. (2018). Social justice in UX: Centering marginalized users. In *Proceedings of the 36th ACM International Conference on the Design of Communication* (p. 21). ACM.

Rose, E. J., Racadio, R., Wong, K., Nguyen, S., Kim, J. & Zahler, A. (2017). Community-based user experience: Evaluating the usability of health insurance information with immigrant patients. *IEEE Transactions on Professional Communication, 60*(2), 214–231. https://digitalcommons.tacoma.uw.edu/cgi/viewcontent.cgi?article=1755&context=ias_pub.

Shipka, J. (2016). Transmodality in/and processes of making: Changing dispositions and practice. *College English, 78*(3), 250–257.

Shivers-McNair, A., Phillips, J., Campbell, A., Mai, H. H., Yan, A., Macy, J. F. & Guan, Y. (2018). User-centered design in and beyond the classroom: Toward an accountable practice. *Computers and Composition, 49*, 36–47.

Spyridakis, J. H. & Fukuoka, W. (2002). The effect of inductively versus deductively organized text on American and Japanese readers. *IEEE Transactions on Professional Communication, 45*(2) 99–114.

Stornaiuolo, A., Smith, A. & Phillips, N. C. (2016). Developing a transliteracies framework for a connected world. *Journal of Literacy Research, 49*(1), 68–91.

Sun, H. (2012). *Cross-cultural technology design: Creating culture-sensitive technology for local users*. Oxford University Press.

Thomas, S., Joseph, C., Laccetti, J., Mason, B., Mills, S., Perril, S. & Pullinger, K. (2007). Transliteracy: Crossing divides. *First Monday, 12*. http://firstmonday.org/article/view/2060/1908.

Trompenaars, F. & Hampden-Turner, C. (1993). *Riding the waves of culture: Understanding diversity in global business*. Irwin Professional.

Vertovec, S. (2017). Super-diversity and its implications. *Ethnic and Racial Studies, 30*(6), 1024–1054.

Walwema, J. (2018). Transliteracies in intercultural professional communication. *IEEE Transactions on Professional Communication, 61*(3), 330–345.

Young, I. (2015). *Practical empathy: For collaboration and creativity in your work*. Rosenfeld Media.

Zdenek, S. (2015). *Reading sounds: Closed-captioned media and popular culture*. University of Chicago Press.

5. Using Student-Experience Mapping in Academic Programs: Two Case Studies

Tharon W. Howard
CLEMSON UNIVERSITY

Abstract: This chapter examines two examples of cases where my colleagues and I used user experience (UX) mapping to improve students' academic experiences. The first case discusses a graduate seminar in which students followed a seven-phase process model to produce a user experience map that enabled their client, the School of Architecture, to completely redesign the school's website to meet prospective architecture student needs. The first case exemplifies ways that courses in our technical and professional communication (TPC) programs can have students utilize UX principles with academic clients. The second case involves faculty using journey mapping as a means to examine and critique the design of an entire curriculum. This case describes how faculty in a professional communication master's program met weekly over the course of a semester in 2002 in order to create a journey map of graduate students' progress through the curriculum. This journey mapping exercise demonstrates how faculty made several key decisions about gaps in the curriculum where students needed new courses in order to help them prepare for their capstone experience, and provided the scaffolding for second semester courses like Visual Communication, allowing the faculty to focus on visual communication theories rather than the tools needed to produce visual communication projects. The exercise also led faculty to reduce the number of required "core" courses to give students more flexibility in developing specialty areas. Finally, creating the journey map also resulted in a "Timeline Handout," which faculty used as an aid for advising that our annual program evaluations actually contributed significantly to more students graduating on time. Ultimately, the goal of this chapter is to demonstrate that the kind of research that goes into UX mapping enables programs to make informed, data-driven curricular decisions based on student advocacy.

Keywords: journey mapping, user experience mapping, service learning, persona design

Key Takeaways:

- Going through the process of creating UX maps enables faculty to think like "student advocates."
- The research needed to create UX maps leads to data-driven, student-oriented curricular decisions.

- UX mapping can follow a rigorous seven-step process, but a "guerilla approach" can also be used to produce impactful results.

Back in the early 1990s, when usability was just beginning to have an impact on technical communication practice in industry and on technical and professional communication (TPC) pedagogy in academe, one of the ways nascent usability professionals like myself sought to both justify and define our roles on product development teams was as the "user advocate." The user, we argued, needed the same advocacy in the decision-making process on a development team as stakeholders such as product support, marketing, manufacturing, engineering, and management. If we allowed functionality and content alone to drive the development of our products, and if we continued to ignore the key role that the user's voice had to play as "co-developer" in a product's design, then we deserved the "feature creep," "bloatware," and "technologies in search of a problem/customer" which had plagued product design throughout the previous decade. In their work on institutional change, James Porter et al. (2000) described how Mary Dieli, the first usability manager at Microsoft Corporation, made similar arguments during this period in order to change Microsoft's institutional culture, "establishing users and user testing as a more integral part of the software development process in a company that is the world's leading developer of operating system software (Windows), Internet web browsers, and business software generally" (p. 611). Porter et al. held that Dieli's work as a user advocate was the type of "rhetorical action" which serves "as the means by which institutions can be changed" and expressed hope "that institutions can be sensitized to users, people, systemically from within and that this sensitizing can potentially change the way an entire industry perceives its relationship to the public" (p. 611).

Ironically, despite the fact that we were extremely successful in making the case for user advocacy in mainstream product design, and in spite of the fact that it's a pretty short journey from "user advocate" to "student advocate," our use of UX design principles in the creation of services and instructional materials intended for students has lagged behind mainstream industry practices, as the editors of this book have observed. Indeed, Aimée Knight et al.'s (2009) "About Face: Mapping Our Institutional Presence," which examined 150 academic program websites, found that "student subjectivities" were missing. The authors concluded that "Many of the program websites make students invisible" (p. 194). Consequently, in this chapter, I examine two examples of cases where my colleagues, students, and I used both a formal and an informal form of user experience mapping to improve the students' academic experiences through the inclusion of students' voices in the design of websites and curricula for academic programs. *Ultimately, my goal in this chapter is to demonstrate that the kind of research that goes into UX mapping enables programs to make curricular decisions based on student advocacy.* I hope to show that the map itself is, in reality, just a byproduct and it's experiencing the process of creating the map(s) which has the greatest value.

Before I describe the case studies, I should explain that my favorite definition of UX mapping comes from Alice Walker's (2018) *UX Collective* blog entry, "User Experience Mapping for Dummies." Walker explains that "*A user experience map shows the users' needs, expectations, wants, and potential route to reach a particular goal. It's like a behavioral blueprint that defines how your customer may interact with your product or service*" (n.p., emphasis added). Figure 5.5 provides an example of a UX map, and for those teaching undergraduate courses who are looking for books with lots of examples, some to consider include Peter Szabo's (2017) *User Experience Mapping* or Jim Tincher and Nicole Newton's (2019) *How Hard Is It to Be Your Customer? Using Journey Mapping to Drive Customer Focused Change*. For my graduate seminar, I chose to use Jim Kalbach's (2016) famous "grizzly bear book," *Mapping Experiences: A Complete Guide to Creating Value through Journeys, Blueprints, and Diagrams*. But for those seeking a quick, high-level overview of what UX mapping entails and how it differs from similar mapping techniques, I would recommend Sarah Gibbons' (2017) "UX Mapping Methods Compared: A Cheat Sheet." Gibbons is Nielsen Norman Group's Chief Designer, and she provides a high-level overview and visual examples of the four commonly used types of mapping in industry: 1) empathy mapping, 2) customer journey mapping, 3) user experience mapping, and 4) service blueprinting. Gibbons also offers a more recent (2019) introduction to the evolution of UX mapping by tracing its origins from Edward Tolman's (1948) work on the "cognitive maps" of rats working through mazes in the 1940s to Tony Buzan's (1974/2010) popularization of the term "mind mapping" to Joseph Novak's (1984) use of concept mapping in the 1970s. Gibbons (2017) shows that cognitive mapping, mind mapping, and concept mapping "are three different ways of visualizing a [user's] mental model" and "are three powerful visual-mapping strategies for organizing, communicating, and retaining knowledge" (n.p.). And in the same way that UX maps serve as "a behavioral blueprint" (Walker, 2018), these early precursors to the UX maps "help us lay out complex ideas, processes, and recognize patterns and relationships" (Gibbons, 2019, n.p.).

In the first case examined in this chapter, I describe a full-blown, semester-long project where graduate students used formal user experience research methods to help the School of Architecture redesign its website. Because of the depth and complexity involved, the discussion of this case will take up the bulk of this chapter. However, while the second case study I discuss is shorter because it involves an informal and far less complex case, I offer the second case as a sort of "discount" user experience mapping exercise which faculty can easily use to examine and describe their curriculum. The second case is less complicated, but the return on investment for our graduate program was significant. As one of the blind, external reviewers of this chapter put it, the "guerilla testing" which went into the second case demonstrates that "the kind of research that goes into UX mapping is especially helpful in allowing programs to make data-based and student-oriented design decisions rather than the anecdote-based and turf-oriented decisions that we so frequently make instead." Ultimately, in discussing both cases, I will make the case that user experience mapping is an indispensable tool for academic professionals, whether they're looking to attract prospective students or to provide an outstanding user experience for the students they already have.

Case Study One: Redesigning the School of Architecture Website

This first case involves a graduate seminar in which students from the M.A. in Professional Communication (MAPC) program followed a formal, seven-phase process to produce a user experience map which enabled their client, the School of Architecture, to completely redesign the school's website to meet prospective architecture student needs. The course the graduate students were taking was a usability testing and user experience design (UUX) seminar, and their first client-based project for the course involved conducting a needs assessment. Subsequent client projects involved using think-aloud protocol analyses; however, in this first project, the goal was to conduct a needs assessment study which would provide a real client with an understanding of the tasks, goals, and attitudes of the users the client was seeking to serve.

Our client for this needs assessment was the School of Architecture. In 2017, the manager of the College of Architecture, Arts, and Humanities (CAAH) website, the Director of the School of Architecture, and the WebCurator responsible for the Architecture site approached me for assistance because previously in 2009, a team of MAPC graduate students and I had used persona design methods to create the design templates for the original CAAH website. In that project—which can still be seen at http://media.clemson.edu/caah/caah_mockups/index.html—we used surveys, interviews, and Google Analytics data to create 12 different personas of users of the CAAH website (Howard, 2009). Next, based on the understanding of the goals and tasks each user persona revealed, the team created static mock-ups of webpages designed specifically for each persona. The mock-ups were then aggregated and became the template used for the college's content management system, which the School of Architecture and the other ten departments in the college used for their sites.

That original 2009 persona design approach and the research on which it had been based were considered so successful that, eight years later for their redesign, the School of Architecture and the webmaster for the college approached me once again to collect more detailed data on users not just of the whole CAAH website, as had been done in 2009, but more specifically, on prospective students for Architecture's graduate and undergraduate degree programs. As a result, the School of Architecture became the client for the professional communication graduate students who were taking my seminar on usability and UX design.

Figure 5.1 is the introduction to one of the seminar's final recommendation reports; it overviews the problem the graduate student team sought to address, the research questions they pursued, and the UX methods they used to resolve it. The excerpt in Figure 5.1 was from the report written by Valerie Smith, Ciara Marshall & Lauren Eubanks, who worked on the prospective undergraduate demographic segment for their final report.

Introduction:

The School of Architecture wants to redesign the undergraduate program portion of their website; however, they feel they need a better understanding of prospective undergraduate architecture students' needs to improve the user experience and meet user goals for the undergraduate programs section of the website.

Therefore, the purpose of this study was to examine the needs and goals of prospective undergraduate architecture students and provide a persona and a user experience map to highlight the prospective students' needs.

The persona shows demographic information about the user (prospective undergraduate Architecture students) along with what the user's needs, motivations, and expectations are for the Clemson School of Architecture's undergraduate programs website, including the tasks the user wants to perform.

The user experience map illustrates prospective students' interactions—their wants, needs, actions, expectations, and overall experience—with the School of Architecture website. Touchpoints are identified in the user experience map, showing the sequence and location of interactions between the prospective undergraduate student user and the School of Architecture website.

In this needs assessment, we sought to answer the following research questions:

1. What tasks do users (prospective undergraduate students) want to perform when searching for information about undergraduate Architecture programs? What are the needs of the users, and how do they interact with the website?
2. How can the School of Architecture improve their website to best fit the needs of the users and enhance the user experience?

Figure 5.1. Excerpt from student recommendation report by Valerie Smith, Ciara Marshall, and Lauren Eubanks.

In order to prepare students for this work—and. in fact, before they had even met with our clients from the School of Architecture and produced the introduction above—we first read and discussed several key texts from the usability and UX research and design literature. One of my pedagogical goals was to impress on the students that UX maps come *at the end* of a long, rigorous research process. Both my industry clients and my students want to jump right in and start creating maps, so I wanted them to recognize that maps are the result of scaffolding; i.e., maps can't be created without first creating personas, and personas can't be created without data resulting from triangulated empirical inquiries. So first, because I knew the students would need to familiarize themselves with the Architecture website and because I wanted them to begin thinking about the kinds of usability metrics which would need to be considered in the site's redesign, I had them read about heuristic analysis as an approach to UX data collection. Initially, they read Jakob Nielsen's classic 1994 piece "Heuristic Evaluation," in which Nielson describes his ten characteristics for evaluating software (and websites) and how the ten characteristics were developed from a factor analysis of 249 previous research studies. Then, in order to help them better understand the application of Nielsen's ten factors to modern websites, they read SaiChandan Duggirala's (2016) excellent blog entry which provides a thorough exemplification of how to apply Nielsen's heuristic analysis to websites. Finally, in order to show students how they could consider creating visuals of their heuristic analyses, students reviewed excerpts from *Homepage Usability: 50 Websites Deconstructed* by Jakob Nielsen and Marie Tahir (2001).

Next, to prepare students for the personas they would need to create, they began by reading the "People, People, People" chapter in Janice Redish's (2012) *Letting Go of the Words*. They reviewed the personas developed for the original CAAH website[1] and they read selected excerpts from John Pruitt and Tamara Adlin's (2006) *The Persona Lifecycle: Keeping People in Mind Throughout Product Design*. Students were also introduced to Xtensio.com and shown how they could edit the templates found there in order to interactively create personas of different types of Architecture website users. In 2017, when we were working for the School of Architecture and at the time of this writing, Xtensio.com was a site which worked on the "Freemium" model. The site allowed users to create free persona designs from a wide variety of templates and then charged additional monthly fees for "premium" services, such as removing Xtensio's branding from exported files, the number of personas which can be created, removing limitations on the size of image files which can be used in the personas, a collaborative workspace for teams, etc. (Xtensio, n.d.). Even if students decided to build their personas in programs like Photoshop, Illustrator, or InDesign, an examination of Xtensio's templates was a useful exercise in having them examine the types of information they can include in a persona and how to display that information most effectively.

---

1. CAAH website: http://media.clemson.edu/caah/caah_mockups/index.html.

Finally, the last reading which prepared students for the project was Jim Kalbach's (2016) famous "grizzly bear" book, *Mapping Experiences: A Complete Guide to Creating Value through Journeys, Blueprints, and Diagrams*. Students read Chapters 1–5, where Kalbach describes how to conduct the empirical research necessary to create UX maps, and they read Chapters 10 and 11, which describe and illustrate "Customer Journey Maps" and "Experience Maps."

Once they were armed with the theoretical and research tools they needed to complete the needs assessment for our client, the students followed seven phases in order to create the UX maps. The phases were the following:

1. Meet with clients to define the problem.
2. Complete a heuristic analysis of the School of Architecture's website using Nielsen's "10 Usability Heuristics."
3. Use Google Analytics to compile data on browser use, geographic location, length of time spent on pages, and unique page views and examine demographics about all students in Clemson's undergraduate and graduate architecture programs provided by the School of Architecture and by the Office of Institutional Research.
4. Interview a representative sample of Architecture student participants based on the demographics provided from Phase 3.
5. Create a persona based on the information and data collected from interviews.
6. Develop a user experience map laying out the journey of a user and identifying common themes and "touchpoints" of prospective students' experiences as they use the School of Architecture's website.
7. Provide recommendations for redesigning the site by using the UX map to identify strengths, weaknesses, and opportunities for improvement (SWOT).

After we met with the client and obtained data from them on the types of academic programs they offered and the demographics of students in the programs, the class divided into three teams working on the project. Because we learned that the numbers of international students in the undergraduate degree were low and weren't as high a recruiting priority as they were for the graduate programs, we decided to organize as follows: 1) one team for prospective undergraduates, 2) one team for domestic graduate students, and 3) one team for international graduate students.

An important point to note here is that the teams were *not* organized around the personas they would ultimately create. Instead, each of the teams would need to decide, *based on the data they collected*, whether they would need more than one persona to represent their program area. For example, would there need to be personas for in-state versus out-of-state domestic students, and would the graduate student teams need different personas for the two-year degree programs versus the three-year degree option? Would the international graduate students need different personas for different countries or regions of the world? At this point in the process, we couldn't answer these questions since we had only met with the director of the school, the school's senior administrative assistant, and the WebCurator for the Architecture website. And while these individuals certainly knew their programs well and could describe their curricula and the application processes prospective students used, they couldn't provide us with statistical data and hard empirical evidence which would enable us to make informed decisions about how many personas would be needed in order to represent the demographics for each of the respective program areas. Thus, in order to avoid premature closure and to ensure that our personas and journey maps were data-driven rather than client-driven, we chose to defer decisions about how many personas each team would make.

As I mentioned previously, our next step was for each team member to conduct a heuristic evaluation of the existing Architecture website in order to familiarize themselves with the site so that they could begin developing questions for interviews with users. Students also worked with the administrative assistant to collect data about the demographics of applicants to the program, and with the WebCurator to obtain data from Google Analytics about which pages were the most popular, where users came from, bounce rates, etc. Finally, the students worked with the Office of Institutional Research to obtain data about the Architecture programs which wasn't immediately accessible to the Administrative Assistant. For example, the team working on international graduate students learned that, in recent years, the program accepted 46 students in total (including 43 from China, 2 from India, and 1 from Iran) out of 107 international applicants. As a result, that team decided to interview at least ten percent of the entering class (i.e., 6–8 students) in order to develop a representative sample of incoming international students. Furthermore, they sought participants who had only been in the program for a single semester and who were students from China, India, and Iran.

It should be noted at this point that we knew we weren't collecting our data from the ideal user groups for the site. In an ideal world, we would have been able to show the existing website to *prospective* students and then interview them; however, since we lacked any funding to travel to international sites and since no means of identifying potential students for the site existed, we were limited to collecting data from students who had already used the website and who had already chosen to accept their admission into the program. We were unable to collect information from potential applicants who chose not to apply to the program or applicants from countries like Germany, Italy, or other parts of the world whose data didn't appear in Google Analytics. We could not, therefore, provide our client with information about why individuals in those countries didn't discover and view the site, and we couldn't collect data on why individuals chose not to pursue an application to the program. However, we were able to provide data on which geographical locations were generating applicants, we could collect

Using Student-Experience Mapping in Academic Programs   95

data on what were "decision triggers" for successful applicants, and (because we limited our interviews to students who had only just completed the application process) we were able to collect data on what difficulties and concerns the applicants encountered during their use of the website. So even though our data wasn't based on an ideal sample of prospective students, we were able to collect useful data for our clients.

In Figure 5.2, the type of data provided by Google Analytics shows one of the ways students on the international student team were able to collect data on which countries were generating the highest number of new visitors to the site ("New Users"), the highest numbers of repeat visitors ("Users" and "Sessions"), how many pages users viewed during each session ("Pages/Session"), how long the sessions lasted ("Avg. Session Duration"), and the percentage of visits where users abandoned the website from the landing page without browsing any further ("Bounce Rate").

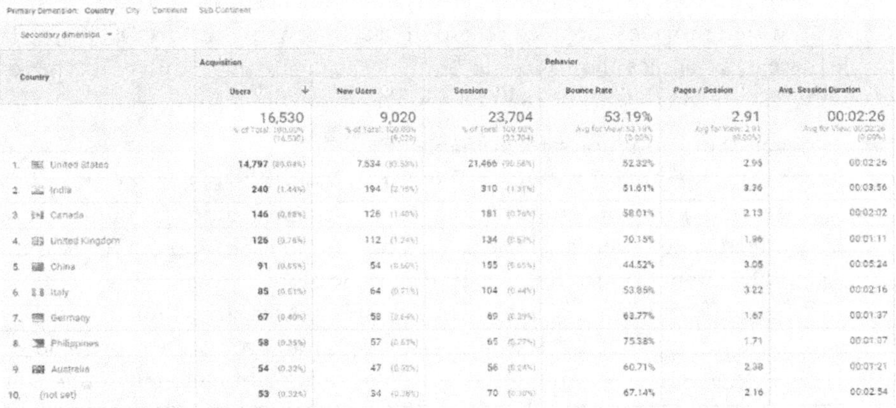

Country	Users	New Users	Sessions	Bounce Rate	Pages / Session	Avg. Session Duration
	16,530	9,020	23,704	53.19%	2.91	00:02:26
1. United States	14,797	7,534	21,466	52.32%	2.95	00:02:26
2. India	240	194	310	51.61%	3.36	00:03:56
3. Canada	146	126	181	58.01%	2.13	00:02:02
4. United Kingdom	126	112	134	70.15%	1.96	00:01:11
5. China	91	54	155	44.52%	3.05	00:05:24
6. Italy	85	64	104	53.85%	3.22	00:02:16
7. Germany	67	58	89	62.77%	1.67	00:01:37
8. Philippines	58	57	65	75.38%	1.71	00:01:07
9. Australia	54	47	56	60.71%	2.38	00:01:21
10. (not set)	53	34	70	67.14%	2.16	00:02:54

Figure 5.2. Partial screen capture of Google Analytics report on users' countries on the site.

Students on the other two teams were also able to obtain the same data for domestic users of the site; however, their data was broken down by state in the US and then by city. And students on all three teams were able to correlate these data with the demographic information we had collected from the Office of Institutional Research and the administrative assistant about actual admissions. In terms of the international graduate student team, we knew, for example, the program accepted 46 students in total (including 43 from China, 2 from India, and 1 from Iran) out of 107 international applicants, and this information correlated well with the fact that users from China had the lowest bounce rate at 44.52 percent, visited the highest number of pages at 3.05, and spent the most time on the site at 5:04 minutes. Conversely, no Philippine students had been admitted in that past year, and Google Analytics showed that users from the Philippines had the highest bounce rate, the second lowest number of pages per session, and lowest time on site. Thus, while we were able to collect information from newly admitted Chinese students about their experiences as prospects, we couldn't provide our clients with information about what prospects from the Philippines (and Germany) did or did not see on the landing page which may have kept them on the site longer. We could only say that those users had been on the site briefly and left quickly.

Google Analytics also provided us with similar data about user demographics which many internet users don't realize they are providing to the owners of webservers. We were able to collect data on users' age, gender, and interests from Google Analytics, as Figure 5.3 illustrates. As Jonathan Ellins (2017) explains on the blog entry "Google Analytics Demographic Data on Age, Gender and Interests," approximately 67 percent of the traffic which goes through a site provides data on personal factors like users' age and gender. These data are primarily collected from Google accounts which users might have used such as YouTube, Gmail, Google Drive, and of course, the Chrome browser itself; however, a significant amount of the data are also collected from "third-party DoubleClick cookies (user tracking cookies)" which provide a detailed record of users' browsing history (Ellins, 2017, n.p.). These data sources allow Google Analytics to create seven different types of standard reports. As the online help for Google Analytics states,

> Seven standard reports are available:
> - **Demographics Overview**: The distribution of Sessions (or other key metrics) on your property by age group and gender. Sessions is the default key metric. You can also use % New Sessions, Avg. Session Duration, Bounce Rate, or Pages per Session.
> - **Age**: Acquisition, Behavior, and Conversions metrics broken down by age group. When you drill into an age group, you see the breakdown by gender, then by interest. Ages below 18 are not included in the data.
> - **Gender**: Acquisition, Behavior, and Conversions metrics broken down by gender. When you drill into a gender, you see the breakdown by age group, then by interest.
> - **Interests Overview**: The distribution of Sessions (or other key metrics) on your property by the top-10 interests in Affinity Categories, In-Market Segments, and Other Categories.
> - **Affinity Categories (reach)**: Acquisition, Behavior, and Conversions metrics broken down by Affinity Categories.
> - **In-Market Segments**: Acquisition, Behavior, and Conversions metrics broken down by In-Market Segments.
> - **Other Categories**: Acquisition, Behavior, and Conversions metrics broken down by Other Categories. (Google, 2019)

Even though they only represent approximately 67 percent of the users, data like those detailed above can be correlated with the admissions data we received from the Architecture School's administrative assistant in order to help the students make informed decisions about details to include in their personas. For example,

Figure 5.3 shows that there was very little difference in the browsing behaviors and bounce rates between males and females, but the fact that 52.67 percent of the sessions were with females gave a slight edge toward choosing a female persona.

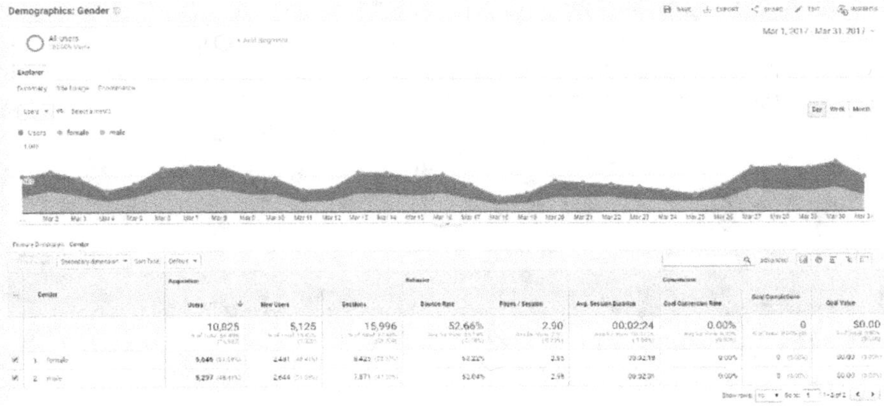

Figure 5.3. Partial screen capture of Google Analytics report on gender.

Armed with information from Google Analytics about topics like which pages on the website were producing the highest bounce rate for users from, say, Charleston, South Carlina, or Beijing, China, each of the three teams developed their own set of interview procedures based on the particular and contingent needs of their user groups. However, because all our interviews requested users to engage in retrospection, we asked them to use the website during the interview in order to prompt them, to stimulate their memories, and to guide their recollection of issues both pro and con which they found on the site. In other words, we used a version of the "Stimulated Retrospective Think-Aloud Method" in which Judy Ramey's team of graduate students at the University of Washington showed that "the logical inference and strategy explanation information in people's verbalization also provide valid information about users' task performance" (Guan et al., 2006, p. 1261). We also asked them to overview the steps they followed as they went through the application process to better help us understand the phases we needed to show on the experience maps we were creating. Figure 5.4 shows an example of a persona which was developed by the international graduate student team using a modified version of Xtensio's "Software Developer Persona" template.

In modifying the template to meet their needs, Nidhi and Doris primarily chose to enhance information collected during their interviews which would help the Architecture website design team make informed decisions about content to include and privilege in the site. For example, the original template included sections on favorite "Brands" that the persona followed (i.e., brands like Nike, Apple, and Nestlé), but Nidhi and Doris reasoned that it was more important to their client to know that the majority of the international students they had interviewed were more interested in the three-year program track in the architecture school than they were in the two-year track. Indeed, in our early meetings with our clients, they told us that they were attempting to decide if they needed to redesign the website so that there was a whole section of the site dedicated to the two-year track and another to the three-year (the current site combined information for both programs on the same pages). Thus, rather than providing information that said that the persona's favorite candy was Nestlé's Butterfinger, the students chose to replace the brand portion of the basic template with information about the "Key Attributes" their interviews revealed about important information (like the reputation of the program) which helped the students decide to apply for the program.

Yi Fang

"Every contribution of effort will reward as gains."

Gender: Female
Age: 26
Ethnicity: Chinese
Family Status: In a relationship
Location: Shanghai, China

Personality

Introvert — Extrovert
Analytical — Creative
Conservative — Liberal
Passive — Active

Determined   Creative   Amiable

Goals

- to apply for a graduate program in architecture (Master of Architecutre)
- to look for information about
  - program reputation (ranking, certified program)
  - tuition (&living expenses)
  - study abroad opportunities
  - campus environment
  - application requirements
- to learn about the difference between 2-year and 3-year tracks
- to be able to get access to student works/projects
- to adapt to a foreign environment

About Yi

Yi Fang has been working for Tengyuan Design as a residential designer for two years. She has a bachlor's degree in urban design. She is a very hard-working and determined woman who is now planning to apply for a graduate program in the United States so that she could get a degree in Master in Architecture. After completing the program, she wants to work as an architect in the U.S. That is why she values the experience of learning abroad and hopes to attend one of the most outstanding programs in the U.S.

Computer Information

Computer: PC
Preferred Browser: Chrome
Mobile phone: iPhone

Preferred Channels

Traditional Ads

Online & Social Media

Referral

Study-Abroad Agency

Key Attributes

- Likes fine arts since a young age
- Has an area of interest in residential design
- Intends to apply for three-year graduate programs related to the field of architecture (especially residential design) and hopes to graduate within three years
- Cares about program reputation and its association with famous architecture companies

Figure 5.4. Sample persona for an international graduate student by Nidhi Verma and Doris Xue Ding.

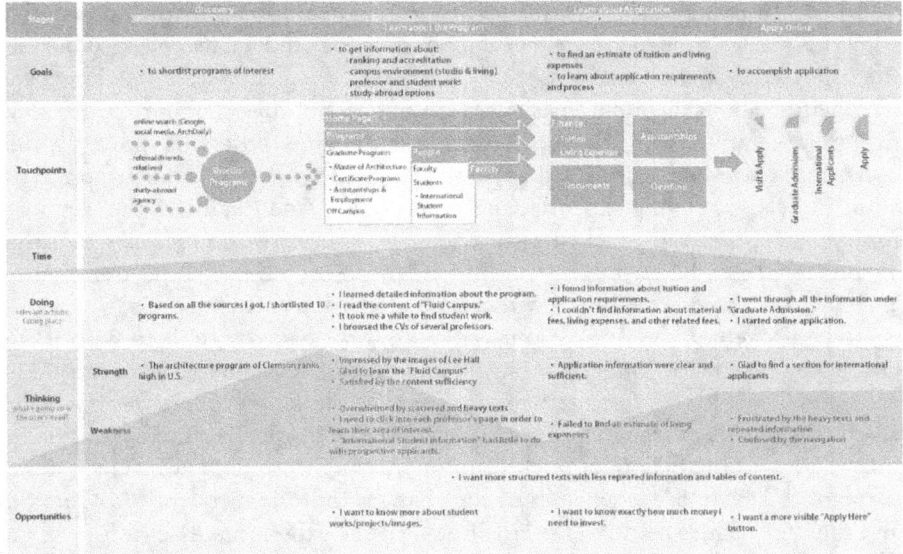

Figure 5.5. Sample user experience map for international graduate students by Nidhi Verma & Doris Xue Ding.

Once the personas had been created using the demographic information collected from the interviews and other sources, the teams then created their experience maps. At this point, students were ready to use their readings from Kalbach's (2016) *Mapping Experiences* book to decide how best to visually display all the empirical data they had collected. Figure 5.5 is an example of a UX map produced by the team working on international graduate students in architecture.

Along the top of the map are the "Stages," or major events that the users experienced during the application process. Next are the goals the users indicated they had at each stage in the process. The information here is of value for the redesign of the website because it shows that users are seeking content such as the program's ranking, accreditation, cost of living, study abroad programs, etc. The third line of the map provides the "touchpoints." Touchpoints are defined as any way a customer or user can interact with a business, service, website, etc. Basically, it's any time that a user "touches" the product being mapped. In this particular case, the team chose to map all of the items of the website which the users chose to touch at each of the phases in the map. The fourth line of the map shows the amount of time users spend at each phase. In this case, the map shows that users spend the most time learning about the program and how to complete an application. The "Doing" line explains what the users were doing with the website at each phase. It's worth noting here that the students chose to use actual first-person quotes from their interviews for these entries in order to help reinforce to our clients that the user experience map is capturing the voice of the user. The "Thinking" line of the map is interesting because it attempts to map the strengths and weaknesses found at each phase based on the data collected during the interviews. It shows that users were pleased when they were seeking basic information about the program, such as ranking, travel abroad opportunities (i.e., the "fluid campus"), and descriptions of the academic programs; however, the users were frustrated by the lack of information about how to actually apply for admission, cost of living expenses, and other topics. And finally, on the "Opportunities" line, the team tracked recommendations users made for ways that the WebCurator could improve the website. In other words, we used the user experience maps to provide the client with a kind of visual SWOT analysis.

Taken together, the five personas from all three teams combined with three user experience maps (one for domestic undergraduates, one for domestic graduate students, and one for international graduate students) collectively gave our clients a clear and thorough understanding of the needs that required attention in the redesign of the School of Architecture's website. It would be well beyond the scope of this chapter to detail all of the changes that the director, WebCurator, and their colleagues made to the site; however, the experience map in Figure 5.6 illustrates just a few of the topics addressed.

Figure 5.6. Sample user experience map for international graduate students.

The experience map contained complaints about the "text-heavy" nature of the website. This was something all the teams found and was addressed by the use of visuals shown in Figure 5.6. The map also called for a "more visible 'Apply Here' button," which figures prominently in the redesign. It called for more information about student projects, which is addressed under the links for "News,"

"Undergraduate Architecture," and, most particularly, under the "People" link. Also, to address the concerns about living expenses and costs, on the "Campus" page, the line "For information about Application, Placement, Housing, Visas and Tuition please visit our Fluid Campus program information page" is centered and highlighted on the bottom of the page to make it easier for users to find that information. These are just a few examples of the hundreds of changes that went into the redesign of the site, changes which were at least in part informed by the detailed information our clients received about their users' needs.

■ Case Study Two: Mapping a Graduate Curriculum

Program directors of technical and professional communication (TPC) programs would almost certainly benefit from the same sort of formal needs assessment study produced by the graduate students for the School of Architecture in the first case study. However, without students having completed the work as a client-based project for a course, few of us who direct TPC programs could assemble the resources needed to conduct such a study. Consequently, unlike the first case, which provides a model for ways that courses in our TPC programs can have students use UX principles with academic clients, the second case I will discuss involves faculty using a simplified form of journey mapping as a means to examine and critique the design of an entire curriculum. In this "guerilla approach" to journey mapping, I will discuss how the entire faculty in our M.A. in Professional Communication (MAPC) program met weekly over the course of a semester in 2002 in order to create a journey map of graduate students' progress through the curriculum.

In the interest of full disclosure, however, I should say that the MAPC faculty didn't set out to create a journey map originally. The fact that we created any sort of map could probably be best described as "a happy accident," and thus, unlike the very formal and complex process I described in the first case study, the process here was decidedly informal, and the problem we were trying to solve was much less complex. Instead, the problem we were originally trying to tackle was how to make sure that all the MAPC faculty had access to the same advising information needed to help students choose between completing the degree in either the traditional two-year sequence (i.e., four semesters) or the more challenging one-and-a-half-year sequence (or three semesters). Each year, as the graduate program director, I conducted focus group meetings with all of the students in the program as part of our annual program evaluation, and one topic which kept recurring was students' concerns about differences in advising information from the faculty. Since all of the MAPC faculty were engaged in advising, we wanted to ensure that they were all able to provide a fairly consistent advising experience for the students.

So in January of 2002, we began to investigate the advising experiences of both the faculty and the students. We began by conducting what, today, we would call a "content audit" and surveyed and compiled all of the advising handbooks, webpages, and materials available for both students and faculty. Not surprisingly, we found that the information was "all there" and available; however, it was scattered across a variety of sources and not compiled in a user-friendly format. For example, key dates for creating a thesis committee; completing a thesis; submitting the thesis to the committee members; defending the thesis; meeting the Graduate School's formatting requirements for a thesis; submitting the signed forms showing that the candidate had met all the program, department, and college requirements for the degree; submitting forms applying for a diploma; and many other documents were scattered across the MAPC program's handbook, different pages on the Graduate School's website, the program's website, and even the university bookstore's website. Additionally, we discovered that key information about common practices in the program, such as when core courses required for graduation would be offered, was known to faculty because they had to staff the courses; however, students weren't always aware of these routine practices. The students didn't know, for example, that the Research Methodologies seminar was only taught in the fall semester and wasn't repeated again in the spring. This meant that students who missed the class in the fall would get their curriculum out of sequence and missed important concepts they were expected to know in subsequent courses.

In order to address some of these concerns, someone on the MAPC Committee suggested that we could really use an "advising calendar." This suggestion was well received, and the committee decided that it would begin creating a calendar that faculty could use to know when to meet with students during a semester and what topics to discuss with their advisees. And, in fact, we did actually create an advising calendar; however, it evolved into a "tickle file" (i.e., an automated calendaring tool that reminds you of key dates when events should happen or when content should be distributed). Ultimately, the program director used the tickle file to send out email reminders to faculty letting them know about timely advising information. Additionally, the exercise resulted in the creation of an advising sheet we named the "Timeline Handout," which is shown in the appendix. More importantly than the tickle file and Timeline Handout, however, is that the committee began looking at what information students needed in order to graduate successfully, beginning with their orientation to the program upon admission through to their graduation. In effect, they began to consider what students were doing and, more critically, what they *ought* to be doing at specific points throughout their academic experience.

We began the process by mapping out the semesters in an Excel spreadsheet. Once we created these events, we began mapping out the major "touchpoints" in the curriculum, focusing at first on the core courses and elective courses in the curriculum, and then later adding other types of information we felt students needed to know or activities they needed to be working on outside of their classroom experiences. This resulted in the very simple spreadsheet table shown in Table 5.1.

Table 5.1. Curriculum Touchpoints

First Semester	Second Semester
Required courses?	Required courses?
Elective courses?	Elective courses?
Grad School / Dept. Forms which are due?	Grad School / Dept. Forms which are due?
Thesis/Project Committee activity?	Thesis/Project Committee activity?
Other activity students should be doing?	Other activity students should be doing?

At this point, in the experience mapping exercise, faculty made several key decisions about gaps in the curriculum where students needed new courses in order to help them prepare for their capstone experiences. For example, during our discussions about required courses, we realized that students needed better technological scaffolding in their first semester in order to prepare them for second semester courses like Visual Communication. Rather than having to cover the technological tools needed to produce visual communication projects, faculty wanted to focus on visual communication theories and concepts in the second semester course. Consequently, we introduced a new seminar called "Digital Rhetorics Across Media" that students would take in their first semester in order to prepare them for work with tools like Photoshop, InDesign, Audition, and Premiere. The Digital Rhetorics course also prepared students for structured authoring and coding in XHTML and CSS so that they could create the final web-based portfolios needed for graduation.

The mapping exercise also led faculty to reduce the number of required "core" courses from five to four to give students more flexibility in the number of "cognate" courses they could take. The faculty wanted the students to be able to build a cognate, or specialist area, on top of the strong foundation in technical and professional communication that the core courses provided. We wanted students to be able to develop expertise in areas such as UX design, health communication, technical editing, rhetoric and composition, science writing, digital publishing, and social media authoring. Developing a cognate area in any of these areas would require that students take at least three, and preferably four, courses in their chosen area. Taking a single class, such as the Usability Testing and UX Design seminar I described in the first case, didn't really allow students to demonstrate "expertise" in the area. They needed more coursework. However, until the faculty engaged in this mapping exercise, we didn't realize that students were often unable to take three courses in a cognate area because of the demands of the five core courses: two required thesis research courses and at least one course required for students to obtain graduate teaching assistantships. We knew from our annual program evaluations that a significant number of students were actually taking 36 credit hours rather than the 30 required for graduation and they were taking an extra semester to graduate; however, it took this mapping exercise to demonstrate *for the whole faculty* that it was our core course requirements which failed to provide students with the flexibility they needed to develop their cognate areas. In other words, it took the mapping exercise to convince the faculty to make the painful decision to drop core TPC courses in favor of cognate courses. The mapping exercise turned faculty who had been advocates for their own privileged core course topics into student advocates.

Finally, as was mentioned previously, creating the experience map also resulted in a "Timeline Handout," which appears in the appendix. Prior to the Timeline Handout, students weren't really considering topics for their theses or putting their thesis committees together until late in their third semester, and, as a result, many were missing the deadlines for graduation in their fourth semester. Mapping out what students needed to be doing above and beyond the courses they were taking each semester enabled faculty to do a much more effective job advising students. Because students had the timeline, they approached faculty much earlier in the process about how to put together a committee, how to select a thesis topic, how to start their job search, and forms that were required before graduation. Because faculty didn't have "to run students down" in order to provide this information, faculty were able to provide such high quality advising that our annual program evaluations showed a significant improvement in more students graduating on time. We experienced a 30 percent increase in the number of students graduating on time the year after we started using the Timeline Handout.

■ Conclusion

I began this chapter by observing that it's a pretty short journey from "user advocate" to "student advocate." As I hope this chapter has shown, our use of UX design principles in the creation of services and instructional materials intended for students can have a dramatic impact on our students' experiences in our programs. The two cases discussed in this chapter show that user experience mapping can improve students' academic experiences, and is well worth the effort, regardless of whether one decides to invest in a formal, full-blown needs assessment program as the School of Architecture chose to do in the first case, or whether one chooses an informal, guerilla style mapping exercise like the one outlined in the second case study. Both formal and informal forms of user experience mapping improve students' academic experiences through the inclusion of students' voices in the design of websites and curricula for academic programs. Beyond the fact that serving as a student advocate is simply the right thing to do as an ethical and professional program administrator, the consequences for recruiting new prospective students, for meeting the advising and information needs of current students, for building a clear understanding among faculty of student experiences in the curriculum so that they can make informed decisions about program changes—all of these are just a few of the reasons that user experience mapping of academic programs will yield a significant return on their investment.

References

Buzan, T. (2010). *The mind map book*. BBC Books. (Original work published 1974)

Duggirala, S. (2016). 10 usability heuristics with examples. *Prototypr*. https://blog.proto typr.io/10-usability-heuristics-with-examples-4a81ada920c.

Ellins, J. (2017). Google Analytics demographic data on age, gender and interests. *Hallam*. https://www.hallaminternet.com/google-analytics-demographic-data-age-gender-interests/.

Gibbons, S. (2017). *UX mapping methods compared: A cheat sheet*. Nielsen Norman Group. https://www.nngroup.com/articles/ux-mapping-cheat-sheet/.

Gibbons, S. (2019). *Cognitive maps, mind maps, and concept maps: Definitions*. Nielsen Norman Group. https://www.nngroup.com/articles/cognitive-mind-concept/.

Google. (2019). *About demographics and interests*. Analytics Help. https://support.google.com/analytics/answer/2799357?hl=en.

Guan, Z., Lee, S., Cuddihy, E. & Ramey, J. (2006). The validity of the stimulated retrospective think-aloud method as measured by eye tracking. In *CHI '06 Proceedings of the SIGCHI Conference on Human Factors in Computing Systems* (pp. 1253–1262). Association for Computing Machinery.

Howard, T. (2009). *College of Architecture, Arts and Humanities (CAAH) website mock-ups*. Clemson University. http://media.clemson.edu/caah/caah_mockups/index.html.

Kalbach, J. (2016). *Mapping experiences: A complete guide to creating value through journeys, blueprints, and diagrams*. O'Reilly.

Knight, A., Rife, M. C., Alexander, P., Loncharich, L., DeVoss, D. N. (2009). About face: Mapping our institutional presence. *Computers and Composition*, 26, 190–202.

Nielsen, J. (1994). Heuristic evaluation. In J. Nielsen & R. L. Mack (Eds.), *Usability inspection methods* (pp. 25–62). John Wiley & Sons.

Nielsen, J. & Tahir, M. (2001). *Homepage usability: 50 websites deconstructed*. New Riders.

Novak, J. D. & Gowin, D. B. (1984). *Learning how to learn*. Cambridge University Press.

Porter, J., Sullivan, P., Blythe, S., Grabill, J. T. & Miles, L. (2000). Institutional critique: A rhetorical methodology for change. *College Composition and Communication*, 45(4), 610–642.

Pruitt, J. & Adlin, T. (2006). *The persona lifecycle: Keeping people in mind throughout product design* (1st ed.). Morgan Kaufmann.

Redish, J. (2012). *Letting go of the words: Writing web content that works* (2nd ed.). Morgan Kaufmann.

Szabo, P. W. (2017). *User experience mapping* (1st ed.). PACKT Publishing.

Tincher, J. & Newton, N. (2019). *How hard is it to be your customer? Using journey mapping to drive customer focused change*. Paramount Market Publishing.

Tolman, E. C. (1948, July). Cognitive maps in rats and men. *Psychological Review*. 55(4), 189–208.

Walker, A. (2018). User experience mapping for dummies: Understand the user's journey before you start building. *UX Collective*. https://uxdesign.cc/user-experience-map ping-alice-emma-walker-868259547ba8.

Xtensio. (n.d.). *User persona template and examples*. https://xtensio.com/user-persona/.

■ Appendix: The Timeline Handout

▓ Typical Timeline for the Thesis Option Over Four Semesters

(created 2/25/02; revised 7/1/03)

The timeline below outlines a **conventional** path that a student might follow. The actual path a student will follow can vary dramatically, and students should always seek advising in order to address individual needs. Note that, to be considered "full status," students should enroll in 9 credit hours per semester.

Fall Semester, First Year	
ENGL 851	This is one of the 5 core courses and is only offered in the Fall.
ENGL 852	This is one of the 5 core courses and is only offered in the Fall.
ENGL 853 or COMM 664	Students have the option of choosing one of these since ENGL 853 is offered in both the Spring and Fall semesters. Students also have the option of choosing either COMM 664 or ENGL 856.
Spring Advising	Before enrolling for the Spring/Summer, students should seek out their academic advisors for assistance in choosing the non-core courses.
Spring Semester, First Year	
ENGL 850	This is one of the 5 core courses and is only offered in the Spring.
ENGL 856 or 853	Students who chose COMM 664 in the Fall will need to take ENGL 853 here. Students who chose 853 in the Fall will take 856. ENGL 856 is only offered in the Spring.
Approved non-core course	See "Spring Advising" above.
Fall Advising	Before enrolling for the Fall, students should seek out their academic advisors for assistance in choosing the non-core courses.
Consult faculty members about potential thesis topics.	This should occur sometime near the end of the semester and before many faculty leave for the summer.
First Summer, First Year	
Approved non-core course	See "Spring Advising" above.
Begin writing thesis proposal.	Start reading the literature on thesis topic and begin thinking about possible members for the thesis committee. Begin drafting thesis proposal. See MAPC Handbook for proposal format.
Second Summer, First Year	
Foreign language requirement	Usually, the Language Dept. offers intensive language courses this semester. See MAPC Handbook or advisor for alternative ways to meet the language requirement.

Fall Semester, Second Year	
File GS2.	See MAPC Program Director for assistance and signatures. Check Graduate School's deadlines for filing GS2 forms.
One approved non-core course	See "Fall Advising" above.
ENGL 891	These are thesis research hours.
Submit thesis proposal to full committee.	This should occur at the beginning of the semester.
Thesis proposal approved. File Thesis/Project Committee Request Form with MAPC Program Director.	This needs to be approved 1–2 weeks after the beginning of the semester.
Begin working on the thesis.	Set up regular meetings with the thesis committee chair to review draft chapters.
File GS4 with Graduate School.	GS4 forms are available in E-106 Martin. Check Graduate School's deadlines for filing GS4 forms.
Spring Semester, Second Year	
ENGL 891	These are thesis research hours.
Meeting with committee chair	Usually weekly or bi-weekly.
Schedule oral exam.	Once oral exam has been scheduled with committee members, the MAPC Program Director needs to be notified of the date, time, and location for the exam.
Complete thesis.	The thesis is normally completed around the middle of the semester.
Take oral exam. File MAPC Oral Report Form and signed GS7 form with the MAPC Program Director.	Usually before April 15; however, check the Graduate School's deadline for taking oral or written exams.
Submit final thesis to committee for defense.	Give unbound copies of the thesis to committee members at least one week prior to the scheduled defense date.
Defend thesis.	This should be done at least one week prior to the Graduate School deadline for taking the oral or written exams.

Notification of successful defense.	The committee chair must notify the MAPC Program Director that the thesis has been successfully defended at least one day prior to the Graduate School deadline for taking the oral or written exams. The Program Director will file the GS_7 form with the Graduate School.
Obtain thesis format approval from the Graduate School.	This cannot take place until after the thesis has been successfully defended. Check the Graduate School's deadline for completing this step.
Submit duplicated copies of the approved thesis to the Graduate School.	Check the Graduate School's deadline for completing this step.

6. "A Nice Change of Pace": Involving Students-as-Course-Users Early and Often

Beau Pihlaja
TEXAS TECH UNIVERSITY

Abstract: Thinking of students as "users" of a course's key elements (e.g., syllabus or learning management system) requires that instructors include students in the design process for crucial course elements "early and often." However, expectations often are that instructors' central course architecture, materials, and hence students' user experience be complete and usable before a class begins. Indeed, many instructors without a prior background in user experience (UX) research and practice might find the approach difficult to integrate with their current best practices. In this chapter, an instructor with preliminary expertise in UX shares how he sought to center students-as-users in a new pilot course by having them contribute to the design of the course syllabus and digital component delivered through Blackboard's learning management system (LMS) at the beginning as well as throughout the semester. This chapter explores both the challenges and possibilities of adopting an "early and often" approach to including students in designing a course's architecture. It describes the relevant activities and students' preliminary responses, and critically evaluates potential revised future application. Additionally, it discusses potential instructor resistance and institutional limitations to taking this approach. Finally, it draws attention to the possibilities for even a basic and provisional UX approach to support course content as well.

Keywords: UX pedagogy, user-centered design pedagogy, syllabus design, learning management system (LMS) design

Key Takeaways:

- Think of a course as a "user experience" and the assignments and key experience architecture elements—especially the syllabus and LMS—as integrated with institutional rules, norms, and expectations.
- Consider students expert end users of course materials when it comes to their experience and day-to-day use of course elements, that is, how they will (or won't) ultimately use them throughout the semester.
- Give students an opportunity to contribute early and often to the design and revision of course materials for which they will be held responsible, especially the syllabus and LMS organization.
- Consider, where possible, ways to integrate user experience perspectives with the course content and not simply its functional delivery, for example as part of a course exploring what it means to be "culturally competent."

■ Including Students in Course Design

As a new assistant professor in Texas Tech University's (TTU) Technical Communication and Rhetoric program (housed in the English department in the College of Arts & Sciences), I was assigned to teach "ENGL 2312: Texts and Technologies that Connect the World." This second-year English course, designed to help meet TTU's institutional "multicultural core requirement," had students explore the use and consumption of texts and technologies around the world. The course was designed to be flexible, with the pilot syllabus bringing together two challenging core concepts: "intercultural communication" and "usability." As I developed the course's first iteration, two questions persisted:

- How could I deploy insights from usability or the larger umbrella discipline of user experience research (Potts & Salvo, 2017) to better teach these concepts to undergraduates?
- How could I better design individual in-class experiences for undergraduate students to facilitate their learning?

Pedagogical instruction has long emphasized "student-centered" approaches using "backwards design" methods to identify that course's student-learning outcomes (Ambrose et al., 2010; Davidovitch, 2013; Hannafin & Land, 1997; Wright, 2011). However, thinking of user experience as an "academic practice" (Crane & Cargile Cook, this collection) can more effectively refine how we help students achieve these learning outcomes. User experience (UX) thinking expands our attention to identify often obscured material and relational dynamics intersecting in students' experience of our courses. For me, positioning the students as course "users" complemented and improved upon traditional approaches to student engagement early on in class as well as throughout the semester.

In this chapter, I demonstrate how thinking of the ENGL 2312 class as a "user experience" inspired two early class activities focused on the syllabus' design and the course Blackboard site. My description and analysis of these classroom activities' design and students' engagement with them in this project fell within TTU's Institutional Review Board (IRB) exemption for studies in "established or commonly accepted educational settings" (#IRB2020-870). The activities also illustrated for students the complex, real-world dynamics of our course topic, "cultural usability." Additionally, students began practicing critical mindfulness as they engaged with the course's texts/technologies. This experience provided me with a foundation for deploying this approach in future versions of this class and others, including in asynchronous, 100 percent online courses, and even graduate courses. This approach, too, creates interesting possibilities for pedagogy in a wide-range of courses, departments, and disciplines, regardless of whether instructors have a background in UX research.

■ Texts and Technologies that Connect the World

Developed and approved prior to my joining the Technical Communication and Rhetoric (TCR) faculty in Texas Tech University's English department, ENGL 2312 fit nicely into our program's Bachelor of Arts in Technical Communication (BATC) major and minor. As determined by the university, courses had to help students develop and demonstrate "intercultural awareness" as well as "exhibit the ability to engage constructively with individuals and groups, across diverse social contexts" by the end of the course (Texas Tech University, n.d.-a, n.p.).

ENGL 2312 was designed to be flexible, allowing individual instructors to approach it from their unique perspectives while meeting core requirements. Teaching the course in the fall of my second year at TTU, I closely followed the sample syllabus provided to me in the original course proposal. Because this was to be the first time this version of the course was taught, I treated it as a "pilot" course and invited students to think similarly throughout the semester.

Institutionally, the course grew out of the fact that:

> Technology increasingly extends the reach of individuals and groups across borders: national/political borders, linguistic borders, and cultural borders. Engineers, technical communicators, and professionals are asked more and more to design texts and technologies that reach and work across those borders. (Texas Tech University, 2021)

The class aimed to help students:

> explore the definition and role of "culture" and what it means to be "culturally competent." . . . [To] learn about the ways writing and writing technologies shape and are shaped by the cultures in which they are used. . . . [T]o understand that technologies are developed for particular users in particular contexts and that in order to effectively design technologies and documents, technical communicators must become invested in cross-cultural communication and mindfulness. (Texas Tech University, 2021)

We used two textbooks, *Cultural Intelligence* (Thomas & Inkson, 2017) and *Cross-Cultural Technology Design* (Sun, 2012), supplemented with readings from technical communication and inter/cultural studies. Students completed four major assignments: two "praxis papers," an individual research project, and a final design group project. The two praxis papers had students practice analyzing specific texts and technologies and then asked them to engage in and reflect upon a cross- or intercultural interaction. The individual research project required students to use Stuart Selber's (2010) categories for organizing digital instruction sets to identify and analyze an instruction set for its potential delivery across cultures. The final project asked groups to identify a text or technology and redesign it for cross-cultural use in accordance with the insights, skills, and frameworks we had discussed, analyzed, and used in class.

The course essentially covered two complex concepts in conjunction, both potentially unfamiliar to undergraduates: cultural competence and usability. Culture is a challenging enough concept to teach on its own as it is broad and all-encompassing in terms of what it defines and influences. Adding to this the concept of usability only compounded the challenge. While user-centered design, usability, and user experience stand as distinct, discrete objects of study and methodological approaches to design and inquiry, they share a common concern with the *user*. In wrestling with how to think with my students about "culture" and how texts and technologies are used in any given context, it became obvious that the way forward was to begin with the first two "commandments" of the user-centered design process: "thou must involve users early and often" (Still & Crane, 2016). So I began by asking *students* how they thought we might best approach the questions, and what they would prefer as users of the course apparatus and content.

Ultimately, I most explicitly involved students at the beginning, consulting them about the material presentation and configuration of the syllabus and our course home page delivered through the university-designed learning management system (LMS), Blackboard. This approach disclosed to me how thinking about user experience as an academic practice held a great deal of potential for student engagement and deeper learning. It also fits with the growing desire to apply "user" engagement to pedagogy and to build on traditional pedagogical approaches to active student learning.

■ Conceptual Frameworks/Precursors

Liza Potts and Michael Salvo (2017), introducing the concept of *experience architecture* (XA), recognize the slippery, conceptual porousness with which XA, UX, user-centered design (UCD), and human-centered design (HCD) are deployed. Theirs is a big-tent, "global" perspective on XA. They aim to support researchers and practitioners who are "putting work in usability together with an ecological approach to genre, information architecture, and document design to create a coherent approach to the complex work of the technical and professional communicator in emergent environments of work and play" (p. 11). They recognize similarities between their work in XA and the "work being done in educational technology under the banner of learning experience (LX)" (p. 7).

However, while *usability* as a research method and testing practice for developing end products has been applied to classroom artifacts, plenty of potential remains untapped for thinking about students as users of course documents as well as other elements (Crane, 2015). Furthermore, potential remains to connect usability—more narrowly focused on the product's "usefulness" as well as the method that tests that usefulness at a specific point in time (Crane & Cargile

Cook, this collection; Lallemand et al., 2015; Nielsen, 2012)—to the larger "experience" or "architecture" of student users.

User-centered design (UCD) is similarly concerned with keeping users central to product design and innovation and may rely on any number of methods to do so (Still & Crane, 2016). UCD, like usability, has been applied to the design of classroom contexts and especially online learning environments (Greer & Harris, 2018). However—like usability—UCD remains more narrowly concerned with users' and distinct products' interactions.

This distinction between UCD/usability and the larger user experience is important because course elements like syllabi and an LMS remain complex systems (Crane, 2015), integrated into other intersecting, networked systems, with many stakeholders that may not share instructors' or students' needs as users. Of course, keeping users at the center of any product design (UCD) as well as testing the specific usability functions of any course element is important when developing a more usable experience architecture for students. But given the complexity of the system and pressures instructors often feel, it can be easier to simply focus in a general way on a document's, assignment instruction set's, or LMS's design's "usability" for students without consulting students (UCD) or connecting the notion of students-as-users to their larger experience as course users (UX).

My contribution here shows how instructors can begin including UCD and usability concerns in our course designs. Instructors with even minimal experience with UX concepts can begin using the basic principles immediately. Additionally, I illustrate how this connects to the larger user experience students have in a class, a department, and at a university as a whole. The principle that designers must consult users at the beginning of and throughout their design process is most clearly applicable to the act of designing a course, course unit, and even a daily activity. Thinking at the outset about how users will take up the texts or technologies we might design for them is crucial to developing the successful uptake of any product. As Brian Still and Kate Crane (2016) note, users' "mental models of the world" make product navigation possible. Designs must "integrate into [users'] models" or be adapted with "not a lot of effort" (p. 46). Furthermore, this process of consulting users should be iterative and ongoing. As components are added to a design or even after a design has "gone live," designers "still learn from users by involving them" (Still & Crane, 2016, pp. 46–47).

Extending this insight to include "cultural" dynamics enables us to see the wide range of minute, banal, overlapping but often divergent ways people around the globe might take up anything we designed. While *cultural usability* is a complex topic, historically, it is concerned with the design of products for usability "cross-culturally," requiring critical analysis of the wider global context for any given local users (Sun, 2012). My prior work studying digitally mediated intercultural professional communication provided me with numerous opportunities to think through communication technology use in and across cultural contexts (Pihlaja, 2018).

What a broader UX perspective can offer pedagogically is a more nuanced perspective on students—namely, that they are operating within larger institutional and cultural ecologies or architecture that must be considered along with usability concerns or even student-centered approaches (Crane, 2015; Crane & Cargile Cook, this collection). Students take up every syllabus, textbook, instruction set, and LMS, putting it to use in order to navigate or implement the process of learning. Engagement with instructors, in class or even via comments on student writing, is also something that students have to put to use in some form or fashion (Still & Koerber, 2010). Recognizing this reveals the need to position students as active users of anything instructors produce for or transmit to them.

Since many instructors do not get formal pedagogical instruction in graduate programs, only subject area expertise, their early teaching career focuses on "what I (or my discipline) want(s) students to understand or be able to do." As instructors gain more experience semester-to-semester and year-to-year, student "personas," students as actual users, are iteratively re-imagined based on those who have taken the course before, succeeding or failing in various ways each year. Syllabi, instruction sets, and assignments are then refined prior to the next semester in order to improve outcomes this time around (and hopefully heading off negative student evaluations). Developing insight into students as users over years of teaching experience in order to adapt is certainly part of an instructor's professionalization process. However, adopting a UX approach to working with students earlier in one's career can potentially provide faster, more efficient insights into what students in any given semester or academic year might need from an instructor.

Uniquely, UCD recognizes that you have to include users directly in the design process if you are to head off design disasters or poor overall UX environments before implementation. Indeed, the qualification "early and often" (Still & Crane, 2016) asks designers to include users not only before but throughout the implementation of a design, be it product or process. Ideally, students become co-creators of the course architecture, and the overall effect is that of a more participatory design approach (Spinuzzi, 2005) to developing course materials and in the case of the LMS, something like Michael Salvo et al.'s (2009) "discursive technology."

It makes sense that design affects usability in educational contexts, which in turn must impact success in learning (Jones, 2018). Indeed, when it comes to syllabus design in particular, Natasha Jones (2018) makes a compelling case that students should be positioned as "expert end-users" of the documents in the course "ecology." We might also see students as expert end-users of the whole course as a product. A course exemplifies experience architecture in that it is a "process of building a variety of experiences for a wide range of users, and then accounting for strategic decisions with stakeholders who determine whether these projects and programs are worth maintaining" (Potts & Salvo, 2017, p. 6). And as Kate

Crane (2015) argued, the usability of the syllabus must be considered along with the larger ecological experience of students at a university.

Of course, instructors might be hesitant to position students as "experts" because they may feel it doesn't match their experiences with students over the years. It may also cut at the heart of how instructors see themselves: as imparting expertise where there is little or none. Acceding expert status to students may feel like conceding instructors' role and status—one's whole reason for being a teacher. Significantly, students may also feel this way and be suspicious of instructors who do not perform competence and confidence in the learning environment or class-as-product in ways they have been enculturated to expect.

Again Jones (2018) draws attention to the fact that students are, by definition, experts in how they will (or won't) ultimately use any given course element. They can also articulate to some extent what it is that facilitates or impedes their comprehension of and engagement with course document designs and structures (Jones, 2018). Additionally, students can articulate how they are "using" course activities and assignments to pursue their learning in a given semester. Furthermore, the process of consulting, testing, and reflecting on course elements with students has the potential to aid the pedagogical goals of the course, using students' agency as "expert end users" of a course as learning product to engage course content itself more critically and deeply.

Syllabi and LMSs are both known quantities whose role in American university course culture is accepted and ubiquitous, both as concrete tools for course delivery (e.g., Blackboard is the required LMS for all undergraduate courses at TTU) and in our cultural lore ("It's on the *syllabus*!"). Because these elements are introduced early in the semester, it makes having an early discussion about their design and functionality more feasible. Yet precisely because we need them early, the syllabus typically must already be written when a class starts. Because this is often a requirement of institutions, including students in its composition or design process can be a challenge.

Syllabus co-construction is by no means an original concept (Buchanan et al., 2017; Hudd, 2003; Kaplan & Renard, 2015). Teachers have incorporated it in a variety of disciplinary fields, recognizing not only its value for fostering student engagement, but also its ability to build a new layer of accountability into the learning process. Still, concerns remain that—however noble one's intentions—students are either too socialized to certain kinds of practices/activities to express much creativity in their contributions (Hudd, 2003) or are simply not prepared for the challenge, especially given the material complexity and likely confusion amidst a student's first weeks on campus in a given semester (Fornaciari & Dean, 2014).

Here, thinking of students as users or end-users and not simply as individuals to be motivated or to be held (however creatively) "accountable" for course materials may be more productive. It recognizes possible reasons for students' lack of engagement separate from either intrinsic psychological concepts of motivation or the somewhat paternalistic moral framework of "accountability." Instead, it acknowledges that a student's "hang-ups" engaging with course material might be at the point of use (usability), or because documents were not designed with them in mind (UCD), or because course elements fit awkwardly or at odds with the larger experience architecture of the university in which they move, and work, and have their academic being (UX).

Any attempt at participatory design, or collaboration, or co-construction is a risk. But UX as an innovative academic practice requires reasonable risk-taking. In the case of the ENGL 2312 course I taught, the fact that the course was something of a pilot design that I had taken over somewhat unexpectedly freed me to embrace the uncertainty and invite my students to do the same by drawing attention to the risk and the purposes for it, and asking them to join me in thinking critically about the course document design and organization. Consequently, I let these two artifacts "hang out there," partially unfinished and open, as we engaged them together during early class periods. What did this look like? Next, I give examples from my own experience provisionally practicing this approach.

Students as Users of the Course Syllabus and Blackboard Site

When my pilot course commenced in the fall of 2018, 17 students were enrolled. The majority (ten) of the students were technical communication majors and were familiar with usability as a disciplinary area of research and testing. Four, however, were majoring in STEM or STEM-related fields: mathematics, computer science, biology, and architecture. One student was a university studies major with English designated as one of their three areas of focus. Another was a sociology major. One student was undeclared at the time the course began. All were second-year students and above. Three were in their final year as undergraduates.

I wanted to build our 120-minute, twice-weekly course meetings around a mixture of small and large group discussions of the assigned texts while actively engaging with the technologies that we had used previously. Drawing attention to texts and technologies that showed up serendipitously in our world over the course of the semester was one possible way to generate discussion about course-related topics and themes. It would enable us to move back and forth between a more abstract academic mode of inquiry and our shared material experience.

Whether online or in person, any class will already share cultural expectations and practices around one text and one technology in particular: the course syllabus and the LMS. So over two separate class periods early in the semester, I guided students as they reviewed the course syllabus and the Blackboard shell from their perspective as users of that text and technology. We looked first at the syllabus and then at the shared Blackboard course shell.

Re-Designing the Syllabus

To enable students' participation in (re-)designing the syllabus, at the beginning of an early class period, I placed students in groups of three to four and assigned each group a subsection of the syllabus to review. One group focused on the course description, objectives, and materials section; another, the assessment criteria for grading; another, the course policies; and finally, another, the course calendar.

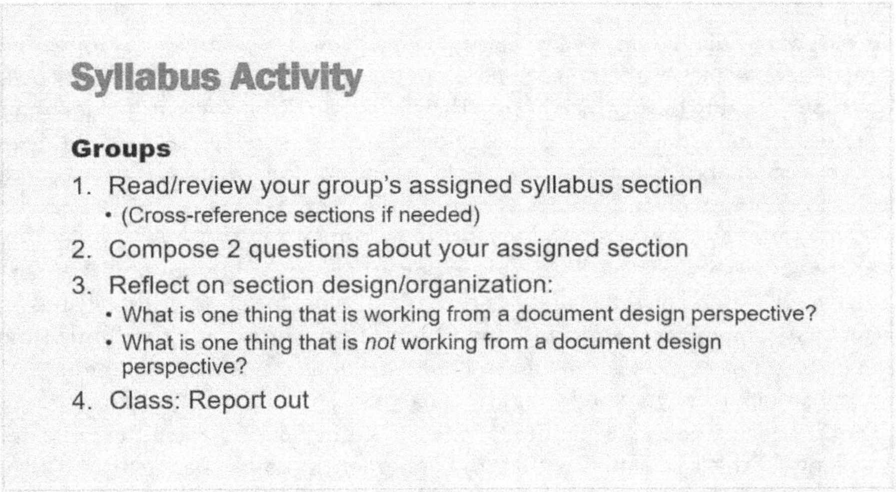

> **Syllabus Activity**
>
> **Groups**
> 1. Read/review your group's assigned syllabus section
>   - (Cross-reference sections if needed)
> 2. Compose 2 questions about your assigned section
> 3. Reflect on section design/organization:
>   - What is one thing that is working from a document design perspective?
>   - What is one thing that is *not* working from a document design perspective?
> 4. Class: Report out

Figure 6.1. PowerPoint instructions slide from Fall 2018 syllabus redesign activity.

I first asked students to articulate the syllabus section's content as they understood it, putting the substance of the section in their own words. This was akin to a "syllabus quiz" an instructor might assign in the first week or two to make sure students had read and understood the syllabus. I then required them to articulate two questions they had about the content (Figure 6.1). Finally, I asked them to identify something they liked about the design of their assigned section of the syllabus and something that made it easier to use, as well as something they didn't like about the design and something that made the document difficult for them personally to use. These last two activity requirements followed Brian Still's (2016) assertion regarding UCD that "by focusing as soon as possible on user needs and wants, the design is exposed to more eyeballs, the important eyeballs of the users, and potential big problems are discovered and addressed before they become too big to be fixed" (p. 26).

At the end of the class period, we came back together to discuss each group's summary, their questions, and their positive and negative insights regarding the documents' design. Outside of class, I also assigned them to complete a reflection on their experience of the activity using guiding questions about the act of conducting the exercise/activity itself (see Appendix A). Students then uploaded these reflections to Blackboard. These activity questions and responses also served as a record and prompt in the manner of a "retrospective recall" method for priming study participants to think about their recent use of a particular tool (Russell & Oren, 2009). I could also refer students to their individual activity reflections to initiate discussions specific to the syllabus in later classes.

Student Response to and Discussion about Syllabus Redesign Activity

As part of our discussion, I asked clarifying questions about students' summaries. I made sure to answer their questions about the content, but I also asked my own questions, seeking deeper insight into their likes and dislikes about the design of the document. Additionally, I proposed design changes to see if they would help improve students' capacity to "use" each section on the syllabus. I also made a point to then actually implement as many of their suggestions as I could after the exercise (refer to Figures 6.2 and 6.3 for comparisons).

The activity was especially useful for obtaining insight into my students' perspectives as "users" of the course content I had built, specifically the syllabus as a text. As Crane (2015) and Jones (2018) previously argued, it also afforded me the opportunity to make visible to students the kinds of institutional limitations or obligations I had in composing my syllabus (e.g., including specific language regarding plagiarism or accommodations and citing specific operating policies). Incidentally, this also supported our discussion of the course's content as it gave us a shared object around which we could explore a university, a department, a major, even a single class as a "culture" that "uses" a text in certain ways, under certain limitations, to certain ends.

Some of the students' design insights were admittedly basic. For example, they complained that several sections were text heavy combined with minimal paragraph "chunking," making reading a section all the way through with comprehension difficult. Like most instructors, I suspect, I had originally composed the syllabus with a focus on content, on what I wanted to say about each component. As a professional writer, I also know I am longwinded, given to running over my word limits with stunning regularity. But hearing in an immediate way from students that the syllabus was hard to engage—that is, to *use*—precisely because it was so wordy made concrete and real something I would no doubt have identified abstractly as a design problem with all my syllabi if asked to provide a self-critique of the document.

Our discussion drew to the forefront how cumbersome the original text of certain sections was (Figure 6.2). Engaging with students about, say, whether the explanatory preface for each course goal area was *really* necessary in this document for what they would use it for (it wasn't) led me to revise that section in particular to make later reference to it easier (Figure 6.3).

> **Course Goals**
> This course is organized around three areas captured in the title "Texts and technologies that connect the world":
>
> **1. Culture ("the world")**
> The world is a big place with lots of different kinds of individuals and groups in it. One key objective for this course will be that students be able to analyze differences we commonly think of as "cultural differences" in complex, critical, and evidence-based ways. At the end of the course students should be able to:
> - Analyze one's own "cultural identity" as a starting point for thinking about "the world"
> - Analyze one's own "cultural identity" provisionally and relative to other "cultural identities"
> - Demonstrate intercultural awareness, knowledge and skills in written, verbal, and behavioral activities
> - Exhibit the ability to engage constructively with individuals and groups, across diverse social contexts.
> - Appraise, privilege relationships at different levels (interpersonal, local, regional, national, and international) and explain how these relationships affect the sociocultural status of individuals and groups.
>
> **2. Texts and Technologies**
> Our world is filled with an ever increasing number of texts and technologies. In our class, "texts" need to be defined very broadly. A "text" can be a book or article, yes, but it can also be a tweet, a WhatsApp message, a website. It can also be more metaphorically considered; For example, a YouTube video may function as a "text" that we read as a tool or argument in a larger network of social, political, and economic relationships. The same is true for "technologies." Here, again, we will think about technologies in very broad terms. Yes, a cell phone is a technology, but so is a specific app or program run on the phone to message others or watch content or manage one's time. At the same time a "book" (physical or electronic) can be a kind of "technology" with the same kinds of relationships as texts. Students need to think about the texts and technologies in the world in complex, critical, and evidence-based ways. At the end of the course students should be able to:
> - Analyze text/technology use/practices in one's own culture/community
>
> **3. Connection ("that connect")**
> Not only is our world "filled" with increasing texts/technologies, we tend to believe it is becoming more "connected" as a consequence. We can now be connected instantaneously via a vast telecommunication network and a wide array of specific communication apps and programs with people living (seemingly) very different lives from us. But the fact that we can be put in contact with one another does not mean we are "connected" in necessarily positive ways. Certainly the goal of our class is to think about how texts and technologies *can* be used to facilitate positive connection across cultures. But we will want to think carefully and critically about the ethical dimensions of our "connections": possible unintended consequences, how our good intentions might result in bad effects, and so on. We will then think about redesigning our texts/technologies and our *use* of those tools to improve our connections across cultures in positive, ethical, and holistic ways. At the end of the course students should be able to:
> - Identify texts/technologies that are "connecting the world"

Figure 6.2. Original design of Fall 2018 syllabus course goals.

This process of modeling revision also allowed me to call attention to how groups organize their cultural expectations around power, who can exercise it, how they can exercise it, what its limitations are, and how people view it differently even within groups who share other characteristics (language, ethnicity, geography, etc.). This discussion was especially valuable, given the content of the class (i.e., considering the role of one's culture on a text or technology's usability). We could discuss the discomfort they felt either with being asked to help design this core course element or with my expressing uncertainty (given my status both culturally and institutionally) as an "expert" about what should be in this document or what they needed.

> **Course Goals**
> This course is organized around three areas captured in the title "Texts and technologies that connect the world":
>
> **1. Culture ("the world")**
> At the end of the course students should be able to:
> - Analyze one's own "cultural identity" as a starting point for thinking about "the world"
> - Analyze one's own "cultural identity" provisionally and relative to other "cultural identities"
> - Demonstrate intercultural awareness, knowledge and skills in written, verbal, and behavioral activities
> - Exhibit the ability to engage constructively with individuals and groups, across diverse social contexts.
> - Appraise, privilege relationships at different levels (interpersonal, local, regional, national, and international) and explain how these relationships affect the sociocultural status of individuals and groups.
>
> **2. Texts and Technologies**
> At the end of the course students should be able to:
> - Analyze text/technology use/practices in one's own culture/community
>
> **3. Connection ("that connect")**
> At the end of the course students should be able to:
> - Identify texts/technologies that are "connecting the world"
> - Recommend specific design choices that facilitate connection for at least one text/technology across diverse social contexts

Figure 6.3. Redesigned Fall 2018 syllabus course goals.

As a class, we found some shared humor in an instance of "cultural miscommunication" whereby I, as a new faculty member at TTU, had thought myself quite clever using the university's red and black color scheme to render headings and points of emphasis throughout the document (Figure 6.4). Without realizing my intention, students asserted (quite forcefully and in one instance with a hint of disgust if not horror) that red was an "angry" or anxiety-producing color—especially when I used it to highlight assignment due dates. After some discussion, while we agreed that the red-black color scheme made a kind of sense from a design perspective, from an affective perspective connected to the document's use (i.e., knowing when an assignment was due without getting excessively anxious), we decided I would use a "cooler" shade of blue to emphasize key points (Figure 6.5).

In reflecting on the activity itself, students did not seem particularly taken with the process. Most of their reflections were of the banal sort one sometimes gets early in a semester when students are still getting acclimated to instructors' expectations, such as "it was interesting," with no further detail provided. This, too, may have been because a syllabus is a fairly well-known cultural artifact, one students use frequently (cultural lore notwithstanding) and are often quizzed about.

But the benefit of taking this approach to me as an instructor should not be discounted. It helped position students not as incorrigibly ignoring the syllabus, but as end users who may find the document or text unwieldy in very specific ways. And while students certainly had obligations to consult and use the syllabus in the shared activity or our class, taking the stance of a designer relative to students' positions as end users and making changes in response to their insights only increased the likelihood that they would actually use the text I had created. Their insights into their reaction to the colors, a suggestion they made to shorten the titles for assigned readings in the course calendar, and a suggestion to adjust the amount of white space in the "to do" sections of the calendar all aided my revisions (refer to Figures 6.2 and 6.3)—and, in fact, gave me insights I also applied to other classes' syllabi.

UNIT II: Culture, Texts/Technology, Connection	
Week 5	
Tuesday, 9/25	Topic: Culture Reading: • Thomas & Inkson, Chapter 3, "Mindfulness and Cross-Cultural Skills" Due: Complete/Upload Reading/Activity Reflections (if applicable)
Thursday, 9/27	Topic: Culture Reading: • Thomas & Inkson, Chapter 4, "Making Decisions Across Cultures" Due: Complete/Upload Reading/Activity Reflections (if applicable)
Week 6	
Tuesday, 10/2	Topic: Culture Reading: • Thomas & Inkson, Chapter 5, "Communicating and Negotiating Across Cultures" Due: Complete/Upload Reading/Activity Reflections (if applicable)
Thursday, 10/4	Topic: Culture Reading: • Thomas & Inkson, Chapter 6, "Motivating and Leading Across Cultures" Due: Complete/Upload Reading/Activity Reflections (if applicable)
Week 7	
Tuesday, 10/9	Topic: Texts/Technology Reading: • Selber, S. A. (2010). A rhetoric of electronic instruction sets. *Technical Communication Quarterly, 19*(2), 95-117. Due: Complete/Upload Reading/Activity Reflections (if applicable)
Thursday, 10/11	Topic: Connection Reading: • St. Amant, K. (2015) "What do Technical Communicators Need to know about International Environments?" Due: Complete/Upload Reading/Activity Reflections (if applicable)
Week 8	
Tuesday, 10/16	Topic: Connection Reading: • Chapter 3 and 4, Sun, "Integrating Action and Meaning into Cross-Cultural User-Experience" and "CLUE As a Framework for Cross-Cultural User Experience," in *Cross-Cultural Technology Design*. Due: Complete/Upload Reading/Activity Reflections (if applicable)
Thursday, 10/18	Topic: Connection Reading: • Chapter 5, Sun, "Sophie's Story: New Chocolate at Work" in *Cross-Cultural Technology Design*. Due: Praxis Paper #2; Complete/Upload Reading/Activity Reflections (if applicable)

Figure 6.4. Original Fall 2018 syllabus schedule design.

UNIT II: Culture, Texts/Technology, Connection	
Week 5	
Tuesday, 9/25	Topic: Culture Reading: • Thomas & Inkson, Chapter 3
Thursday, 9/27	Topic: Culture Reading: • Thomas & Inkson, Chapter 4
Week 6	
Tuesday, 10/2	Topic: Culture Reading: • Thomas & Inkson, Chapter 5
Thursday, 10/4	Due: *Praxis Paper #1* Topic: Culture Reading: • Thomas & Inkson, Chapter 6
Week 7	
Tuesday, 10/9	Topic: Texts/Technology Reading: • Selber, S. A. (2010). A rhetoric of electronic instruction sets. (linked on Blackboard)
Thursday, 10/11	Topic: Connection Reading: • St. Amant, K. (2015) "What do Technical Communicators Need to know about International Environments?" (linked on Blackboard)
Week 8	
Tuesday, 10/16	Topic: Connection Reading: • Sun, Chapters 3 and 4
Thursday, 10/18	Due: *Praxis Paper #2* Topic: Connection Reading: • Sun, Chapter 5

Figure 6.5. Redesigned Fall 2018 syllabus schedule design.

More substantively, this exercise set the stage for us to consult with each other about the arrangement of the schedule, when things were due, and how they worked to scaffold and relate to one another, culminating in the final project. While we agreed to complete the class as initially designed and planned, we talked about the relationship of assignments to one another and the due dates, and whether there was enough time to reasonably complete one assignment before the next, in some cases actually shifting due dates around. These discussions indicate the potential a UX approach, particularly in assessment, might have for class design and pedagogy.

On the last day of class, while debriefing the course, we explored more radical redesign options—for example, requiring the "final" project be completed *first* and using it as a shared artifact to work collectively towards deeper understanding of cultural competence applied to text and technology design. Whatever objections they or I had to these kinds of negotiations, the status of the course as a new "pilot" course helped us extend leeway to one another. But I do wonder whether we could take this approach *every* semester, regardless of the status of the class. Indeed, to ask these questions every time is to accept that students' needs and user practices are not all the same and that the culture of the class changes from semester to semester, if not more frequently.

Designing Blackboard for Student Use

To position students as the users of Blackboard for the class, I took a similar approach as with the syllabus. I first asked students to describe how they had used Blackboard in previous classes. Because instructors' LMS use across campus can be especially idiosyncratic (or non-existent), students' user experience with it can be uneven. I then invited students to engage in a simple paper prototyping activity (Snyder, 2003). Students first drew their own "ideal" LMS interface, for example, sketching out a course site's home page, labeling links and content areas, listing out subfolders, even sketching buttons or images. Finally, I asked them to draw their ideal *Blackboard* interface. We discussed their answers to my initial questions in class. Later, I had students reflect on this activity as well, uploading it to Blackboard (see Appendix A).

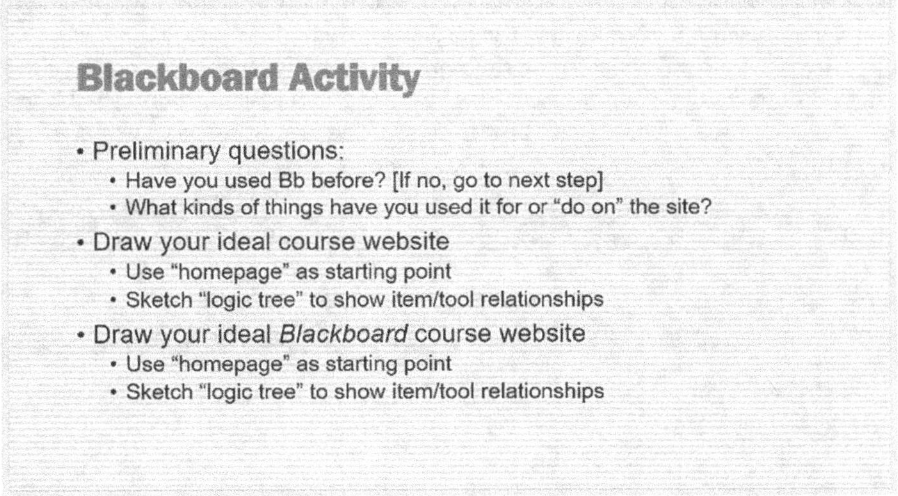

Blackboard Activity

- Preliminary questions:
    - Have you used Bb before? [If no, go to next step]
    - What kinds of things have you used it for or "do on" the site?
- Draw your ideal course website
    - Use "homepage" as starting point
    - Sketch "logic tree" to show item/tool relationships
- Draw your ideal *Blackboard* course website
    - Use "homepage" as starting point
    - Sketch "logic tree" to show item/tool relationships

Figure 6.6. PowerPoint instructions slide from Fall 2018 Blackboard design activity.

Student Response to Discussion About Blackboard Design

The in-class discussion regarding how students might use and design their course Blackboard shells was markedly livelier than our discussion around the syllabus. Based on several student reflections, which I will discuss in a moment, I suspect this reaction was because the exercise was relatively novel—they had never been invited to comment on how their course website was or should be organized or designed (whether hybrid, online, or as supplement to in-person courses). However, the drawing exercise proved minimally useful. Many of their sketches were incoherent or incomplete and did not support our follow-up discussion especially well. This may have been because I did not provide them with examples of what such drawings should look like or really much other guidance about what their drawings *could* look like. At the time, I was more concerned that I not inadvertently telegraph that I was looking for something in particular or otherwise distort their original ideas with my suggestions. Consequently, the activity was also likely overwhelming for most students—drawing a whole web page in only a few minutes. As I discuss below, in a second version of the class, I have focused the activity on drawing a page with their ideal path for completing a significant but discrete task (see Appendix C).

Whereas students are more familiar with a syllabus and its possibilities and purposes as a text or cultural artifact, the Blackboard back end is something of a mystery—or at least it was for my students in the fall of 2018. However, this activity allowed me to make visible some of the constraining limitations that shape a technology like Blackboard in a way I had never done before. In terms of engaging course content, it also proved a useful starting point for talking about how we as technical communicators were learning to be culturally competent consumers, users, and producers of texts and technologies.

After the students reflected on their previous use of Blackboard and imagined an ideal organization for a course LMS, I brought up the blank course shell home page in edit mode to show them how things looked to me and what was involved in setting up assignments in this context (Figure 6.7).

Figure 6.7. Blank Fall 2019 Blackboard home page shell (identical to Fall 2018, which was filled in as class went).

"A Nice Change of Pace" 125

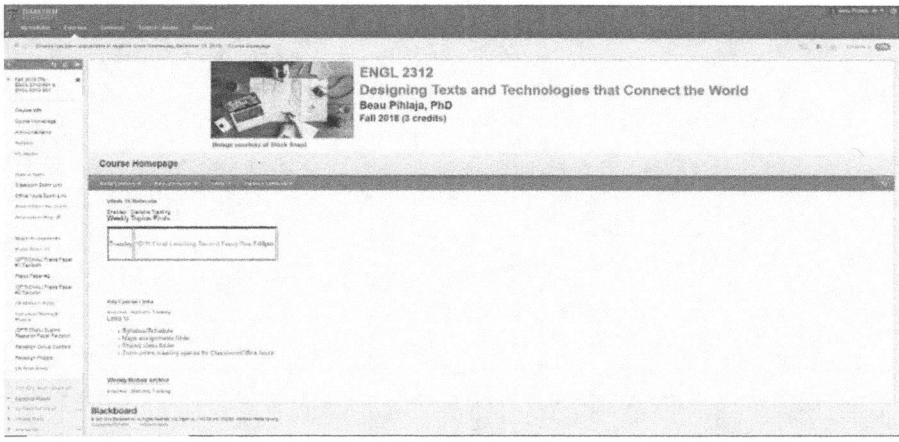

Figure 6.8. Completed Fall 2018 Blackboard home page.

Because I had left it blank, I was able to walk them through the material mechanics of setting up assignments, uploading documents, making announcements, etc. We were able to discuss what information would be most useful where and how it might best be presented so they could navigate it most easily. This gave students a say in the final layout (Figure 6.8) as well as set the groundwork for discussing cultural expectations and usability for a course LMS.

We discussed at length how they would like the frequent reading response assignments to be organized and labeled online such that they would know what response was due when. Here, my students provided perfectly reasonable suggestions from a *user's* perspective—many of which I applied (e.g., shortening the titles to "RR[#]"). But I also took the time to show them the process for creating an assignment and what options and affordances were available to me in Blackboard's instructor view (Figure 6.9). This activity also gave me an opportunity to explain the difference between using a folder/sub-folder organization method vs. my preferred approach of using weekly learning modules to organize content and assignments together. I was also able to discuss principles of "modularity," that is, how instructors-as-users segment content as much as possible to facilitate *re*use from semester to semester.

One student initially suggested I designate each reading response "RR[#]"—which I did—followed by the date the response was due (e.g., "RR1 9/3/18"). This made perfect sense, again from a *user* perspective. But I drew their attention to the fact that, while adding the date to a title was perfectly viable for *this* semester, as an instructor, I had to use this template from semester-to-semester or build it from scratch every time. Putting the dates in the title meant I would have to go and manually edit the new due dates in each title every semester, as in the area designated "Due Dates" in Figure 6.9.

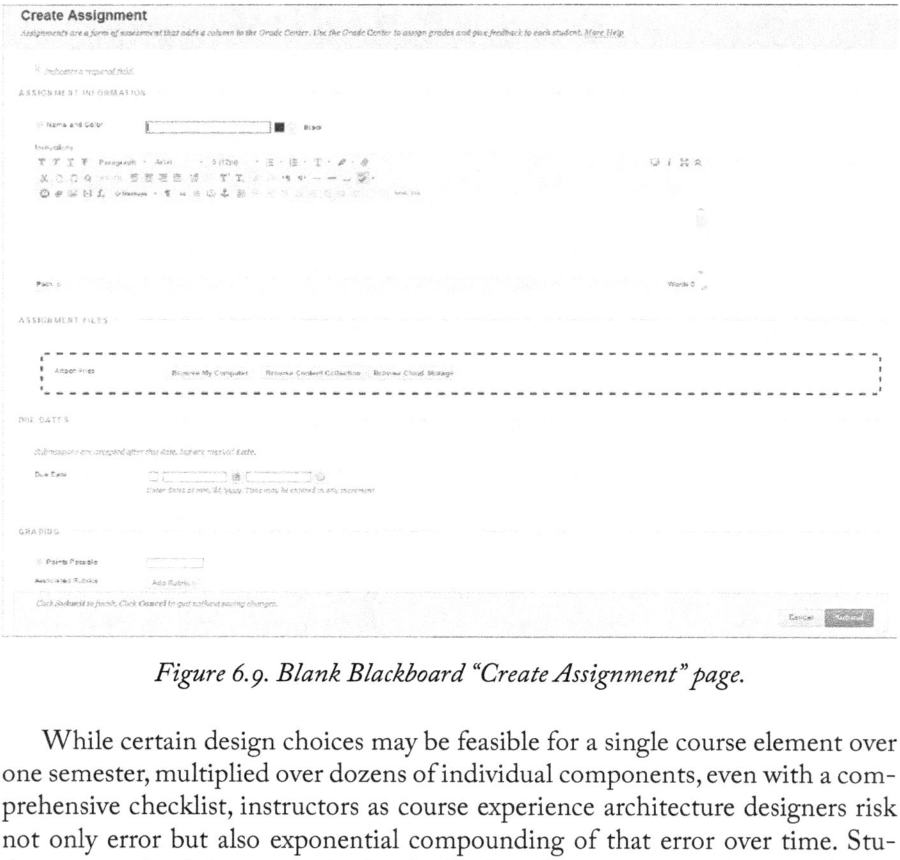

Figure 6.9. Blank Blackboard "Create Assignment" page.

While certain design choices may be feasible for a single course element over one semester, multiplied over dozens of individual components, even with a comprehensive checklist, instructors as course experience architecture designers risk not only error but also exponential compounding of that error over time. Students recognized the constraint for the final reading response assignment layout (Figure 6.10) as a reasonable trade-off between usability and technical limitations. I also tried to assist them by placing the reading responses in the module for the week they were due. That said, students still struggled a bit to determine what reading response assignment was due when.

This allowed me to illustrate how different users' needs/preferences might clash as we hashed out a design that worked. It also enabled me to remind them that—in addition to my desire to think of *students* as users—as an instructor, I, too, am a user of these texts and technologies with constraints, needs, and desires for how I use them day-by-day or semester-by-semester.

This particular example also dovetailed nicely with our course content discussions around possible cultural differences that show up even in mundane, everyday ways (e.g., how we represent dates and time). While it is customary in the United States to represent months and days in that order, many other nations represent them in the reverse: day then month. This added a cultural competence dimension to the discussion.

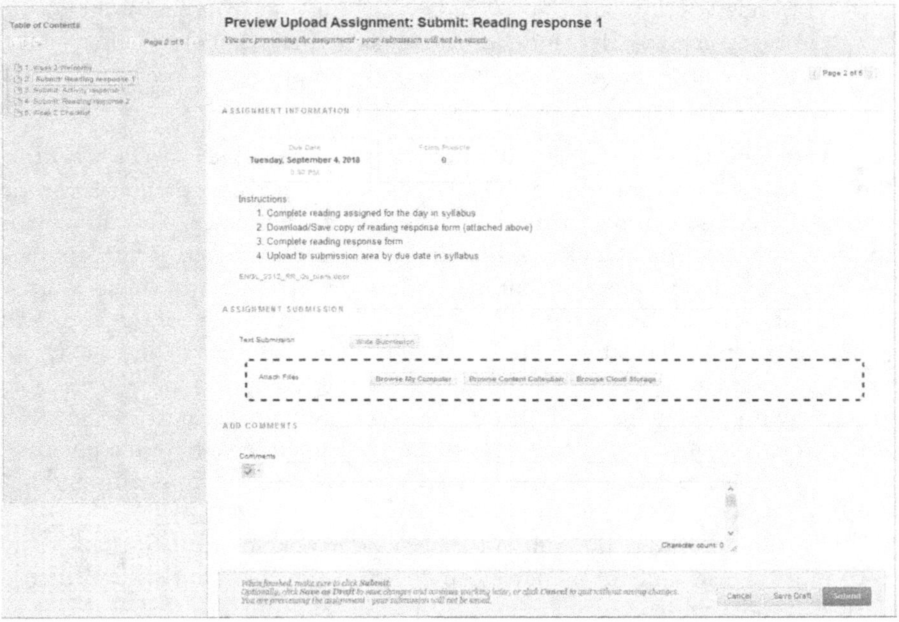

Figure 6.10. Original assignment upload preview screen for reading response assignment.

Students were able to see that not only did we have to contend with the individual preferences and constraints we had in the class at TTU in the fall of 2018, but if the class, its texts, and technologies were to "connect the world" per our course description, we would have to consider the potentially global impact of even small differences. Indeed, we returned to the day-month example several times throughout the semester. In explaining what a "redesign for cross-cultural connection" of some existing text or technology might look like for their final projects, I called back to this example. I suggested that if one were to "redesign for cross-cultural connection" our course website, they might develop a plug-in or module that would enable assignments on a course calendar to be updated automatically any time an assignment's due date/time was changed. You could also propose a toggle that would allow users to convert the representation from month-day to day-month automatically, per the preference of any student.

In contrast to students' largely ambivalent reflections on the syllabus redesign activity, the response from several students to the Blackboard design activity was starkly stronger and positive. More than that, however, students seemed to recognize how strange it was that they'd never been asked to contribute to the design of either Blackboard or its use in an individual class. Mason, who was especially thoughtful in his responses throughout the semester, commented,

> I wondered why a professor would ask the students what they want in Blackboard.... This is definitely a positive thing, but every other college course has just been dealing with the professor's preferred Blackboard layouts. It's a nice change of pace.[1]

It's not especially surprising that learning environments are instructor-centric. But it is important to note that being brought into the activity as a user, someone who might have something to say about course delivery, can be a pleasant one for students ("a nice change of pace"). This suggests to me a UX perspective's potential to improve student engagement with course topics and in individual courses.

Another student, Emily, put an even finer point on the value of this approach in her reflection on the activity: "It's really important that we are able to navigate this page, so I'm glad we were able to have a say in its composition." She was able to see why it was important, given that they were going to have to *use* the technology for the course. This demonstrated to me that students have the potential to see themselves as *users* of course materials and learning environments and not simply *consumers* of their content.

These responses were the fruit of the decision to position students not simply as consumers or recipients of course content from an expert, but as users whose capacities and experience would shape their success as students. The process gave us shared objects and artifacts to ground our learning together. This may not be a potential benefit available for every class. However, that possibility should not be dismissed out of hand. Where the student is thought of as a user and brought into the process of designing courses, the prospects for student engagement, learning, persistence, and success are substantial.

■ Implications, Limitations, and Future Trajectories

My description and analysis of my experience in this pilot course outlined in this chapter suggests that a UX approach is useful for thinking through every level of course design and delivery. Neither of these exercises was remotely close to a full-fledged "usability test" or "user experience" analysis. Instructors looking to include these kinds of activities should certainly formalize the process further, taking a more structured approach to testing discrete elements.

In the Fall 2019 version of the class, I provided students with a much more structured form to guide their test of the syllabus' usability, assigning different roles to group members and narrowing the tasks they had to complete (see Appendix B). The assignment remained a challenging icebreaker to implement in the first

---

1. Both Mason and Emily, whom I also quote below, were kind enough to grant me explicit permission to quote their responses to this activity as well as to use their names in this publication. I am grateful to them as well as the rest of their colleagues in the Fall 2018 section of ENGL 2312 at TTU for being such thoughtful, serious, critical, and yet joyful good sports as we worked our way through a very challenging topic.

week. Completing five separate tests in a somewhat crowded room with two students joining the class online via video conference made the process that much more complicated. But it appears to have still gotten students thinking about a syllabus as part of their experience as students-as-users in a similar way to the Fall 2018 cohort. It allowed me again to model revision and to highlight centering users' needs as a key practice in UX analysis and research.

I also revised the Blackboard design activity assignment. Again, I provided students with a more structured form for completing the activity and narrowed the required task for suggesting a redesigned LMS interface (see Appendix C). I also asked them more directly to compare their experience as Blackboard users with their experiences with other sites they use, perhaps for different purposes (see question four in Appendix C).

Instructors can no doubt develop different and better ways to design or incorporate these kinds of activities. However, my experience pressed me to refine my thinking overall about students as individuals to work *with* as opposed to *on*. Thinking of students as course "users" has the potential to serve as another path away from the deficit model of student needs and capacities.

From an assessment perspective, thinking of students as users of course content and tools was an effective way to test their prior knowledge while disclosing (to both the instructor and students themselves) their tacit understanding of the course topic *and* tracking learning over the course of a semester. It has the ability to help clarify why a student might not be succeeding. Rather than simply assuming the problem is cognitive—"they just don't get it"—or a moral deficiency, e.g., "laziness," it frames and tracks learning relative to potential difficulty using the course architecture. That said, it is another way instructors can build accountability for students who will have participated in and, therefore, ideally taken responsibility for, the design of key class elements (Shivers-McNair et al., 2018).

Finally, this framing of students as users who need to be included early and often in the process may also help instructors meet accessibility needs (broadly defined). It can enable instructors to organize content delivery in ways that are flexible enough to meet diverse students' needs (Borgman & Dockter, 2018). It might also prove a useful way to test a course's content and tools for accessibility throughout a semester/quarter.

The pilot nature of the course was also somewhat freeing, enabling me to take what, to me, felt like risks in how I approached the topic and course structure precisely because the course had yet to be deployed in this particular configuration before. This enabled me to connect Still and Crane's (2016) commandment to involve users in design early to my students' potential experience in my class. I was already comfortable thinking of *myself* as a user, especially of Blackboard's interface and as a course designer. I knew experientially the iterative dynamics inherent to course design and improvement. Indeed, every instructor of any skill level engages in a kind of elongated user experience assessment of their classes when they develop course goals and track students' engagement, points of confusion, successes, and failures in any given lecture, assignment, or discussion.

But what thinking of students as users reveals is that in the hurly-burly of day-to-day instruction, we may not always or explicitly think of students as users who need to be engaged early and iteratively in course design—regardless of a course's status as a "pilot" or "established" course. It reveals that we should aim to connect the discrete usability (or lack thereof) of a course and its elements to the larger architecture of their user *experience*, including the contextual differences we might think of as "cultural."

Inviting student input on course element design no doubt renders one vulnerable. To show up on day one of a course expecting to be able to teach the class only after you've had substantial input on how students will or will not be able to "use" its organization and environment may feel like risking one's identity as a teacher. And to be clear, it is not a risk equally available to everyone, knowing what we do about the ways in which instructors' subject positions shape their reception by students who interpret the same things differently (Boring, 2017; see also "Being a Black Academic in America," 2019).

Given several of my students' responses to being engaged in this way about the very design of the course texts/technologies, it makes sense that we test the impact of taking this stance towards students, i.e., as users, first on student success—both as a matter of depth and breadth. We might also test the impact of this approach on student retention at a school, in a major, or in a course sequence. It also seems wise, given the pitfalls I noted above around instructor subjectivities and the impact they may have on student perceptions, to test the impact of this approach on semester course evaluations and student perceptions of instructor competence *before* using these attempts as grounds for assessing instructors.

Furthermore, institutional structures are not always conducive to applying Still and Crane's (2016) first and second commandments of UCD. The historically determined commitments to course design and delivery demand courses be fully planned and deployable at the outset. The user experience, in other words, is expected to be fully formed and used immediately. This is especially true for courses delivered 100 percent online—particularly asynchronously. Institutional and even student expectations are such that everyone shows up to class on day one "ready to go."2

---

2. I have attempted to build this same conceptual perspective into my 100 percent asynchronous course sections. While the course design still has to be completed prior to the start of a term, I have included a designated "usability/UX discussion board" in the LMS. Students can—for extra credit—post insights about what is or is not working in their navigating the course site, content, and requirements from a user's perspective. In order to receive full extra credit, I ask that they complete all assigned work and post three times: once at the beginning, middle, and end of the semester. Students in two separate sections over the two separate semesters in which I have adopted this assignment have spontaneously expressed the same kind of pleased surprise that Mason did at being

Regarding digital learning environments, Blackboard no doubt has user-tested the LMS with faculty and students in context as part of the product's proprietary development and iterative redesign. But if students are in fact enculturated users (Crane, 2015; Sun, 2012), then their diverse, ever-changing contexts of use are a crucial component of their capacity to engage the experience architecture of a course, be it the LMS, syllabus, or instruction sets. Lab-testing a product's use can only take designers and instructors so far. Every class will be unique to some extent.

Given the rapid proliferation and customization of so much content delivery outside the university, there's also little reason to believe our capacities to replicate Fordist models of course delivery and quality control inside the university will do anything but grow weaker without more flexible models of student engagement. Of course, there's no guarantee that UCD approaches themselves will be able to move beyond the more apolitical, individualist thinking regarding student engagement that leads Collin Bjork (2018) to propose we supplement usability-type approaches with insights from digital rhetoric, identifying the inherently rhetorical dynamics at work in any user interface, such as audience, persuasion, and credibility.

Yet my hope is that this chapter connects with those instructors interested in taking a user-centered approach to the design and deployment of their courses and their pedagogical practices more broadly, especially in those courses that have a significant intercultural, cross-cultural, or multicultural component. My work here seeks to extend insights gained by traditional student-centered pedagogies, usability and UX studies generally, and those who have already begun to apply usability and UX approaches to writing studies—especially online writing instruction (Bjork, 2018; Borgman & Dockter, 2018; Crane, 2015; Greer & Harris, 2018; Shivers-McNair et al., 2018).

Writing studies, technical communication studies, and UX studies are well positioned to adopt and extend this thinking and, in many ways, already have. Each already recognizes the constitutive role of revision and audience in composing anything, whether that is writing an essay, crafting an instruction set, or designing a web interface. Further turning our content knowledge and the process insights of our field to see students themselves as users with potential insight into the class they are taking may grow our capacity to engage a more diverse group of students in a wider range of topics and environments.

Any instructor could theoretically, at this moment, start thinking of their students as "users" at the center of and in their course. However, instructors might object to how much time this process of engaging students as users takes if it does not also directly advance toward course goals and outcomes. This is a valid concern, especially for instructors in tightly integrated sequence courses with a lot of content to cover to prepare students for their next course. Exploring ways

---

included in thinking through how the course is designed and organized.

to fold the process into the content of the course in the ways I was provisionally able to do might head off complaints that it takes away from content instruction.

Hopefully my own foray into this pedagogical framing will encourage others, even those new to thinking of students as users, to begin incorporating it into their teaching processes, their syllabus design, term planning, and daily activity development. Instructors with this mindset will be a critical part of supporting and advocating for the broader institutional and disciplinary shifts called for by the editors and authors of this volume.

■ References

Ambrose, S. A., Bridges, M. W., DiPetro, M., Lovett, M. C. & Norman, M. K. (2010). *How learning works: Seven research-based principles for smart teaching*. Jossey-Bass.

Being a Black academic in America. (2019, April 18). *The Chronicle of Higher Education*. https://www.chronicle.com/interactives/20190418-black-academic.

Bjork, C. (2018). Integrating usability testing with digital rhetoric in OWI. *Computers and Composition, 49*, 4–13. https://doi.org/10.1016/j.compcom.2018.05.009.

Borgman, J. & Dockter, J. (2018). Considerations of access and design in the online writing classroom. *Computers and Composition, 49*, 94–105. https://doi.org/10.1016/j.compcom.2018.05.001.

Boring, A. (2017). Gender biases in student evaluations of teaching. *Journal of Public Economics, 145*, 27–41. https://doi.org/10.1016/j.jpubeco.2016.11.006.

Buchanan, S. A., Bullard, J., Aspray, W., Bailey, D., Barker, L., Carter, D., Clement, T., Gottschlich, N., Howison, J., McLaughlin, S., Ocepek, M., Sholler, D., Trace, C. B. (2017). Collaborative syllabus design for studying information work. *Proceedings of the Association for Information Science and Technology, 54*(1), 630–632. https://doi.org/10.1002/pra2.2017.14505401094.

Crane, K. (2015). *The usability of the course syllabus: Testing syllabi modality and comprehension* [Doctoral dissertation, Texas Tech University]. Texas Tech University Libraries. https://ttu-ir.tdl.org/handle/2346/64572.

Davidovitch, N. (2013). Learning-centered teaching and backward course design from transferring knowledge to teaching skills. *Journal of International Education Research (JIER), 9*(4), 329–338. https://doi.org/10.19030/jier.v9i4.8084.

Fornaciari, C. J. & Dean, K. L. (2014). The 21st-century syllabus: From pedagogy to andragogy. *Journal of Management Education, 38*(5), 701–723. https://doi.org/10.1177/1052562913504763.

Greer, M. & Harris, H. S. (2018). User-centered design as a foundation for effective online writing instruction. *Computers and Composition, 49*, 14–24. https://doi.org/10.1016/j.compcom.2018.05.006.

Hannafin, M. J. & Land, S. M. (1997). The foundations and assumptions of technology-enhanced student-centered learning environments. *Instructional Science, 25*(3), 167–202. https://doi.org/10.1023/A:1002997414652.

Hudd, S. S. (2003). Syllabus under construction: Involving students in the creation of class assignments. *Teaching Sociology, 31*(2), 195–202. https://doi.org/10.2307/3211308.

Jones, N. N. (2018). Human centered syllabus design: Positioning our students as expert end-users. *Computers and Composition, 49*, 25–35. https://doi.org/10.1016/j.compcom.2018.05.002.

Kaplan, D. M. & Renard, M. K. (2015). Negotiating your syllabus: Building a collaborative contract. *Journal of Management Education, 39*(3), 400–421. https://doi.org/10.1177/1052562914564788.

Lallemand, C., Gronier, G. & Koenig, V. (2015). User experience: A concept without consensus? Exploring practitioners' perspective through an international survey. *Computers in Human Behavior, 43*, 35–48.

Nielsen, J. (2012, January 3). *Usability 101: Introduction to usability*. Nielsen Norman Group. https://www.nngroup.com/articles/usability-101-introduction-to-usability/.

Pihlaja, B. (2018). Activity theory, Actor-network theory, and culture in the twenty-first century. In R. Rice & K. St. Amant (Eds.), *Thinking globally, composing locally: Rethinking online writing in the age of the global internet* (pp. 182–203). Utah State University Press.

Potts, L. & Salvo, M. J. (2017). Introduction. In L. Potts & M. J. Salvo (Eds.), *Rhetoric and experience architecture* (pp. 3–13). Parlor Press.

Russell, D. M. & Oren, M. (2009). Retrospective cued recall: A method for accurately recalling previous user behaviors. In *2009 42nd Hawaii International Conference on System Sciences* (pp. 1–9). IEEE. https://doi.org/10.1109/HICSS.2009.370.

Salvo, M. J., Ren, J., Brizee, H. A. & Conard-Salvo, T. S. (2009). Usability research in the writing lab: Sustaining discourse and pedagogy. *Computers and Composition, 26*(2), 107–121. https://doi.org/10.1016/j.compcom.2008.10.001.

Selber, S. A. (2010). A rhetoric of electronic instruction sets. *Technical Communication Quarterly, 19*(2), 95–117. https://doi.org/10.1080/10572250903559340.

Shivers-McNair, A., Phillips, J., Campbell, A., Mai, H. H., Yan, A., Macy, J. F., Wenlock, J., Fry, S. & Guan, Y. (2018). User-centered design in and beyond the classroom: Toward an accountable practice. *Computers and Composition, 49*, 36–47. https://doi.org/10.1016/j.compcom.2018.05.003.

Snyder, C. (2003). *Paper prototyping: The fast and easy way to design and refine user interfaces*. Morgan Kaufmann.

Spinuzzi, C. (2005). The methodology of participatory design. *Technical Communication, 52*(2), 163–174.

Still, B. (2016). Fundamentals of user-centered design. *Intercom, 63*(3), 26–27.

Still, B. & Crane, K. (2016). *Fundamentals of user-centered design: A practical approach*. CRC Press.

Still, B. & Koerber, A. (2010). Listening to students: A usability evaluation of instructor commentary. *Journal of Business and Technical Communication, 24*(2), 206–233. https://doi.org/10.1177/1050651909353304.

Sun, H. (2012). *Cross-cultural technology design: Creating culture-sensitive technology for local users*. Oxford University Press.

Texas Tech University. (n.d.-a). *Multicultural requirement learning outcomes*. https://www.depts.ttu.edu/provost/curriculum/core-curriculum/requirements.php.

Texas Tech University (n.d.-b). *Undergraduate course offerings*. https://www.depts.ttu.edu/english/degree_resources/courses/past_course_offerings/2018_fall_undergrad_tcr.php.

Thomas, D. C. & Inkson, K. (2017). *Cultural intelligence: Surviving and thriving in the global village* (3rd ed.). Berrett-Koehler Publishers.

Wright, G. B. (2011). Student-centered learning in higher education. *International Journal of Teaching and Learning in Higher Education*, 23(1), 92–97.

■ Appendix A: ENGL 2312 Activity Reflection Questions

Save copy for your records: Last_name_ENGL2312_Activity Reflection_1

Activity:

Date of Activity:

Respond to the following questions for any activity conducted in class (or smaller activity conducted outside of a course in a given week). Answers need not be long, but need to show serious, genuine, honest, and thoughtful engagement with the texts.

1. Briefly summarize your experience doing the activity.
2. How do you think the activity connected with our course topic, readings, other activities (either completed or yet to come)?
3. What is the most interesting/important part of the experience for you? Why did this part seem interesting or important to you? Provide specific example(s).
4. What is something that confused you about the activity? Is there something you still don't understand having completed the activity?
5. What is something you can do to clear up any confusion you still have? Provide specific example(s).

Upload copy to course LMS (e.g., Blackboard). Retain a copy for your records.

■ Appendix B: Revised Syllabus Design Activity (Fall 2019)

Syllabus "user test"

Date: _____

Student user name: _____

Observer name: _____

Role [check only one]:

____ Administrator/observer

____ Time keeper/observer

____ External observer

Syllabus format (circle all that apply): Single-sided/double sided, loose/stapled, digital copy

Task 1: Identify **2 ways** to contact your instructor if you have questions/issues
  Successful? **Y/N**   Time to completion: _____
  TAP notes:

Task 2: Identify what **books, other readings/materials** are needed for this course
  Successful? **Y/N**   Time to completion: _____
  TAP notes:

Task 3: *Identify when the* Final group presentations *are due*
  Successful? **Y/N**   Time to completion: _____
  TAP notes:

Task 4: *Identify* **whether or not** *you can turn in assignments* **late** in this class
  Successful? **Y/N**   Time to completion: _____
  TAP notes:

Task 5: Identify what it takes to get a "**B**" in this course
  Successful? **Y/N**   Time to completion: _____
  TAP notes:

Appendix C: Revised Blackboard Design Activity (Fall 2019)

Date: _____
Student name: _____

1. Have you used Blackboard before in other classes? (If answer is "no" go to question #2.)
2. How have instructors used Blackboard in classes before? What kinds of things have you had to do on Blackboard as a student?
   a. What worked/was easy to use/did you like using Blackboard to do in classes?
   b. What didn't work/wasn't easy to use/you didn't like using Blackboard previously? Why?
3. Have you used learning management systems (LMS) other than Blackboard? What system did you use: _____ (If answer is "no" go to #3 below.)
   a. What worked/was easy to use/did you like using _____ to do in classes?

      b. What didn't work/wasn't easy to use/you didn't like using _____ previously? Why?
4. Draw an "ideal pathway" from a course homepage to submitting our first major assignment (e.g., LRSA). How would you get from the home page to submitting the assignment? What links, tools, information, etc. would you want to have available/see? Be creative!
5. Compare the purpose of Blackboard to one other site/app you use regularly. How do those differences/similarities in purpose impact the interface design? The way you think about either? The way you use them? (Example: Blackboard cp. to Snapchat):

7. Learning from the Learners: Incorporating User Experience into the Development of an Oral Communication Lab

Lindsay Clark and Traci Austin
SAM HOUSTON STATE UNIVERSITY

Abstract: Much current research has shown that oral communication skills are crucial to success in the workplace, regardless of the field or discipline (e.g., Archer & Davison, 2008; Kesner, 2008; Reinsch & Gardner, 2014). Unfortunately, employers have expressed frustration with what they see as a lack of proficiency with oral communication in employees (Bauer-Wolf, 2018). To address this issue, many professional communication programs around the country have created communication labs or centers. This chapter presents a case study of an oral communication lab created in a college of business which, due to limited resources, lacked the sophisticated technologies found in similar facilities at other universities. Rather than focusing on technology, we focused on providing feedback, including individualized grader input and user experience (UX) and usability metrics. In this article, we share details from the development of this lab, particularly the challenges and affordances of researching our users and the impact of successive intervention on their abilities as presenters. In the process, we learned that even a low-tech lab can be successful if we include users as co-creators in the process of designing, implementing, and assessing the lab and its services.

Keywords: oral communication, communication lab, user experience, UX

Key Takeaways:

- Our assumptions about the needs, goals, skills, and motivations of users can limit the kinds of questions we ask and the information we seek from and about those users.
- As faculty and administrators, we must recognize the value of seeing our student users as co-creators of resources intended to serve them.
- Engaging student users as co-creators requires thoughtful, formal, and iterative mechanisms for including their feedback and experiences.
- Acting on student-user feedback and experiences may upend assumptions and initial planning but, consequently, improve design and effectiveness.
- Even best practices may need to be adjusted to the unique experiences, expectations, skills, and ideas of a particular group of student users.

DOI: https://doi.org/10.37514/TPC-B.2022.1367.2.07

Much current research has shown that oral communication skills are crucial to success in the workplace, regardless of the field or discipline (e.g., Archer & Davison, 2008; Kesner, 2008; Reinsch & Gardner, 2014). In fact, in a 2018 survey by the Association of American Colleges and Universities, oral communication skills ranked highest in a list of job skills that employers want (Gewertz, 2018). Oral communication includes a number of distinct yet interrelated skills, such as listening, conversing, and presenting (e.g., Brink & Costigan, 2015). As professionals advance in an organization, however, presentation skills become much more important and can become one of the features that separates successful employees from less successful ones (Gray & Murray, 2011; Lin et al., 2010). Unfortunately, many employers have expressed frustration with what they see as a lack of proficiency with oral communication in employees, especially those who are recent graduates (Bauer-Wolf, 2018).

To address this issue, many universities support students' oral communication skill development through coursework that includes different types of professional speaking assignments. In addition, some universities also offer resources such as communication centers and labs. Similar to writing centers, communication labs give students space and resources to develop their speaking and presentation skills outside of the classroom. While our college of business had a long history of integrating oral communication across the curriculum, it had no communication lab or similar resource available to students outside their coursework.

■ The Genesis of the Lab

In Fall 2018, the college administration expressed support for the business communication faculty to develop new initiatives that foster students' *soft skills* (teamwork, leadership, ethics, and communication) and, in particular, oral communication. Because of budget and space constraints, we were also challenged to use existing technological and logistical resources. With these parameters in mind, we proposed the creation of a pilot oral communication lab that would be operated in conjunction with one author's course, a second-year business presentations course. This face-to-face course was held two days a week and had 28 students, mostly sophomores, all of whom were of traditional college age.

One of our first tasks was to find a place for the lab and to acquire the equipment and resources necessary. As mentioned above, our lab was comparatively "low tech." The college leadership allocated a large, unused office located in the faculty suite for the lab. The room was large enough to accommodate the main activities: particularly, students presenting formally in front of visual aids. We were given a projector and a desktop computer with a webcam attached to the monitor, all of which came from college surplus; students were to record their presentations using the webcam and would project any visual aids onto a blank white wall behind them. We acquired a table and chairs as a workspace for individual students and (later) student teams, a portable whiteboard, and pens and notepads for brainstorming.

In order for the lab to run smoothly, it was crucial that students be able to use the technology independently since the lab was not staffed and the instructor or the other faculty were not always present to show students how to use or troubleshoot the technology. It was also important to choose technology that was free to students and offered the privacy, confidentiality, and options for technical support expected in a university environment. We chose Blackboard, our university's learning management system (LMS), to house the activities in the lab. Next, we chose Kaltura, our LMS-integrated video management platform, for students to create, edit, and share their presentation videos. The plan was for students to submit their videos through an assignment portal in Blackboard, receive feedback on their videos from the external reviewer through an integrated rubric, and apply this feedback to prepare for their graded, face-to-face presentations in class.

In designing the lab's activities, we drew upon Susan Miller-Cochran and Rochelle Rodrigo's (2009) definition of *usability*: a process of "anticipating users' needs and expectations, as well as designing texts, documents, systems, platforms, spaces, software—and many other things—with a purpose in mind that is appropriate to and tailored for that audience of users" (as cited in Shivers-McNair et al., 2018, p. 3). We also considered how we might incentivize our students to use the lab to practice their presentations. According to Keshab Acharya (2016), understanding the idea of *value* from a user perspective includes considering what motivates users to use a product and how or why that product is deemed important to the user. For our pilot project, we made scheduling and access to the lab easy, and offered course credit for students' use of the lab for half of their required presentations. Additionally, in order to secure continued support of the lab, we needed to measure and demonstrate this intervention's impact on students' oral communication skills. We identified three primary research-informed areas of intervention to incorporate into the lab: practicing/overlearning, expert feedback, and video recording.

Benefits of Practicing and Overlearning

The students came to the course with a variety of oral presentation skills and experiences. Some had experience with public speaking before taking the class, but many did not; some were fluent speakers, while others faced challenges in this arena. While the majority of students in the course had room for improvement when it came to their oral communication skills, some felt themselves to be—and perhaps truly were—effective and confident presenters. The question arose early on about exempting these students from having to practice in the lab. However, continuing to practice a skill or task even after improvement has plateaued can make that skill easier to perform in terms of the energy and cognitive effort expended (Huang et al., 2012). In other words, even though already effective speakers' raw skills may not improve, the amount of effort and thought required to maintain their level of performance will decrease. Therefore, we decided that students would be asked to practice multiple times in the lab, regardless of their initial or ultimate skill level.

Repeated practice would, we believed, benefit students in other ways as well. Research has shown that practicing a speech can reduce the apprehension students feel when delivering their presentations to in-class audiences (e.g., Ayres et al., 1998). In informal discussions during the first week of class, a few students expressed comfort with presenting in front of an audience, and most acknowledged some degree of anxiety; with some students, this anxiety was overwhelming. Most were aware that, as business majors, they would be required to create and deliver substantial presentations in their upper-level courses. This awareness contributed to the students' sense of the importance of the second-year class (and, to a degree, to the amount of anxiety they reported).

It has long been recognized that anxiety or worry can make the performance of complex tasks worse (e.g., Derakshan & Eysenck, 2009; Eysenck, 1992; Humphreys & Revelle, 1984); however, today's traditional-age college students face some additional challenges. This generation—alternatively called Generation Z or the iGeneration—is more assertive than previous ones and more likely to believe that they can "be anything [they] want to be" (Twenge, 2014). However, they also show higher levels of stress and anxiety, and they are less likely to be self-reliant. Thus, when faced with a situation for which they have little practice and experience, such as public speaking, members of the iGeneration can experience crippling levels of anxiety. One function of the lab would be to provide a space where students could privately practice without fear of grades or evaluation; this would, we hoped, positively impact both their actual performance and their attitudes toward public speaking in general.

Expert Feedback

The idea of a communication lab is perhaps not unique; however, ours had marked differences from the beginning. Many oral communication labs at other universities feature sophisticated technology and facilities that allow students to create, edit, and record a variety of speaking-related events, like the One Button Studio (Lone Star College, n.d.; University of Minnesota Libraries, n.d.). Others incorporate artificial intelligence platforms that can offer some analysis of delivery features, such as eye contact and tone of voice (e.g., PitchVantage, n.d.). While some communication labs offer students the opportunity for feedback from human experts, many do not, reflecting the long-standing approach that individual practice is among the more important elements in improving oral presentation skills. However, when we surveyed students in our courses to help us determine the kinds of activities and resources they would like to see in a college-based oral communication center, 98 percent (n = 101) indicated they would like a space to get comprehensive feedback on their speaking-related assignments and out-of-class activities.

Oral communication pedagogy often incorporates feedback from teachers, peers, and the students themselves. Research has shown, however, that feedback from teachers is of higher quality in terms of its impact on student improvement. In addition, students *believe* that feedback from teachers is "better" than the feedback they receive from peer- or self-review (van Glinkel et al., 2019). If the review of student practice presentations in the lab was to be conducted by their course instructors, we felt it might limit the number of faculty who would encourage their students to use the lab; those instructors who did not want to address oral communication skills in their classes or review the practice videos of their students might simply opt to not participate.

Fortunately, the college was able to draw upon the success of another communication endeavor to address this issue. In 2015, the college established a Writing Initiative, in which expert graders were provided to faculty who wanted to incorporate extensive written assignments in their courses but did not want to take on the additional grading burden. While the instructors graded content and organization, the outside reviewers evaluated language, grammar, and mechanical issues. To implement this model in the lab, the Writing Initiative grader was assigned to review student presentations as well, using a rubric developed by the business communication faculty and commonly used in sections of the presentations course (see Appendix A).

Video Recording

The external reviewer would serve as the audience for the practice presentations, and, early on, the decision was made to have her review videos rather than live presentations. This decision had practical aspects in that it eliminated the need to schedule the reviewer and the students in the lab at the same time. More importantly, research shows that recording presentations offers students a number of benefits that ultimately improve their performance, including the ability to review their videos, more opportunity to practice, and reduced communication apprehension (Leeds & Maurer, 2009). Additionally, with an asynchronous, recorded presentation, we intuitively felt students would be in complete control of the presentation process and could start, stop, and re-start their presentations at their own pace and according to their own comfort level. A live audience, either present in the room or on a live video feed, would not allow students this degree of control and comfort.

Although we felt that our proposed pilot was grounded in current pedagogical research, established best practices, and UX and usability principles, the college administration—and we ourselves—wanted to have evidence of its effectiveness in helping students develop their oral communication skills before allocating substantial physical and personnel resources to the venture. At the outset, our original research questions focused on measuring and reporting back to the administration data on the impact of the lab experience on students' oral presentation skills and confidence, as well as the usability of our instructional materials, to have a clear understanding of our logistical needs. In the process of developing, managing, and evaluating the pilot project, however, our research question evolved into one more focused on user feedback: *What impact did incorporating user experience throughout the development process have on the overall success of our Oral Communication Lab?*

Early on, we observed how our assumptions of our users' wants and needs—and, therefore, the ultimate impact of the lab—were challenged by our users' feedback, prompting us to adjust materials, texts, and processes. As we engaged in a cycle of implementation, reflection, adjustment, and re-implementation, we realized the importance of including students in the development process. As such, our new approach echoed the approach to *usability testing* modeled by Shivers-McNair et al. (2018), which they define as "an empathetic, flexible, ongoing engagement with our audiences and users" (p. 39). Our original plans and processes were modeled on established communication-lab best practices; however, by listening to and learning from our students through formal and informal feedback mechanisms, we learned that even best practices need to be adjusted to the unique experiences, expectations, skills, and ideas of our particular group of users. This chapter presents a case study of how this realization changed the course of the pilot study, revealed the challenges and affordances that exist when integrating user experience, and, ultimately, led to a more successful and impactful experience for our students.

■ Methods

After receiving Institutional Review Board approval to research the lab (REF# IRB-2019-113), our next step was to develop or identify tools to assess the impact of the lab as we defined it above. Also, the assessment instruments were intended to help us as instructors refine the experience in the lab to better meet students' needs and expectations as well as create a body of data which could be reported to the college administration with the goal of continuing or even expanding the lab's services.

At the outset of the semester, we planned to use the following assessment instruments: an observations/electronic journal, the Personal Report of Communication Apprehension (PRCA-24) as a pre-test and post-test, the Shannon Cooper Technology Profile, the Instructional Video Usability Survey, Speech Anxiety Thoughts Inventory (SATI), Lab Technology Usability Survey, and the final Logistics Survey. As will be shown in the Findings section, the information gathered from these instruments prompted the creation and/or implementation of additional interventions and assessments based on feedback from our users.

Observations/Electronic Journal

Observation is recognized as one of the most powerful tools for understanding how users see, hear, and interpret the environment they are working in and how they act and react to the reality of that environment (Still & Crane, 2016). To better understand the users' experience in the lab, we conducted a *cognitive walkthrough* by "defining the task or tasks that [our] user would be expected to carry out" and then using the space and technology to practice and record our own conference presentation (Interactive Design Foundation, 2018, para. 3). In an electronic journal, we noted our experience and any logistical problems we could address before making the space available to the students. We also recorded our observations of student interactions with the space and technology when we met them in the lab for their first (and subsequent) visits. Our goal was to try to anticipate what information and tools the students would need to use the lab successfully; however, as will be seen below, further interactions with students would make it clear that our interpretations of those needs were not always on the mark.

Personal Report of Communication Apprehension (PRCA-24): Pre/Post-test

In the presentations course, we discuss *communicator anxiety* with our students, which their textbook defines as the "feeling of butterflies or sick feeling in stomach" (Hamilton & Kroll, 2018, p. 160). As mentioned earlier, many students stated reticence to public speaking; therefore, we anticipated that this nervousness might create a barrier to students using the lab. To help us as instructors and the students themselves recognize and address the nature and extent of their communication apprehension, we created a packet of self-assessments and peer activities to raise students' awareness of how their individual anxiety manifests itself.

The first assessment instrument administered to the students was the Personal Report of Communication Apprehension (PRCA-24) developed by James McCroskey (Hamilton & Kroll, 2018). This survey helps students identify their own brand of anxiety and its manifestations during specific oral communication situations, such as group settings, meetings, dyadic interactions, and public speaking (e.g., "I feel relaxed while giving a speech," with 1 = Strongly Agree and 5 = Strongly Disagree). The survey also included Likert-scale questions and open-ended reflection questions that encouraged students to think about how and why they feel anxious when speaking to others and to reflect on ways that they might manage or reduce that anxiety. To measure any changes in communication apprehension levels among students, we re-administered the PRCA-24 survey at the end of the semester.

Shannon-Cooper Technology Profile

Based on the 2006 National Education Technology Standards for Students, Li-Jen Shannon et al. (2006) condensed the findings of several studies to create a model that asks learners to assess their skill and comfort level in a number of technological areas on a scale of 0 to 10, with 0 being the lowest and 10 being the highest. The Shannon-Cooper Technology Profile (SCTP) covers technological areas such as communication tools, video/audio/graphics software, social media, and learning management systems (see Appendix B). We adapted the SCTP to include the categories of technology that we planned for the students to use, both in the pilot program and in potential expansions of the lab's services. These categories include virtual conference tools, social media, presentation software, screen capture/video creation, web creation software, and video and audio editing software. We asked students to rate their skills and comfort with specific platforms in these categories (e.g., the category of presentation software included PowerPoint, Prezi, and an Other category). Our intention was to confirm that the students were proficient in the technology we would be using in the lab; however, the results of these initial surveys informed the development of additional support materials and assessment instruments.

Instructional Video Usability Survey

Based on the results of the cognitive walkthrough and the Shannon-Cooper Technology Profile, we created an instructional video that explained the location of the lab space and presented step-by-step visual instructions for recording and uploading videos. Before students used the lab for the first time, the instructor asked them to informally evaluate the video after watching it twice during class. Based on that feedback, we revised the video prior to students actually using it in the lab and designed a more complete post-semester usability survey, which we discuss in the Lab Technology Usability section.

Speech Anxiety Thoughts Inventory (SATI)

Due to the results of the PRCA-24, which indicated high levels of communication apprehension in the class, we hoped to better understand the nature of these feelings and to respond, if possible, in the lab. Therefore, we sought out an additional instrument, the Speech Anxiety Thoughts Inventory (SATI) tool, adapted from Cho et al. (2018; Appendix C). The tool asks students to indicate their level of agreement (1–5) with different statements related to oral communication concerns, such as "If I make a mistake, the audience will think I'm stupid," and "I'll get tongue-tied." Based on their responses, students were asked to reflect on the types of worries they have with regard to public speaking and brainstorm reasons why they may feel this way (past experiences, lack of preparation, etc.).

These results helped us identify the origin of the anxiety—e.g., general anxiety, technology, or confidence issues—and apply potential responses.

Lab Technology Usability Survey

To assess the usability of the lab technology, including Blackboard, Kaltura, and the revised instructional video, we administered a survey at the end of the semester based on usability criteria from Jakob Nielsen (2012; Appendix D). According to Nielsen, *usability* refers to how easy it is for users to use a certain website, software, or other technology, and involves at least six criteria:

- **Learnability**: how easy it is for learners to use the software for the first time
- **Efficiency**: how quickly learners can actually use the software after learning how
- **Memorability**: how easily learners can use the software after not using it for a while
- **Errors**: how often learners make mistakes and how easily they can troubleshoot or fix the errors
- **Satisfaction**: how attractive or pleasant the design and navigation of the software is
- **Utility**: to what degree the software does what the learners need or want

The survey included questions that correspond to the six elements from Nielsen's usability standards and are modeled on a survey used by Parmanto et al. (2016). Students were asked to indicate how much they agreed with a series of statements, and each section included a line for open-ended comments. We analyzed these usability findings alongside a post-semester logistics survey assessing students' perceptions of the availability of the lab as well as the impact of practicing on their oral presentation skills.

Logistics Survey

Students also evaluated several logistical aspects of the lab to inform continued program development and sustainability, such as their perceptions of the procedures, lab access and support, physical lab space, and the likelihood of sustained engagement for future utilization of the lab. Analyzing these data points demonstrated the rich opportunities available when including user input in the developmental process. However, we also learned new challenges and affordances that come from intentionally engaging in iterative user-centered design.

Findings

The assessments we implemented during and after the pilot study provided valuable insight that both informed the development of lab resources during the semester and also provided guidance for future iterations of this oral communication initiative. In this section, we describe how first understanding our students' (the users') attitudes toward presenting and technology helped us make intentional decisions about how we would prepare and support the lab initiatives. The findings also showed us the importance of incorporating usability and user experience feedback during the development of initiatives like the lab. As a result of the inclusion of user experience assessments, we were able to make adjustments during the development process that aligned more with the needs of our current users.

To better understand our students' experience, we first used the lab ourselves to practice a conference presentation. During our cognitive walkthrough, our first goal was to see the lab from a user's point of view and to gather information and data from that perspective, specifically any challenges our users may encounter in the space. Conducting a cognitive walkthrough of the lab processes taught us a great deal. For example, the projector light was nearly blinding, and, given the narrowness of the room, there was no real way to avoid having it shine in our eyes. Also, the microphone was across the room from us as speakers, and, because of this, the audio was not as clear as we would have liked. Background noises also interfered; the air conditioner was loud when running, which caused us to have to speak more loudly to overcome it. Also, the lab shares a ventilation system with the faculty lounge, so the noise of the lounge's television (and the occasional college birthday celebration) bled through. All of these proved distracting to us, and, though few students communicated with us about these issues, we recognized that they may potentially impact students' experience in the lab. We requested additional insulation for the space and alerted the grader to these potential challenges.

In the observation journal are several instances in which the students clearly made the space their own. While we intended the whiteboard in the lab as a place to write our instructions or announcements, students used it to write each other encouraging messages. They left each other inspirational or instructional notes on paper on the table. They rearranged the furniture to best suit their preferences. We also recorded the observation that the students overwhelmingly dressed casually, in spite of the practice rubric including a section on professional dress and the expectation that they were to dress professionally for the graded class presentation. We even observed one student, who had worn shorts and a T-shirt to practice in the lab, walking around campus a short time later the same day dressed in a jacket and tie for another event. Clearly, students were envisioning the lab and its services in a unique and different way than we had originally expected.

Other day-to-day observations led us to rethink how students viewed and used the lab. For example, we assumed that students would start the recording when they came to the lab and just let it run as they practiced their presentation over and over. However, students wanted to submit a more polished final product rather than a video of their entire process, so they ended up recording, deleting, and re-starting their Kaltura videos several times over until they had a single shorter video they considered the "best." Some even wanted to upload more than one video, because each had "different good points" that they wanted feedback on. We also overheard students practicing their presentations when we knew the camera wasn't running, and even heard a few instances of motivational self-talk from students before they began "formally" practicing.

The users of the lab, mostly sophomores, brought a range of speaking and presentation skills to the course. Considering the composite results of the PRCA-24, students' anxiety scores ranged from low to high; however, a shared perception among the students was lower situational anxiety towards dyadic communication situations and higher anxiety towards group communication situations (meetings, presentations, networking). The composite scores from the pretest PRCA-24 indicated an overall class average of 59.6 (n = 27, range 24-120), and the posttest overall average was 52.3, representing a 12 percent reduction of communication anxiety. Moreover, by examining specifically the public speaking subtotal scores, we found that the pretest average was 18.3 and the posttest average was 14.3 (n = 27, range 6–30), indicating a 22 percent decrease in communication anxiety.

Not only did we assume student attitudes toward dress, but we also assumed they would be proficient in the technologies we planned to use in the lab. The results from the Shannon-Cooper Technology Profile (Appendix B) indicated that students self-reported high proficiency in social media, basic computing programs, and the Blackboard LMS platform. For example, Facebook scored an average of 7.4/10, Twitter scored 7.3/10, and Instagram scored 8.8/10. In contrast, Kaltura, our integrated video recording platform, scored an average of .59/10, with 22 of the 28 students giving it a score of zero. Because the Shannon-Cooper Technology Profile showed that students were not familiar with Kaltura, we felt it was important to meet each student in the lab during that student's first visit in order to lead them through, click by click, the process of recording and uploading their videos. Additionally, we created an instructional video to assist students with the process of recording and submitting their videos in the lab. Using Kaltura, a cell phone, and VideoPad video editing software, we created a five-minute instructional video that guided students through locating the lab space, using Kaltura to record their videos, and submitting those videos for feedback through Blackboard. To make sure that students had easy access to the video, we posted it on the course Blackboard site and published it on YouTube, where it could be easily viewed on mobile devices.

The students evaluated the instructional video for using the technology twice—once before using the lab and again at the end of the semester. Prior to using the lab, students evaluated the instructional video in class by completing the Instructional Video Usability Survey. The students wrote down their feedback in a two-column format (liked, disliked) after viewing the video twice. Our intention was to use the students' feedback to edit or adjust the video prior to them using it to navigate the software and hardware in the lab. Many students responded positively to the detailed, step-by-step format of the video, commenting that it was clear, detailed, and helpful. However, when reporting their "dislikes," we received several comments about the background music being distracting and the process appearing complicated and overwhelming. One student even noted, "it seems like there are about 35 steps to just upload my video." The entire process, in fact, was relatively simple to us (approximately eight steps), but in our effort to be detailed, we created a perception of the process as overwhelming and adverse for our users. We considered this feedback and revised the video in several ways: lowered the volume of the music, numbered the steps on-screen, and added transitions that divided the video into three major tasks.

At the end of the semester, students completed the lab Technology Usability Survey, an anonymous Blackboard survey that used Nielsen's (2012) usability criteria of learnability, efficiency, memorability, errors, and satisfaction. The survey included questions related to the usability of the revised instructional video, as well as the Kaltura program used in the lab. The most notable insight from this second round of testing was informal feedback from the students that they did not actually use the video during their time in the lab. When commenting on learnability and memorability, several said they remembered the basic steps from their initial viewing and then "just figured it out." Interestingly, while the revised video was no shorter than the previous version, the feedback from the students indicated that it was clear and organized. In the final usability survey, 82 percent of students reported satisfaction with the instructional video. Although we gleaned that most did not use the video while in the lab, the survey results indicated a preference towards this instructional medium: 68 percent ($n = 28$) agreed that the video is a better way to get instructions than a written handout, and 68 percent agreed that the video is a better way to get instructions than written directions on a website. These findings also supported our perception that students were learning the technology quickly and intuitively. Our observations in the lab provided another example of this technological intuitiveness on the part of students. Once we showed the students where to open the My Media tab on Blackboard (where Kaltura is housed), many students actually started to lead us; they would find and click on the proper buttons before we pointed them out. While we know from the survey that students did not know the details of using Kaltura, we do not know if it was their intuitive ability to navigate unfamiliar software or their perceived value of the video that caused them not to use this resource.

At the end of the semester, we asked the students to complete the anonymous Logistics Survey evaluating several aspects of the lab to inform continued program development and sustainability, such as their perceptions of the procedures, lab access and support, physical lab space, usability of technology, and the likelihood of sustained engagement for future utilization of the lab. Not only did 93 percent of the users indicate that they would use the lab again for future presentations, but they also surprised us by suggesting extended operating hours, extended appointment times, and additional uses for the space related to professional development. We had assumed a 9:00 a.m. to 5:00 p.m. schedule would work best for our student population, many of whom work after classes or commute to campus only two or three days a week. However, on the survey, 76 percent indicated they preferred weekday evening hours to practice in the lab, with 59 percent requesting weekend hours. While we recognized early on that our assumptions of our users' needs and wants were not always correct, we were so focused on scaffolding skills that we did not create an opportunity for gathering feedback on basic scheduling and process logistics.

▪ Discussion

The experience of developing, implementing, and assessing our communication lab highlighted how much our assumptions informed the original conception of students' needs and experiences, prompting us to evaluate those assumptions through the lens of evidence-based inquiry to allow the voices of the users to take precedence in the development process. This iterative process included more opportunities for user feedback and more flexibility in our design, echoing Alexander Osterwalder et al.'s (2014) notion of a *value proposition design* that includes "designing, testing, building, and managing value" (p. 79) by "test[ing] ideas as quickly as possible in order to learn, create better design, and test again" (p. 50). While most of our user feedback concerned our support materials, we now recognize the potential for additional metrics that elicit feedback on students' preferences and experiences related to the lab space, logistics, and access.

Students had the opportunity to visit the lab at four points during the semester: optionally, for their first and fourth presentations, and required, for their second and third presentations. When the lab was initially advertised to the students, they were given the opportunity over the next two weeks to schedule sessions, but none chose to do so. This was not surprising to us given the students' self-reported anxiety levels and resistance to or lack of recognition of the value of practice. However, when students were incentivized to schedule a lab session through nominal participation points, 89 percent ($n = 28$) of the students successfully recorded and uploaded their videos for review by our external reviewer. By the third presentation, attendance in the lab dropped to 75 percent (-14%); however, we noted three specific incidents of sickness and family situations that could have prevented students from scheduling an appointment. Most notable of these usage statistics is the 75 percent usage for the fourth and final presentation, which was optional. However, what was still unknown to us is why students chose to practice (for no course points), and if their motivation was related to grades, increased confidence, decreased anxiety, or a combination of factors. These numbers suggest that most students came to realize the value of practicing their presentations prior to delivering them in class, and that perhaps incentivizing students to practice can move them past initial resistance and anxiety. Still, more feedback opportunities related to students' motivations and preferences may have given us additional direction for adjustments that could enrich their use of the lab during the semester.

The results of the Speech Anxiety Thoughts Inventory (Cho et al., 2004) indicated that students predominantly express worry about negative judgment from others. Regardless of their initial or ultimate level of reported anxiety, 97 percent ($n = 27$) of the students "strongly agree" or "agree" with the seven statements that coalesce around the idea of an audience (e.g., "If I make a mistake, the audience will think I'm stupid"). This phenomenon addresses one issue that had been discussed among college administration, i.e., the benefits of having a "live" audience vs. recording presentations on video. Members of the college's advisory board, for example, volunteered to come to the lab to serve as audience members for the students' practice sessions. However, the responses on the PCRA suggested that students would see such live-audience situations not as practice, but as "final" presentations that undermine the lab's value as a neutral, low-risk practice space. The advisory board members' offer to serve as audiences was intended as a good-faith effort to increase the value of the lab for students; however, the reported value of the lab for the students themselves lies in the ability to practice privately and to remain in complete control of the experience. This insight has the potential to impact staffing decisions for the lab in the future. If asynchronous feedback from a human expert is truly preferable and more useful for students—as it appears to be—then the pressure to staff the communication lab with those experts at all times is reduced. Instead, the lab can be either unstaffed or staffed by non-specialist personnel, as long as it is accessible to students

After practicing and recording their presentations, the students were expected to review the feedback from the outside expert and apply it to the performance of their graded presentations in the course, which usually took place a few days after they completed their practice videos. Regardless of where the students began the semester in terms of proficiency or confidence, by the end of the semester, they demonstrated and reported gains in all areas. The most marked improvement came in delivery—voice fluency, pitch, and pacing, as well as eye contact and body language. Students also seemed more proficient when interacting with their visual aids, referring to them instead of reading from them and effortlessly positioning themselves so as not to block them. The lowest in-class presentation scores were associated with those who did not practice in the lab at all or those who only used it once. This finding reinforces the original concept that repeated practice, followed by feedback, and then followed in turn by reflective integration, is an effective approach for improving student oral communication skills.

Perhaps the most marked example of the lab's potential for success comes from the student with the highest anxiety score, "Henry." On his PCRA prior to using the lab, Henry reported high apprehension for nearly every kind of speaking situation: in groups, in meetings, dyadic (one-on-one), and public situations (e.g., at networking events or parties). He also expressed low confidence in creating and delivering presentations for class. In his first presentation in class, given before students were allowed to practice in the lab, he showed severe anxiety in his voice, eye contact, and other nonverbal behaviors. Even when he came to his first appointment in the lab, he was reticent when interacting with the instructor and seemed anxious about using the lab's technologies, even though no one else was going to be present.

With each practice session, however, Henry's confidence and fluency grew. He used the lab at least twice for each presentation, at one point staying for more than two hours (when the appointments at that time were only half an hour long). With each in-class presentation, his delivery improved; his voice was louder, his eye contact was more direct, his interaction with visual aids more effective, and his demeanor more confident and relaxed. He received a perfect score on his last individual presentation and expressed the view that the lab truly helped him to grow as a speaker. His experience supports the idea of overlearning, in that he practiced again and again until he had mastered the basic mechanics of presenting. He then continued to practice until the act of presenting became less intimidating, and he was able to add nuances of tone and delivery on the top of his performance.

Educational theory and pedagogical best practices encourage us as teachers to use assessment instruments to gather information about the success (or lack thereof) of our teaching endeavors—*formative* assessments for when instruction is ongoing and *summative* assessment at the end (Harlen & James, 1997). Both allow us to make adjustments during and after our classes in preparation for future iterations. However, we also must recognize that our assumptions about the needs, goals, skills, and motivations of learners can limit the kinds of questions we ask and the information we seek from and about our student users when creating feedback and assessment interventions. Perhaps we should view our students as co-creators of knowledge when developing materials and resources, considering not only the usability of our tools but also the motivation and value that influence user experience.

▎Conclusion

Though this project had a relatively small sample size, i.e., 28 students who constitute one section of a multi-section course at our university, the research findings emphasize the importance of including our students in the developmental process of initiatives aimed at supporting their professional development. All of our students were traditional college age, and all had chosen to take a face-to-face class. Overall, though, the university has a growing number of non-traditional students and students who take all or nearly all of their classes online. If the lab is to be made available to all students, the needs and schedules of these students will have to be considered.

Because of the successful impact of the lab on students' presentation skills and confidence levels, and the enthusiasm the students expressed about the lab, the college's administration is open to extensions of lab services. In considering expansions, we will once again take guidance from the students. For example, in the Logistics Survey, students expressed interest in such activities as face-to-face interviewing practice (57%), networking practice (48%), and virtual interviewing practice (29%). With the expansion of the services comes the opportunity for further research into the communication-related needs, wants, skills, and motivations of our students. As we consider the next steps, we can see how the larger lab project will have a number of benefits; by creating a robust, pedagogically sound framework for the lab—by continuing to learn from the learners—the project will ensure that students have the most effective experience possible and will see significant improvements in their communication skills and communication-related confidence.

This experience has taught us that our assumptions about what our students (the users) need and want did not always align with what they indicated informally and formally during the semester. Had we not incorporated user feedback checkpoints or kept our eyes open during informal interactions with students, the lab and its activities would have had a much lower chance of success. First of all, we would have created more work for ourselves as teachers (and likely for the students as well) by using unsuccessful, ineffective instructional strategies. Secondly, we would have missed the innovative and insightful comments, ideas, and actions expressed by students as they navigated, learned from, and contributed to the lab. Though we hope the lab will always be a dynamic and evolving place, the contributions students have made through this pilot study will help to ensure that, as it opens to the rest of the college, the communication lab can have a true and real impact on students as speakers and presenters.

Acknowledgments

This work is supported by the College of Business Administration Summer Research Grant Program at Sam Houston State University.

References

Acharya, K. R. (2016). User value and usability in technical communication: A value-proposition design model. *Communication Design Quarterly, 4*(3), 26–34.

Archer, W. & Davison, J. (2008). *Graduate employability: What do employers think and want?* The Council for Industry and Higher Education. https://www.voced.edu.au/content/ngv%3A25673.

Ayres, J., Schliesman, T. & Sonandré, D. A. (1998). Practice makes perfect but does it help reduce communication apprehension? *Communication Research Reports, 15*(2), 170–179. https://doi.org/10.1080/08824099809362111.

Bauer-Wolf, J. (2018, February 23). Overconfident students, dubious employers. *Inside Higher Ed.* https://www.insidehighered.com/news/2018/02/23/study-students-believe-they-are-prepared-workplace-employers-disagree.

Brink, K. E. & Costigan, R. D. (2015). Oral communication skills: Are the priorities of the workplace and AACSB-accredited business programs aligned? *Academy of Management Learning & Education, 2*, 205–221.

Cho, Y., Smits, J. A. & Telch, M. J. (2004). The Speech Anxiety Thoughts Inventory: Scale development and preliminary psychometric data. *Behaviour Research and Therapy, 42*(1), 13–25. https://doi.org/10.1016/s0005-7967(03)00067-6.

Derakshan, N. & Eysenck, M. W. (2009). Anxiety, processing efficiency, and cognitive performance: New developments from attentional control theory. *European Psychologist, 14*(2), 168–176. https://doi.org/10.1027/1016-9040.14.2.168.

Eysenck, M. W. (1992). *Anxiety: The cognitive perspective.* Erlbaum.

Gewertz, C. (2018, September 25). Speaking skills top employer wish lists, but schools don't teach them; Strong speaking skills are in high demand in the workplace. *Education Week, 38*(06), 7–9.

Gray, F. E. & Murray, N. (2011). "A distinguishing factor": Oral communication skills in new accountancy graduates. *Accounting Education, 20*, 275–294.

Hamilton, C. & Kroll, T. L. (2018). *Communicating for results: A guide for business and the professions* (11th ed.). Wadsworth; Cengage Learning.

Harlen, W. & James, M. (1997). Assessment and learning: Differences and relationships between formative and summative assessment. *Assessment in Education: Principles, Policy & Practice, 4*(3), 365–379. https://doi.org/10.1080/0969594970040304.

Huang, H., Kram, R. & Ahmed, A. (2012). Reduction of metabolic cost during motor learning of arm reaching dynamics. *Journal of Neuroscience, 32*(6), 2182–2190. https://doi.org/10.1523/JNEUROSCI.4003-11.2012.

Humphreys, M. S. & Revelle, W. (1984). Personality, motivation, and performance: A theory of the relationship between individual differences and information processing. *Psychological Review, 91*(2), 153–184. http://doi.org/10.1037/0033-295X.91.2.153.

Interactive Design Foundation. (2018). *How to conduct a cognitive walkthrough.* https://www.interaction-design.org/literature/article/how-to-conduct-a-cognitive-walkthrough.

Kesner, R. M. (2008). Business school undergraduate information management competencies: A study of employer expectations and associated curricular recommendations. *Communications of the Association for Information Systems, 23*, 633–654.

Leeds, E. M. & Maurer, R. A. (2009). Using digital video technology to reduce communication apprehension in business education. *INFORMS Transactions on Education, 2*, 84–92.

Lin, P., Grace, D., Krishnan, S. & Gilsdorf, J. (2010). Failure to communicate: Why accounting students don't measure up to professionals' expectations. *CPA Journal, 80*(1), 63–65.

Lone Star College. (n.d.). *One Button Studio/VR Lab.* https://www.lonestar.edu/TomballOBS.htm#:~:text=One%20Button%20Studio%2FVR%20Lab%20How%20Does%20it%20Work%3F,if%20you%20have%20no%20previous%20video%20production%20experience.

Miller-Cochran, S. & Rodrigo, R. L. (Eds.). (2009). *Rhetorically rethinking usability: Theories, practices, and methodologies.* Hampton Press.

Nielsen, J. (2012, January 4). *Usability 101: Introduction to usability.* Nielsen Norman Group. https://www.nngroup.com/articles/usability-101-introduction-to-usability/.

Osterwalder, A., Pigneur, Y., Bernarda, G. & Smith, A. (2014). *Value proposition design: How to create products and services customers want.* John Wiley & Sons.

Parmanto, B., Lewis, A. N., Graham, K. M. & Bertolet, M. H. (2016). Development of the Telehealth Usability Questionnaire (TUQ). *International Journal of Telerehabilitation, 8*(1), 3–10. https://doi.org/10.5195/ijt.2016.6196.

PitchVantage. (n.d.). https://pitchvantage.com/#team.

Reinsch, N. L. & Gardner, J. A. (2014). Do communication abilities affect promotion decisions? Some data from the C-suite. *Journal of Business and Technical Communication, 28*(1), 31–57. https://doi.org/10.1177/1050651913502357.

Shannon, L., Polnick, B. & Cooper, P. (2006). *Millennial generation leads changes in higher education* [Paper presentation]. APERA Conference, Hong Kong.

Shivers-McNair, A., Phillips, J., Campbell, A., Mai, H. H., Yan, A., Macy, J. F., Wenlock, J., Fry, S. & Guan, Y. (2018). User-centered design in and beyond the classroom: Toward an accountable practice. *Computers and Composition, 49*, 36–47. https://doi.org/10.1016/j.compcom.2018.05.003.

Still, B. & Crane, K. (2016). *Fundamentals of user-centered design: A practical approach.* CRC Press.

Twenge, J. W. (2014). *Generation Me: Why today's young Americans are more confident, assertive, entitled—and more miserable than ever before* (2nd ed.). Atria.

University of Minnesota Libraries. (n.d.). *1:Button Studio*. https://www.lib.umn.edu/1button.

Van Ginkel, S., Gulikers, J., Biemens, H., Noroozi, O., Roozen, M., Bos, T., van Tilborg, R., van Halteren, M. & Mulder, M. (2019). Fostering oral presentation competence through a virtual reality-based task for delivering feedback. *Computers & Education, 134*, 78–97.

■ Appendix A: Presentation Evaluation Rubric

Presentation Evaluation Rubric

Name: _____ Topic: _____ Evaluator: _____

Performance Element	Below Expectations	Meets Expectations	Exceeds Expectations
Opening			
Attention	❏ No attempt to gain audience's attention	❏ Gains audience's attention with a startling statement, anecdote, question, humor, or quotation	❏ Gains audience's attention with a startling statement, anecdote, question, humor, or quotation and establishes common ground
Purpose	❏ No clear purpose statement	❏ Provides a general purpose statement	❏ Provides a statement of purpose – describing the problem and question to be answered
Motivation to Listen	❏ No indication of benefits for the audience	❏ Identifies at least one benefit for the audience	❏ Identifies benefit to audience and the rhetorical purpose of the presentation
Preview	❏ No preview of main points	❏ Provides a general preview of topics	❏ Provides preview of topics, notes the expected length of the presentation, suggests a plan for handling questions
Body	**Below Expectations**	**Meets Expectations**	**Exceeds Expectations**
Organization	❏ Haphazard or inappropriate pattern of organization; no use of transitions; requires effort to follow	❏ Pattern is generally clear and organized; uses transitions to connect most major points; a few minor points may be confusing	❏ Uses a clear, appropriate pattern of organization; uses transitions to make the presentation easy to follow
Audience-Centered Content	❏ Too many points unrelated to audience's interest, or needs	❏ Makes 3 or 4 major points relevant to the audience	❏ Makes 3 or 4 major points; tailors the message to audience's interests and needs; uses appropriate language and examples
Credibility	❏ Does not establish credibility	❏ Establishes trustworthiness and expertise	❏ Provides 3+ reasons for credibility by contextualizing sources and evidence sources
Support	❏ Provides only limited or weak facts or data to support thesis	❏ Uses appropriate facts, evidence, data, or financial analysis to support thesis	❏ Uses appropriate facts, evidence, data, or financial analysis to support thesis; interprets meaning and draws conclusions

Learning from the Learners 155

	Below Expectations	Meets Expectations	Exceeds Expectations
Closing Summary	❏ No summary of main points	❏ Summarizes main points	❏ Summarizes main points and reinforces the central idea of the presentation
Call to Action	❏ No call or weak call to action	❏ Asks for a specific, realistic action in a direct manner (e.g., "I recommend")	❏ Asks for specific realistic action in a direct manner, suggests timeline, restates benefits
Memorable Ending	❏ Stops abruptly or uses trite closing	❏ Ends on a strong memorable note	❏ Ends on a strong, memorable note and links back to opening
Visual Content	❏ Multiple points per slide (text-heavy); irrelevant or hard to see images; difficult to quickly understand slide	❏ Several major points per slide; relevant, quality visuals included to explain points; fairly easy to quickly understand slide	❏ Few major point per slides/speaking points; thoughtful, quality visuals included to explain points; easy to quickly understand slide
Clarity	❏ Difficult to read; full sentences; charts/graphs too complex	❏ Easy to read: simple charts/ graphs	❏ Easy to read; simple charts/ graphs; appropriate use of "white space"
Consistency	❏ Mix of type fonts, colors, clip art or photo styles on one or more slides	❏ Consistent font type, colors, and clip art/photo styles	❏ Consistent font type, colors, clip art and photo style, and use of upper/ lower case
Correctness	❏ More than two mechanical errors – spelling, typos, formatting, etc.	❏ One or two mechanical errors	❏ Free of mechanical errors
Delivery Appearance	❏ Inappropriate grooming or dress for business presentation	❏ Business/professional appearance	❏ Men: dress shirt/tie, slacks, sport coat Women: tailored jacket, skirt or slacks
Eye Contact	❏ Limited eye contact; uses note cards; stares at ceiling or focuses on screen	❏ Tries to maintain eye contact but frequently looks at screen or notes	❏ Maintains eye contact, seldom refers to slides or notes
Poise and Confidence	❏ Distracting sways, paces or fidgets; poor use of hands (e.g., clicking pen, clapping)	❏ Neutral; uses hand and body movements but appears stiff, uneasy	❏ Engaging. Uses gestures and expressions; looks comfortable, confident, and natural
Voice	❏ Difficult to understand; mumbles; too loud or soft; too fast or slow, lots of "umms" and verbal distraction	❏ Easy to understand. Appropriate pace and volume; few verbal distractions	❏ Engaging. Uses conversational tone, modulates voice
Enthusiasm	❏ Delivery lacks enthusiasm/ energy	❏ Projects a feeling of enthusiasm about the topic	❏ Projects a feeling of enthusiasm about the topic combined with high energy delivery

TIMING: _____   COMMENTS:

■ Appendix B: Shannon-Cooper Technology Profile

Part I:

On a scale of 0 to 10 (0 is lowest, 10 is highest), please rate your skill and comfort level with the following:

Application and Software Usage:

1. Virtual conference tools:
   _____ Skype for Business
   _____ Zoom
   _____ Other (please specify):
2. Social Media:
   _____ Facebook
   _____ Twitter
   _____ Instagram
   _____ Other (please specify):
3. Presentation Software:
   _____ Microsoft PowerPoint
   _____ Prezi
   _____ Other (please specify):
4. Screen Capture/Video Creation:
   _____ Kaltura

  ____ Screencastify
  ____ Camtasia
  ____ Adobe Spark
  ____ Other (please specify):

5. Web creation platforms:
  ____ Wix
  ____ Weebly
  ____ Google Sites
  ____ Other (please specify):

6. Video Software:
  ____ Media Player
  ____ Movie Maker
  ____ iMovie
  ____ Adobe Premiere
  ____ Other (please specify):

7. Audio software
  ____ Audacity
  ____ Sound Recorder
  ____ Other (please specify):

Technology Levels: (0 is lowest, 10 is highest)

 ____ 1. Hardware troubleshooting skills: Keyboard, mouse, monitor, printer, etc.
 ____ 2. Software troubleshooting skills: Operating system (Windows/macOS), Microsoft Office Suite, Graphics, Audio, etc.
 ____ 3. Network troubleshooting skills: Internet connection, network printers, Internet browsers, etc.
 ____ 4. Connecting peripheral devices: printer, scanner, camera, etc.
 ____ 5. Installing software: Installing software by CD, USB, or download, etc.
 ____ 6. Transferring files through Internet: Upload/download files to the network or Blackboard

Part II:

On a scale of 0 to 10 (0 is lowest, 10 is highest), please rate your comfort level with the following:

Training:
 ____ 1. Are you willing to learn new technologies to update with the most recent development?
 ____ 2. Are you willing to attend face-to-face training sessions on the Huntsville campus, outside of your class time, to learn new technology applications?
 ____ 3. Do you believe that learning new technologies could enhance your skills?
 ____ 4. Are you willing to complete virtual, no-credit tutorials to learn new technologies?

_____ 5. Are you willing to complete virtual tutorials for class credit to learn new technologies?

Multimedia Interest:
_____ 1. Do you enjoy creating new ideas or materials either on computers or mobile devices?
_____ 2. Do you enjoy creating multimedia projects (audio, video, or graphics)?
_____ 3. Are you willing to try new software or tools for creating multimedia?
_____ 4. Are you familiar with the ethics and privacy issues around technology usage?

Part I average score: _____   Part II average score: _____

■ Appendix C: Speech Anxiety Thoughts Inventory (SATI)[1]

Thinking about your previous responses and specific experiences you have had giving presentations in professional situations, complete the questionnaire below about the different worries that often contribute to communicator anxiety.

(1) Strongly Agree   (2) Agree   (3) Undecided   (4) Disagree   (5) Strongly Disagree

When you are anxious about giving a presentation, what do you worry about?
_____ 1. I'll get tongue-tied.
_____ 2. My speech won't impress the audience.
_____ 3. My speech will be incoherent.
_____ 4. I won't be able to speak as well as others.
_____ 5. When others are not paying attention to my speech, I worry that the audience is thinking poorly of me.
_____ 6. If I perform poorly, then the audience will remember me negatively.
_____ 7. It would be terrible if my voice will tremble.
_____ 8. If I make a mistake, the audience will think I'm stupid.
_____ 9. If I am anxious in this situation, the audience will not like me.
_____ 10. I won't know what to say when I'm called on to make a speech.
_____ 11. If I don't speak well, the audience will reject me.
_____ 12. What I say will sound stupid.
_____ 13. It would be terrible if others think I'm not intelligent.
_____ 14. It would be terrible if I make a mistake during my speech.
_____ 15. I will not be able to control my anxiety.
_____ 16. It would be terrible if people notice that I'm anxious.
_____ 17. My behavior will appear awkward to the audience.
_____ 18. I will be unable to give a good speech.
_____ 19. I won't be able to complete my speech.
_____ 20. My mind will go blank.
_____ 21. I must deliver a good speech in order to gain approval from the audience.

---

1. Adapted from Cho et al. (2004)

_____ 22. I worry that I will be asked to give a speech.
_____ 23. I won't be able to answer questions from the audience.

■ Appendix D: Lab Technology Usability Survey

Formative Assessment of Kaltura Usability

(1) Strongly Agree   (2) Agree   (3) Undecided   (4) Disagree   (5) Strongly Disagree

		1	2	3	4	5
Utility	Kaltura is a great tool for recording video assignments to class.					
	Kaltura is a better way to record videos for class than other methods.					
	I can imagine uses for Kaltura beyond making videos for class assignments.					
	Comments:					
Learnability/ Memorability	It was easy to use Kaltura.					
	It was easy to learn how to use Kaltura.					
	I believe I could become proficient in using Kaltura in a short time.					
	I believe that I will be able to use Kaltura again without additional help or instructions.					
	When I didn't know how to do something in Kaltura, I could figure out how to do it on my own (i.e., without asking the teacher for help).					
	Comments:					
Errors/ Reliability	Whenever I made a mistake using Kaltura, I could fix the problem easily and quickly without help.					
	Whenever I made a mistake using Kaltura, I could fix the problem easily and quickly with help from an instructor or fellow student.					
	When something didn't work as I expected, the system gave me a clear error message to let me know how to fix the problem.					
	Comments:					
Efficiency	Once I learned how to use Kaltura, I could complete tasks quickly.					
	Using Kaltura to record and upload my video took less time than I expected.					
	Comments:					

Satis-faction/ Media Quality	I could see myself clearly in the video when I played it back.					
	I could hear myself clearly in the video when I played it back.					
	I could see my visual aids clearly in the video when I played it back.					
	The video has a professional appearance.					
	I can envision using Kaltura to create a video for use in the job-search process or other professional context.					
	Comments:					
Satis-faction/ Interface	I like using Kaltura.					
	Kaltura is simple to understand.					
	Kaltura can do everything I want it to do.					
	Overall, I am satisfied with Kaltura.					
	Comments:					

Usability of Instructional Video

(1) Strongly Agree   (2) Agree   (3) Undecided   (4) Disagree   (5) Strongly Disagree

		1	2	3	4	5
Utility	The video was a great tool for learning how to find and use the COBA Communication Lab.					
	The video is a better way to get instructions than a written handout.					
	The video is a better way to get instructions than written directions on a website.					
	Comments					
Learn-ability/ Memo-rability	It was easy to find the video.					
	It was easy to access and play the video.					
	I replayed the entire video more than once to help me learn how to use Kaltura.					
	I will be able to use Kaltura again after viewing the video only once.					
	I replayed parts of the video to help me learn how to use the lab.					
	Comments:					

Errors/ Reliability	The video provided accurate instructions for finding and using the lab.					
	The screencast section of the video matched what I saw on my screen when I was using Kaltura and/or Blackboard.					
	When the video gave inaccurate or confusing instructions, I was able to figure out the right way on my own.					
	Comments:					
Satisfaction/ Media Quality	The video quality was good.					
	The video's audio quality was good.					
	The video was the right length.					
	The video was too long.					
	The video was too short.					
	Comments:					
Efficiency	Having access to the video helped me complete tasks (i.e., recording and uploading the video) quickly.					
	Comments:					
Satisfaction/ Overall	I liked the video.					
	The video is simple to understand.					
	The video helped me do everything I wanted to do.					
	Overall, I am satisfied with Kaltura.					
	Comments:					

8. Ideating a New Program: Implementing Design Thinking Approaches to Develop Program Student Learning Outcomes

Luke Thominet
FLORIDA INTERNATIONAL UNIVERSITY

Abstract: This chapter discusses how a design thinking process was used to create student learning outcomes for an undergraduate writing and rhetoric program. Design thinking is a creative process for solving complex problems through divergent thinking and active, collaborative design practices. The chapter traces the creation of the program student learning outcomes through five project phases: empathizing, defining, ideating, prototyping and testing, and implementing. The chapter demonstrates how users were actively involved with the design of outcomes and how their ideas were taken up throughout every phase of the process. Ultimately, the chapter builds a model for programmatic design thinking to create opportunities for building more representative and inclusive visions for our curricula.

Keywords: design thinking, student learning outcomes, academic program development, problem setting, divergent thinking

Key Takeaways:

- Design thinking can act as a flexible heuristic for creating curricular design projects.
- Divergent thinking practices create space for including students' and other participants' perspectives in curricular design.
- Design thinking activities, such as problem setting, highlight the need to identify and focus on curricular issues that matter to stakeholders, including students.
- Design thinking is iterative, and, as such, it works best when solutions are modeled, tested, and changed over time.
- While user experience (UX) practice is more time-consuming than relying solely on faculty expertise, UX data provides unique situational insights about specific contexts and student users.

From 2017 to 2018, the writing and rhetoric program at my institution used design thinking and user experience (UX) methods to develop program student learning outcomes for a new writing and rhetoric major track. *Program student learning outcomes (PSLOs)* define the desired "skills, knowledge, and other attributes" for a graduate of an academic program (Carter et al., 2003, p. 105). Regional accreditation agencies have argued that PSLOs are "the principal gauge of higher education's effectiveness" (Ewell, 2001, p. 1) and a key element in programmatic assessment (Southern Association of Colleges and Schools Commission on Colleges, 2020). The academic literature has also emphasized the uses of PSLOs beyond assessment, including for explaining programmatic identity and for "[helping] our students explain what skills they bring with them to the workplace and how they orient themselves as citizens" (Clegg et al., 2021, p. 30).

Despite the acknowledged importance of PSLOs, there has only been limited attention to the PSLO design process. And as Paul Anderson (2010) argued, the typical PLSO design process relies on expert and disciplinary knowledge: "We generally construct our objectives by consulting several sources, including our faculty's interests and knowledge of our field, the needs of the employers who hire our graduates, and the objectives adopted by programs at other institutions" (p. 58). Notably, this process does not include space for participatory UX methods that would intentionally include the voices and perspectives of diverse stakeholders, including students. Evidence of the typical approach is also reflected in the numerous institutional guides for developing PSLOs. For example, a guide developed by the University of Florida focused much of its attention on using Bloom's Taxonomy verbs for phrasing outcomes as S.M.A.R.T. (Specific, Measurable, Achievable, Relevant, and Time-bound) goals (Brophy, 2017). However, this guide only spent a quarter of a page to outline a design process which asked faculty to review and revise existing PSLOs to align them with Bloom's Taxonomy verbs. Still, some other guides do spend more time describing PSLO design processes. For example, a guide developed by the University of Nebraska-Lincoln described six strategies for creating PSLOs, including holding conversations with department faculty, examining existing instructional materials, and reviewing similar units or programs (Jonson, 2006). Yet these varied strategies still emphasized a closed, faculty-centric approach rather than a UX design methodology.

Meanwhile, recent assessment literature has signaled a potential shift toward more inclusive and iterative PSLO design methods. For example, Chris Anson (2010) recommended a recursive process that combined outside-in and inside-out approaches for PSLO development. In the outside-in approach, committees and administrators define PSLOs and then assess and refine those outcomes based on evidence. In the inside-out approach, individual teachers define outcomes based on their own experiences and instructional strategies. While Anson's model still relied heavily on faculty input, it opened the design process to additional participants and emphasized an iterative process. Jo Allen (2010) also created a heuristic that mapped institutional values to program outcomes to curricular content and extra-curricular learning opportunities in order to create a coherent educational vision. In doing so, she showed how PSLOs could respond to the local context of a program. Likewise, Geoffrey Clegg et al. (2021) argued for fitting outcomes to local exigencies and for "a continuous improvement model [that] consistently [revisits] the PSLOs to determine how well they are working for students, faculty, programs, and external stakeholders" (p. 11). Other technical communication literature has also discussed UX-inspired academic program design without explicit reference to PSLOs. For example, Deb Balzhiser et al. (2015) described the application of participatory design, through a questionnaire and focus group, to create a master's program definition. They also used the information sources to align their program with the expectations of their primary audience of working professionals. And Teena Carnegie and Kate Crane (2019) described how they used interviews with graduates to regularly iterate on their undergraduate curriculum and to ensure that it remained responsive to current professional needs.

This chapter contributes to the program development literature by describing how a UX mindset can alter the PSLO design process. As Cargile Cook and Crane argue in this collection, UX reorients us toward continual, recursive, highly contextual attention to students' needs and motivations rather than experts' assumptions. To meet these UX goals, this chapter describes how a design thinking process can support active and collaborative methods that integrate the knowledges and experiences of numerous stakeholders. In this way, *adopting design-thinking practices can help to move us away from a faculty-centered committee model and toward a participatory approach to PSLO design that focuses on students' experiences, needs, and goals.* Ideally, this process will result in more responsive, representative, and inclusive program definitions.

In the sections that follow, I review the field's literature on design thinking and situate it in relation to UX. Then I describe the history of my institution's writing and rhetoric program and explain how we used a design thinking process to create PSLOs. Next, I discuss the challenges we encountered during this PSLO project. Finally, I close by sketching a rough model for adapting design thinking to programmatic work.

■ Design Thinking in Writing Studies and User Experience

This literature review explores definitions of design thinking, situates design thinking within technical communication and writing studies research, and compares it to UX. Broadly speaking, *design thinking* is defined as follows:

> the human-centered process of imagining, creating, testing, and revising responses to critical, highly contextual, dynamic, and messy problems.... Design thinking is a way of problem framing and problem solving that values empathy with audiences and users, "radical" collaboration, ambiguity, a bias toward action, productive failure, iteration, and regular feedback. (Pope-Ruark, Tham, et al., 2019, p. 371)

However, there is still significant disagreement between competing definitions of design thinking. Lucy Kimbell (2011) divided definitions into three categories: "design thinking as a cognitive style, as a general theory of design, and as a [managerial] resource for organizations" (p. 285). She noted that, while the first two definitions were drawn from academic studies of the practices of designers, the managerial approach was the most common implementation of design thinking but "[lacked] a wider research base" (p. 294).

This managerial approach has proliferated over the past two decades, and in that time, various design consultants have promoted their own flavors of design thinking. For example, the British Design Council represented design as a double diamond with two sets of paired stages: discover and define, then develop and deliver (Tschimmel, 2012). IDEO depicted it as three spaces of inspiration, ideation, and implementation (Brown, 2008). IBM Enterprise Design used the model of a loop with recurrent phases of observing, reflecting, and making (IBM, n.d.). And the Stanford d.school described it as a five-step process of empathizing, defining, ideating, prototyping, and testing (*An Introduction to design thinking: Process guide*, 2010). While I adopt the d.school structure in this chapter due to its ability to open space for critical reflections on my PSLO design project, it is important to note that all these formulations of managerial design thinking share the same core practices. First, designers observe and interview stakeholders to better understand their needs. Based on this information, designers seek to clearly define the design problem. Next, large multidisciplinary teams use active, collaborative, and visual design exercises to imagine many potential solutions to the design problem. Then the teams prototype and test select ideas with potential users. Through several iterations, the prototypes are narrowed and refined until one design is finalized and implemented as a product or service. Two further points should be made about these phases. First, each phase is treated as cyclical and recursive, so further user research can occur after the product implementation, which can lead to further ideation and prototyping, etc. Second, the phases are often conceptualized as cycles of divergence and convergence: designers intentionally open up to a multiplicity of ideas and then move toward defining or narrowing solutions. For example, divergent thinking is often the focus of the ideation stage, while convergence to a singular design solution is a goal of the testing and iteration phase.

It is important to note here that there has also been significant pushback on managerial design thinking. Designers and academics have argued that it does not accurately reflect professional design work (Vinsel, 2017), that the various phases have become overly formalized (Nussbaum, 2011), and that it can reinforce colonialist worldviews of global salvation (Khandwala, 2019). In some cases, new design thinking methodologies have been developed to address these issues. For example, Kimbell (2012) situated design in local contexts, recognized contributions from non-human actors, and de-centered the agency of the designer. Likewise, Lucía Durá et al. (2019) integrated design thinking with positive deviance inquiries to offer better approaches for advocating for users. And Amollo Ambole (2020) argued for decentering Western paradigms for projects in Africa in favor of design thinking approaches that attended to the specific sociocultural

Ideating a New Program 165

contexts of local communities. Together, this literature can help designers better attend to local cultures and exigencies.

Despite the criticisms, there has also been a growing interest in managerial design thinking in writing studies scholarship. This interest likely stems from the field's extended discussion of design, which can be traced back to Charles Kostelnick's (1989) comparison of the writing and design processes (Leverenz, 2014). The writing studies literature now includes more than 26 articles with various frames, including design as digital or multimodal writing and design as the process of creating course structures (Purdy, 2014). Recent articles have also offered practical approaches for adapting design thinking to the work of creating courses and assignments. Richard Marback (2009) argued for framing writing assignments as wicked design problems, which are contingent problems "of deciding what is better when the situation is ambiguous at best" (p. 399). James Purdy (2014) aligned the d.school formulation of design thinking with the writing process to demonstrate how we might reframe writing classes as design work. And Carrie Leverenz (2014) argued that adopting design thinking practices, such as prototyping and design briefs, could help connect the writing classroom to the outside world. Numerous others have taken up these arguments to explore the application of design thinking to a variety of specific writing classes (Belcher, 2017; Cooke et al., 2020; Khadka, 2018; Lane, 2018; McCarthy, 2016; VanKooten & Berkley, 2016; Wickman, 2014). Further information on many of these papers can be found in Rebecca Pope-Ruark, Joe Moses, and Jason Tham's (2019) useful bibliography of the design thinking literature.

Meanwhile, the exact relationship between design thinking and UX remains contested. Articles in professional trade publications have compared the concepts, but they have not always agreed on the relationship between them. For example, Dirk Knemeyer (2015) argued that UX is focused on tactical design decisions for specific products, while design thinking is focused on open-ended, strategic decisions, thus differentiating between the concepts based on their intended scope. Charan Singh (2016) described the difference as a relationship between methodology and process. He depicted UX as a methodology for user-centered design that evaluates a user's quality of experience while focusing on a single technology. As such, he likened it to other user-centered design methodologies such as interface and system design. On the other hand, he described design thinking as a process that could be used for any of these methodologies. While these articles offered interesting comparisons between the concepts, they also used constrained definitions of UX. Academic publications typically use a broader definition of *UX* that includes "the architecture of systems both above and below the surface (i.e., architecture of interactions, visuals, content, structure, and policy)" and also "how an individual component is part of a larger ecosystem [of] multiple technologies, devices, websites, organizations, people, and events" (Potts, 2014, p. 3).

Using this perspective, Ehren Pflugfelder (2017) built a strong connection between UX and design thinking through the rhetorical frame of *techne*. First, he differentiated between design thinking and design science: whereas design thinking uses divergent approaches to develop creative solutions to potentially ambiguous problems, design science seeks to create a rational, consistent, and empirical system for solving problems in specific fields. After building this differentiation, he used the rhetorical frame of *techne* to connect design to UX. Drawing on the work of David Roochnik (1996) and Kelly Pender (2011), Pflugfelder described two kinds of *techne*. *Techne 1* "is a determinate, universal, infallible set of techniques used to accomplish something" that "resembles an instruction set" (Pflugfelder, 2017, p. 173). This kind of *techne* included both usability testing and design science. Meanwhile, Pflugfelder defined *techne 2* as "an abstract process to be consciously employed in variable-rich contexts" (2017, p. 174). *Techne 2*, then, represented both UX and design thinking: they are both methodologies for handling messy problems, and they both have associated methods that can be flexibly employed according to the situation and problem definition. Pflugfelder further emphasized the overlap of the two concepts by using the design thinking methods of problem setting and divergent thinking to create a user-needs gap model for UX work.

In short, this chapter takes up Pflugfelder's argument by reframing PSLO development from a design science to a design thinking perspective. The traditional faculty-centered approach treats PSLO development as a neat problem that can be rationalized efficiently and effectively through a universal set of techniques. But this approach elided the complexities of the localized knowledges, values, and experiences of program stakeholders. Instead, I discuss and reflect on my program's effort to use a flexible design thinking process that integrated problem definition, divergent thinking, and iteration as a response to the inherently messy problem of curricular design.

■ Institutional Context

The English department at my institution houses four relatively independent programs in creative writing, linguistics, literature, and writing and rhetoric. Traditionally, the department awarded undergraduate degrees in literature and English education, and it offered M.A. degrees in literature and linguistics, and an M.F.A. in creative writing. The writing and rhetoric program did not have strong representation in either the undergraduate or graduate degrees. A reflection of this can be found in the description of electives in the 2010–2011 undergraduate catalog:

> Upper-division electives [are offered] in writing, film, literature, and/or linguistics. The English Department recognizes a continuing obligation to ensure that its majors write well. The Chairperson may require any English major to take the appropriate composition course. English majors may choose to take a general program

of English studies or may select one of the Department's three areas of emphasis: literature, language and linguistics, or creative writing. (Florida International University, 2010, pp. 197–198)

In this description, composition courses were mentioned primarily as an obligatory support for some students, while the other programs were described as potential areas of emphasis and interest. While the Writing and Rhetoric Program still offered a few upper-division electives at this time, it focused primarily on the first-year composition sequence and the technical communication service course. This focus was logical. The department is part of a very large (more than 45,000 undergraduate students) public, minority-majority, urban research, Hispanic-serving institution. Each year, we offer approximately 300 sections of first-year composition and 60 sections of the technical communication service course. To manage this workload, the program supports approximately 40 full-time faculty, and it coordinates with other programs across campus, including the Global First-Year Program and the Writing Across the Curriculum Initiative.

In 2012, the writing and rhetoric program created a new professional and public writing certificate that drew interest from students across the campus and graduated 30–40 students each year. The certificate created a demand for new upper-division courses and supported requests for new tenure-track hires. Ultimately, the certificate acted as proof that there would be student interest in a full writing and rhetoric degree.

The program's first attempt involved the creation of a writing and rhetoric M.A. In 2014, program faculty researched local demand and drafted a proposal for the new degree. It was initially approved by the department before being halted due to a broader freeze on new M.A degrees.

Over the next few years, the program began to focus instead on the creation of an undergraduate degree. Then in Fall 2017, the department introduced a new version of the English major with a shared core of four classes (one in each program) and extended tracks in each of the four programs. Students specifically enrolled in the writing and rhetoric track were required to take survey courses in rhetorical theory, writing studies, and technical communication as well as three additional upper-division electives. These electives were initially based on faculty members' individual interests and were often built from pilot sections into official courses. From 2017–2019, the program offered at least 20 different electives, including Writing as Social Action, Community Writing, Alternative Writing & Rhetorics, Writing Across Borders, Writing About the Environment, Advanced Business Writing, and Queer Rhetorics.

While the faculty were excited about the new undergraduate degree, we also expected growing pains. At program meetings during the 2016–2017 academic year, we discussed methods for promoting the new major track and for recruiting students. Still, only limited progress had been made on these tasks when the major track began enrolling students in Fall 2017.

During that same semester, several of our faculty attended the Council for Programs in Technical and Scientific Communication (CPTSC) conference, where presentations discussed methods for applying UX research techniques to assist with academic program design (e.g., Moore et al., 2017; Shalamova et al., 2017). In particular, Jennifer Sano-Franchini et al. (2017) facilitated a useful workshop on collaborative ideation and curricular assessment techniques that included an affinity clustering activity. These presentations acted as an inspiration for our program's work over the following year.

■ A Design Thinking Approach to Curricular Design

We began our project intending to explore the perspectives and experiences of program stakeholders to find ways to promote the new major track. The use of data from this project was approved as an exempted study by my university's institutional review board for human subjects research (#18-0178). The subsections that follow will be framed specifically according to the d.school process of design thinking, which includes specific stages for empathizing, defining, ideating, prototyping, and implementing. I am using this structure here primarily because it offers a means to organize the discussion and to reflect on areas of revision in future iterations of this work.

Empathizing with Program Stakeholders

A common first step in design thinking is getting to know stakeholders and understanding problems from their point of view. The d.school has argued for the centrality of this phase:

> As a design thinker, the problems you are trying to solve are rarely your own—they are those of a particular group of people; in order to design for them, you must gain empathy for who they are and what is important to them. (*An Introduction to design thinking: Process guide*, 2010, p. 2)

Some practitioners have also essentially described this phase as qualitative UX research:

> Focus on users' experiences, especially their emotional ones. To build empathy with users, [designers] observe behavior and draw conclusions about what people want and need. Those conclusions are tremendously hard to express in quantitative language. Instead [designers] that "get" design use emotional language (words that concern desires, aspirations, engagement, and experience) to describe products and users. (Kolko, 2015)

The research methods for this phase vary based on the design brief, but they often include observations of environments or tasks, interviews with stakeholders, focus groups, questionnaires, and card sorts (IDEO, 2015). Still, most of these qualitative methods are focused on rapid results and often lack the depth of prolonged ethnographic studies (Beckman, 2020).

For the empathize phase of the curriculum design project, I interviewed faculty and students about their experiences in the program. First, I recruited faculty who had designed and taught at least one upper-division writing and rhetoric course. Student participants were then recruited directly by those faculty. Student participants included recent graduates and current members of the literature major and the professional and public writing certificate as well as a few students in the new major track. The only strict requirement was that student participants had to have completed at least one upper-division writing and rhetoric course. During this phase, I interviewed 7 faculty and 12 students.

The interviews were relatively short (15–20 minutes) and were focused on three areas: (a) participants' favorite topics in rhetoric, (b) participants' best experiences in our courses, and (c) existing programmatic needs. A full list of the questions for each participant group can be found in Appendix A. After the interviews were complete, I developed a summary of the responses and distributed it to all participants and to the rest of the program faculty. This summary acted as a starting point for the project's subsequent design thinking phases.

A few trends from these interviews are worth mentioning. First, faculty participants described the ideal track broadly and included rhetorical theory, academic and professional research methods, professional communication, digital media, and community writing as core topics. Likewise, there was not a consensus among faculty about the likely career outcomes for students: they mentioned academic, nonprofit, teaching, and professional writing careers but largely avoided specific technical specializations. Finally, faculty reported enjoying their teaching work: they liked the variety of classes and spoke highly of the students.

Students also spoke positively about the program and the faculty and staff. Their best experiences were interactions with faculty members and other students. Their ideal curriculum was focused on the practical application of rhetoric to everyday and professional life, but they also enjoyed researching topics related to personal interests. They emphasized broad writing practices and rarely mentioned specific theoretical concepts. Students also described a range of career goals including academia, copywriting, editing, publishing, law, technical writing, public relations, and teaching.

Since the participants were not a representative sample and because we wanted to get students actively involved in our design process, we did not use the interview results as generalizable data to support specific programmatic changes. Instead, we used them to understand the situation more clearly and as an inspiration for our subsequent work. In that way, the interviews played a significant role in the next phase of problem definition, which, in turn, informed the ideation methods that followed.

Defining the Goals for the Project

The definition phase "brings clarity and focus to the design space" with the goal of "[crafting] a meaningful and actionable problem statement" (*An Introduction to design thinking: Process guide*, 2010, p. 4). This phase is often associated with the activity of *problem setting*, which has been contrasted with the design field's traditional focus on problem-solving:

> We ignore problem setting, the process by which we define the decision to be made, the ends to be achieved, the means which may be chosen. In real-world practice, problems do not present themselves to the practitioner as givens. They must be constructed from the materials of problematic situations which are puzzling, troubling, and uncertain. (Schön, 1983, pp. 39–40)

Problem setting has also been discussed in relation to technical communication work. Jeremy Cushman (2014) framed it as a largely invisible rhetorical practice that could add value to our work, and Pflugfelder (2017) developed a user-needs gap model for problem setting in UX work.

For the PSLO project, three elements of the interviews contributed to the problem-setting phase: the broad program definitions by faculty, the emphasis on practical application by students, and the lack of a shared vision among the participants. While these elements suggested some marketing strategies (e.g., tying classes to specific jobs or highlighting student testimonials), they also demonstrated the need for a clear and specific vision for the program. In other words, the interviews largely shifted our attention from marketing to program definition as our core problem.

This problem-setting move was not unexpected. Because the program was created as a new track within an existing major, the institutional proposal required less documentation. Broadly, the proposal used a circular definition, saying the writing and rhetoric track was "designed for students who have a particular interest in writing and rhetoric." It then offered a wide range of potential career goals for students, including:

> a variety of academic, professional, and community contexts, including professional and technical writing positions within South Florida and beyond; K–12 teaching positions in language arts and writing; graduate study in rhetoric and composition, writing studies, law, and other professional, multimodal, or writing-related fields; and work in a variety of other writing-intensive non-profit and for-profit professions.

Finally, it described the curriculum as "six specialized courses in the field of rhetoric and composition, including a nine-credit required sequence that introduces [students] to writing studies as a field, the discipline of rhetoric, and professional and technical writing." This abbreviated documentation accelerated the creation of the track, but it also created ambiguous program definitions at the outset. On the other hand, tacit program definitions were more developed due to the previous attempt to create a master's program, but these definitions were never made explicit for the undergraduate program. Therefore, the interviews with faculty and students reintroduced the program definition as a concern that preceded work to promote a specific vision of the program. After consulting with the program administrator and other faculty, I refocused the design brief on creating PSLOs with the goal of helping students conceptualize and explain their achievements in the program.

Ideating Potential Program Outcomes

Once the problem is defined in relation to stakeholder needs, design thinking shifts to an ideation phase that focuses on developing a range of potential solutions to the problem (Pflugfelder, 2017; Purdy, 2014). This phase is often depicted as a process of *divergent thinking* or of "[seeking] multiple perspectives and multiple possible answers to questions and problems" (Kim & Pierce, 2013, p. 245). Divergent thinking has been contrasted with the analytical thinking method, where options are narrowed logically and incrementally until a single solution becomes obvious (Brown & Wyatt, 2010). Conversely, divergent thinking makes space for more voices in a way that can lead to creative and innovative solutions (Leverenz, 2014). To foster divergent thinking, ideation typically takes place in multidisciplinary teams or workshops where participants use active collaboration techniques to conceptualize and prioritize potential solutions to a given problem. The exact methods vary, but organizational guides and popular press books have offered numerous ideation exercises (Gray et al., 2010; IDEO, 2015; Mattimore, 2012).

The ideation phase for the PSLO project consisted of two identical workshops that lasted two hours each. Initially, the phase was planned as a single workshop, but conflicting schedules made it impossible to locate a single time that would work for all participants, so two smaller, identical workshops were used instead.

Workshop participants reflected the diverse disciplinary, institutional, community, and cultural identities of members of our academic program. Three tenure-track faculty, three non-tenure-track faculty, a staff member (the department's long-serving academic advisor), and four students participated in the workshops. Faculty participants were recruited to reflect a range of disciplinary emphases, including professional communication, cultural rhetoric, and community writing. Student participants were also intentionally recruited to reflect the predominantly Latinx and Black student population of the university. Finally, two local industry representatives were also recruited, though both withdrew before participating in the workshops. The goal of this approach to recruitment was to develop more inclusive visions for the program while also reflecting the range of specialized knowledge of participants.

The workshops had six stages: 1) introduction, 2) warmup, 3) ideation, 4) categorization and prioritization, 5) prototyping, and 6) reflection. I will discuss each of these stages below.

I used a brief introductory presentation to establish the goals of the workshop and to explain the design thinking process. None of the participants had previously used design thinking methods, and the student participants were unfamiliar with curricular development. Therefore, I reviewed the history of the local problem and the results of the interviews. Then I briefly summarized the literature on PSLOs and design thinking. I primarily used this presentation to encourage positive orientations toward the work we were doing.

Next, we used a warmup brainwriting exercise to energize participants and to get them thinking about the problem space for the workshop (Gray et al., 2010). In brainwriting exercises, each participant writes down an answer to a prompt and then passes the answer to the next participant, who uses it as a new starting point; after several rounds, the paper is returned to the original owner, who selects and presents their favorite ideas to the group (Mattimore, 2012). To allow for more variety, I gave participants several different prompts, which covered topics related to effective writing and rhetorical practice. A complete list of the brainwriting prompts can be found in Appendix B. Among other things, participants discussed building a growth mindset, using journaling to ease into writing projects, and designing succinct texts to communicate complex information. The responses from this exercise were not used directly in later steps but were, instead, primarily intended to get ideas flowing so that the subsequent ideation stage would be less daunting.

Next, the workshop moved into a rapid ideation exercise where participants responded to a series of prompts by writing or drawing ideas on sticky notes. While there are numerous ways to conduct this exercise, research has suggested that alternating individual and group ideation allows for more creative ideas while also helping participants to build on each other's contributions (Korde & Paulus, 2017). Participants were given the following typical ideation guidelines (Dam & Siang, 2018):

Write only one idea per sticky note.
- Work rapidly and aim for quantity.
- Defer any criticism (including self-judgment) during idea generation.
- Aim for unconventional, creative, and wild ideas.

Participants had five minutes per prompt to write down as many ideas as possible. Timing this exercise effectively can be difficult: the demand to continually and rapidly write new ideas can be exhausting for participants, but people often develop their most creative ideas only after recording more obvious or mundane ideas first (Mattimore, 2012). The key with timing, then, is to find a happy medium between creativity and exhaustion. The five-minute time limit seemed to work well to balance between the participants who stopped around the three- or four-minute mark and the other participants who continued working until the very end.

Since participants had varied experience and knowledge, I presented prompts in sets, which included questions customized for students, faculty, and practitioners. Each participant was still free to respond to any version of the prompt. Broadly, the first three prompt sets asked about the skills, knowledge, values, and experiences that graduates of the program should have. The fourth set asked for anti-definitions of our program. A full list of these prompts can also be found in Appendix B.

In total, participants in the two workshops developed 247 ideas about graduates of the writing and rhetoric degree. Some ideas described specific genres that graduates should know, including "write an effective resume/CV" and "create a website, podcast, or app." Participants also discussed rhetorically aware communication practices, including "thinking usefully about the reader's experience" and "practicing rhetorical listening." And they talked about productive values and mindsets, including "cultivating empathy for others" and "valuing a diversity of thought and style." Finally, they identified experiences that they hoped graduates would have, including "managing an extended writing project" and "having a meaningful mentorship experience." The ideas ranged from the typical goals of writing programs to more inventive visions for what our program could be.

There were so many ideas that the space required to cover them all would be prohibitive. So instead, I will trace one set of ideas from this early ideation stage through the rest of our project. Specifically, participants in both workshops recorded ideas related to writing about personal experiences and values. The following list shows examples of these ideas from each workshop.

Workshop 1

1. Have the freedom to conduct research about something we truly care about.
2. Students should engage in meaningful projects connected to their life, goals, values, etc.
3. More opportunities for personal writing.
4. The personal/untellable is still important.
5. Students should know who they are and what they believe and why.
6. Explore commitments, interests, expertise, values.
7. The time, energy, and focus it takes to craft pieces of effective writing.

Workshop 2

1. Graduates should have had a rewarding, or even fun, writing experience.
2. Find some joy in rigor.

3. Be okay with failing at writing.
4. Learn to be naked (become comfortable with critique).
5. Be willing to take creative risks.
6. Work really hard on a personally meaningful project.
7. Write what we want to write about.

This focus on personal interests and experimentation had been left out of our previous conversations about the curriculum, which focused more on the standard areas of rhetorical theory, professional writing, etc. As such, it represented a direction for the program that we discovered primarily through the workshops.

In the next workshop stage, participants categorized ideas using an affinity diagramming method where they first grouped sticky notes together without discussing their reasons, then named the groups, and finally, voted for the most important groups (Spool, 2004). In our workshops, participants initially created many different idea clusters, but they were subsequently asked to consolidate them whenever possible. Once the participants were satisfied with the clusters, they named them. Overall, each workshop created 15 named categories, with some similar or shared names across the workshops. For example, both workshops had a category named "Collaboration," and both had similarly named categories in "Rhetorical Theory and Lenses" and "Rhetoric and Theory." However, these similar category names sometimes belied differences in the underlying ideas. For example, the "Networked/Digital" category from Workshop 1 had a strong emphasis on UX research and design, while the "Digital Media" category from Workshop 2 emphasized multimodal and new media writing.

The personal writing ideas in the list of examples were primarily clustered together. In the first workshop, the category was named "Personal/Reflective Writing," and, in the second workshop, it was named "Personally meaningful writing/attitude." However, ideas 1 and 2 from the first workshop were placed in a research category alongside ideas related to research methods and citation styles.

After the categorization step was complete, participants prioritized ideas. During a design thinking process, this step is typically used to converge from the multiplicity of initial ideas to a list of concepts for prototyping and testing. Workshop participants were given five stickers and were asked to vote for the ideas that represented the most innovative or essential aspects of our program. Given the range of options, only a few ideas received more than one vote. In the first workshop, "The power of rhetoric" received three votes, and "Writing for the real world" received two votes. In the second workshop, "Writing has rules but does not have rules" received three votes, and three ideas each received two votes: "Writing belongs to the reader, not the author," "Know and value the difference between genres of writing," and "Be able to make connections between courses." After prioritizing ideas, participants had a brief discussion about which ideas were most valued and why. Categories were then ranked based on the number of votes that their constituent ideas received.

Participants voted for several of the ideas in the list of examples from the workshop (see above), including ideas 1 and 3 from the first workshop and ideas 8, 11, and 13 from the second workshop. Since the prioritized ideas were placed in separate categories in the first workshop, each category was ranked lowly. However, the consolidation of the prioritized ideas in the second workshop made "Personally Meaningful Writing/Attitude" the highest-ranked category there.

Next, participants each selected a category with at least two votes and drafted a program outcome based on the language of any prioritized ideas. Unfortunately, this was an abbreviated exercise, and it often did not result in usable learning outcomes. For example, since the personal writing ideas were in relatively low-ranked categories in the first workshop, no one created outcomes related to those ideas. In the second workshop, the following outcome was created: "Graduates will work really hard on a meaningful project," which suggests that the participant drew mainly from idea 13 in the workshop ideas list. Unfortunately, this outcome draft did not represent the complexities of the ideas developed in the workshop, nor did it fulfill the goals of a PSLO. Institutional guides typically state that outcomes need to be directly related to the specific academic discipline, be measurable and observable, and focus on outcomes rather than inputs (Georgia Tech Office of Academic Effectiveness, n.d.). The above outcome statement could have related to any discipline, it identified an input or experience, and it was not measurable. This issue was the result of a design flaw in the workshops, which I will discuss in more detail below.

The workshops concluded with a collective debrief. Participants discussed the ideas that were most surprising in the workshop, the exercises that worked best, and the exercises they would change. Some people were surprised at the potential outcomes that received relatively limited attention and prioritization, including teamwork and reading. Others commented on how the workshop was a positive experience, saying that they felt it valued everyone's voice and gave everyone a chance to speak. One student also commented that she began to see more connections between the courses she had taken in our program after doing the workshop. The only consistent criticism of the workshops was related to the need for more time for several of the exercises.

Prototyping and Testing Program Student Learning Outcomes

Prototyping is the process of creating quick representations of products or services to test specific attributes or variables. In design thinking projects, prototypes are tested with stakeholders and then iterated upon, which leads to further testing. Leverenz (2014) also likened writing drafts to prototyping when those drafts had intentional variety and were produced with minimal initial cost or time investment.

Since the outcome drafts made during the workshops were incomplete, I collaborated with another faculty member to condense the ideas from the workshops into cohesive PSLOs and to test those PSLOs with other faculty members.

First, we combined analogous categories between the two workshops, and then we combined similar ideas within each category while maintaining wording from the original ideas. Next, we eliminated ideas that did not align with realistic program outcomes. For example, we removed the ideas "Writing as brutalist design" and "Design as an attack on the senses" from the Visual Design category of Workshop 2. In both ideas, participants had expressed views of what our program should not be. As such, they provided insight into the kinds of visual design that participants did value. However, because we were working primarily from the wording of the ideas, there was no direct way to integrate either idea into a measurable outcome.

Once the data was more manageable, we wrote two to four outcome drafts for each category. Ideas that had been prioritized by workshop participants had to be present in at least one of the drafts. We also included other workshop ideas whenever possible. For example, Table 8.1 demonstrates how ideas from the personally meaningful writing categories were translated into initial outcome drafts.

Table 8.1. Translation of Source Ideas from Workshops to Outcome Drafts

Ideas from Workshops	Draft of Outcomes
"Had a rewarding, or even fun, writing experience" "Work really hard on a personally meaningful project" "Find some joy in rigor" "The time, energy, and focus it takes to craft pieces of effective writing"	Graduates will be able to pursue personally rewarding, rigorous writing projects that use time, energy, and focus to craft pieces of effective writing.
"Be okay with failing at writing" "Learning to be naked (becoming comfortable with critique)"	Graduates will appreciate the values of failure and criticism while defining good writing.

At the end of this process, the initial 247 ideas were narrowed into 90 outcome statements. At that point, we moved the outcomes into one (very long) list, which can be found in Appendix C. Because this list included a significant amount of repetition, we began to consolidate the outcome statements. First, we searched for repeated terminology in the outcomes. For example, 11 of the initial outcomes used the word "audience," and five of these outcomes focused explicitly on tailoring documents for a variety of audiences (see outcomes 9, 63, 64, 78, and 79 in Appendix C). Once we identified these repeated concepts, we combined the outcomes to address small differences between them and eliminated any leftover repetition. Then, we named the new outcome based on the identified concept (e.g., audience analysis, collaborative writing, rhetorical theory, etc.), sought out any remaining outcomes in the list that shared that goal, and continued to combine outcomes and eliminate repetition. Once we had a more manageable number of outcomes, we began sharing drafts with colleagues for feedback and critique. Based on their feedback, we narrowed the list to 14 program outcomes. At that point, we considered the initial draft of the PSLOs to be complete. During this process, the drafts in Table 8.1 were combined into the following outcome: "Graduates will be able to produce rigorous, personally meaningful writing projects that demonstrate flexibility and a willingness to take creative risks."

The prototyping stage took about one month to get from our initial list to the final version of the outcomes. It was a messy process, and we could not include all the ideas from the workshops in the final outcomes. There was also a significant amount of individual interpretation and prioritization, similar to the kind that occurs in more traditional methods for developing PSLOs. I explore this difficulty and potential alternative approaches to the prototyping stage in the evaluation section.

Implementing the Program Student Learning Outcomes

While an *implementation phase* is not always included in design thinking models, it is sometimes appended as a sixth step at the end of the d.school model. During the implementation phase, designers "put [their] vision into effect. [They] ensure that [their] solution is materialized and touches the lives of end users" (Gibbons, 2016). As with the other phases, implementation is often described as part of an ongoing cycle, wherein designers return to researching users' experiences even while they implement a solution.

The process of implementation for the PSLOs primarily involved moving the work from ad hoc workshops and collaborations back into official program committees. The first step was to re-form the defunct major track committee. For the new instantiation, the committee membership was kept small. The five members of the committee represented both tenure-track and non-tenure-track faculty as well as various research areas, including writing center studies, legal writing, cultural rhetorics, feminist rhetorics, and professional communication. It took only two meetings for the committee to revise the outcomes into a final version. During this work, the outcomes were organized into four categories, and two new outcomes were added: collaborative writing and community literacy. Other outcomes had only slight changes in wording. For example, the personally meaningful writing outcome had a few words added: "Graduates will be able to produce rigorous, personally meaningful writing projects that draw on their own experiences and demonstrate both flexibility and a willingness to take creative risks."

Once the committee agreed, the final 16 PSLOs were distributed to the full program faculty for review and discussion. The committee received no substantial feedback beyond the approval of the outcomes. The outcomes were then discussed and voted on during the subsequent program meeting. They were unanimously accepted and became official PSLOs in Fall 2018. The final list of outcomes from this process can be found in Appendix D.

■ Evaluation of the Design Thinking Approach

Throughout the design thinking process, 12 faculty, 16 students, and one staff member contributed to our PSLOs. Since participants built on the ideas of the various stakeholders throughout the process, the 16 final PSLOs represented a broad definition for the curriculum. However, this breadth also helped to create a more inclusive vision for our program, and several of the outcomes—such as the emphasis on personally meaningful writing and visual rhetoric—represented shared values that were not explicit in prior conversations about the program. This breadth would likely be problematic for many academic programs, which would necessitate a stronger control over idea prioritization in the workshops. However, in our program, this breadth helped to secure faculty support for the new PSLOs.

After establishing the outcomes, the major track committee used them to map our existing curriculum. We collected syllabi and assignment sheets for all our classes and analyzed the documents for evidence of attention to each of the outcome areas. Ultimately, this analysis identified several gaps in our core curriculum and electives. As a result, we designed two new courses: Visual Rhetorics, which addressed the visual design PSLO, and a senior capstone, which emphasized the personally meaningful writing and metacognition PSLOs. We also developed a plan to integrate community literacy projects into our core major track courses and ethical writing projects more broadly across the curriculum. For example, rhetorical theory instructors began to add projects working with local elementary schools, and the legal writing instructor added an ethics unit to the course.

The committee's next major task is developing an assessment plan for the outcomes. With 16 PSLOs, assessment will not be easy. However, since the major track is a sub-degree level program (i.e., it is a track within the pre-existing English major rather than a new, standalone major), we are not subject to institutional oversight on assessment, which gives us more flexibility in our plans. Currently, we plan to assess outcome categories one at a time and to collaborate with other program committees (e.g., the technical writing committee) on assessment. For example, the first year of assessment will focus on the "Writing Our Communities and Ourselves" outcome category. Over the coming months, the major track committee will collect examples of student work from core classes and will then do a traditional assessment reading process to understand how well our program is meeting these outcomes. At the same time, we do not plan to abandon design thinking in our move to assessment. Both design thinking and UX are inherently built on an iterative approach that emphasizes direct feedback from major stakeholders. For that reason, the committee is also planning on using some indirect assessment practices, including exploratory exit interviews with graduating students, to supplement our more traditional assessment methods.

While design thinking was useful for building a shared vision for our program, it also introduced some new challenges. In the sub-sections that follow, I will discuss some of the problems we encountered in more detail, including the relative inefficiency of the approach, the difficulty of building buy-in with stakeholders, and the need for more open prototyping and testing methods.

Managing Inefficiency in Design Thinking

Design thinking is not an efficient process. It takes time to explore stakeholder views, foster divergent thinking, and work collaboratively. Lisa Melonçon offered a similar criticism of her experience in a project that sought to use design thinking:

> The [design thinking] framework lost its power in an attempt to just get through the steps. It was flattened because to truly implement design thinking requires lots of time, and that time costs money. Most organizations simply don't have the time or money to fully invest in it nor do they have someone who understands the idea enough to facilitate the conversations—at every stage—that are necessary. (Pope-Ruark, 2019, pp. 452–453)

The design thinking process we used to create our outcomes was not exempt from this criticism of inefficiency. I spent approximately 15–20 hours setting up, conducting, and analyzing the interviews. Then I spent another 20–25 hours coordinating, designing, and facilitating the workshops. Finally, revising these results into the various drafts of the outcomes and formalizing them through the major track committee took another 15 hours. All told, I spent over 60 hours on the project. And the other participants collectively spent an additional 50 hours doing interviews, workshops, and other meetings, though no other person spent more than 5–6 hours on the project.

So, from one perspective, this process might appear to be incredibly inefficient. A faculty member likely could have sat down and drafted a reasonable set of outcomes in a few hours. And even a traditional committee likely could have completed the work in fewer person-hours. On the other hand, there were aspects of the design thinking process that were relatively quick and easy. For example, we used templated language (e.g., "Graduates will be able to") and wording from the workshop ideas to rapidly draft our initial outcome statements. And committee approaches can sometimes become bogged down in intractable disagreements, while single-faculty approaches are likely to reify a limited view of the academic program. In short, there is no perfect approach, and the design thinking process offered us some advantages that could not be reduced solely to efficiency.

Building Buy-In

Numerous practitioners have commented on the difficulty of building stakeholder and organizational buy-in for UX research and design (Anderson et al.,

2010; Sharon, 2012). Their recommendations have included demonstrating a clear return on investment and integrating UX work into existing institutional structures and processes.

For the PSLO project, I sought to construct buy-in with four groups of stakeholders: program administration, program faculty, students, and industry representatives. Through a recursive and continual effort, I was able to secure buy-in from the first three groups, but not from industry representatives.

Securing agreement from the program administrator was a crucial first step. In retrospect, a combination of factors likely facilitated this step. First, I was already researching UX, so I framed this work as an extension of my existing expertise. Second, the major track committee was not actively making progress, which created space for alternative approaches. Finally, other faculty had also spoken positively about the presentations at CPTSC, thus lending additional credence to the design thinking process.

Building faculty buy-in was also essential because the program employs strong collective governance and because each phase required contributions of time and effort from other faculty members. Several of my methods here were also successful. First, I voluntarily carried the workload for the project. Given the amount of time and effort that design thinking requires, this may not be possible in all situations. Second, we referred to the ad hoc collaborations and workshops as a "workgroup," which allowed faculty participants to count their contributions toward their service requirements for the year. Finally, I kept the project processes and data transparent throughout by providing progress updates regularly at program meetings and sending summaries from each phase to program faculty.

Finally, encouraging student buy-in was also relatively straightforward. Students were generally happy to contribute to the program. They repeatedly thanked us for talking with them and for including them in the workshops. Beyond this, I designed the interviews and workshops to be relatively user-friendly. The interviews were short, and they focused on students' individual preferences and experiences. And students were positioned as equal contributors in the workshops, with their ideas being discussed openly, and without judgment, by all participants.

Despite the success of building buy-in with the above stakeholders, we failed to get contributions from industry representatives. There were likely two primary causes of this failure. First, there was no financial support for the project, and some form of compensation might have encouraged industry representatives to attend the workshops. Second, the diffuse program focus meant that we did not have clear connections to specific industries and local organizations. While technical communication programs have been able to achieve this sort of buy-in through the creation of industry advisory boards (Söderlund et al., 2017; Spartz & Watts, 2016), we had not established this structure before the project. However, the noticeable lack of industry contributions has also helped us identify this as a potential area of growth for the program. We are currently working to build more sustained relationships through our internship and service-learning courses and are considering other ways to get industry and community feedback on our curriculum.

Opening Up Prototyping and Testing

We adopted a traditional approach to creating PSLOs during the prototyping and testing phase. While the outcomes were based on the ideas and input of a broader group of stakeholders, the actual work of prototyping them still occurred in a closed faculty collaboration. While it was necessary to tame the vast amount of data from the workshops, we still might have undertaken this work in more open and participatory ways.

A different model could have focused the workshops more directly on the work of drafting full PSLOs. This either would have taken more time or a reorientation of the second workshop, but it would have been possible. For example, the workshop could have split participants into two groups. Each group could then have selected eight to ten sticky notes to create their own list of PSLOs. This shorter list could then be prototyped by each team into an initial rough draft of outcomes and presented back to the other group to explore a possible range of emphases.

Design thinking also typically relies on visual or physical prototypes that can be actively tested with real stakeholders. Again, the limited testing in our process could have been improved by seeking feedback from students and industry or community representatives. Either as part of the workshops or as a follow-up, the initial PSLO lists could have been prototyped into physical artifacts such as flyers for the program or fictional graduate resumes. These artifacts could then be more easily tested with non-faculty stakeholders. As we continue to iterate on our program design in the coming years, we will be supplementing traditional assessment with these kinds of active testing methods to gain a broader perspective on our curriculum.

■ A Heuristic Model for Programmatic Design Thinking

While the single PSLO project described here is not sufficient to offer a universal framework applying design thinking to curricular development, I would like to close by sketching a general model for curricular projects adapting a design thinking process.

First, a design thinking model should be a flexible heuristic rather than a linear process. Drawing on Ben Lauren's work, we might say that faculty and administrators using design thinking "have to build a capacity for seeing design as a kind of detective work in which logistics and exigencies can change or be discovered in a nonlinear fashion" (Greenwood et al., 2019, p. 406). Therefore, the model for programmatic design thinking must first acknowledge the cyclical and iterative nature of the work. It has no inherent starting point and no definitive end. A program that specifically needs to design PSLOs could easily begin in ideation and loop back toward problem setting in later stages of the project. And testing and iteration could also become the focus for a program with existing outcomes. In other words, the phases can help us think of the kinds of tasks and work we need to do, but they do not provide us an exact roadmap of how to carry out that work.

Second, a design thinking model must also emphasize cycles of divergence and convergence. For example, in the PSLO project, the initial interviews offered an opportunity for divergence by including a range of experiences in and perspectives on the program. The information from interviews led to a convergence around the need for better program definitions. This led to another cycle where a diverse group of participants imagined a range of goals for our program and where those ideas were formalized into PSLOs and approved by program committees. These cycles of divergence and convergence create space for multiple perspectives and encourage the testing and iteration of specific solutions over time.

In building a heuristic model, I also simplified the process into four activities: listening, problem setting, ideating, and iterating, as shown in Figure 8.1. In this model, the implementation phase is incorporated into the process of iteration as a recognition that programmatic design projects do not have a clear start or end point.

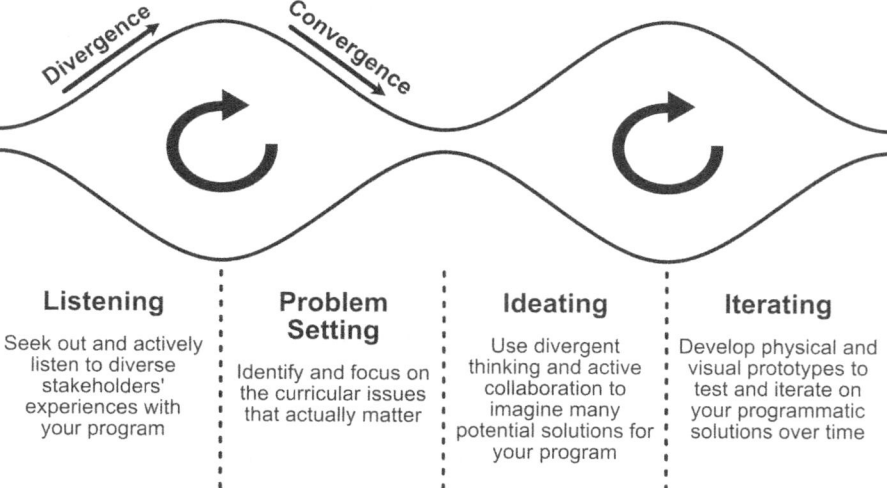

Figure 8.1. Heuristic for programmatic design thinking.

In the listening activity, faculty and administrators seek out and actively attend to diverse stakeholders' experiences with and perspectives on our academic programs. This activity is a recognition of our own positionality as well as the limits of our knowledge and perspectives. It helps us see and hear the experiences of others more clearly and it opens programmatic design to non-faculty participants.

The problem-setting activity highlights the need to identify and focus on curricular issues that matter to stakeholders. Sometimes, traditional models of curricular design seem like a teleological process of checking off the requisite institutional and bureaucratic boxes, and, as such, solutions might be assumed before the problem space is even explored. But, as Christian Bason and Robert Austin (2019) argued, "Design thinking is challenging because it involves something more fundamental than just managing change: It involves discovering what kind of change is needed" (p. 91). Ultimately, when faculty and administrators can make space for intentional problem setting, we can focus our efforts on the real problems that students (and other stakeholders) encounter in academic programs.

Ideation creates space for active participation and divergent thinking. Intentionally supporting divergent thinking can slow down the design process, but it also opens up new possibilities. As writing studies and technical communication continue to build stronger support for cultural and linguistic inclusivity across our academic programs (Gonzales & Baca, 2017), curricular design needs to create space for more voices. And active participatory and divergent thinking models can help to create this kind of space.

Finally, design thinking is, fundamentally, a process of iteration. It is a process that works best when solutions are modeled, tested, and changed over time. To accomplish this activity, faculty and administrators can experiment with physical and visual prototypes of the curriculum to encourage non-faculty stakeholders to actively engage in the design process.

In closing, and in the spirit of iteration, I would like to offer this heuristic model itself as an initial prototype in need of further testing, experimentation, and revision. Design thinking alone certainly is not a magic instrument for fixing curricular problems. But with appropriate attention and intention, it can operate as a flexible guide for finding new futures for our programs.

■ References

Allen, J. (2010). Mapping institutional values and the technical communication curriculum: A strategy for grounding assessment. In M. Hundleby & J. Allen (Eds.), *Assessment in technical and professional communication* (pp. 39–56). Routledge.

Ambole, A. (2020). Rethinking Design Making and Design Thinking in Africa. *Design and Culture*, *12*(3), 331–350. https://doi.org/10.1080/17547075.2020.1788257.

Anderson, J., McRee, J., Wilson, R. & The EffectiveUI Team. (2010). *Effective UI: The art of building great user experience in software*. O'Reilly.

Anderson, P. V. (2010). The benefits and challenges of adopting a new standpoint while assessing technical communication programs: A response to Jo Allen. In M. Hundleby & J. Allen (Eds.), *Assessment in technical and professional communication* (pp. 57–62). Routledge.

Anson, C. (2010). Assessment in action: A Möbius tale. In M. Hundleby & J. Allen (Eds.), *Assessment in technical and professional communication* (pp. 3–15). Routledge.

Balzhiser, D., Sawyer, P., Womack-Smith, S. & Smith, J. A. (2015). Participatory design research for curriculum development of graduate programs for workplace professionals. *Programmatic Perspectives*, 7(2), 79–133.

Bason, C. & Austin, R. D. (2019). The right way to lead design thinking. *Harvard Business Review*, 97(2), 82–91.

Beckman, S. L. (2020). To frame or reframe: Where might design thinking research go next? *California Management Review*, 62(2), 144–162. https://doi.org/10.1177/000812 5620906620.

Belcher, D. D. (2017). On becoming facilitators of multimodal composing and digital design. *Journal of Second Language Writing*, 38, 80–85. https://doi.org/10.1016/j.jslw .2017.10.004.

Brophy, T. (2017). *Developing program goals and student learning outcomes*. Office of the Provost. University of Florida. https://fora.aa.ufl.edu/docs/89/Meeting-Materials /DevelopingPGsandSLOsGuide.pdf.

Brown, T. (2008). Design thinking. *Harvard Business Review*, 86(6), 84–92.

Brown, T. & Wyatt, J. (2010). Design thinking for social innovation. *Stanford Social Innovation Review*, 8(1), 31–35.

Carnegie, T. A. M. & Crane, K. (2019). Responsive curriculum change: Going beyond occupation demands. *Communication Design Quarterly*, 6(3), 25–31. https://doi.org/10 .1145/3309578.3309581.

Carter, M., Anson, C. M. & Miller, C. R. (2003). Assessing technical writing in institutional contexts: Using outcomes-based assessment for programmatic thinking. *Technical Communication Quarterly*, 12(1), 101–114. https://doi.org/10.1207/s15427625 tcq1201_7.

Clegg, G., Lauer, J., Phelps, J. & Melonçon, L. (2021). Programmatic Outcomes in Undergraduate Technical and Professional Communication Programs. *Technical Communication Quarterly*, 30(1), 19–33. https://doi.org/10.1080/10572252.2020.1774662.

Cooke, L., Dusenberry, L. & Robinson, J. (2020). Gaming design thinking: Wicked problems, sufficient solutions, and the possibility space of games. *Technical Communication Quarterly*, 29(4), 327–340. https://doi.org/10.1080/10572252.2020.1738555.

Cushman, J. (2014). Our unstable artistry: Donald Schön's counterprofessional practice of problem setting. *Journal of Business and Technical Communication*, 28(3), 327–351. https://doi.org/10.1177/1050651914524778.

Dam, R. & Siang, T. (2018, November 29). *Stage 3 in the design thinking process: Ideate*. Interaction Design Foundation. https://www.interaction-design.org/literature/art icle/stage-3-in-the-design-thinking-process-ideate.

Durá, L., Perez, L. & Chaparro, M. (2019). Positive deviance as design thinking: Challenging notions of stasis in technical and professional communication. *Journal of Business and Technical Communication*, 33(4), 376–399.

Ewell, P. T. (2001). *Accreditation and student learning outcomes: A proposed point of departure*. Council for Higher Education Accreditation. https://www.chea.org/accredita tion-and-student-learning-outcomes-proposed-point-departure.

Florida International University. (2010). Undergraduate course catalog 2010–2011. https://digitalcommons.fiu.edu/catalogs/41/.

Georgia Tech Office of Academic Effectiveness. (n.d.). *Guidelines for writing program outcomes*. https://academiceffectiveness.gatech.edu/assessment-toolkit/developing -student-learning-outcome-statements.

Gibbons, S. (2016, July 31). *Design thinking 101*. Nielsen Norman Group. https://www.nngroup.com/articles/design-thinking/.

Gonzales, L. & Baca, I. (2017). Developing culturally and linguistically diverse online technical communication programs: Emerging frameworks at University of Texas at El Paso. *Technical Communication Quarterly, 26*(3), 273–286. https://doi.org/10.1080/10572252.2017.1339488.

Gray, D., Brown, S. & Macanufo, J. (2010). *Gamestorming: A playbook for innovators, rulebreakers, and changemakers*. O'Reilly Media.

Greenwood, A., Lauren, B., Knott, J. & DeVoss, D. N. (2019). Dissensus, resistance, and ideology: Design thinking as a rhetorical methodology. *Journal of Business & Technical Communication, 33*(4), 400–424. https://doi.org/10.1177/1050651919854063.

IBM. (n.d.). *Enterprise design thinking field guide*. https://www.ibm.com/cloud/garage/content/field-guide/design-thinking-field-guide/.

IDEO. (2015). *The field guide to human-centered design*. http://www.designkit.org/resources/1.

Jonson, J. (2006). *Guidebook for programmatic assessment of student learning outcomes*. University of Nebraska-Lincoln. https://svcaa.unl.edu/assessment/learningoutcomes_guidebook.pdf.

Khadka, S. (2018). A broad-based multiliteracies theory and praxis for a diverse writing classroom. *Computers and Composition, 47*, 93–110. https://doi.org/10.1016/j.compcom.2017.12.002.

Khandwala, A. (2019, June 5). What does it mean to decolonize design? *AIGA Eye on Design*. https://eyeondesign.aiga.org/what-does-it-mean-to-decolonize-design/.

Kim, K. H. & Pierce, R. A. (2013). Convergent versus divergent thinking. In E. G. Carayannis (Ed.), *Encyclopedia of creativity, invention, innovation and entrepreneurship* (pp. 245–250). Springer. https://doi.org/10.1007/978-1-4614-3858-8_22.

Kimbell, L. (2011). Rethinking design thinking: Part I. *Design and Culture, 3*(3), 285–306. https://doi.org/10.2752/175470811X13071166525216.

Kimbell, L. (2012). Rethinking design thinking: Part II. *Design and Culture, 4*(2), 129-148. https://doi.org/10.2752/175470812X13281948975413.

Knemeyer, D. (2015). Design thinking and UX: Two sides of the same coin. *ACM Interactions, 22*(5), 66–68. https://doi.org/10.1145/2802679.

Kolko, J. (2015). Design thinking comes of age. *Harvard Business Review, 93*(9), 3–7.

Korde, R. & Paulus, P. B. (2017). Alternating individual and group idea generation: Finding the elusive synergy. *Journal of Experimental Social Psychology, 70*, 177–190. https://doi.org/10.1016/j.jesp.2016.11.002.

Kostelnick, C. (1989). Process paradigms in design and composition: Affinities and directions. *College Composition and Communication, 40*(3), 267–281.

Lane, L. (2018). Iteration for impact: Exploring design thinking: Designing for social change in client projects. In *Proceedings of the 36th ACM International Conference on the Design of Communication* (pp. 1–6). Association for Computing Machinery. https://doi.org/10.1145/3233756.3233952.

Leverenz, C. S. (2014). Design thinking and the wicked problem of teaching writing. *Computers and Composition, 33*, 1–12. https://doi.org/10.1016/j.compcom.2014.07.001.

Marback, R. (2009). Embracing wicked problems: The turn to design in composition studies. *College Composition and Communication, 61*(2), 385–385 JSTOR. https://www.jstor.org/stable/40593465.

Mattimore, B. W. (2012). *Idea stormers: How to lead and inspire creative breakthroughs.* Wiley.

McCarthy, S. (2016). Designing an engaged swarm: Toward a techne for multi-class, interdisciplinary collaborations with nonprofit partners. *Community Literacy Journal, 11*(1), 106–117. https://doi.org/10.1353/clj.2016.0019.

Moore, K., Young, D., Pitchford, B. & Cargile Cook, K. C. (2017, October). *Just ask them: User-centered design activities for program development* [Conference presentation]. Council for Programs in Technical and Scientific Communication. Annual Conference, Savannah, GA, United States.

Nussbaum, B. (2011). Design thinking is a failed experiment. So what's next? *Fast Company.* https://www.fastcompany.com/1663558/design-thinking-is-a-failed-experiment-so-whats-next.

Pender, K. (2011). *Techne, from neoclassicism to postmodernism: Understanding writing as a useful, teachable art.* Parlor Press.

Pflugfelder, E. (2017). Methodologies: Design studies and techne. In L. Potts & M. J. Salvo (Eds.), *Rhetoric and experience architecture* (pp. 166–183). Parlor Press.

An Introduction to design thinking: Process guide. (2010). Institute of Design at Stanford. https://web.stanford.edu/~mshanks/MichaelShanks/files/509554.pdf.

Pope-Ruark, R. (2019). Design thinking in technical and professional communication: Four perspectives. *Journal of Business & Technical Communication, 33*(4), 437–455. https://doi.org/10.1177/1050651919854094.

Pope-Ruark, R., Moses, J. & Tham, J. (2019). Iterating the literature: An early annotated bibliography of design-thinking resources. *Journal of Business and Technical Communication, 33*(4), 456–465. https://doi.org/10.1177/1050651919854096.

Pope-Ruark, R., Tham, J., Moses, J. & Conner, T. (2019). Introduction to special issue: Design-thinking approaches in technical and professional communication. *Journal of Business & Technical Communication, 33*(4), 370–375. https://doi.org/10.1177/1050651919854054.

Potts, L. (2014). *Social media in disaster response: How experience architects can build for participation.* Routledge.

Purdy, J. P. (2014). What can design thinking offer writing studies? *College Composition and Communication, 65*(4), 612-641. JSTOR. https://www.jstor.org/stable/43490875.

Roochnik, D. (1996). *Of art and wisdom: Plato's understanding of techne.* Penn State University Press.

Sano-Franchini, J., Moore, K. R. & Kulak, A. (2017, October). *Rhetoric and experience architecture* [Conference presentation]. Council for Programs in Technical and Scientific Communication. Annual Conference, Savannah, GA, United States.

Schön, D. A. (1983). *The reflective practitioner: How professionals think in action.* Basic Books.

Shalamova, N., Rice-Bailey, T. & Domack, A. (2017, October). *Launching a 21st century program in user experience (UX): Leveraging lean methodology to redesign our technical communication program* [Conference presentation]. Council for Programs in Technical and Scientific Communication Annual Conference, Savannah, GA, United States.

Sharon, T. (2012). *It's our research: Getting stakeholder buy-in for user experience research projects.* Elsevier.

Singh, C. (2016, December 28). HCD vs design thinking vs service design vs UX .... What do they all mean? *Medium.* https://medium.com/@charan3/hcd-vs-design-thinking-vs-service-design-vs-ux-what-do-they-all-mean-4927fb248fa1.

Söderlund, L., Spartz, J. & Weber, R. (2017). Taken under advisement: Perspectives on advisory boards from across technical communication. *IEEE Transactions on Professional Communication, 60*(1), 76–96. https://doi.org/10.1109/TPC.2016.2635693.

Southern Association of Colleges and Schools Commission on Colleges. (2020). *Resource manual for the principles of accreditation: Foundations for quality enhancement* (3rd ed.). https://sacscoc.org/app/uploads/2019/08/2018-POA-Resource-Manual.pdf.

Spartz, J. M. & Watts, J. (2016). Towards a participatory action research model for extending programmatic assessment with industry advisory boards. *Programmatic Perspectives, 8*(2), 163–185.

Spool, J. (2004, May 11). The KJ-technique: A group process for establishing priorities. *Center Centre—UIE.* https://articles.uie.com/kj_technique/.

Tschimmel, K. (2012). Design thinking as an effective toolkit for innovation. In *Proceedings of the XXIII ISPIM Conference: Action for Innovation: Innovating from Experience* (pp. 1–20). The International Society for Professional Innovation Management (ISPIM).

VanKooten, C. & Berkley, A. (2016). Messy problem-exploring through video in first-year writing: Assessing what counts. *Computers and Composition, 40,* 151–163. https://doi.org/10.1016/j.compcom.2016.04.001.

Vinsel, L. (2017, December 6). Design thinking is kind of like syphilis — It's contagious and rots your brains. *Medium.* https://medium.com/@sts_news/design-thinking-is-kind-of-like-syphilis-its-contagious-and-rots-your-brains-842ed078af29.

Wickman, C. (2014). Wicked problems in technical communication. *Journal of Technical Writing and Communication, 44*(1), 23–42. https://doi.org/10.2190/TW.44.1.c.

■ Appendix A: Interview Questions

Faculty Interview Questions

1. What is your primary area of academic expertise?
2. What upper-division courses have you taught?
3. What was your favorite course to teach? Why?
4. What has been your best experience in teaching for our program?
5. Describe an ideal writing and rhetoric track student or graduate. What do they know? How do they think? What can they do?
6. What is a key experience for students in our program?
7. What is your least favorite part of our current program?
8. What is something we should add to our program?

Student Interview Questions

1. What upper-division courses have you taken?
2. What has been your favorite writing and rhetoric course?
3. How did you learn about our program? What attracted you to writing and rhetoric courses?

4. What are the most useful skills you learned in our courses? What are the most important concepts you learned in our courses?
5. What was your best experience in one of our courses?
6. What is something you still hope to learn in a Writing and Rhetoric course? Or if you already graduated, what is something you wish you had learned in a Writing and Rhetoric course?
7. What would you like to see changed in our courses?

Appendix B: Workshop Prompts

Brainwriting Prompts

- Who is the most effective writer that you know? What makes them effective?
- How has (good) writing changed over the past 10–20 years?
- What is something you wish you could improve in your own writing?
- What aspect of effective writing is most often overlooked?
- Explain the importance of rhetoric as if you were speaking to a friend who has not studied it.
- How do your values intersect with your understanding of effective writing and/or rhetoric?
- How have you seen writing and/or rhetoric being used in your local community?

Ideation Prompts Set 1: Skills

- **Faculty:** What should a student be able to do before they graduate from a Writing and Rhetoric Program? What skills are most important for a writing and rhetoric student? What skills do you see as most important to their future work?
- **Professionals:** What writing or communication skills would you list on a job ad for an entry-level position? What writing or communication skills are most important to your own work?
- **Students:** What can you do now that you could not do before taking writing and rhetoric classes? What do you still want to learn how to do?

Ideation Prompts Set 2: Knowledge and Values

- **Faculty:** What should a student know before they graduate from a Writing and Rhetoric Program? What are the core concepts you teach in your courses? What values do you hope graduates will hold? What are the key values of writing and rhetoric as a field?
- **Professionals:** What knowledge do you want new hires to have? What concepts help you communicate effectively in professional settings? What are the key values of your profession or organization?

- **Students:** What are the most important concepts or ideas you have learned about in writing and rhetoric courses? What are the key values that teachers have talked about in class? What kind of values do you think are important for success?

Ideation Prompts Set 3: Experiences

- **Faculty:** What should a student have done before graduating from a writing and rhetoric major? What are key educational experiences for most students? What do you think are the best experiences for students in your classes?
- **Professionals:** What kinds of experiences do you want a new hire to have? What experiences have been essential to your own growth as a writer or communicator?
- **Students:** What have been your best experiences in our program so far? What do you still want to do before you graduate from our program?

Ideation Prompts Set 4: Anti-Definitions

- **Faculty:** What is something students should not learn in our program?
- **Professionals:** What would make a recent graduate a bad fit for a writing position?
- **Students:** What is something you do not want to learn more about in our program?
- **Wildcards:** What is the worst possible focus for our program? What is the opposite of a Writing and Rhetoric Program?

■ Appendix C: Initial List of Outcome Statements

1. Graduates will learn the complexities and power of rhetoric.
2. Graduates will be able to pursue personally rewarding, rigorous writing projects that use time, energy, and focus to craft pieces of effective writing.
3. Graduates will appreciate the values of failure and criticism while defining good writing.
4. Graduates will take creative risks within the writing process.
5. Graduates will value writing as products of considerable, process-driven efforts affected by time and deadlines.
6. Graduates will conduct constant writing assignments.
7. Graduates will adapt their style to their rhetorical situation, purpose, and audience, keeping in mind that writing belongs to the reader, not the author.
8. Graduates will think usefully about the reader's experience (of both the text and the author as communicator).

9. Graduates will analyze the effects a text may have on different audiences.
10. Graduates will examine interdisciplinary studies in writing, including the differences and nuances between disciplines' genres of writing.
11. Graduates will collaborate in teams on interdisciplinary writing situations to negotiate different writing styles.
12. Graduates will evaluate peer writing to become reflective practitioners of their own writing.
13. Graduates will practice divergent and convergent thinking.
14. Graduates will understand how writing is as important a skill as math and science.
15. Graduates will understand how pedagogical and theoretical strategies help with understanding how to write.
16. Graduates will take classes from multiple professors and know their professors' names.
17. Graduates will be able to make connections between courses and understand/identify outcomes from different types of writing classes.
18. Graduates will read documents to evaluate strengths and weaknesses, thinking critically to synthesize ideas in context and making connections across contexts and cultures.
19. Graduates will practice analyzing structures in texts for the purpose of identifying how these structures value and save readers' time.
20. Graduates will be able to conduct primary and secondary research by interacting with and managing the breadth, depth, and historical communion of the interrelated nature of sources.
21. Graduates will effectively analyze sources for credibility/biases, accuracy, depth/loaded writing and sophistication of content focusing clearly enough to identify nuances in rhetoric, tone, and argument.
22. Graduates will accurately, professionally cite sources through strong, comprehensive summary, paraphrase, and quotes of both traditional and alternative, modern research sources.
23. Graduates will be able to clearly delineate and state objective source material from subjective opinions in their writing practices.
24. Graduates will understand the complexities of situational plagiarism.
25. Graduates will be exposed to a range of foundational and modern writing theory, rhetorical theory, and interdisciplinary theory, and critical thinking.
26. Graduates will value rhetoric at work in everything and everywhere, identifying the complexities of rhetoric as power and communication.
27. Graduates will understand the purposes, rhetorical strategies and audiences for mediums and messages.
28. Graduates can establish proper mediums (websites, podcasts, apps) and compose texts for messages.

29. Graduates will write for public audiences and engage audiences through public speaking/public reading/performance.
30. Graduates will write for the assessment of someone other than the teacher.
31. Graduates will create writing projects requiring effective expansion/editing practices.
32. Graduates will write engaging introductions.
33. Graduates will have the ability to self-regulate strategies for time management and "how to get through your paper in a single sitting and a single draft."
34. Graduates will be able to read a book and create prompts for response.
35. Graduates will have a clear understanding of careers and graduate programs available for their degrees.
36. Graduates will engage in internships.
37. Graduates will work at a writing center or tutor peers.
38. Graduates will articulate (qualify and quantify) their writing skills as professional skills.
39. Graduates will know what types of jobs are suitable for their expertise and how to sell their skills through branding.
40. Graduates will have experience with practical, tangible genres of professional writing like resumes and CVs.
41. Graduates will recognize, examine, and appreciate gaps in their own education.
42. Graduates will conduct a thorough, accurate self-review.
43. Graduates will be able to recognize, use, and proofread/edit standard and non-standard English practices, the cultural and political values associated with them, and the historical constructs of power within them.
44. Graduates will understand the value of non-standard Englishes and the power dynamics associated with these values.
45. Graduates will understand that there are no rules, only conventions.
46. Graduates will appreciate diversity of thought and style in writing through cultural examinations of texts.
47. Graduates will understand the production of rhetoric through appropriate messages, methods, and mediums (social media/press releases/popular writing/personal writing/ public writing/academic writing).
48. Graduates will have engaged in rewarding and engaging writing experiences.
49. Graduates will develop a personal connection to the power and complexity of rhetorical practice.
50. Graduates will demonstrate comfort with having their writing critiqued. They will develop effective ways of managing and responding to critique.
51. Graduates will show a willingness to take risks in writing.

52. Graduates will write effectively for a range of real audiences and tasks outside of academia.
53. Graduates will market and promote their skills and experience effectively.
54. Graduates will use rhetorical concepts and strategies to craft powerful and effective communication.
55. Graduates will recognize how rhetorical concepts and strategies are being used in a range of communications.
56. Graduates will use effective strategies for communicating across cultures.
57. Graduates will value and demonstrate respect for others' opinions.
58. Graduates will employ communication strategies that demonstrate empathy for others.
59. Graduates will employ effective strategies for managing projects and for working collaboratively with others, both in person and online.
60. Graduates will have significant experience with working collaboratively in teams and groups.
61. Graduates will know how to employ the fundamentals of visual design to craft effective page layouts and integrate visuals into a variety of texts.
62. Graduates will be able to create effective visual displays of data and use visual rhetoric effectively to achieve their goals.
63. Graduates will be able to analyze various audiences and tailor writing to their needs and preferences.
64. Graduates will be able to effectively represent themselves in writing for a variety of audiences.
65. Graduates will know how to use a range of digital writing tools.
66. Graduates will be able to write effectively for a range of networked and digital environments.
67. Graduates will have engaged in extended research projects tied to individual goals and values.
68. Graduates will know how to conduct research responsibly and ethically.
69. Graduates will know a range of research methods appropriate both for academic and professional settings.
70. Graduates will have experience editing others' work.
71. Graduates will know how to carefully and comprehensively edit work.
72. Graduates will have significant experience with presenting information orally.
73. Graduates will have engaged in personal writing.
74. Graduates will understand the ethical implications of writing.
75. Graduates will value both their and others' writing styles.
76. Graduates will know how to bring all their resources to writing practice, including multilingual and multicultural resources.
77. Graduates will have a flexible knowledge of genre conventions and know how to analyze and adapt newly encountered genres.

78. Graduates will be able to adapt their writing to a variety of contexts and audiences.
79. Graduates will know how to moderate their tone to match a range of situations and audiences.
80. Graduates will have a deep understanding of community and engagement.
81. Graduates will be better communicators after collaborating with peers in writing projects.
82. Graduates will work very hard on a meaningful project.
83. Graduates will know and value various genres of writing, types of writing, and disciplines of writing.
84. Graduates will be able to analyze their rhetorical situation and adapt their writing accordingly.
85. Graduates will be able to identify and effectively use standard and non-standard Englishes.
86. Graduates will be able to articulate how their writing courses relate to each other (and the logic of the curriculum).
87. Graduates will be able to value/appreciate the diversity of thoughts, genres, and styles.
88. Graduates will learn to communicate in ways that are not just textual. They should be encouraged to use technology and new media to gain these skills. They should understand that their content is not the only important part of their communication but that the context in which it is told and the medium that is used hold rhetorical value.
89. Graduates will be able to write for a variety of real-world audiences and purposes using a variety of mediums such as emails, memos, proposals, resumes.
90. Graduates will engage with and understand the power of rhetoric, alternative and mainstream rhetorical histories, theories and practices, and apply these analytical lenses and approaches to communicate effectively.

Appendix D: Final List of Program Student Learning Outcomes

Developing Rhetorical Awareness

- **Rhetoric and Composition Theory:** Graduates will be able to explain the value, power, and complexity of theoretical perspectives, including classical, alternative, feminist, multilingual, and/or multicultural rhetorics and composition. They will be able to compose rhetorically-effective communications.
- **Textual Analysis:** Graduates will be able to analyze a variety of everyday and academic texts for their strengths and weaknesses according to rhetorical, contextual, and cultural parameters.

- **Audience:** Graduates will be able to analyze various audiences' needs and adapt writing to the expectations of those audiences.
- **Ethics:** Graduates will be able to analyze the ethical implications of writing situations and practices. They will know how to take appropriate ethical action when faced with complex communication situations.

Building a Writing Process for Academic and Nonacademic Contexts

- **Writing Process:** Graduates will be able to employ a flexible writing process. They will be able to invent rhetorically appropriate content; provide and incorporate constructive feedback; proofread, revise, and edit their own and others' work; and address stylistic preferences of various audiences.
- **Research:** Graduates will be able to conduct primary and secondary research. They will be able to analyze sources for credibility, biases, accuracy, depth, and sophistication. And they will be able to professionally integrate research and sources in ways that support their project's goals.
- **Collaborative Writing:** Graduates will be able to work on complex projects with team members. They will be able to employ a range of strategies for managing projects and negotiating team dynamics.

Enhancing Workplace Writing Practices

- **Professional Writing:** Graduates will be able to employ the genres and qualities typical to professional audiences and situations. They will be able to articulate and market their writing skills and to position themselves for their desired career or graduate program.
- **Visual Design:** Graduates will be able to employ the fundamentals of visual design to display data, to craft page layouts, and to integrate visuals into a variety of texts.
- **Digital Media:** Graduates will be able to use digital media, select rhetorically fit mediums, and design strategies appropriate to those mediums.
- **Oral Presentation:** Graduates will be able to present information orally both individually and in teams for a range of situations, topics, and audiences. They will also be able to craft visual and/or textual supports for their presentations.

Writing our Communities and Ourselves

- **Personally Meaningful Writing:** Graduates will be able to produce rigorous, personally meaningful writing projects that draw on their own experiences and demonstrate both flexibility and a willingness to take creative risks.
- **Community Literacy:** Graduates will be able to develop best practices for participating in community writing and service-learning projects in and beyond the South Florida community that work toward community engagement and social action.

- **Cross-Cultural Communication:** Graduates will demonstrate respect for others' views. They will be able to craft communications for members of other cultures and to bring their own resources to writing practices, including their multilingual and multicultural resources. Graduates will be able to work within and across language standards and conventions and the cultural and political values associated with them.
- **Interdisciplinarity:** Graduates will be able to write for other disciplines. They will be able to research and adapt to the conventions, goals, and constraints of other disciplines.
- **Metacognition:** Graduates will be able to self-identify gaps in their education and knowledge and create plans to address these gaps when necessary.

9. Using UX Methods to Gauge Degree Efficacy

Kelli Cargile Cook
TEXAS TECH UNIVERSITY

Abstract: This chapter describes a four-year longitudinal study of a new degree program in professional communication. It describes study methods and reports preliminary findings from the first year. Throughout the chapter, the author argues that student data collected through user experience methods enriches the assessment process as well as benefits students by providing insights into program design and outcomes.

Keywords: program assessment, user experience methods, longitudinal study design, degree efficacy, iterative design

Key Takeaways:

- Programmatic assessment is a continuous improvement process that informs curricular decisions and ideally increases student outcome achievement.
- Student voices are frequently absent from programmatic assessment processes, data collection, and curricular design decision-making.
- Adding user experience (UX) methods to the programmatic assessment mix affords program administrators a means to collect student experiences and use these data to inform program design, assessment, and redesign decisions.
- UX methods are intended to be local, ungeneralizable, and fit to specific situations, to specific products, and to the specific users who engage with products.
- Even though UX methods do not produce generalizable results, the data collected can guide faculty and administrators as they seek continuous improvement of a program's design and outcomes.

Program assessment is a common practice on public university campuses. The Office of Planning and Assessment (OPA) at Texas Tech University (TTU) provides guidance on how program outcomes and assessment should be conducted on this campus; its guidance is comparable to peer institutions of higher education and compliant with the *Principles of Accreditation: Foundations for Quality Enhancement* guidelines of the Southern Association of Colleges and Schools Commission on Colleges (SACSCOC, 2018). Section 7 of the *Principles of Accreditation* specifically provides guidance for institutional planning and assessment:

> Effective institutions demonstrate a commitment to principles of continuous improvement, based on a systematic and documented process of assessing institutional performance with respect to

mission in all aspects of the institution. An institutional planning and effectiveness process involves all programs, services, and constituencies; is linked to the decision-making process at all levels; and provides a sound basis for budgetary decisions and resource allocations (SACSCOC, 2018, p. 19).

While accreditation associations do not require specific methods of assessment, they do encourage a variety of methods. For example, OPA (2017–2018) reported that course level assessments, exams, and capstone assignments or projects were the most common means of assessing student learning outcomes in both graduate and undergraduate courses. Other means of assessment are described in the 2017–2018 OPA infographic in Figure 9.1.

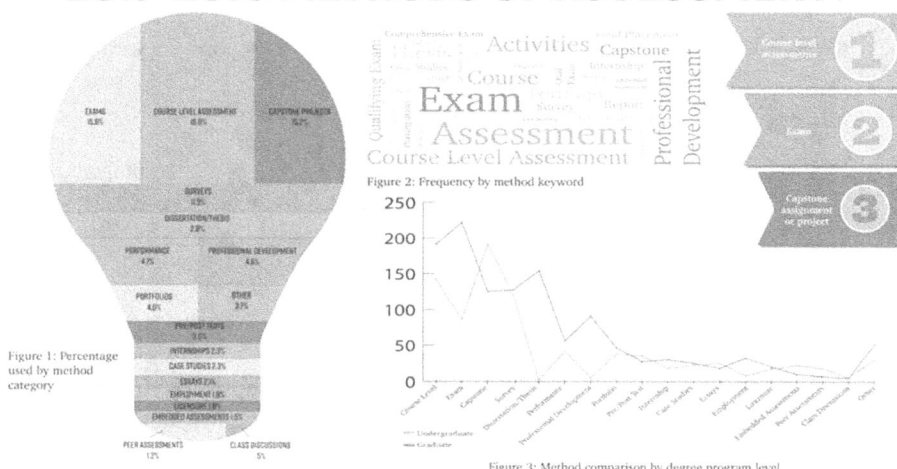

Figure 9.1. TTU Office of Planning and Assessment 2017-2018 means of program assessment infographic.

As Figure 9.1 illustrates, most assessment is performed at faculty and administrative levels. Instructors assess student learning outcomes by evaluating students' work or work products. Only the data collected through surveys, such as teaching evaluations and peer assessments, give any quantifiable insights into how students think or feel about their programmatic successes. As Christine Masters-Wheeler and Gracemarie Mike Fillenwarth's chapter in this collection specifically details, program assessment typically begins with a subject matter expert(s)—often a faculty member or team—deciding on a set of identifiable, measurable objectives that will demonstrate student learning. What is notable about this common educational procedure (as well as in Figure 9.1) is that the individuals being assessed—students engaged in degree programs—are rarely consulted during curricular design, assessment, and redesign processes. While graduate and alumni surveys as well as exit interviews are sometimes employed in program assessment (see, for example, Carnegie and Crane, 2019), most curricular and assessment plans focus on expert or faculty input. Student input, perceived as lacking subject matter expertise, is absent. Yet students have first-hand knowledge of how well a program is working. They can discuss whether courses are working holistically to build knowledge and support skills-development or are disconnecting in ways that a single instructor could not foresee or even imagine. Engaging students adds an important and often silenced voice in the assessment process. This study addresses student silence by centering on student experience while completing a degree: it directly engages students in curricular development and assessment.

The site for this case study is the professional communication department (PCOM) at Texas Tech University. The program studied is the digital media and professional communication (DMPC) degree, which was officially approved and created along with the professional communication department in September 2018. The PCOM department and DMPC degree were inspired by a group of College of Media and Communication alumni who brought their career changes to administrators' attention: they had all earned bachelor's degrees in communication studies, journalism, public relations, or advertising; yet they found, as the years passed, that job opportunities or market pressures had required them to transition from one communication field to another. They encouraged administrators to design a degree—which became the DMPC—that was broader in scope, offering upper-level courses across communication fields rather than educating students with a deep knowledge of a single field. The PCOM department was formed to house these majors and to house the faculty who would provide students with knowledge of business and professional communication practices undergirding courses.

Initiating a new department and a new degree simultaneously provides a unique longitudinal research opportunity to employ user experience (UX) methods to gauge the efficacy of the degree plan and its outcomes through extended input from students from their matriculation to graduation. To take advantage of this opportunity, PCOM department administrators designed a four-year longitudinal research project to study the first four years of the DMPC program by following its majors as they progress through their degrees. The first class of DMPC majors is the cohort of undergraduate majors who declared under the 2018–2019 calendar; these students and those who join them in 2019–2020, 2020–2021, and 2021–2022 will comprise the population of the study. This population of majors may attend Texas Tech at either the Lubbock, Texas or the Waco, Texas campus, where the DMPC degree is approved for delivery. This study employs user experience research methods to gather the perspectives of these majors over time and to use that data to design a viable assessment plan, develop curriculum, and generate recruiting and marketing materials for the DMPC. Using Patricia Sullivan's (1989) definition of *longitudinal field studies* as a guide, this research project is designed to "employ qualitative methods to study a group or a number of individuals over a period of time" (p. 13). In her discussion of such studies, Sullivan cautions researchers who choose to use this method: longitudinal field studies are resource-, time-, and labor-intensive.

Further complicating the decision to conduct longitudinal research with user experience methods was the awareness that using UX and longitudinal methods may seem contradictory. As this collection's first two chapters argue, *UX methods* are intended to be local, ungeneralizable, and fit to specific situations, to specific products, and to the specific users who engage with products. UX methods, consequently, are associated with lean principles and agile design processes, while a longitudinal study, by definition, examines change over extended periods of time. Put in racing terms, UX research is a series of sprints, while longitudinal research is a marathon. Slightly modifying the race metaphor, however, alleviates the contradiction; if one thinks of the sprints as legs of a distance relay, then each leg (or sprint) moves the research forward until the final leg is completed and the research is done. Planning and conducting a longitudinal study with UX methods thus requires a researcher to set goals for each leg as well as for reaching the finish line.

This chapter (TTU IRB #2019-58) reports the findings of the first sprint, the first completed year, of the longitudinal study. Unlike other chapters in this collection, this chapter is not retrospective; it is a study in progress—or as SACSCOC (2018) notes, a study in "continuous improvement"—as assessment projects should be. This chapter focuses on the study's design and its initial findings. It details the five user experience methods/activities in the study's design, provides a rationale for their use, and maps these methods into a four-year timeframe. It then provides results from initial data collected in order to present a student-user profile. Finally, it discusses the value of including UX methods as assessment tools for degrees in professional and technical communication.

This chapter, on the other hand, does not claim to report generalizable findings or claim to be a complete picture of the program under study or of its students. The findings reported are, unquestionably, the first of a four-year study. Furthermore, the initial findings are meager, at best. Yet the findings do provide insights about programmatic longitudinal study design that can aid program administrators, and they also provide preliminary insights into the experiences of student-users who engage in programmatic study.

■ User Experience and Program Assessment

As other authors in this collection have noted, user experience research engages actual users in the design, assessment, and redesign of products, most commonly technological ones. It is the culmination of research, design, and testing to understand the user's experience before, during, and after their encounter with a product. It focuses on the users' motivations for selecting and using a product rather than experts' assumptions of users' needs (Getto & Beecher, 2016; Rose et al., 2017; Still & Crane, 2016).

The design product in this study is not a technological product, per se; it is a degree program, the DMPC. The population under study are the first four years of DMPC majors. In addition to participating in annual surveys and focus groups, samples of DMPC majors will engage with program administrators using three other user experience methods: user profiles, personas, and journey mapping. Through these methods, program administrators hope to gain insights into student decisions and other experiences as they engage with the program's faculty, advisors, and staff, seeking guidance on the degree plan, internship opportunities, and job market opportunities. The insights gained, in turn, will allow programmatic faculty to assess the degree program, to identify strengths and weaknesses, and potentially to modify the program and its curriculum to improve its efficacy. Thus, the research design not only informs the program stakeholders, such as the department chair and faculty who serve on the curriculum committee, but it also has the potential to improve student knowledge of how to fulfill degree plans, how to identify and select internships, and how to market themselves for post-graduation employment. Because of its potential to inform programmatic decisions and bolster student educational success, this study seems well worth the required investments in time, resources, and labor.

UX Methods Deployed in the Study

This study will proceed in four phases, from January 2019 through the December 2022 semester, excluding summers. Program administrators will gather student data using five UX methods: *surveys, user profiles, personas, journey mapping,* and *focus groups*. These methods and their phases are depicted in Figure 9.2 and detailed in this section.

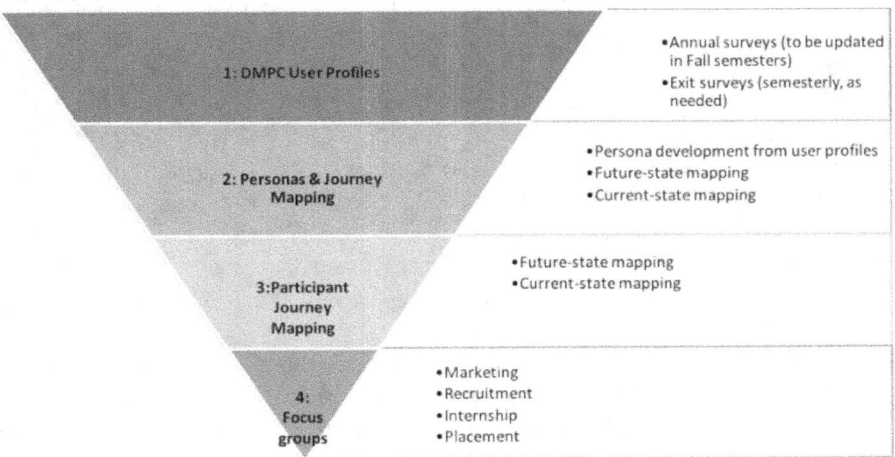

Figure 9.2. Study longitudinal phases and UX methods.

Surveys and Focus Groups (Phases 1 and 4)

Surveys and focus groups are useful for collecting aggregate data on DMPC majors as a whole, including their attitudes and experiences. Phase 1 of this research relies on annual surveys to collect both quantitative and qualitative data about DMPC majors' demographics and attitudes. These data will be aggregated to develop user profiles and personas. Students who leave the DMPC program will be asked to complete an exit survey to discover their attitudes and motivations for leaving or changing majors. This survey will also assist in identifying program competitors. Phase 1 of this project will be *iterative*, repeating on a semesterly (exit survey) or yearly rotation (annual survey).

While surveys are the first interaction students will have with this research, focus groups will be their last. Conducted in Phase 4 of the study, a *focus group* is an interview with a group of people who are "brought together to discuss their experiences or opinions around topics introduced by a skilled moderator who facilitates an open, nonjudgmental atmosphere" (Baxter et al., 2015, p. 340). Each focus group session will last approximately two hours and be held in a designated focus group room with audio and video recording capabilities. The focus group team will include the moderator and at least one additional researcher to take notes. The focus group will provide a concluding snapshot of student experiences with DMPC courses, degree plans, advisors, and administrators. It will also ask majors for their ideas on degree revisions, innovations, and marketing and recruiting materials.

User Profiles and Personas (Phases 1 and 2)

User profiles are summaries of the mindset, motivations, and goals of a group of product users. *User profiles* demarcate the characteristics that all or most of the individuals within the group possess; they are developed from actual data collected from the group.

What distinguishes profiles from personas is the difference between group and individual characteristics as illustrated in Figure 9.3. The user profile provides actual data about all or most DMPC majors, while *personas* are fictionalized stand-ins that user experience researchers create to remind them of their actual users. "Personas take a user profile and then fill in the details to create a 'typical' user" (Baxter et al., 2015, p. 41). As such, personas share characteristics of the group, but they also have distinguishing features that extend beyond group characteristics.

For example, based on university advising demographics, the user profile of DMPC majors would have several easily identifiable commonalities: they are all undergraduates at Texas Tech, and, thus far, they are all Texas residents. Individually, however, Persona 1 might be a first-year student from an urban area who resides on the Lubbock campus; Persona 2 might be a first-year student from a rural community who commutes from home to Lubbock to attend classes; and Persona 3 might be a junior transfer student from an urban area who attends classes online. So while user profiles provide designers with the big picture of the group, personas focus on key differences, such as means of attending classes and classifications. The DMPC user profile design concludes the first iteration of Phase 1. Because the annual survey will be repeated twice more, user profiles may be updated after each survey.

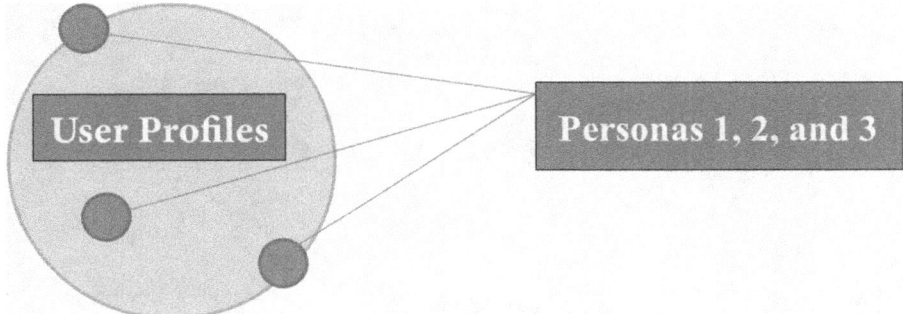

Figure 9.3. Distinguishing between user profiles and personas.

Personas

In the spring semester of 2020, program administrators will invite a random sample of DMPC majors to meet for the first time in a persona development workshop. This workshop begins Phase 2 of the study. After completing the required Institutional Review Board (IRB) informed consent procedures, administrators will report the aggregate survey results—the user profile—to participants, explaining how user profiles inform user experience research and how they lead to the development of personas. They will then explain how to construct personas of DMPC majors from key demographics, interests, and opinions.

After this introductory discussion, administrators will ask participants to work in groups to generate a specific persona for the study—a "typical" DMPC major. To generate a persona, DMPC majors will complete the following steps as defined in Luma Institute's (2012) *Innovating for People*:

- Write a personal description of each type.
- Give them realistic names.
- Include a representative portrait for each persona.
- Describe their distinguishing characteristics.
- Establish their needs and goals.
- Summarize their mindset with a memorable quote.
- Compose a one-page summary sheet for each type (n.p.).

Using examples like Figure 9.4, administrators will prepare students to construct their own personas of DMPC majors.

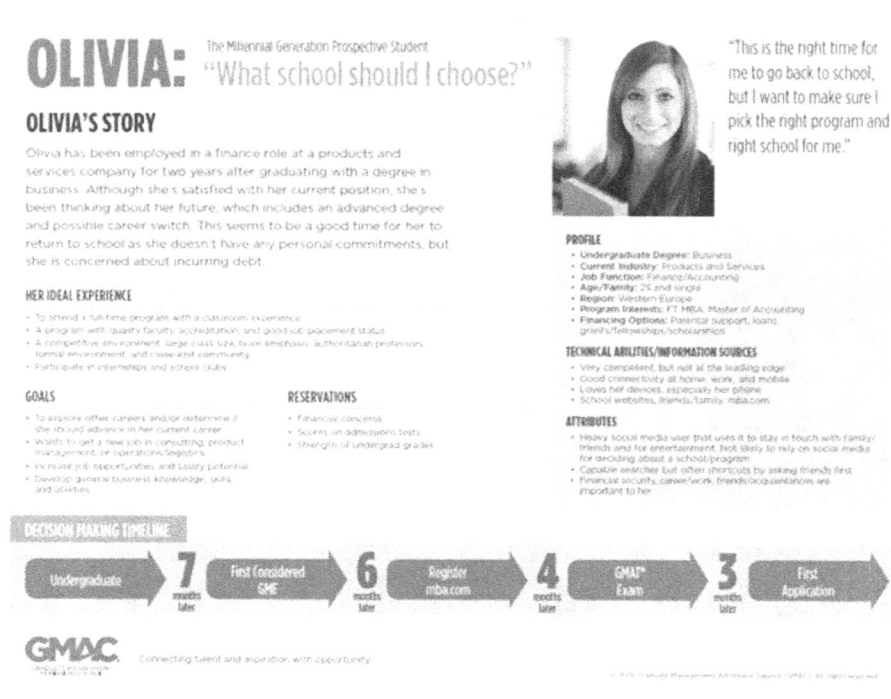

Figure 9.4. Persona of student, Olivia (McKay, 2015).

The first spring meeting will conclude with the development of three to five personas that will be used in the next meeting. These personas will also be used for training purposes as participants learn more about journey mapping, which is described in the next subsection.

Journey Mapping (Phase 3)

Phase 3 of the study requires participants to create two kinds of journey maps, one for their fictional personas and a second for themselves. A *journey map* is a "visual depiction of what users need and what steps they take to fulfill those needs as they interact with a product" (Still & Crane, 2016 p. 95) from first interaction to last. Journey maps generated in this study focus on how personas (and eventually participants) begin their journey with the declaration of the DMPC major and end with their leaving the major or graduation. *Maps of experience*, as James Kalbach (2016) defines them, allow designers to "focus on the story you need to tell in your organization" (p. 274). Through their stories or timelines, these maps allow designers to track a user's experience "not only for pain points, struggles, and fears in an experience, but also aspects that motivate and encourage" (Kalbach, p. 275). Figure 9.5 provides an example of a persona's journey map. Customer Linda's journey to find specific information is mapped: stages of the experience, activities completed and attempted, feelings and needs, and potential opportunities for improvement (Monroe & Chronister, 2015).

Using UX Methods to Gauge Degree Efficacy   205

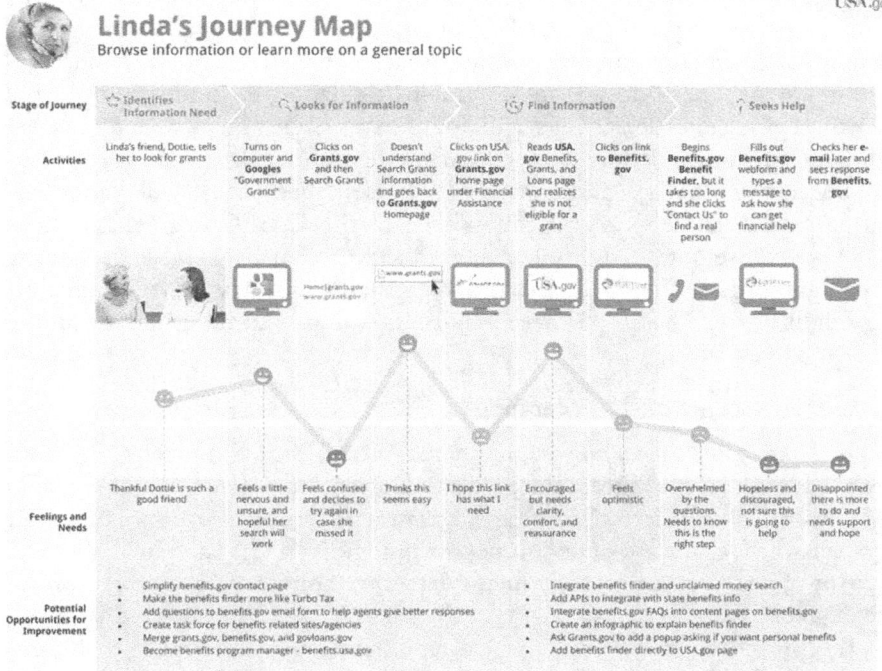

Figure 9.5. Journey map example (Monroe & Chronister, 2015).

As Figure 9.5 illustrates, journey maps often look like timelines with interactions drawn and described on them, but they can also include emoticons that depict how the user feels about the interaction. DMPC majors will engage in two journey-mapping activities over the course of the study: future-state and current-state journey mapping.

Future-State Journey Mapping

After completion of their fictionalized personas, participants will be asked to return for a second meeting. Participants will learn about and practice future-state journey mapping in this session. *Future-state journey mapping* asks participants to imagine a future journey/path that their persona might take to complete a specific goal, or, in this case, graduation with a DMPC degree. Future-state journey mapping will also be used in later research sessions (Fall 2020 and Fall 2021) when participants are asked to map their own future-state journeys.

In future-mapping sessions, program administrators will explain journey mapping as a concept and practice and then provide participants with supplies they need to complete the activity: poster-size paper or post-it notes, markers, degree plans, elective lists, and undergraduate catalogs. They will ask participants to map their persona's journey from choosing the DMPC program to graduating with the DMPC degree. Participants will have to puzzle through degree plan requirements and catalog course descriptions to successfully map their persona's journey from matriculation to graduation. At the end of the session, debriefings will follow, describing maps and discussing different paths and rationales used. After the debriefing, future-state maps will be used for analysis. These maps will be useful because they depict potential paths that students might follow to earn the DMPC degree. The maps may also expose potential problems ahead as well as participant expectations, hopes, and dreams. They may also provide insights into how DMPC scheduling might proceed based on these majors' intentions and their understanding of the degree plan.

Current-State Journey Mapping

Current-state journey mapping depicts actual interactions and touchpoints with the product instead of future interactions. Current-state maps can be updated as the user's actual interactions progress toward graduation. After walking their personas through future-state journey mapping, DMPC majors will generate their own current-state journey maps, depicting how they have progressed in the degree.

The procedures for completing current-state maps are similar to future-state maps. To remind students how journey maps work, administrators will use the persona maps that students generated previously and explain how participants will create their own journey maps in this session. After the review, administrators will provide participants with the supplies they need to complete the activity and ask them to map their personal journey from choosing the DMPC program to the current semester. Participants will again puzzle through related documents to successfully map their journeys from beginning to current-state. At the end of the session, participants will debrief the maps, describing their journeys. When journey maps are employed in later years, participants will update their maps to include additional touchpoints (advising meetings, courses, internships, and other activities) that have occurred since their last mapping session. After each session, program administrators will collect the maps for analysis and use in future sessions.

Summary of Phases, Methods, and Anticipated Outcomes

As noted earlier, this longitudinal study will continue for at least four years, beginning in 2019 and ending in 2022. While the four study phases will be deployed chronologically (first, surveys and user profiles; second, personas; third, journey mapping; and fourth, focus groups), some phases, such as annual surveys and current-state journey mapping, will be repeated iteratively to refine further what we know about our population of DMPC majors. To encourage students to participate in these activities, program administrators will provide three incentives: all group meetings will include popular meals, such as pizza or burgers; at the end of each session, one student from each group will be randomly selected to receive a $50 gift certificate; and all group meetings will include opportunities to meet and work with administrators, faculty, and advisors in the PCOM program. (Funds for six gift certificates were generously provided by an assessment award from TTU's Office of Planning and Assessment.)

Table 9.1 provides a summary of the phases: phase/focus, research questions, methods, and anticipated outcomes. Of particular note in Table 9.1 are the foci for each phase, as each phase's focus is designed to collect data from majors but also to educate majors about degree planning, internship preparation, and job placement opportunities.

Table 9.1. Summary of study phases, foci, research questions, and outcomes

Phase/Focus	Research questions	Methods	Outcomes
Phase 1: Focus on DMPC majors	• Who are DMPC majors? • What are their career goals? • Why did they major in DMPC?	• Annual survey • User profile development	• Collect demographic information and attitudes about department, college, and university in order to create a DMPC user profile. • Create user profile.
Phase 1, cont.: Focus on retention	• Why do majors change or leave the DMPC program?	• Exit survey	• Identify pain points. • Identify competitors.
Phase 2: Focus on personas	• What are the characteristics of personas needed to track typical user experience in the DMPC program?	• Persona development	• Develop 4–5 personas.
Phase 3: Focus on personas' journeys from degree plans to specializations/minors	• By their sophomore year, what courses would these personas have taken and what experiences would these personas have had with faculty, advisors, and peers?	• Persona current- and future-state journey mapping	• 1. DMPC majors identify pathways personas need for major, minor, and/or specializations.

Phase/Focus	Research questions	Methods	Outcomes
Phase 3, cont.: Focus on personas' journeys from degree plans to specializations/minors	• What courses should DMPC majors take to complete degree plans? • What courses should DMPC majors take to graduate with a minor and/or specialization?	• DMPC major current-and future-state journey mapping	• DMPC majors identify pathways needed for major, minor, and/or specializations.
Phase 3, cont.: Focus on internships	• How will/do courses prepare students for internships? What kinds of internships appeal to DMPC majors?	• DMPC major current- and future-state journey mapping	• Update current- and future-state DMPC journey maps. • Compare students' identified skills and coursework with those requested in internship opportunities. • Understand students' internship interests and connect to career plans.
Phase 4: Focus on degree innovations	• What recommendations do DMPC majors have for improving degree offerings and student support?	• Focus group	• Collect recommendations for degree design changes and course improvement.
Phase 4, cont.: Focus on marketing and recruitment	• What information should marketing and recruitment materials contain to attract students to this major?	• Focus group	• Collect recommendations for marketing and recruiting materials.

▪ Phase 1 Findings: Surveys and User Profile Development

To begin this study, DMPC majors were invited to complete the initial Qualtrics survey in Spring 2019, and the survey was repeated in early Fall 2019. Responses from both surveys were used to generate a user profile of the current DMPC major. Survey responses included student classifications, genders, ethnicity/races, and motivations for majoring in DMPC. Both Qualtrics surveys required a log-in, which prevented participants from submitting multiple submissions to either survey. Survey settings allowed anonymous responses, protecting student identity. Data from these surveys combined with data collected from the TTU Office of Planning and Assessment have been used to gain insights into the group's demographics, personal motivations, and goals. Those insights have been used to generate a profile that fits the DMPC first class as a whole. Specific insights from the surveys—the DMPC user-profile characteristics—are reported later in this chapter. Currently, the first iteration of Phase 1 is complete. The annual surveys have been launched, and a preliminary user profile has been developed. In addition, program administrators have gathered data from our DMPC advisor and the Texas Tech University FactBook to expand and compare survey findings. This section of the chapter details the results of this data collection phase.

An Opening Word About Response Rates and the Challenges of Surveys

Without question, the most important findings from Phase 1 are methodological: Using surveys to gauge student opinion and motivations is challenging. By the time program administrators received IRB approval, they had less than one month in which to launch the survey in Spring 2019. To be sure that the survey did not land in students' email junk folders, they requested that the DMPC advisor send the survey to students using software that allows her to send blanket emails to all majors. The survey was distributed to the approximately 30 majors at that time. In addition, the DMPC advisor sent two survey reminders after seven and ten days. At the end of the semester, two weeks later, administrators closed the survey. Five majors responded, a response rate of 17 percent. As required by the study's iterative design, the survey was reopened, and a request to respond was sent to majors again in Fall 2019. The number of majors had increased at the time of the survey to 61. Two reminders were sent following the initial request, but responses were again disappointing. Only eight majors responded, for a response rate of 13 percent. While these response rates certainly are not as high as administrators would have liked, online survey instruments, such as SurveyMonkey (Porter, 2020) and SurveyGizmo (Fryrear, 2015), suggest that online surveys typically have no higher than 15–20 percent response rates.

Because survey results provide useful information about DMPC majors, the results are reported in this section in spite of the low response rates. While such low rates may be criticized for their lack of generalizability, ignoring the results of those majors who did respond, from administrators' perspectives, would be indefensible. In other words, administrators realized that although the response rate was low, even a low response rate was user data that offered important insights about programmatic efficacy. To ignore the data would be to, once again, ignore the student-users who participated. If the image of students provided by these results was unclear, the image, inexact as it was, was the only one available. Further, administrators knew they would be repeating the survey annually and hoped that the picture would become clearer as the research progressed and other methods were deployed.

A related problem to lack of response is the moving target that is the number of majors in an academic program. When administrators designed the study, they proposed following the first 17 students who chose the major at the time of its first approval. By the time they had deployed the first survey, eight months after the degree was approved, the number of majors had grown to 30. Over the summer into the early fall semester, the number of majors continued to increase. In December of 2019, the number of majors had grown to 91. Although the major has a mix of undergraduates at all classifications, administrators have yet to graduate any majors, and the number of majors is increasing at the rate of approximately 30 students per semester. This growth is a result of the popularity of the DMPC major, which allows students to take courses broadly across the five departments in our College of Media and Communication: advertising and brand strategy, communication studies, journalism and creative media industries, professional communication, and public relations. Another factor that has added to the DMPC major's popularity is its design that appeals to transfer students. The DMPC program is designed so that students can enter the degree with a 60-hour core-complete associate's degree from a Texas university and complete the DMPC program with only an additional 60 credit hours. This "core-complete option" has made it a popular choice for transfer students both at the Lubbock and Waco campuses.

While the degree's growth is a boon to the department and college, its effects on the study design have been complicating. Administrators had intended initially to follow the first 17 majors, but that number had increased to 30 by the time the study was approved by the IRB. Of those original 17, only 13 were still in the major (three have changed majors and one has left the university). Because of the increase, administrators decided to send the survey to all majors, regardless of when they chose the major.

Survey and Other Data Analysis

The desired outcome of the initial annual surveys in Spring and Fall 2019 was to construct a workable user profile of DMPC majors. This profile would provide a snapshot of the common features of survey participants. From data collected in the initial surveys and from advising records, administrators are now able to identify these commonalities:

- All of the current DMPC majors are Texas residents.

- They have an average GPA of 2.85, with a median of 2.82, and a mode of 2.85.
- One-third of majors selected the DMPC program in academic year 2018–2019 when it was first approved; the other two-thirds selected the major in 2019–2020.
- First-year and junior classifications were the highest growth classifications for the DMPC major in 2019.
- DMPC student ethnicities were on par with TTU overall ethnicity figures, although the DMPC program had higher percentages of Hispanic and Black (Not of Hispanic Origin) than university averages.
- Sixty-three percent of DMPC majors have permanent residences in urban Texas cities and metroplexes, including Dallas-Fort Worth, San Antonio, and Houston. The other 37 percent are from rural areas and mid-size urban cities in West and Central Texas, such as Lubbock and Waco.

While these demographics provide us with a relatively broad swath of information about our majors, the two surveys provided more details. Three questions on the survey asked respondents about factors that influenced their choice of a major generally and their choice of the DMPC major specifically.

Factors Affecting Major Choice

Majors were asked to rank factors that affected their choice of major from 1 (least important) to 5 (most important). A summary of results appears in Figure 9.6.

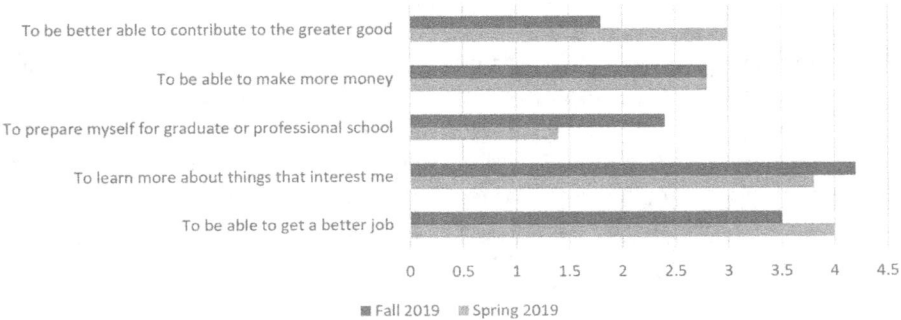

Figure 9.6. Factors affecting choice of major. 0=least important to 5=most important.

Respondents in both surveys identified two factors—to learn more about things that interest me and to be able to get a better job—as most important. Preparing for graduate school was the least important factor, while the other two factors—to make more money and to contribute to the greater good—were rated mid-field. These results, considered with the results of the more specific choices question, provide a clearer picture of survey participants' motivations. Figure 9.7 summarizes the factors affecting their choice of the DMPC program.

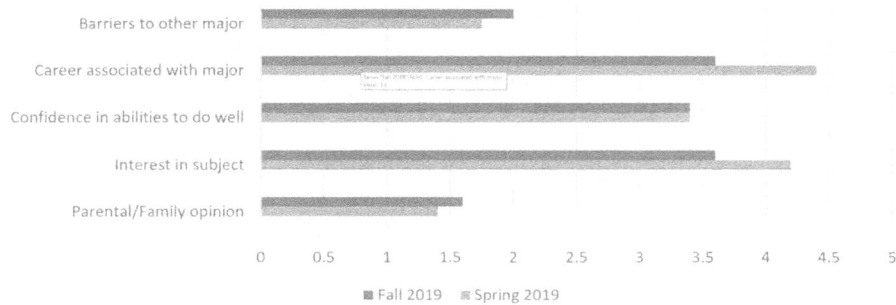

Figure 9.7. Factors affecting DMPC choice. 0=least important to 5=most important.

In response to these choices, respondents ranked career opportunities, confidence in ability to do well, and interest in subject as highly important, while barriers to another major and parental/family opinion were ranked least important.

An open question asked respondents to explain, in their own words, why they chose the DMPC major. All respondents completed this question, and three themes emerged in their answers: breadth of coursework, flexibility of scheduling, and career opportunities from the major. Sample responses from the survey are listed below:

- Because it encompassed all of the majors offered in the college, making me a well-rounded student
- It encompasses all of the educational aspects that I have the most interest in for my career.
- I initially liked this major because it seemed broad and I wasn't sure what I wanted to do in my professional career. Now that I have a couple internships under my belt as well as a few classes, I recognize the value of this degree because of where the communication industry is headed: using more broad skills and requiring me to have knowledge in several areas, including but not limited to: writing, photography, cinematography, graphic design, media relations, advertising, and public speaking.
- I chose this major because it gave me more freedom to choose other classes in the college. I wanted knowledge in more than one area of study and this was a flexible degree plan to do so.

These quotes provided insight into the ways these DMPC majors were thinking about their major as well as how the program was marketing the major to students.

Satisfaction With the Major

In addition to asking students about their choice of major, the survey asked participants about their satisfaction with a number of institutional and programmatic interactions. On a scale of 1 (least satisfied) to 3 (very satisfied), majors were asked to rank their satisfaction with faculty, peers, and classes. Figure 9.8 summarizes their opinions.

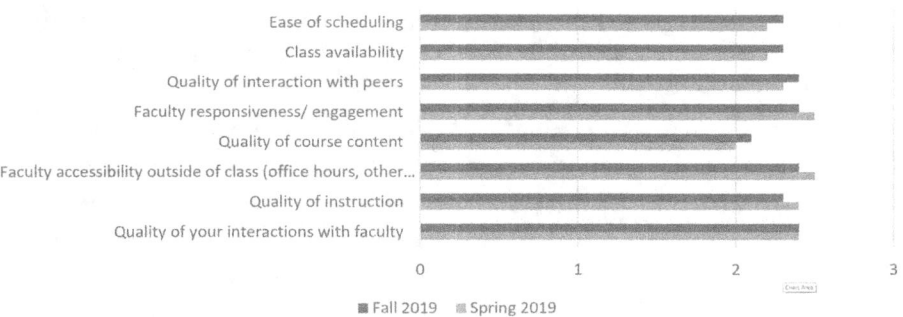

Figure 9.8. Satisfaction with faculty, peers, and courses. 0=satisfied to 3=satisfied.

In general, results from this question illustrated that respondents are satisfied to very satisfied with their courses and instructors. Of all the categories, course content was ranked lowest in satisfaction; however, this lower ranking may be a result of most of these students still taking required courses. Even juniors and seniors who transfer into the program must complete approximately 12 hours of lecture-style, large-format courses before they can take smaller, more specific courses related to their major.

A second satisfaction question asked specifically about academic advising. The College of Media and Communication has a central advising unit, but each major has a designated advisor who works closely with all students in that major. In addition, the college and the department have regular recruitment and study-abroad fairs where majors are invited to meet and converse with college deans, department chairs, and faculty. As with the previous satisfaction question, survey respondents were satisfied to very satisfied with academic advising they had received. Figure 9.9 summarizes these results.

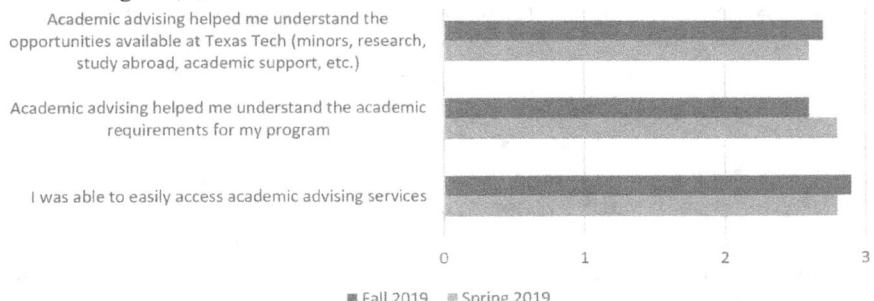

Figure 9.9. DMPC majors' satisfaction with academic advising. 0=least disagree to 5 =agree.

Proficiency Perceptions

The survey included a question asking students to evaluate their preparation for specific career-related requirements. Their evaluation was based on a three-point

Likert scale, ranking their preparation from "not prepared" to "very prepared." Student responses indicated that they felt prepared to very prepared in almost every requirement, as summarized in Figure 9.10.

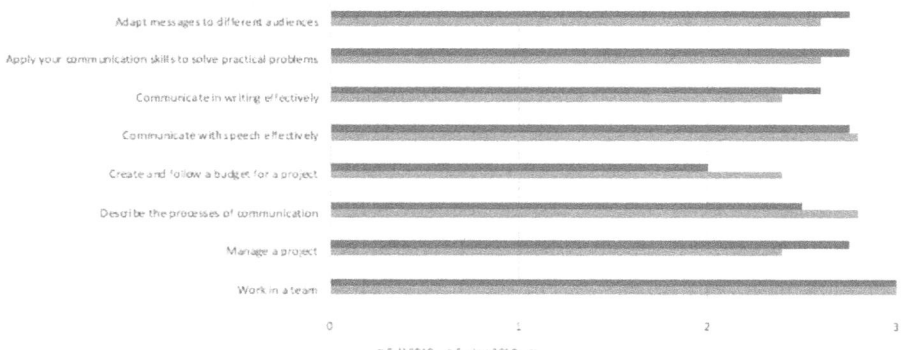

Figure 9.10. DMPC majors' perceptions of profic. 0=not prepared to 3-very prepared.

Moving From Survey Data to DMPC Major Profile

Although the survey responses were meager, a snapshot appears from the data collected. All of these respondents are from the same state, but their homes are spread across a wide geographic area. Most respondents live in or near large urban areas within the state, but they are attending a university with campuses in smaller cities (Lubbock and Waco). The majority of respondents are White, but a growing number have Hispanic and Black ethnicities. They range across all classifications, but most respondents come into the DMPC program as first-year students or juniors who transfer from a two-year college or another major.

The majors who responded are unified about the decisions they made to choose the DMPC degree. They indicate that they have chosen the degree because they want careers in a field that interests them. They are not interested in seeking a graduate degree or attending a professional school after graduation. They are only moderately motivated by money, and they have chosen their majors based on their interests, not their parents' influence. Thus far, they are fairly satisfied with their teachers, their advisors, their courses, and their peer interactions. They would like to take more courses with content that interests them. Finally, they are confident in their career skills preparation. They are most confident in their ability to work with others in teams and their speaking abilities. Their project management skills are an area where they feel they need more preparation. Overall, however, the survey respondents are happy with their choices, their degree requirements, and the individuals associated with them. Figure 9.11 is an example of a DMPC user profile.

Using UX Methods to Gauge Degree Efficacy   215

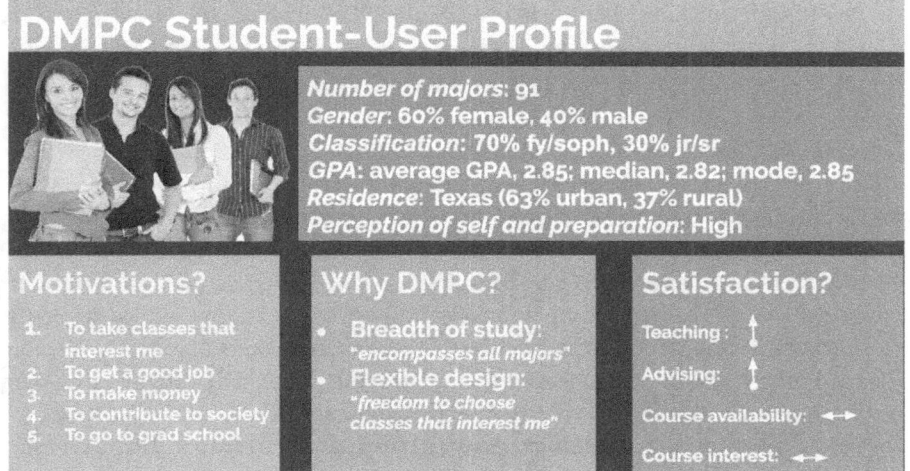

Figure 9.11. DMPC user profile.

■ The View from Here and Moving Forward

While the surveys and other data collected have given us an opening profile of DMPC majors, not all aspects of the snapshot are perfectly clear. Several of these problem areas are discussed in this section as well as the solutions being implemented to address them.

The Problem of Low Response Rates

As discussed in the previous section, the question of low student response rates is complicated: was the low response rate tied to time constraints, apathy to responding to emails, a dislike or oversaturation of survey requests, something else, or a combination of the above? Whatever students' reasons, one answer seems clear: DMPC majors, as a whole, do not see themselves as co-designers of this curriculum. Or as Kate Crane (personal communication, 2020) questioned, "How do we reprogram students when they've been programmed to receive academic plans, not be partners in creating them?" One possible remedy is to increase student engagement in the process. Incentives may lead to student engagement and help them gain a better understanding of the degree program and its opportunities. This understanding should lead to increased participation, but only time will tell. Another possible reason for low response rates is that students do not respond to email, preferring other channels to communicate. This possibility has led administrators to consider other means of survey completion, such as the classroom touchpoints described next.

Response Rate Solution: Classroom Touchpoints

Although the low survey response rate is an obvious weakness of the study, this problem has already led to curricular action. PCOM faculty and administrators have developed and are in the process of approval for two first-year courses (four hours total). The first one, Introduction to Professional Communication, will be a one-hour course which introduces students to the major, provides them with opportunities to speak with college alumni who work in professional communications, and offers the curricular pathways to complete their degree plans. A second three-hour course, Foundations in Professional Communication, will offer a broad survey of careers, competencies, and case studies to introduce students to concepts encountered in their degree plans. Taken as their first courses in the major, both the Introductions and Foundations courses will provide students with a broad foundation for the rest of their coursework. A final course, Capstone in Professional Communication, will conclude their degree. The Capstone will follow the organization of *Managing the Communication Function* (Gayeski, 2016), a publication of the International Association of Business Communicators. This textbook will prepare majors to move from coursework into the professional or corporate communication workplace. These courses will bookend students' degree experiences; but, more importantly from an assessment standpoint, these courses will provide opportunities to survey and interview students in classes as they begin and end their degrees. Having dedicated classroom touchpoints in the major where surveys can be included should help to solve the response rate problem.

Perception vs. Reality

As noted in the DMPC major profile, DMPC majors who responded to the surveys have high confidence in their career preparation. Although administrators are pleased to know that DMPC majors feel confident about their preparation, their overall GPAs (2.85 average) and their coursework status (primarily still being in first- and second-year required courses as opposed to advanced courses) suggest that administrators need measures other than student self-report to assess these skills. Student data about their perceptions of preparation is important; it lets program administrators and advisors know that they are moving them in the right direction, but they need more than student perceptions to evaluate a program's efficacy. The DMPC degree was approved with viable assessment outcomes, but administrators have very little data thus far on those outcomes. The first DMPC majors will graduate no sooner than August 2020. In addition to plans for assessment that were built into an overall assessment plan, the focus groups that are planned for the final phase of the study will help to gather more student input as will the data the college eventually collects on student placement in its annual survey.

Finally, this preliminary snapshot will become more focused as the study progresses into Phases 2, 3, and 4 to collect more student data via journey-mapping and focus group user experience activities. Through these activities, program administrators will gain more insight into who DMPC majors are, who they want to be when they graduate, and which courses best prepare students for those careers. Administrators will also gain valuable information about students' successes as students seek and accept internships and job offers.

The Value of User Experience Data in Program Assessment

For now, the results of this study are inconclusive and provide only first impressions of DMPC majors. Through iterative studies and multiple methods, DMPC administrators recognize that program assessment is an inexact art: Some methods deployed work better than others. Some results provide better data than others. Failures are part of any UX process and cannot be avoided, but UX processes also produce successes. Furthermore, innovation is not a linear process, and continuous improvement requires longitudinal study whatever methods are used to collect and report data.

The decision to seek student input for assessment requires time, preparation, and a budget. Fortunately, administrators at this institution, with IRB approval, may bring in food for students who participate and offer small rewards for participation. As such, these administrators are particularly thankful for the Office of Planning and Assessment's Innovation in Assessment Award, which seeded their budget with an internal grant.

This study, with its UX emphasis, has moved administrative thinking in this department to another level, one where faculty and student inputs are included regularly and often within the assessment process. Whether the longitudinal study will empower students to become co-designers of the curriculum is yet to be seen. Unquestionably, engaging students and convincing them to participate in this research remains a challenge. If administrators can convince them to engage, they are optimistic that student experiences will influence their programmatic decision-making by introducing ideas and feedback that faculty and administrators could not have foreseen had they simply forged ahead with typical expert assessment mechanisms. Employing user experience methods offers a methodological rationale for including student voices and experiences in program assessment that other means of assessment simply do not. Departmental administrators also feel optimistic that adding student user experience research into the assessment mix will establish an academic culture in the department where students are truly at the center of curricular design and where participation there will inform student choices about courses to take and avenues to explore in the College of Media and Communication and beyond.

■ References

Baxter, K., Courage, C. & Caine, K. (2015). *Understanding your users: A practical guide to user research methods* (2nd ed.). Morgan Kaufmann.

Carnegie, T. A. & Crane, K. (2019). Responsive curriculum change: Going beyond occupation demands. *Communication Design Quarterly Review, 6*(3), 25–31.

Fryrear, A. (2015). Increasing your survey response rates. *Alchemer, formerly SurveyGizmo.* https://www.surveygizmo.com/resources/blog/survey-response-rates/.

Gayeski, D. (2016). *Managing the communication function* (3rd ed.). International Association of Business Communicators.

Getto, G. & Beecher, F. (2016). Toward a model of UX education: Training UX designers within the academy. *IEEE Transactions on Professional Communication, 59*(2), 153-164.

Graduate Management Admission Council. (2021). Free Persona Templates. https://www.gmac.com/reach-and-recruit-students/recruit-students-for-your-program/free-persona-templates.

Kalbach, J. (2016). *Mapping experiences: A complete guide to creating value through journeys, blueprints & diagrams.* O'Reilly.

Luma Institute. (2012). *Innovating for people: Human-centered design planning cards.*

Monroe, M. A. & Chronister, M. (2015). *Journey mapping the customer experience: A USA.gov case study.* Digital.gov. https://digital.gov/2015/08/12/journey-mapping-the-customer-experience-a-usa-gov-case-study/.

Office of Planning and Assessment. (2017-18). *2017-2018 methods of assessment.* Texas Tech University. https://www.depts.ttu.edu/opa/assessments/2017-2018-Methods-of-Assessment-Infographic.jpg.

Porter, B. (n.d.). *Tips and tricks to improve survey response rates.* SurveyMonkey. https://www.surveymonkey.com/curiosity/improve-survey-response-rate/.

Rose, J., Racadio, R., Wong, K. & Nguyen, S. (2017). Community-based user experience: Evaluating the usability of health insurance information with immigrant patients. *IEEE Transaction on Professional Communication, 60*(2), 214–231.

Southern Association of Colleges and Schools Commission on Colleges. (2018). *Principles of accreditation: Foundations for quality enhancement.* SACSCOC. https://sacscoc.org/app/uploads/2019/08/2018PrinciplesOfAcreditation.pdf.

Still, B. & Crane, K. (2016). *Fundamentals of user-centered design: A practical approach.* CRC Press.

Sullivan, P. (1989, October). Usability in the computer industry: What contribution can longitudinal field studies make? In *International Professional Communication Conference Communicating to the World* (pp. 12–16). IEEE.

10. Real-World User Experience: Engaging Students and Industry Professionals Through a Mentor Program

Lee-Ann Kastman Breuch, Ann Hill Duin, and Emily Gresbrink
UNIVERSITY OF MINNESOTA

Abstract: This case study investigates user perspectives of a "joint enterprise" that resulted from strategic interaction of students and industry professionals in a pilot mentor program. We were chiefly concerned with this question: *How might user experience in a mentor program address the academic-industry gap?* Sub-questions included the following: *What is the "user experience" of participating in a mentor program? And how can we make improvements to a mentor program based on user/participant feedback?* Findings from survey and interview responses indicated that the mentor program specifically addressed the "gap" in two ways: by providing a key learning opportunity outside of the classroom that could inform students about the field and careers and by building professional relationships and networks. Designing a mentor program from a user experience perspective proved useful as a means to cultivate real-world user experience and position students for successful entry into technical communication. Prominent themes were that community, duration, clarity of goals, and pairings are critical to mentor program success.

Keywords: advisory board, community, mentoring, students, technical communication, user experience

Key Takeaways:

- Few studies have investigated mentor relationships between students and mentors in technical communication programs.
- Mentor programs that overlap with technical communication advisory boards can be guided by the foundation of communities of practice to encourage collaboration between students and workplace professionals in a "joint enterprise."
- Mentor programs benefit from user-based design and planning that gathers perspectives of students and professionals that contribute to continuous improvement.
- This case study shares user experience results from a mentor program that resulted in recommendations for community, duration, clarity, and pairing.

- Collecting student and mentor user experience data before, during, and after participation in a mentor program allows program directors to evaluate program effectiveness from the perspective of all stakeholders.

Academia exists within a bubble. Real-world workplaces are difficult to recreate in an academic setting without students taking on intern/externships or working roles. In our experience at a large midwestern research university, engaging students with technical communication advisory board (TCAB) members and alumni is the closest that students can get to real-world hands-on experience while remaining embedded in academia. Such engagement represents an innovative approach to instructional design and assessment, one that moves both students and workplace professionals to the center of academic practice. Industry professionals provide an intimate view of workplace trends and topics, making these accessible and relevant for students via industry-academia course projects, informational interviews, webinars, and onsite visits. In turn, our vision is that engagement with academia and students increases the effectiveness of industry professionals and their industries. To encourage this kind of engagement, we decided to launch a user-centered pilot mentor program involving our students and TCAB members. In this chapter, we share our investigation of user feedback from specific mentor-mentee interaction of students and professionals in a pilot mentor program.

Our mentor program strives to narrow the gap between academic and industry understandings of technical communication, and to do so, it is informed by community of practice theory and framework. In earlier research, Ann Hill Duin and Jason Tham (2018) used Etienne Wenger's (1998) three dimensions for establishing a community of practice—joint enterprise, mutual engagement, and shared repertoire—along with Joel Kline and Thomas Barker's (2012) model for academic/practitioner collaboration that suggests that "effective collaboration among the academic and practitioner communities will improve professionalism through better research, better education, and a more comprehensive body of knowledge" (p. 33). Kline and Barker emphasized that community of practice (CoP) theory "strongly emphasizes the interactively constructed nature of engaging, belonging, and sharing tools" and "the three dimensions of community can help us to identify and understand the kinds of activities, engendered through membership in a community of practice, that lead to professionalism" (p. 35).

Our pilot mentor program was also designed and developed through the lens of user experience and user-centered design (Gould & Lewis, 1985). John Gould and Clayton Lewis (1985) coined the phrase "user-centered design" and defined it as having three central characteristics: (1) early focus on users, (2) systematic data collection, and (3) iterative design. Using this model, we wanted to investigate the "joint enterprise" that results from strategic interaction of students and industry professionals (TCAB members and program alumni) through a mentor program. We conducted a detailed case study on the impact of designing a mentor program from a user experience (UX) perspective, focusing on both what students and industry professionals want and acquire from such a program.

In theory, such a mentor program should provide students with an experience not otherwise available within a course; such external experience should strengthen their overall academic and professional experience before they enter the workforce or continue in their education. Indeed, we began this mentor program because it was a strong request from TCAB members. We then asked students and learned that they were very enthusiastic about the idea as well. We asked both parties about what each would want from a mentor program, and they mentioned the need for structure and clear delineation of roles and responsibilities: Who initiates? What is the student role? What is the mentor role? In response, we provided structural parameters for the mentor program that included the expectation that each pair meet three times in a 15-week period, that they articulate goals together, and that they let us know how they decided to structure their mentor-mentee engagement. We launched our pilot mentor program with a get-together event on campus, at which time we shared program goals and mentor resources, and their engagement began. This "interactively constructed nature of engaging, belonging, and sharing tools" allowed for both an open-ended and user-centered approach to the mentor program in that the student and paired mentor decided how they wanted to shape their meetings. For example, one pair decided to do a job shadowing, another decided to have coffee, and another decided to have a resume review. The three-meeting framework allowed for both structure and freedom to address student and mentor needs.

With Institutional Review Board (IRB) exemption approval, we gathered survey responses from participants as the pilot ended, and we conducted follow-up interviews. Throughout the pilot, we were chiefly concerned with this question: *How might user experience in a mentor program address the academic-industry gap?* Sub-questions included the following: *What is the "user experience" of participating in a mentor program? And how can we make improvements to a mentor program based on user/participant feedback?* Our goal was to integrate user feedback with instructional design to find ways to better bridge industry and academia and to engage students and industry practitioners. This approach is indeed innovative and useful as we actively practice student-practitioner engagement as a method for cultivating real-world user experience through such joint enterprise activity.

In the remainder of this chapter, we further discuss mentor programs as communities of practice, we discuss our user-based approach to this pilot study, and we share results and findings from the participants of our mentor program.

Mentor Programs, Communities of Practice, and User Experience

Most scholarship on mentor programs focuses on programs within workplaces or within academia rather than across academia and industry. Several studies have addressed mentoring for graduate students and early career faculty members in academia (Finch & Fernandez, 2014; Metzger et al., 2015; Pardun et al., 2015). Others have addressed workplace mentor programs; for example, Stephen Baer (2018) suggested that mentor programs are common within workplaces, as they can provide ongoing learning, support, and training for employees (see also Allen et al., 2009; Jones, 2012; QualComm, n.d.). Within workplace mentor programs, learning can be positively associated with factors such as affective trust (sharing bonds) and perceived organizational support (perceptions of how employees are valued; Baer, 2018). In addition, learning can be more impactful when mentor dyads are paired carefully to address similarities and differences, when expectations are clear, when participants reflect on the experience, or when mentor training is provided (Jones, 2013). Mentor experiences can be enhanced by using metaphors to facilitate conversations about complex situations, as well as questions about workplace practices or contexts (Seto & Geithner, 2018).

Very few studies in technical and professional communication have addressed mentor programs between students and workplace mentors; however, a common and related topic involves student internship programs in technical communication and ways that those programs can address the gap between academia and industry (Bloch, 2011; Henze, 2006; Kramer-Simpson, 2018; Munger, 2006; Sapp & Zhang, 2009; Sullivan & Moore, 2013). In a qualitative study of four student interns, Elisabeth Kramer-Simpson (2018) identified elements of successful internship programs that benefit students. A recurring finding was that successful internship experiences provide students with important workplace tasks while also providing freedom as well as opportunities for mistakes as learning moments. Patricia Sullivan and Kristen Moore (2013) also investigated internships, but they specifically addressed the experiences of female students in engineering programs and technical communication courses. Using feminist methodology, they found that women engineering students did not always thrive in internship situations arranged by engineering programs. Instead, Sullivan and Moore explored mentor strategies that emerged in technical communication courses required for those students and focused on daily work practices. These strategies involved time tracking, project management, and weekly memo updates, and students found these strategies very beneficial in projects involving industry clients. A key finding suggests that alternative mentor strategies may be helpful to female engineering students.

While scholarship on internships is helpful, very few, if any, studies address mentor programs outside of internships or the student/mentor experience of such pairings. Duin and Tham (2018) addressed ways that mentors from an advisory board helped with the curricular revision of a course in digital writing and content management. Using the community of practice (CoP) framework (Wenger, 1998), Duin and Tham explored three dimensions of community of practice—mutual engagement (participation from all parties), joint enterprise (negotiated goals and accountability), and shared repertoire (shared history and richness). In their study, a "shared repertoire" was mainly comprised of faculty and advisory board member discussions surrounding learning outcomes, course goals, and resulting strategic direction and course syllabi. A key conclusion was continued recognition that to keep pace with technological and industry changes, course redesign should be a collaborative endeavor with advisory board members and industry experts. Laura Gonzales and Heather Turner (2019) also examined industry-academic partnerships, specifically through a social justice lens. They described experiences with industry-academic projects involving multilingual students and communities; however, they also discovered that multilingual students experienced anxiety about mentor relationships due to racial and linguistic backgrounds and differences, resulting in labor associated with building professional networks. Gonzales and Turner in turn described several strategies to address this labor, such as grounding collaboration in empathy and listening, and building spaces for sharing stories between students and industry collaborators. Such strategies can be integrated into industry-academic partnerships, including advisory boards.

Advisory boards can indeed be helpful resources for collaborative interactions and discussions that can bridge the gap between academics and practitioners, and they can help form a key "community of practice" for students entering the workplace (Söderlund et al., 2017). Advisory boards can be great resources for mentor programs as well. Indeed, as Gonzales and Turner (2019) noted, we acknowledge the difficulty students may have establishing professional networks, and we saw our TCAB and mentor program as a response to helping students address that challenge. Our TCAB is an intergenerational group of business leaders whose purpose is to provide exemplary networking and experiential learning opportunities for students and to enrich the curriculum and visibility of our programs, students, faculty, and staff. Three of our academic programs—a B.S. in Technical Writing and Communication, a Graduate Certificate in Technical Communication, and an M.S. in Scientific and Technical Communication—have opportunities to interact with TCAB members.[1] At the time of this writing, the board included 18 members. Many serve in upper-levels of management at national/international companies; others have their own businesses; and 11 were graduates of our programs, with two being recent graduates of our B.S. program. Since the inception of our TCAB in 2014, we have created a number of opportunities for students to interact with board members, such as a connect event involving speed networking, a research showcase in which students share research projects with TCAB members for feedback and input, and webinars that feature our TCAB members and their areas of expertise.

---

1. https://cla.umn.edu/writing-studies/alumni-friends/technical-communication-advisory-board/members

Our most recent TCAB addition is the mentor program, which is the focus of our study here. In Fall 2018, we asked students and TCAB members what might best help create engaged experiences. Our TCAB members enthusiastically supported the idea of a mentor program, and when we later asked students, they also indicated strong interest. In response, in 2019, we piloted a mentor program in which we paired interested students with TCAB members (and additional alumni who served as mentors) over a 15-week period. We scheduled an initial launch meeting in which mentors and mentees met each other. At that initial meeting, we provided some background information about mentor programs (see QualComm, n.d.) and our goals of establishing greater engagement across academic and workplace contexts. For example, we mentioned the following goals:

- to build relationships that enhance professional development for both mentors and mentees
- to bridge the gap between academia and industry
- to help students develop a personal learning network (PLN) that contributes to personal, academic, and professional success
- to articulate clear goals for professional development

We provided time for the pairs to meet and asked them to articulate goals for their mentorship pairing, and we also asked them to plan for two additional points of contact in the remaining 15-week period. (See Appendix A for launch meeting worksheet.) We then asked pairs to come back to a large group discussion in which we fielded any additional questions about the program. The mentor-mentee pairs were then on their own to conduct their plans.

We use community of practice theory as a framework for our study of this mentor program, in that we are interested in Wenger's (1998) three dimensions for establishing a community of practice—joint enterprise, mutual engagement, and shared repertoire—as a framework. We are especially interested in examining the mentor program in terms of a "joint enterprise" that requires negotiated goals that are collaboratively constructed. Kline and Barker (2012) also emphasized a community of practice framework for academic-industry partnerships, and they noted the importance of collaboration between academics and practitioners:

> Similarly, industry advisory boards for academic programs, mentorship programs, and certification initiatives are good opportunities. However, their structure needs to build collaborative participation from both communities to succeed. Without collaboration, the knowledge and social presence necessary to negotiate meaning, something that Wenger (1998) notes is critical to community, fails to occur.

In addition to collaboration, an important aspect of community of practice is situated learning, or learning within a specific context. Jean Lave and Etienne Wenger (1991) suggested that new professionals learning on the job must pay attention to the contextual factors around them as they learn new tasks; it is also important for new professionals to establish positive relationships with workplace peers. Technical and professional communication scholars have also addressed the importance of situated and contextual learning in studies of new employees who have transitioned from academic to professional contexts. For example, Liberty Kohn (2015) suggested that students or new employees may feel more motivated when their writing or communication is an embedded part of a community context rather than a separate, individual "paper" in a writing classroom. In her investigation of new employees in communication roles/positions, Susan Katz (1998) also suggested that new employees are successful when they develop literacy techniques that address specific needs of a context. Dorothy Winsor (1996) also reinforced the importance of situated learning in her investigation of new engineers moving from graduation into their first professional jobs. Anne Beaufort (1999) mentioned the importance of context as well in creating appropriate documents and texts for workplaces. In sum, addressing context in new workplaces is an important aspect of belonging in a community of practice (p. 43).

A community of practice framework for the study of our mentor program also aligns well with user experience and user-centered design theory and practice. By integrating "user experience" in our mentor program, we mean understanding not just performance or preference of a specific task but rather the entire user experience before, during, and after their "use" or participation in the mentor program (see Getto & Beecher, 2016; Potts & Salvo, 2018; Rose et al., 2017; Still & Crane, 2017). As an example, Michael Salvo and Liza Potts (2018) described "experience architecture" that is not limited "to one aspect of a product" but rather one's entire experience (p. 6). Conducting this kind of user experience research requires largely qualitative research methods such as interviewing, field inquiries, and participatory design (Johnson et al., 2007; Redish, 2010; Salvo, 2001). In addition, these qualitative approaches in user experience research align with methods that technical communication scholars have advocated to investigate issues of social justice. For example, scholars in technical communication have asserted that researchers must ensure the representativeness of participants, be open to including vulnerable populations that may benefit from participating in designs, and consider qualitative methods such as storytelling to gather information about user experience (Rose et al., 2017; Walton & Jones, 2013).

Our pilot study of the mentor program embraced these user experience approaches in that we used interview methods to learn more about the broader, holistic experiences of students and mentors in the mentor program. In addition, we sought to capture the voices of as many participants in the mentor program as possible to inform the continued development of the program. Specifically, we asked users—in this case, students and mentors—to inform us of ways they believed the mentor program did or did not address the gap between academia and industry and of recommendations they would have to improve the program.

In gathering this input, we approach the mentor program through a collaboratively constructed user-centered design perspective that relies on participant research and takes into account participant contributions that will be addressed as the program continues to improve. This user-centered design approach provides the added benefit of contributing participant feedback as a kind of formative assessment of our pilot mentor program. (As noted by Crane and Cargile Cook, 2019, assessment rarely includes student perspectives or participation. We seek to integrate user-centered design by involving our participants in providing feedback for continual improvement [K. Crane & K. Cargile Cook, January 21, 2019].) Thus, we see community of practice theory as providing a necessary framework for understanding our mentor program, and user experience and user-centered theory and practice as ways to research and evaluate the program.

■ Methods

We conducted a case study of our pilot mentor program in order to gather data that would inform the user experience of students and mentors in the program. Robert Yin (2003) suggested that a case study "investigates a contemporary phenomenon within its real-life context, especially when the boundaries between phenomenon and context are not clearly evident" (p. 13). Yin explained that case studies are useful tools for better understanding contextual situations. Our case study can be explained as a single case study or an intrinsic case study which provides the opportunity to learn about one particular case (Stake, 1995). Case studies can encompass a variety of data collection methods; our case study includes a qualitative, open-ended survey and follow-up interviews, and it was conducted with the intention of evaluating the pilot and identifying ways to strengthen the mentor program. Stake (1995) might identify this case study as a type of formative evaluation that is meant to provide insights for future improvement. We integrated qualitative methods aligned with user experience research to inform our case study.

As mentioned, we began this project as a pilot study of a voluntary mentor program that would last through a 15-week period. We launched the mentor program with an initial meeting in February 2019 in which all students and mentors had the opportunity to meet. This initial meeting included an introduction to the mentor program, including an overview of participation and suggested structure for the mentor pairs. We asked mentors and students to articulate goals for participating in the program and outline three contact meetings that would occur during the program. Mentors and students were given great flexibility for articulating these goals and meetings.

Near the end of the 15-week period, we distributed a questionnaire to all participants that asked questions about the goals of their mentor pair, their meeting choices, their hopes for the program, and whether or not hopes were met. The questionnaire also asked participants for reflections about how the program addressed the academic-industry gap and any recommendations. This study was submitted to our institution's IRB board and was returned with a full exemption, stating that this work was considered program evaluation. We gathered 34 surveys out of 40 participants, or a participation rate of 85 percent. We included a question that asked about a follow-up interview; several participants agreed, and we conducted short 15-minute interviews with 23 participants. (See Appendix B.)

We gathered survey data which was offered in open-ended written responses, and we transcribed interview data in response to the following four questions:

- What was your overall experience in the mentor program?
- How do you believe the mentor program addressed (or not) the gap between academia and industry?
- In what ways did the program help?
- What recommendations do you have for improvement?

We examined responses according to the questions asked and used an emergent coding approach informed by the data rather than any predetermined coding categories. As themes were identified, we reviewed them as a team to either verify or eliminate. In the results section, we highlight results by both question and theme.

Participants

A total of 40 people participated in the mentor program—20 students and 20 mentors. Participating students represented four different academic programs in our department: two students from our M.A./Ph.D. program, six students from our M.S. professional program, six students from our Graduate Certificate program, and six students from our B.S. program in technical communication. Of the mentors, 15 were TCAB members and five were invited alumni from our various programs (see Figure 10.1).

About 12 weeks into the mentor program, we distributed a survey to all 40 participants in the program (see Figure 10.2). The survey included open-ended questions that asked participants to identify the goals they articulated for the program, the meetings they planned, their hopes and dreams for the program, whether their hopes were met, and how they believed the program did or did not address a gap between academia and industry (see Appendix B). Of 40 participants invited, 34 participants responded to the survey, for a participation rate of 85 percent. Of those responding to the questionnaire, participants included the following:

- Ten TCAB members and mentors (30.3%)
- Four invited alumni and mentors (18.2%)
- Six M.S. students (15.2%)
- Six Graduate Certificate students (18.2%)
- Two M.A./Ph.D. students (6.1%)
- Five B.S. students (15.2%)

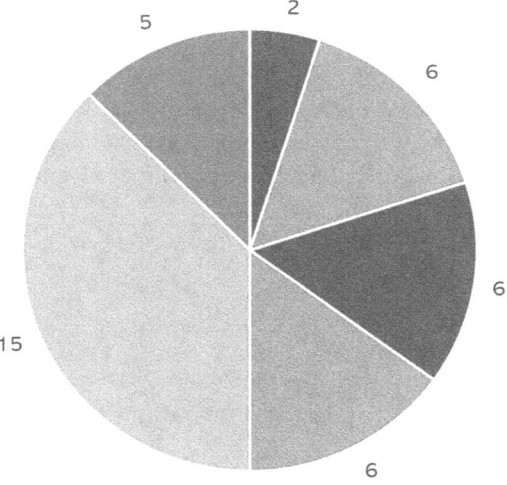

Figure 10.1. Program participants in the mentor program.

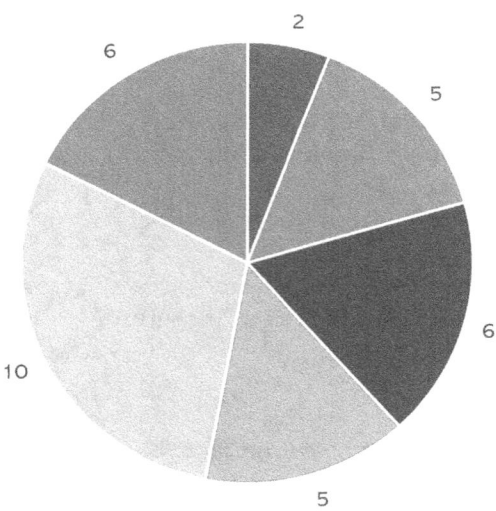

Figure 10.2. Survey participation.

The last item on the survey asked if participants would be willing to participate in a brief interview about their experience. Of the survey participants, 23 agreed to be interviewed. We scheduled brief 15-minute interviews with these participants using whatever method worked best, whether in-person, video conference, or phone. One interview was conducted with two participants at the same time; all others were conducted one-to-one. Of those completing interviews, 11 were mentors and 12 were students. Participants included the following:

- Six TCAB members and mentors
- Five invited alumni and mentors
- Four M.S. students
- Two Graduate Certificate students
- One M.A./Ph.D. student
- Five B.S. students

■ Results

Our guiding research questions addressed the user experience of participants in the mentor program, how well the mentor program addressed the gap between academia and industry, and suggestions from users/participants to improve the program. We discuss results in order of these questions, using responses from our participants from a survey and interviews about the mentor program.

Overall User Experience

Participant responses to the program and overall user experience were overwhelmingly positive. Several participants indicated that their hopes were both met and exceeded in the program. Many used the word "great" to describe their experience. Comments focused on the pairings, rapport, opportunities to engage with professionals, and flexibility of the program. One undergraduate student enthusiastically described her experience as exceeding her expectations:

> My hopes were met and exceeded by this program! I thought it was such a great opportunity to meet and engage with professionals in the field on a personal level. I learned so much from [my mentor] and she helped me feel much more prepared to move forward into my job search and eventually first career.

Graduate students seemed to appreciate having knowledgeable mentors that could help them learn more about opportunities and the field. One graduate certificate student said, "I really enjoy having a mentor that currently works in the field and is incredibly knowledgeable, friendly, and helpful." Some graduate students commented on the flexibility of the program and ways the program could continue, as seen in the following response from an M.A. student:

It was great. I enjoyed my meetings with my mentor. We decided to not continue meeting regularly, but we are staying in touch. For example, my mentor is going to be a guest presenter next week for the course I am teaching.

Mentors commented that they mostly had positive experiences and that they hoped the students would find the experience useful. Several commented on what they hoped might be helpful for students, such as sharing professional contacts. Said one mentor, "I'm here for [the student]."

Of the 34 participants responding to the survey, only six participants indicated dissatisfaction—four students and two mentors. Student comments of dissatisfaction mostly addressed disappointment that very specific expectations were not met, for example, that mentors did not have experience in their particular specialty area (e.g., usability or environmental science), or that mentors did not have advice for them on specific or personal challenge areas. Mentor comments of dissatisfaction indicated some frustration when student mentees did not contact them to set up further meetings or have clear goals for the mentorship, or that student mentees expected them to review their work or resume, like an editor or teacher. Yet, overall, these comments were few, and most participants reported positive experiences.

Interview data reinforced these findings. In response to the question "Tell me about your experience," most participants shared positive comments and gave specific examples such as:

- appreciating free-flowing discussions and the ability to address questions
- enjoying the opportunity to job shadow and/or tour a workplace
- liking the flexibility to shape the mentorship
- appreciating the initial launch meeting
- learning from mentors about everyday work practices
- learning about specialization areas of mentors
- learning from mentors about work experience across multiple industries
- learning from "very knowledgeable" mentors
- learning from mentors who are closer in age and have just graduated
- getting feedback on resumes
- appreciating the relaxed and informal tone of the program
- learning about mentor approaches or philosophies to certain kinds of work

Comments that were not positive indicated disappointment when the pairs did not find ways to meet, unclear expectations or goals, or pairs that did not result in mutual interests.

We further addressed overall user experience by examining responses from the survey or interview about mentor pair goals, meeting structures, hopes, and how hopes were met, as described in the sections that follow.

Mentor Pair Goals

To learn more about the overall user experience, we examined goals articulated by the mentor dyads as reported in the surveys. Responses indicated that goals generally addressed four areas: career and job search, professional networking, specific skill areas, and specific requests. As Table 10.1 shows, we report results according to student-expressed goals for the mentor program, differentiating between undergraduate and graduate students.

Goals related to career and job search were stated most frequently (see Table 10.1), as several students mentioned working on their resume and cover letters, updating LinkedIn profiles, strengthening job portfolios, or preparing for a job search and/or applying for jobs. However, when examined for student population, it was clear that graduate students had more specific goals for job searching than undergraduates, such as questions about part-time work, re-entering the workforce, and exploring career areas. Another strong theme related to goals for the program included professional networking, which was expressed by both undergraduate and graduate students. When examined for student population, survey responses showed that both graduate and undergraduate students expressed goals for increasing their professional networks, such as through joining professional organizations, learning more about the work of technical communicators by talking with mentors and/or other practitioners, or job shadowing. A number of responses indicated goals related to specific skill sets. As Table 10.1 shows, these goals were most frequently related to usability, but also to the medical device industry and other skill areas such as project management, improving writing, marketing, writing proposals, storytelling, writing manuals, etc. Graduate and undergraduate student responses both indicated specific skill set areas. A final category involved very specific requests of mentors such as to provide feedback on student research projects or give personal advice regarding how to productively disclose disabilities in a workplace situation.

In order to create the mentor pairings, we began by reviewing these survey responses for each participant. We also took into consideration a brief one to two paragraph statement written by each student, which expressed their specific interests and reasons for wanting a mentor through this program. Based on the student paragraphs and survey data from students and mentors, we conducted an informal coding process that looked for similar themes, interests, and goals between the students and mentors. When an ideal match surfaced in the themes, the student and mentor were paired together. Thus, while this was not a self-selected mentor pairing process, it was user-guided in that we considered student statements, goals, and interests as guidance while pairing them with mentors.

Table 10.1. Themes and Articulated Goals Reported by Students in Survey Responses

Theme	Mentions by Students (N=18)	Grad Students (N=13)	Undergrad Students (N=5)
Career and Job Search			
Working on resume and cover letter	10	9	1
Preparing for job search / applying for jobs	9	5	4
Updating LinkedIn profile	2	2	0
Strengthening job portfolio	3	3	0
Exploring career paths or directions	5	5	0
Advice on part-time work	2	2	0
Advice on transitioning to workforce	1	1	0
Total	31	26	5
Professional Networking			
Growing a professional network	5	4	1
Learn more about technical communication field	8	5	3
Job shadowing	2	1	1
Network with usability experts	4	1	3
Total	19	11	8
Strengthen Specific Skill Sets			
Learn more about the usability / human factors field	5	2	3
Learn how to create a business plan	2	2	0
Improve writing	2	1	1
Learn about issues in medical device writing	2	2	0
Learn about structured authoring and content management	2	2	0
Learn to market an idea	1	0	1
Learn to formulate a proposal	1	0	1

Theme	Mentions by Students (N=18)	Grad Students (N=13)	Undergrad Students (N=5)
Learn project management skills	1	1	0
Learn more about storytelling	1	1	0
Learn how to manage a technical team	1	1	0
Learn how to become a CTO	1	1	0
Total	19	13	6
Specific Requests of Mentors			
Feedback on B.S. undergraduate capstone project	2	0	2
Feedback on classes and goals for after graduation	1	0	1
Suggestions for how to disclose a disability with employers and develop positive avenues for working with employers	1	1	0
Total	4	1	3

Mentor Pair Meetings

We learned as well from the questionnaire that mentor dyads set up meetings in a variety of formats. For example, some pairs reported meeting virtually through video conferencing (four) and some pairs had phone meetings (two). However, most pairs met in person at least once, either at a coffee shop or restaurant, or at the workplace of the mentor for job shadowing or a tour. Regarding activities or foci of the meetings, participants mentioned reviewing resumes, LinkedIn profiles, and student academic work such as a usability report, paper, or portfolio for class; discussing career paths; touring a mentor's workplace; or job shadowing at a mentor's workplace. Some dyads reported a sequence in which one meeting was focused on the mentor's workplace and experience, and the second meeting was focused on the student's interests, whether resume, portfolio, or academic paper.

Hopes, Expectations, and How the Program Met Hopes

In our post-participation survey, we asked users what their hopes were for the program as it continues and how well their hopes are being met. We report results here according to undergraduate, graduate, and mentor populations.

Undergraduate students were overall very excited and pleased about the program and its opportunities. Most of them found their hopes met by the program;

one participant explicitly mentioned they felt their experience was not rewarding and their hopes were unmet. The undergraduate population expressed a desire to become more connected to individuals in the field and wanted a longer duration of mentorship (discussed later). They wanted to see the program become a stepping stone for undergraduates going into the workforce. One student said, 'I've really enjoyed all of the time I spent with my mentor, and I found this to be one of the most valuable, useful experiences I've had in terms of networking and career building at the U so far."

Like the undergraduate students, graduate students were overall very pleased with their experience in the program, felt their hopes were met and the program went well. Graduate students seemed to want more information about jobs and career searches. Many graduate students also noted ongoing connections with their mentors, whether formally as a mentor-mentee pair or as a connection/resource in the technical communication industry. Some students enjoyed the free structure of the program, while others sought more structure, activity suggestion, and overall guidance as a mentee. As the program continues, graduate students expressed hope in more students participating, more mentors from more industries, greater networking opportunities, and feedback as their careers evolve.

Mentors also echoed the sentiment of a positive experience with overall hopes being met. They expressed a desire to continue mentoring and felt the program was a good chance to connect with students. Some areas of change recommended by mentors included having more in-person meetings, more structure to the program, and more undergraduate-age students signing up for mentorship guidance.

How the Program Helped

A question we asked in follow-up interviews was "How did it help?" This question allowed participants to share their thoughts on how their experience participating in the mentor program helped them as students or as professionals working in industry.

The majority of undergraduate participants found the mentor program, as a whole, helpful. Specifically, the undergraduate students found that one-to-one attention from their mentors with resume and career advice from real-world workers was a helpful takeaway. The specialized attention from a one-to-one pairing allowed undergraduate students to connect with a professional on a more personalized level. One student responded,

> [My mentor was] better than [the university's] Career Center, which I visited before as a sophomore and had them look at my resume. But it was just students working there—they were older students but didn't have much to say about me. I felt they had thousands of resumes to look at so I'm not sure they could help me that much.

Additionally, many undergraduate students felt that their mentors provided a good overview of how technical communications careers could look, feel, and operate. A number of mentees mentioned their mentors walked them through daily job tasks and scenarios, and showed them where their academic careers could take them.

Graduate students shared a similar sentiment as well; many of them found their mentor's real-world experience helpful in their understanding of how a technical communication role may function. One student described their experience as a "snapshot" of what it would be like to work in the industry, having had an opportunity to observe their mentor in the workplace, in real time.

However, graduate students offered different responses than undergraduate students regarding what was helpful. While undergraduates found concrete advice helpful, such as resume editing advice, graduate students found the exchange of skills and information to be specifically helpful in their mentoring pair. A student mentioned that their mentor was helpful because the mentor had skills the mentee did not have; by sharing that information, the mentor helped the mentee to gain a useful skill. Additionally, graduate students found it helpful to have connections with technical communicators in the industry as they began to seek jobs. One student stated that it was good to be put into contact with people from a local company and that they were glad to be able to visit with people at a place where they wanted to potentially work in the near future.

From the mentor perspective, all of the mentors found the insight from students in academia to be informative for their lines of work or perspectives on learning. Many mentors enjoyed speaking one-on-one with their mentees and found their comments on career goals to be insightful. One mentor, a recent graduate, found it interesting to see where they were just a few years ago and felt it was positive to speak to someone about to graduate, since their academic career was relatively fresh as well.

Many of the mentors in this pilot are alumni of the academic program in which they are mentoring. One mentor said the experience was helpful to gain insight into what students are currently learning and experiencing in the classroom and the direction in which the program is leading students. Additionally, another alumnus found it fulfilling to give back to a program that provided a positive student experience, and mentoring was a great way to do so.

Additionally, one mentor used their experience from this pilot program to leverage a new experience in their workplace; the knowledge and skills they learned from mentoring their student translated into an opportunity to lead a mentor program in their workplace. They found the ideas and structure of this program to be informative as they helped pilot another mentoring program in the community.

How the Mentor Program Bridged the Academic-Industry Gap

In both the questionnaire and interviews, we asked a question about how well participants thought the program bridged the gap between academia and industry, and this was a key focus of our study. Again, the responses were overwhelmingly positive, yet open-ended and covered a lot of ground. After reviewing both survey and interview responses from participants, two strong themes emerged: (1) mentor program as a learning opportunity and (2) mentor program as a way to build relationships and network. The word cloud in Figure 10.3 visually depicts the most commonly used words in responses.

As shown by Figure 10.3, frequent words such as "think," "can," "know," "learn," "mentor," and "help," "helps," or "helped" demonstrate the capacity for the mentor program as a learning tool or opportunity for both mentees and mentors. Indeed, responses from participants mentioned the many areas where they gained knowledge, whether about the broad range of career opportunities in technical communication, agencies that hire, or potential career routes. Each of these areas were things that participants deemed "outside of the classroom" and a unique strength of the mentor program.

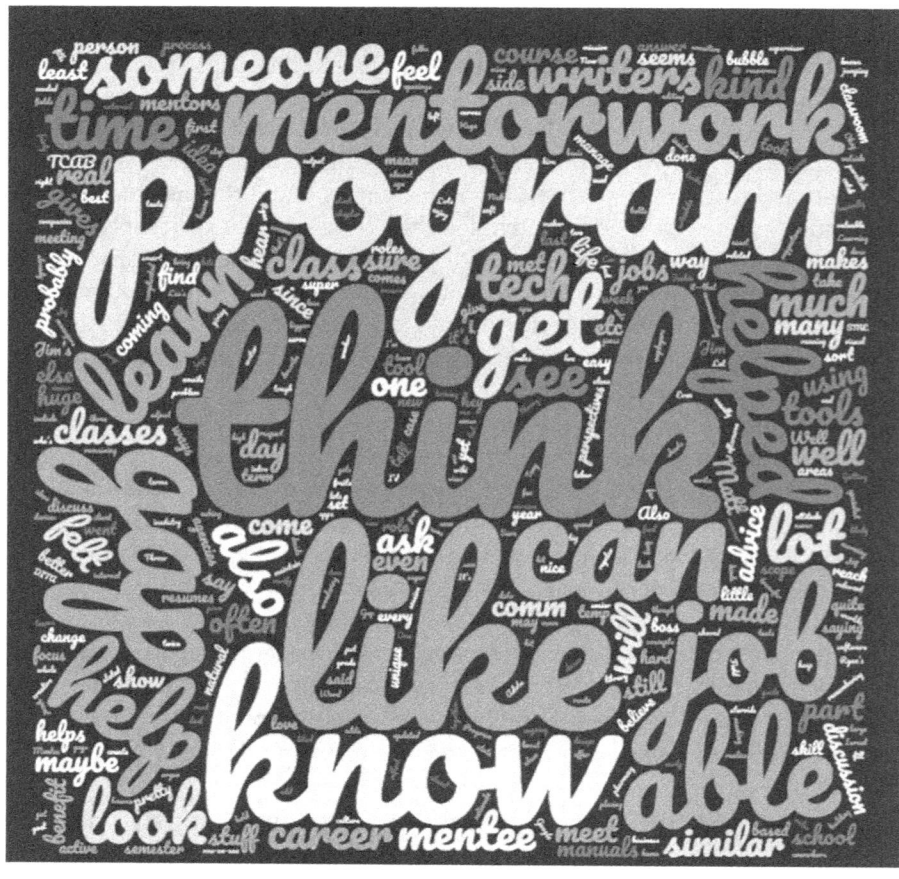

Figure 10.3. Word cloud from responses to gap question.

Undergraduate students seemed to appreciate learning about technical communication as a field and imagining what careers might look like. Many commented that it is difficult to gain this knowledge in the classroom, and they appreciated that their mentors could provide more insight outside of the classroom. Said one student, "Being able to have the opportunity to talk to someone who is outside the university is not something I had the opportunity to do throughout the school year or this internship." Experiences with mentors helped them learn about the field in ways that classrooms could not. One undergraduate student expressed this idea clearly:

> I felt the program definitely addressed the gap between academia and industry. Courses helped with content areas but the mentor program was more personal and a place where I could ask questions about jobs, applications, career. No classes are geared toward jobs necessarily. I could have asked these questions of a professor but felt more natural coming from [my mentor] who had been through things very recently.

Graduate students commented that they learned more details about the technical communication profession, possible career tracks, and specific areas such as usability. They appreciated that the mentor program provided a vehicle for students to reach out, rather than having to do it on their own. Responses included words such as "get information" and "learn about the technical communication profession." One graduate certificate student explained in more detail how the mentor program helped them learn about the field:

> [My mentor] has worked in many different fields and it really opened my eyes to all of the possibilities that tech comm has to offer. [He] was able to reflect on his time as a student and job-hunting as well and also give me advice based on his experience as a hiring manager. It was great to learn more directly about the industry-side of things that is often difficult to accomplish in an online class setting.

Mentors provided a broader perspective and could recognize the value of the learning opportunity for students who are entering or further exploring the field. Some commented on the ways the mentor program allowed flexibility and "comfort" to ask difficult questions. As one mentor said, "This program has opened a window for students to ask large (and sometimes difficult) questions about what their futures may hold." And mentors commented on the ways they learned from students as well, as seen in the following response from an alum and mentor:

> This program is a great tool for students as they prepare for their transition from academic to professional life. As a professional, I found it interesting to learn about classes the students are taking.

It allows me to see how future technical writers are training, and it makes me excited for the future of the field!

A second theme in responses about how the program bridged gaps between academia and industry was building relationships, networks, or community created through the mentor program—a kind of guided experience. It is this sense of community that seemed to bridge the gap between academia and workplace—understanding that there are differences between academia and industry but also working towards transition from one to the next (and back again!).

Undergraduates appreciated the opportunities to network and meet people in ways they would not be able to through classes. One student said that the program has allowed him to meet people in the field and expand his knowledge of the field.

Graduate students articulated how valuable it was to have a personal resource to help navigate the differences between academia and industry. As one graduate student put it, "having someone to guide you . . . that's really helpful." Another graduate student recognized the value of bridging the gap and said it was useful in ways that he would want to continue: "It was helpful in connecting the two worlds. I want to keep doing it."

Mentors had many positive things to say about how the program helped establish relationships. One mentor said that the program "made a person-to-person connection" and commented that the connection helped bridge the gap between academia and industry. Others used words like "engagement," "coaching," and "developing professional skills sets." Some mentors offered that they have introduced their mentees to other professionals to help mentees build their networks. One mentor saw the program as an opportunity for students to work with a professional on a regular basis and make it easier to connect. Mentors definitely valued and acted upon the idea of relationship building as a way to bridge the gap between two worlds. One TCAB member and mentor responded,

> It has afforded the student the opportunity to work with a working tech. comm. professional on a regular basis, and made it convenient for the student and mentor to establish a working relationship whereby topics that are often overlooked or sensitive in nature can be discussed in confidence.

Recommendations for Improvement

The fourth question on our post-participation survey asked users if they had recommendations for future iterations of the mentor program. This question allowed survey participants to share their thoughts on what they feel would make the mentor program better going forward or what they wished they could've had during their time in the program. While participants largely had positive things to say about the mentor program, several suggestions for improvement were given. Themes emerged around areas such as duration and format of the program, flexible mentor-mentee pairings, and clearer goals and expectations.

Undergraduate student participants seemed to like the idea of meeting for a longer duration of time; that is, three meetings were good, but more meetings would have been better. A few students mentioned that the program should be planned for an entire academic year (September to May). The length of time mattered to students because they sought a connection with their mentors; more time with their mentors would create a personalized, tailored experience for the mentees' needs and wants.

Another recommendation from the undergraduate level was the idea of flexibility in mentor assignments. The option to change mentors was mentioned a few times; this was due either to changing interests or a complete clash of interests in the first place. The opportunity to gather as much insight as possible—or find that one perfect fit—was something students valued. Students mentioned these changes could happen at the semester or yearly mark; one mentioned the chance to change as soon as possible.

Much like undergraduate students, graduate students also mentioned the duration and meeting frequency as something to look into in the future. The duration of one year was mentioned by a handful of graduate students; more meetings were recommended as well. Additionally, graduate students specifically made recommendations for in-person, large group meetings alongside more one-to-one time with their mentors. One student suggested large group meetings could be used as icebreaker/"get to know you" time or as connection events to see what other perspectives are out there beyond their mentors.

From the mentor standpoint, duration was also the main recommendation; mentors want more time with their mentees, and vice versa. One mentor suggested that a longer duration with a mentee allows for more focused career development and a tailored mentor experience:

> I think it would be cool if you would have opportunities to have a [mentor] meet with [their mentee] a few times over a longer period of time in their development or their career. So, for example, if somebody thinks they want to be in medical writing . . . Have them meet with[someone] from the medical industry early on. Then maybe a half a year later, you can see some progression and how things how [mentee] ideas change, or how things change [in the industry].

Another concept recommended by mentors was one of clarity in goals and purpose. All mentors appeared to share a positive experience with their mentees, but many seemed to feel that their mentees relied on them for goal setting; in reality, mentees should drive the partnership with their goals and ideas, and mentors should offer their advice and opportunities as appropriate. One mentor mentioned that she felt her student didn't really "know what [they] wanted out of this," but only because the student was younger/undergraduate level. Ideas such as structured activities, printed or online resources, and concrete goal setting were recommended.

Additionally, it was recommended that mentors come prepared too. A handful of mentors mentioned that they have experience with similar scenarios outside of the pilot study (i.e., external mentor programs) which have valuable resources on teaching people how to mentor. Having those resources available was a recommendation, so those who may not know where to start with a mentee would have a starting point. Another recommendation was to provide a list of sample goals to guide mentors and mentees at the launch meeting. Similarly, several commented on making clear expectations about what mentors could and could not do, or rather what goals were realistic for mentor pairs. Mentors also suggested that organizers make clear that mentees need to initiate contact, and that mentors are not expected to serve roles as teachers or professors in evaluating or grading work. Mentors also suggested that the program emphasize networking as a realistic expectation rather than "finding a job." One mentor suggested that students complete a summary of what they learned from the program to inform organizers of the program.

∎ Discussion

In this chapter, through the lens of user experience and user-centered design, we have investigated the "joint enterprise" that comes as a result of strategic interaction of students and industry professionals (TCAB members and program alumni) through a mentor program. This "interactively constructed nature of engaging, belonging, and sharing tools" allowed for both an open-ended and user-centered approach to the mentor program in that the students and mentors determined how they wanted to shape their interaction. Our particular interest focused on the specific user experience of participating in the program, including how such mentor-mentee experience might address the academia-industry gap. We articulated a central research question: *How might user experience in a mentor program address the academic-industry gap?* We also articulated sub-questions: *What is the "user experience" of participating in a mentor program? And how can we make improvements to a mentor program based on user/participant feedback?*

Overall results from the survey and interview data indicate that this program provided a positive framework for establishing effective connections across academic and practitioner communities. Mentor-mentee interaction provided an opportunity for students to engage with mentors from specific industries, working to identify and understand the kinds of activities engendered through membership in the technical communication field. Key findings were based on user feedback about the mentor program and included four themes: community, duration, clarity of goals, and mentor pairing matters (see Figure 10.4).

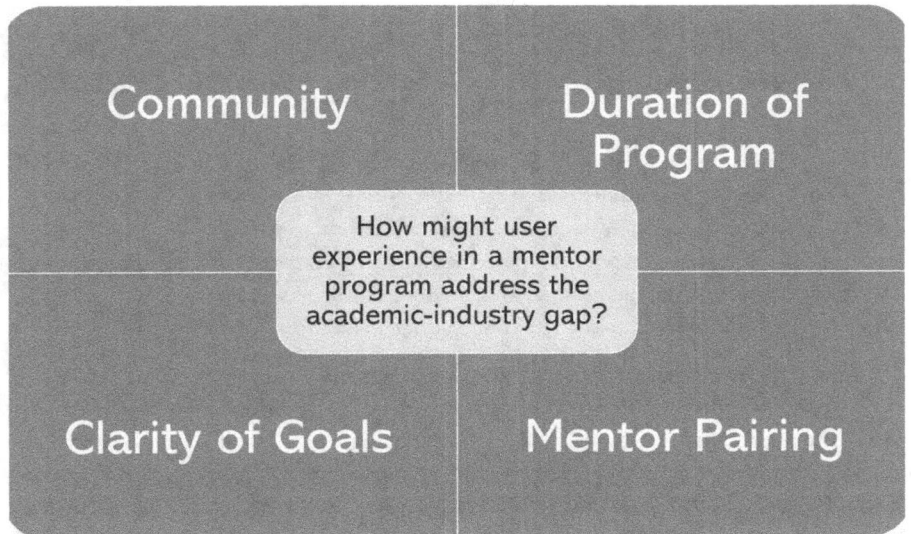

Figure 10.4. Four user-based themes on mentor programs.

In terms of *community*, our findings from survey and interview responses indicated that the mentor program specifically addressed the "gap" between academia and industry in two ways: by providing a key learning opportunity outside of the classroom that could inform students about the field and careers, and by building professional relationships and networks. These two findings connect explicitly with community of practice theory, in particular, that new professionals join communities of practice and that professional relationships are important learning opportunities. As Kline and Barker (2012) suggested, academia and industry must both contribute and collaborate to build positive connections: "Without collaboration, the knowledge and social presence necessary to negotiate meaning, something that Wenger (1998) notes is critical to community, fails to occur" (p. 43). Our findings suggest that mentor dyads provide a key collaborative opportunity for students and professionals to reach out, to learn things outside of the classroom, and to build professional networks.

Related to the idea of community is the theme of *duration*, or the length of the mentor program and opportunity for the community to grow and thrive. In our findings, participants from each group—undergraduates, graduates, and mentors—expressed the need for more time to develop community, asking for the program to continue or that it be offered over a longer timeframe. Some enthusiastically suggested the opportunity to have new mentors each year to build a broader professional community. Another suggestion related to community was the idea of having additional larger group meetings, such as at the end of the year, to bring everyone together and get a sense for the collective community.

Regarding *clarity of goals*, user feedback identified that the program needed to provide clearer goals, both for mentors and participating students. This feedback helped us revisit the following goals we shared at the first mentor-mentee pairing event:

- to build relationships that enhance professional development for both mentors and mentees
- to bridge the gap between academia and industry
- to help students develop a personal learning network (PLN) that contributes to personal, academic, and professional success
- to articulate clear goals for professional development

From surveys and interviews, we identified the need to revisit these goals throughout the program and to add more specificity to these; e.g., what exactly does it mean to "bridge the gap" as a student meets with a technical communication professional for the first time? While academics may use PLN visualizations to indicate resources, tools, and contexts within which they work and learn, such visualizations are not commonly used in either academia or industry. Therefore, we should articulate mentor-mentee strategies that more clearly relate to making connections that build understanding about technical communication industries and how to best develop skills for securing a position and being successful in this profession. We also learned through survey feedback the various goals that dyads articulated, and how those differed for graduate students and undergraduate students. While some goals and expectations that undergraduate students brought to the program surprised us, e.g., requests for mentors to review coursework or to represent the specific industry the student planned to enter (environmental communication), the largest overall goal of discussion was job search and career preparation. The majority of undergraduates were exploring the field; in contrast, the graduate students exhibited greater understanding as well as practice in the field, leading to more focused goals. As facilitators, rather than including one set of goals, we have identified the need to provide more specific mentor-mentee direction based on the student level.

Regarding *mentor pairings*, while TCAB member bios are included on our website, we did not ask students to indicate who they might be most interested in working with, as not all TCAB members were able to participate in this pilot program. We asked students to share a paragraph about themselves for the purposes of our development of mentor-mentee pairings; however, we did not share these with mentors or allow them to request a specific student mentee. Instead, we relied on our collective knowledge of all students and mentors, working to develop pairings that matched student interest with specific industry directions. Again, our goal was to integrate user feedback with instructional design to find ways to better bridge industry and academia, and to engage students and industry practitioners. While the pairings engaged students and industry practitioners, comment and direction from participants indicated the need to clarify expectations to focus on mentee responsibility to generate clear goals for professional development that would allow mentor sharing of expertise.

The user feedback we received from participants in this pilot mentor program offer "lessons learned" that contribute to our next iteration of the program. We plan to implement changes that address each of the four themes of community, duration, clarity, and pairing. In terms of *community*, we will work to foster greater community throughout, clustering mentor groupings by industry if possible, and bringing the full group together one or two additional times. In terms of *duration*, we will extend the duration of the program so that it spans the entire academic year rather than one semester (or a portion of one semester). One idea is to run the mentor program from October to May. We can connect this theme of duration to the theme of community by asking pairs to meet and reflect on their mentor experience at the end of the program. In terms of the theme of *clarity*, we will provide clearer parameters and options for the types of activities mentor pairs might engage in, and we will provide more information to guide students as they articulate goals, outcomes, and/or expectations for the mentor program. These efforts will be informed by current research by technical communication scholars such as Rebekka Anderson, Carlos Evia, and JoAnn Hackos that identifies the industry-academia gap and important conversations and connections that need to be made as we prepare students for professional lives (see Andersen & Hackos, 2018; Evia & Andersen, 2018). As well, we note that sometimes establishing professional network connections is difficult and challenging for students (Gonzales & Turner, 2019; Sullivan & Moore, 2013), and we encourage conversations to be open and supportive of narrative experiences (Gonzales & Turner, 2019). We also will be intentional in following up with students as they (1) develop professional goals, (2) review and work on these with their mentors, (3) share these with a larger community, and (4) develop short- and long-range plans for this work. A final large group mentor meeting would be an appropriate place to address these items. Finally, in terms of the theme of *pairing*, we will provide a mentor program model in which students prepare more for this program (e.g., perhaps require a LinkedIn site) and have more information for their mentors. We also will share more details about the mentor pool with students. These plans of action are generated directly from user feedback that we believe will improve our mentor program.

■ Conclusion

As noted earlier, this program came about as the result of a strong request from TCAB members. Such a program provides a means for "succession planning" and overall strengthening of the field. The mentors—both TCAB members and program alumni—were pleased with the impact of this program as it provided a means to connect with the academic community. This was more than a one-way transfer of knowledge from mentor to mentee; it provided for a transactional knowledge exchange. For example, one mentor used her experience to prepare for another role leading a different mentor program; another mentor learned about disabilities in the workplace, having had no prior exposure working one-to-one with the specific mentee's disabilities. Mentors appreciated the chance to showcase their workplaces, recommending that we identify multiple mentors from a given workplace to allow for creation of a stronger community of practice as multiple mentors and mentees meet together in the workplace setting. Again, we see this collaborative give-and-take in the mentor program as addressing a "joint enterprise" with negotiated goals. We see the mentor program as a key learning opportunity that our target users—students and mentors—find valuable.

Overall, the mentor program in this case provided an innovative way to build academic-industry connections, and we are overwhelmed by its positive impact. The program provided an opportunity for mentors and mentees to engage in joint enterprise and community practice work to bridge the academia-industry gap. User feedback allowed us to better understand the mentor program user experience, and in this case, we learned that the student experience needs to broaden outside the classroom. We see such a user experience perspective as bridging industry and academia, as integrating design and instructional design, as engaging students and industry practitioners. At a time when numerous virtual opportunities exist to build and share knowledge, the impact of a personal one-to-one connection—most often in person—clearly worked to build each mentee's personal and professional network. We know that successful internship experiences provide students with the opportunity to develop important workplace skills; however, unless the student is offered a position and continues to work in the industry, it's rare for the experience to foster a strong mentor-mentee relationship. With expansion of program duration, clearer articulation of goals, and greater attention to mentor-mentee pairings, such a mentor-mentee program will hold even greater impact on students and our field.

∎ References

Allen, T. D., Smith, M. A., Mael, F. A., O'Shea, P. G. & Eby, L. T. (2009). Organization-level mentoring and organizational performance within substance abuse centers. *Journal of Management, 35*(5), 1113–1128. https://doi.org/10.1177/0149206308329969.

Andersen, R. & Hackos, J. (2018). Increasing the value and accessibility of academic research: Perspectives from industry. In *Proceedings of the 36th ACM International Conference on the Design of Communication* (pp.1–10). Association for Computing Machinery.

Baer, S. (2018). Enhancing learning for participants in workplace mentoring programmes. *International Journal of Evidence Based Coaching and Mentoring, 16*(1), 35–46. https://doi.org/10.24384/000462.

Beaufort, A. (1999). *Writing in the real world: Making the transition from school to work.* Teachers College Press.

Bloch, J. (2011). Glorified grammarian or versatile value adder? What internship reports reveal about the professionalization of technical communication. *Technical Communication, 58*(4), 308–327.

Duin, A. H. & Tham, J. (2018). Cultivating code literacy: A case study of course redesign through advisory board engagement. *Communication Design Quarterly, 6*(3), 44–58.

Evia, C. & Andersen, R. (2018). Preparing the next generation of leaders and innovators in technical communication. *Intercom*, July/August, 23–24.

Finch, J. K. & Fernandez, C. (2014). Mentoring graduate students in teaching: The FCCIC model. *Teaching Sociology, 42*, 69–75. https://doi.org/10.1177/0092055X13507781.

Getto, G. & Beecher, F. (2016). Toward a model of UX education: Training UX designers within the academy. *IEEE Transactions on Professional Communication, 59*(2), 153–164.

Gonzales, L. & Turner, H. N. (2019, October). Challenges and insights for fostering academic-industry collaborations in UX. In *Proceedings of the 37th ACM International Conference on the Design of Communication* (pp. 1–6). Association for Computing Machinery.

Gould, J. D. & Lewis, C. (1985). Designing for usability: Key principles and what designers think. *Communications of the ACM, 28*(3), 300–311. http://portal.acm.org/citation.cfm?id=3170&coll=portal&dl=ACM&CFID=11644763&CFTOKEN=46634291.

Henze, B. (2006). The research-experiential internship in professional communication. *Technical Communication, 53*(3), 339–347.

Johnson, R., Salvo, M. & Zoetewey, M. (2007). User-centered technology in participatory culture: Two decades "beyond a narrow conception of usability testing." *IEEE Transactions on Professional Communication, 50*(4), 320–332.

Jones, J. (2012). An analysis of learning outcomes within formal mentoring relationships. *International Journal of Evidence Based Coaching & Mentoring, 10*(1), 57–72.

Jones, J. (2013). Factors influencing mentees' and mentors' learning throughout formal mentoring relationships. *Human Resource Development International, 16*(4), 390–408. https://doi.org/10.1080/13678868.2013.810478.

Katz, S. M. (1998). *The dynamics of writing review: Opportunities for growth and change in the workplace*. Ablex.

Kline, J. & Barker, T. (2012). Negotiating professional consciousness in technical communication: A community of practice approach. *Technical Communication, 59*(1), 32–48.

Kohn, L. (2015). How professional writing pedagogy and university–workplace partnerships can shape the mentoring of workplace writing. *Journal of Technical Writing and Communication, 45*(2), 166–188. /https://doi.org/10.1177/0047281615569484.

Kramer-Simpson, E. (2018). Moving from student to professional: Industry mentors and academic internship coordinators supporting intern learning in the workplace. *Journal of Technical Writing and Communication, 48*(1), 81–103. https://doi.org/10.1177/0047281616646753.

Lave, J. & Wenger, E. (1991). *Situated learning: Legitimate peripheral participation*. Cambridge University Press.

Metzger, A. M., Petit, A. & Sieber, S. (2015). Mentoring as a way to change a culture of academic bullying and mobbing in the humanities. *Higher Education for the Future, 2*, 139–150. https://doi.org/10.1177/2347631115584119.

Munger, R. (2006). Participating in a technical communication internship. *Technical Communication*, *53*(3), 326–338.

Pardun, C. J., McKeever, R., Pressgrove, G. N. & McKeever, B. (2015). Colleagues in training: How senior faculty view doctoral education. *Journalism & Mass Communication Educator*, *70*, 354–366. https://eric.ed.gov/?id=EJ1086563.

Potts, L. & Salvo, M. J. (2018). *Rhetoric and experience architecture*. Parlor Press.

QualComm. (n.d.). *Mentorship program toolkit*. Retrieved October 11, 2021, from https://www.qualcomm.com/media/documents/files/mentorship-program-flip-focus-guide.pdf.

Redish, J. C. (2010). Technical communication and usability: Intertwined strands and mutual influences. *IEEE Transactions on Professional Communication*, *53*(3), 191–201.

Rose, E. J., Racadio, R., Wong, K., Nguyen, S., Kim, J. & Sahler, A. (2017). Community-based user experience: Evaluating the usability of health insurance information with immigrant patients. *IEEE Transactions on Professional Communication*, *60*(2), 214–231.

Salvo, M. J. (2001). Ethics of engagement: User-centered design and rhetorical methodology. *Technical Communication Quarterly*, *10*(3), 273–290. https://doi.org/10.1207/s15427625tcq1003_3.

Sapp D. A. & Zhang, Q. (2009). Trends in industry supervisors' feedback on business communication internships. *Business Communication Quarterly*, *72*(3), 274–288. https://doi.org/10.1177/1080569909336450.

Seto, L. & Geithner, T. (2018). Metaphor magic in coaching and coaching supervision. *International Journal of Evidence Based Coaching and Mentoring*, *16*(2), 99–111. https://doi.org/10.24384/000562.

Söderlund, L., Spartz, J. & Weber, R. (2017). Taken under advisement: Perspectives on advisory boards from across technical communication. *IEEE Transactions on Professional Communication*, *60*(1), 76–96. https://doi.org/10.1109/TPC.2016.2635693.

Stake, R. E. (1995). *The art of case study research*. Sage Publications.

Still, B. & Crane, K. (2016). *Fundamentals of user-centered design: A practical approach*. CRC Press.

Sullivan, P. & Moore, K. (2013). Time talk: On small changes that enact infrastructural mentoring for undergraduate women in technical fields. *Journal of Technical Writing and Communication*, *43*(3), 333–354. https://doi.org/10.2190/TW.43.3.f.

Walton, R. & Jones, N. (2013). Navigating increasingly cross-cultural, cross-disciplinary, and cross-organizational contexts to support social justice. *Communication Design Quarterly*, *1*(4), 31–35.

Wenger, E. (1998). *Communities of practice: Learning, meaning, and identity*. Cambridge University Press.

Winsor, D. A. (1996). *Writing like an engineer: A rhetorical education*. Lawrence Erlbaum Associates.

Yin, R. K. (2003). *Case study research: Design and methods* (3rd ed.). Sage Publications.

Appendix A: Launch Meeting Worksheet

Technical Communication
ADVISORY BOARD
Connecting Students to the Future

Contact Information

Mentor Name: _____ Email: _____

Mentor Phone (Optional): _____ LinkedIn: _____

Mentee Name: _____ Email: _____

Mentee Phone (Optional): _____ LinkedIn: _____

Goal Setting:

What goals would you like achieve this semester? Write down up to **three** goals. If you're stuck, think SMART* – specific, measurable, achievable, relevant, and time-bound. This will help narrow down your focus and write goals that can be achieved by you and your mentor.

1. _____
   _____
   _____
   _____

2. _____
   _____
   _____
   _____

3. _____
   _____
   _____
   _____

Upcoming Meetings:

Next Meeting: _____ Online, or In Person: _____

Next Meeting: _____ Online, or In Person: _____

Subsequent Meetings are Optional, but Encouraged!

Adapted from https://fitsmallbusiness.com/wp-content/uploads/2018/05/SMART-Goals-Template-Worksheet.pdf

Appendix B: Post-Participation Mentor Program Questionnaire

1. Email Address
2. Participant Name
3. How are you participating in the Mentor Program?
   - ○ Undergraduate TWC Student
   - ○ Graduate Certificate Student
   - ○ Graduate M.S. Student
   - ○ Graduate M.A./Ph.D. Student
   - ○ TCAB Member and mentor
   - ○ Invited alumni and mentor
4. What goals did your Mentor Pair articulate for Spring 2019? (Please list up to three goals)
5. The Mentor Program asked each Mentor Pair to set up two meetings or opportunities for connection. Please describe the first of those meetings or opportunities for connection.
6. The Mentor Program asked each Mentor Pair to set up two meetings or opportunities for connection. Please describe the second of those meetings or opportunities for connection.
7. What are your hopes for this program as it continues?
8. How well are your hopes being met and what can be done to improve the program?
9. How has this mentor program engaged the gap between students and industry professionals?
10. Please share any additional information you think may be helpful as we continue this pilot program.
11. Would you be willing to be contacted for a short (15 minute) follow up interview about your experience with the Mentor Program?
    - ○ Yes
    - ○ No
    - ○ Other (free text)

Appendix C: Pre-Participation Mentor Program Questionnaire (Student Version)

1. Are you interested in being paired with a TCAB Member for the 2019 Spring Semester?
   - ○ Yes
   - ○ No

2. Are you able to commit to at least three meetings, including our facilitated event on Monday February 4th, 2019, 6–7 pm?
   ○ Yes
   ○ No
3. What are your areas of interest?
   ○ Business and Professional Writing
   ○ Writing on Issues of Science and Technology
   ○ Technical and Professional Presentations
   ○ Editing, Critique, and Style
   ○ Rhetoric, Technology, and the Internet
   ○ Science, Technology and the Law
   ○ Writing Proposals and Grant management
   ○ International Professional Communication
   ○ Information Design: Theory and Practice
   ○ Technology, Culture, and Communication
   ○ Technical and Professional Writing
   ○ Visual Rhetoric and Document Design
4. Do you have any comments, suggestions, or questions as we move forward in this pilot program?

Appendix D: Pre-Participant Mentor Program Questionnaire (Mentor Version)

1. Are you interested in being paired with an undergraduate or Cert/MS student for the 2019 Spring Semester?
   ○ Yes
   ○ No
2. Are you able to commit to at least three meetings, including our facilitated event on Monday February 4th, 2019, 6–7 pm?
   ○ Yes
   ○ No
3. What are your areas of interest?
   ○ Business and Professional Writing
   ○ Writing on Issues of Science and Technology
   ○ Technical and Professional Presentations
   ○ Editing, Critique, and Style
   ○ Rhetoric, Technology, and the Internet
   ○ Science, Technology and the Law

- Writing Proposals and Grant management
- International Professional Communication
- Information Design: Theory and Practice
- Technology, Culture, and Communication
- Technical and Professional Writing
- Visual Rhetoric and Document Design

4. Do you have any comments, suggestions, or questions as we move forward in this pilot program?

■ Appendix E: Email Script for Mentor Program Students

Hello -

Thank you for applying to join our Workplace Mentor Program. We are so happy to see you are interested in coming together during Spring 2019 for this pilot program between students and TCAB Members.

The next step before pairing you with a TCAB member involves getting to know you better, beyond the survey content. We are asking that you provide us with one paragraph (no more than half a page, double-spaced) telling us more about what interests you, what your educational and career goals are . . . anything that might help us better understand your academic and professional goals and better pair you with a TCAB member/mentor.

Please submit this paragraph to me (gresboo8@umn.edu) by the end of the day Thursday, December 20th. Please note that if you don't submit a paragraph, you will not be able to receive a mentor pairing.

If you have questions, please reach out to me. I am happy to help and advise on this process as needed.

Thanks!

Best,
Emily Gresbrink
Lee-Ann Kastman Breuch
Ann Hill Duin

11. User Experience Design and Double Binds in Course Design

Mark Zachry
UNIVERSITY OF WASHINGTON

Abstract: This chapter explores course design practices based on a user experience (UX) perspective. Drawing on a three-year case study of the evolving design and execution of a senior capstone course, the chapter examines how course assessment data—gathered through both institutional instruments and instructor-developed practices—were used to guide decisions about course design. Using selected examples over the time span of the study, the chapter illustrates techniques for translating student observations and desires into requirements and classroom practices. Turning to an analysis of successes and failures, the chapter explores the idea of *double binds* in designing from user experience perspectives. This analysis addresses the question of what happens when an instructor is willing to make radical course design choices based on expressions of student experiences and desires.

Keywords: Double binds, instructor-designer, design, user experience, capstone

Key Takeaways:

- Effective, artful instruction emerges from learning experiences design informed by attention to student users engaged with that design.
- Listening to students provides insights into what they need or desire to support their learning, but students' needs and desires may be conflicting and even contradictory within any given class.
- These contradictory needs and desires can result in instructors facing double binds, situations in which the designer faces a dilemma due to competing demands.
- This chapter identifies three types of double binds instructor-designers may encounter when attempting to teach from a user experience perspective and recommends that instructors normalize talk about double binds with peers as they consider how double binds might be addressed.

As a faculty member in a department that articulates in its very name a commitment to valuing human needs, I have a strong inclination toward pedagogical practices that prioritize what works best for students in the classroom. Elsewhere (Zachry & Spyridakis, 2016), I have described this commitment and how it helped shaped program and curricular decisions broadly in my home department. In this chapter, however, I will explore some of the inherent challenges in following this approach at a more granular level—that of an individual class. In particular, I will explore the experience of attempting to place student needs and desires as a central concern in the design of a class.

The case for designing our courses in a way that is tuned in to the needs and desires of the students we encounter today is compelling. As advocates for designs that are responsive to the needs of the humans who will be using them, it seems necessary for us to create courses that are designed in this same way. Although as instructors we bring substantial training and often experiences to bear on the courses we offer, it remains true that our perspective does not represent the totality of perspectives in the interactions our courses facilitate. Effective instruction emerges from the artful design of learning experiences that should be meaningfully informed by attention to the people (students) we will engage in that design. As the work of many contributors to this collection suggests, a notable number of educators in our field seek to design their courses in a way that responds to the needs and desires of the students they will encounter. In this regard, it makes sense to think of educators inclined to follow this approach as instructor-designers following the priorities of a user experience approach. In short, instructor-designers use varied techniques to discover the needs and desires of the students with whom they interact toward the end of realizing instructional goals. As suggested in this volume, the techniques take many forms—formal and incidental. Together, though, they represent the impulse to observe and listen to expressions of students and to methodically adjust the design of assignments, classroom experiences, and feedback mechanisms to best support students in their use of our classes to achieve learning goals.

Listening to students clearly provides insights into what they need or desire to support their learning. At the same time, however, experienced instructors know that the insights students offer are often uneven, perhaps reflecting a singular perspective or not accounting for the overall learning context the instructor is working within. Some insights, nevertheless, are relatively easy to address and require negligible effort to implement. Addressing some other needs and desires, though, requires more substantive changes. In some instances, attempting to be responsive to the insights gained from listening to students places the instructor in a dilemma, such as trying to reconcile student needs/desires with contradictory institutional requirements. At other times, instructor-designers discover contradictory student perspectives that demand juxtaposing approaches. In such instances, listening to and being responsive to one or a few students can actually lead to choices that negatively affect the design of the class for the needs and desires of a different set of students in the same class. When the students in a given class represent a heterogeneous collection of stakeholders, an instructor who desires to adjust the design of a course to address their competing needs faces a dilemma. Consider, for example, an instance in which an instructor is asked by some students to drop their grades on a few of the early class assignments because they were confused when the term began, but now feel like they are doing better. A different group of students in the same class objects, saying that they rearranged their schedules to devote time to those early assignments—something they would not have done had they known eliminating those assignments was a possibility. Yet another student mentions that the class syllabus documents those assignments and their point value. Any change to them, the student speculates, may be something worth talking to the educational assessment office about. Over lunch, a pair of colleagues disagree with each other when this story is shared. One colleague cites their routine practice of negotiating with students who have encountered difficulties, while the other colleague argues that the design of the class presented in the syllabus is a contract binding the instructor and students to a plan.

Such dilemmas—those in which an instructor attempts to be responsive to the wants and needs of students, but discovers contractions within those expressions and in the broader context of stakeholders—deserve greater consideration by our field. In this chapter, then, the phenomena that I am particularly interested in exploring is that in which attempting to use feedback from students can lead to double binds for instructors who are attempting to design the best possible learning environments. To facilitate this exploration, I will draw on examples from a class that I routinely teach at my institution. As I present each of the three examples, my focus will be on my attempt to foster a classroom design that is responsive to the experiences of students. I will then expand on the theory of double binds in responding to the needs and desires of students when designing a class-based learning experience.

■ Capstone Course Sequence

To complete their undergraduate degree in Human Centered Design & Engineering (HCDE; my students' designated field of study), all undergraduates must undertake a capstone project. These projects are completed in a two-course sequence in the winter and spring quarters of the senior year. The projects are completed by small teams (three or four students) and are sponsored by an external entity (e.g., a business, a non-profit organization, a governmental office). In the winter quarter, students group themselves into teams and then, as a team, choose a sponsor. During this quarter, each team then focuses on exploring the design challenge related to the sponsor's needs, develops a human-centered design approach to addressing that challenge, and prepares a proposed work plan with milestones to be executed in the following quarter. In the spring quarter, the student teams execute their plan and then present their work to the sponsors and the general public at the department's largest annual event, the spring open house, which is held just a few days before graduation.

By design, many elements of the capstone experience are shaped by the students themselves. The students form their own teams based on the configuration of skill sets they desire; the teams pick their sponsored projects based on their interests; and the teams devise their own design process based on their understanding of the challenge and how best to apply skills and knowledge they have developed during their studies. Over both quarters, student teams routinely interact with members of the instructional team (the lead instructor and a group of teaching assistants) to think through problems they are encountering and to receive feedback on the choices they are making at each juncture. Each quarter includes a mix of individual and team assignments (with team assignments being most dominant), and all the work is graded.

▪ Illustrative Examples

I have selected three examples of feedback received from students over three years of offering the capstone course sequence. These examples are selectively pulled from many conversations over these years. Each is picked to illustrate a different type of the potential double binds that an instructor might encounter when attempting to teach in a way that is responsive to the desires of students.

Example 1: Evaluation

In the first year I taught the capstone sequence, the winter quarter class was offered as a credit/no credit course. The assignments in the class required students to analyze the design challenge presented by their sponsor, develop an appropriate design process to address that challenge, and then prepare a detailed plan to execute that process. This sequence of assignments is demanding, and the instructional team provides extensive feedback to the students. Near the end of the quarter that first year, the instructional team was somewhat perplexed by how casual students were in their execution of these assignments. For many of the student teams, the assignments were executed in a cursory manner with seemingly little attention being paid to the quality of thought as well as the writing. Toward the end of the quarter, I engaged a subset of the students in a discussion about why they were taking such a relaxed approach. Their consensus opinion was that they were taking a cost-benefit approach to time allocation: "You assume that what we are doing is our best work, but this course is not graded." In short, they reported that they were allocating greater time to other courses that were graded and would affect their GPA and that they were taking a sufficing approach to this class that would earn them credit but consume no more time than necessary because they were otherwise too busy. They advised that if I wanted to see work more in line with expectations, then I should have the class changed to a graded course. After considering this input and what would likely be best for students' learning experiences in subsequent years, I worked with the department's curriculum committee to make this change the next year. Making this course a graded course that affected GPAs did result in substantially better work on the assignments in terms of completeness and professionalism. However, this change in demand on student time also became the source of grumbling and even dissatisfaction in end-of-quarter course evaluations. In one evaluation, a student argued,

> C/NC [credit/no credit] makes a lot more sense for this class. It's a 2cr class it shouldn't be graded. Especially for the amount of work that you have to put into this class in order to succeed. It's too much for 2cr.

Yet another student complained,

> I think that there was a lot of confusion about whether the class was graded or not. Everyone I talked to seemed to be confused about this fact. I think that there was also no precedent/warning about how hard the first graded assignments were going to be, because everything before that was "if you did it, you got credit."

For students such as these, implementing a course design feature suggested by students from a previous class immediately surfaced new concerns that countered the suggested feature in an unanticipated way. Clearly, within the broad student population, people held competing—perhaps irreconcilable—thoughts about how course evaluation should be designed.

Example 2: Equivalency

Across the years that I have offered this course, I have required student teams to have an official sponsor for their projects. Most students select their project from a catalog of projects that I have arranged with sponsors from various organizations and from a range of domains (e.g., consumer app development, surgical support devices, community planning, and toys to support emotional development for children). This requirement to have an external project sponsor is intended to facilitate learning about real project constraints (e.g., design politics with stakeholders, economic considerations, and risk-benefit analysis of design options) as well as to develop communicative skills when interacting with people outside the classroom (Ford, 2018; Ford & Teare, 2006). For many students, this requirement is appreciated and sometimes noted in end-of-term course evaluations: "I like having a project that is culminating of my HCDE education. I also like that we have real stakeholders involved and possible restrictions. It resembles the 'real world' better than other HCDE course projects have." Each year, however, at least one student team questions the requirement, expressing a desire to pursue a design vision that they have imagined on their own. The desire of some students for each project to be unique sometimes shows up in end-of-course comments:

> Everything was very formulaic for every different group. All groups were expected to submit the same format of project

proposal even if different sections didn't make sense. Rather than allowing groups to determine what is necessary and actually allow groups to form our own proposal, everyone was forced into a template.

When teams ask to be an exception to the class expectation that all projects have an external sponsor, I guide them to make arrangements with an external entity in their desired domain to become at least a nominal sponsor of the project so that they can complete the same sequence of assignments as their fellow teams. For example, I connected a team that wanted to work on directing prepackaged food waste on campus to local donation sites for those in need with a company working on technologies to use crowd-sourcing in guidance for waste disposal systems. Another group wanted to work on developing a progressive approach to culinary education, so I guided them to work with the proprietor of a local cooking school designed to engage millennials in recreational cooking. Without exception, these teams struggle repeatedly at different junctures in their work, encountering such tricky issues as initial problem definition, scale and scope of design, and identification of design options that work within realistic budgets and/or use contexts. Their self-arranged project sponsors are typically of little help when the teams must work through these issues because they are not invested in the project in the same way as the other sponsors.

Example 3: Expectance

As graduating seniors who are taking the capstone sequence in their final two quarters of their final year, the students in general feel very confident in what they know as they begin their projects. For most, the excitement of getting started on what will be their biggest project in the program is evident from the beginning. Recognizing this enthusiasm and hoping to make it work for the students in what is inevitably a longer and more challenging project than they anticipate, I attempt to design the class sessions in the first quarter to focus on work specifically related to their individual team projects as rapidly as possible. Consequently, all the teams are self-formed and paired with a desired sponsor within three weeks of the class beginning. After that, all class sessions are designed to facilitate hands-on design activities that support initial discovery and brainstorming, identifying and scheduling milestones for the projects, and detailing a plan to execute the project that the team buys into and that can be shared with the sponsors before our spring break and then the final quarter when the design process officially begins. The design of this first quarter capstone is shown in Table 11.1.

Table 11.1. Course Schedule for HCDE Capstone Planning Course in Winter 2019

Week	Date	Topic	Activities	Assignments due
1	1/10	Syllabus review Capstone overview	Overview of the capstone courses and assignments	A1: About Me Slides A2: Personal Inventory Sheet
2	1/17	Project interests	Speedy introductions exercise	
3	1/24	Sponsored projects	Sponsor pitches	A3: Team Formation A4: Sponsor Ranking
4	1/31	Project topics/Design questions	Communicating with sponsors	A5: Team & Project Declaration
5	2/7	Project declaration	Team and project declaration feedback	A6: Design Research Review
6	2/14	How to develop your project intro and methods	Work session	A7: Project Introduction & Methods
7	2/21	Communicating project deliverables and focus	Project intro & methods feedback Work session	A8: Project Deliverables and Timeline
8	2/28	How to write a team contract	Project timeline feedback Work session	A9: Team Contract Draft
9	3/7	Putting together your project proposal	Team contract feedback Work session	A10: Project Madness Slide
10	3/14	Project Madness Presentation	Team project presentations	
F	3/21	Finals Week	No Class	A11: Project Proposal

The topics for this class and the sequence of assignments are designed to achieve the overall goals of 1) forming student teams, 2) pairing teams with project sponsors, 3) having the teams develop an initial understanding of the project design challenge, and 4) having the teams propose an informed process about how they will design and execute a user experience (UX) process to address that challenge. Some of the topics in the syllabus clearly correspond to things that the students have previously received instruction in during prior quarters. For this reason, each year, at least one or two student teams will make time to talk to me about being frustrated that I have shared with them a definition to clarify a term in an assignment or to provide examples of what has helped or hurt teams in past years. While many students in the class appreciate such insights (and will inevitably ask for them if they are not offered to the class as a whole), one or two teams are clearly annoyed by such information and ask, "Why are you talking about things when we just want to be starting our projects faster?" Versions of this complaint are asked both in scheduled office appointments and on end-of-quarter class evaluations. For example, in one end-of-term student evaluation, one student complained about "lecture time spent on reviewing topics of HCDE we have already learned like the different parts of the design process." In a different evaluation, a student lamented, "We know what the UCD process is. We don't need lecture to teach us about these things." At their core, these complaints cut to the very design of the class, indicating that even the most minimal instructional approach will work for many of the students, but not for all. A subset of the students in the class clearly benefits from hearing an explicit discussion of how what they will be doing over the next several weeks maps to concepts and techniques that they have encountered in varied classes taken earlier in the program. Since the teams in the class include mixes of students—some who do not want an explanation of how their capstone work is connected to things they have learned previously and some of whom strongly desire to have those connections drawn—I, as the instructor designing the class, face a decision in which some set of students is going to be less satisfied than the other. In this case, I err on the side of sharing more information to benefit those who want more (and may be in a team with those who want less). I do so knowing that a portion of the class will applaud the choice when they complete their evaluations and that a different portion of the class will complain strongly, such as in the quotes above.

Drawn from my teaching experiences over three years, each of these examples illustrates a variation on dilemmas that I have faced as I have attempted to integrate the experience of learners in these classes into its design. To think productively about these instances and how they might have implications for using a UX approach to class design, I see value in thinking about double binds in UX design. After offering this explanation of double binds, I will return to these three examples to illustrate with details how each of these examples exemplifies a type of double bind that we face as instructor-designers following a user experience approach to course design.

▪ Double Binds

The notion of double binds realized through communicative interactions was first developed in the mid-20th century in the field of anthropology (Bateson et al., 1963) and has usefully been extended to studies of varied communication-intensive contexts since then. One such extension is the work of Conra Gist (2017), who uses the concept of double binds to analyze the experiences of aspiring teachers of color. She addresses the conflicted experiences of teacher candidates who "need to reconcile oppositional tensions between personal ties" related to their complex cultural identities as a person and "systemic ties," such as those associated with the profession and its institutions (Gist, 2017, p. 931). Focused on a different area of inquiry, Ronald Wendt (1998) uses the concept of double binds to examine the nonrational power dynamics that emerge from the communication dynamics in organizations that adopt a participative management approach. In a third example of how double binds have been used to conceptualize communicative interactions, Deborah Tannen (1983), in a presentation to the California Association of Teachers of English to Speakers of Other Languages, suggests that double binds are a common feature of cross-cultural differences in interpersonal communication.

Consideration of double binds in user experience (UX) studies has been more limited. Double binds have been casually considered by a few (e.g., Van Dijck, 2009) and have been used more systematically to consider the ongoing relationship between designer and users (Béguin, 2003). In a related strand of work, the framework of double binds has also been used to level a general critique (Khovanskaya et al., 2015) of Human Computer Interaction (HCI) frameworks that are not sensitive to critical considerations. In this chapter, I extend this notion to the design of learning contexts, using the three examples presented above. I will illustrate how accommodating the priorities of students discovered through conversation and course evaluations yields design priorities that place the course designer in a double-bind situation.

In the context of class design following a UX approach, a *double bind* is a situation in which the designer faces a dilemma due to competing demands. On one hand, the instructor-designer seeks to hear from students about their needs and desires as learners and to incorporate what is discovered into the design of the course. On the other hand, the instructor-designer is positioned within an institutional context that places its own demands (including educational policies and conventions), affecting what may or may not be possible or wise to do in the classroom. In short, the design space is not unconstrained. When the needs and desires of students are irreconcilable with the demands of the institution/profession, the instructor-designer encounters a double bind.

In the context of higher education, where faculty are often both instructors and the designers of the learning experience that their students will have in a given term, it is inevitable that they will experience double binds when taking a UX approach in their work. My three selected examples help demonstrate this.

Example 1: Evaluation

Deeply embedded in the logic of institutional-based instruction is the assumption that learning will be measured and verified. The practices of measurement and verification vary widely from one institution to another (and often even within a given institution), but instructors are almost always the agents that execute this institutional mandate. When acting as designers and following UX priorities, these same instructors will periodically hear from students that the standards for measurement and evaluation should be altered. In my example 1, this recommendation came in the unexpected form of making the standards more demanding. In this instance, upon analyzing the costs and benefits of making such a design change, I decided to follow the institutional process to make the course graded (rather than credit/no-credit). The choice, however, was not clearly or necessarily the right one. To make the choice, I had to face the dilemma of upsetting some students who really counted on the class to be less demanding so that they could balance it against the other demands of completing their senior year requirements and also of upsetting a few of my colleagues. These colleagues had either taught the class previously or had intentions to teach it in the future, and this change represented a new set of requirements in that the work would have to be evaluated more rigorously. In short, teaching the class would now be more demanding. At the moment I was involved in balancing the needs and desires of some of the students against the needs and desires of other students and of other stakeholders, I acutely felt the pressure of this double bind.

Example 2: Equivalence

Connected in many ways to the standards of evaluation is the assumption of equivalence in instructional contexts. Skilled instructors are often artful in using the available degrees of freedom they have in the classroom to adjust learning experiences so that they serve the needs of their students to the greatest degree possible. Sometimes, however, students will express desires that cannot be completely reconciled with the deeper logic of a course design. When seeking to find design accommodations that will address such student desires, instructors can encounter the double bind of allowing something that students anticipate will fit their needs but also making the class expectations equivalent. In my example, the accommodation I have offered is clearly not ideal and is felt as a dilemma in each juncture. Allowing students to pursue a project of their own imagination by adding on a nominal, recruited sponsor to ensure that the course requirements are roughly equivalent is a compromise solution to a double bind. On one hand, I could deny the students' requests to pursue a passion project of their own making and thereby make all the project teams have an equivalent relationship to their project sponsors. Conversely, I could simply comply with the impassioned pleas of a few student teams to be guided by their own interests and thereby allow inequivalences to proliferate across the course assignments. My solution to this double bind—allowing students to pursue a passion project while interacting with an add-on, nominal sponsor—serves a pragmatic need, but predictably yields a result that is less than ideal for the students. Although I can anticipate such an outcome and offer the students a reasoned prediction about the consequences of their choice, one or two teams each year choose to learn if I am right by trying out the compromise option.

Example 3: Expectance

When students arrive in our classes, they have expectations about what they will encounter that are formed from varied information resources and are undoubtedly different from one student to another. Information sources as varied as course catalogs, the perspective of student advisors, experiences shared by peers, and even general lore within the degree program are shared unevenly by students. Further, different learning styles and even personality types play into the varied expectations that students bring to any given class offering. In the example of the senior capstone class that I am drawing on in this chapter, it is also the case that student expectations are shaped by the realities of this juncture in their life: they are literally at a transitional moment when they are finishing as a student and about to embark on whatever their next known (or unknown) venture will be. Most are reasonably anxious and apprehensive. For many of them, the prospect of engaging in a large-scale project in which they can demonstrate their skills and knowledge with a team working with an external sponsor is exciting. For a few others, the realization that this project is the end of their degree and that there are many things they do not yet know and that the horizon holds many unanswered questions creates frustrations that surface in capstone. As the instructor of the course, with several years' worth of experience in both teaching and non-academic professional work, I have thoughts about things that would be useful for students to consider in order for them to get the most benefit out of their capstone project experience. Many students want such a perspective layered into conversations during class meetings. Without exception, though, each year, there are some students whose expectations are that this course should be more singularly about them demonstrating what they have learned during their previous years of coursework. In essence, they expect the course to be about achieving something by pure force of action sans any instruction. Such desires are made explicit in private conversations or sometimes in end-of-course evaluation comments. The double bind I face as the instructor-designer of the course is how best to make the course work for user-learners with such strongly held desires. The somewhat unsatisfactory solution I have arrived at is to reduce most oral instruction to a few strategic forms: explicit, detailed assignment sheets, brief allusions to such details in discussions with the class as a whole, and strategically timed mentoring discussions with teams who are receptive to such ideas during the quarter. Sharing instructional information in this way is far less efficient and even effective than a more centralized mechanism, but it is more complementary to the strongly held expectations of some students.

The details of these three examples are specific to my institutional context, but the types of double binds they represent are almost certainly recognizable to most readers. I could readily point to instances of such double binds in other courses I have taught over recent years, as I anticipate nearly any instructor-designer could.

Recognizing the presence of double binds in course designs following a UX approach has potential value in allowing for instructor-designers to talk across their individual experiences. This framing clearly has a relationship to notions of *constraints* and *competing interests* in design, but it is more specific. In particular, this framing places an emphasis on the conflicted, felt experience of instructor-designers. That is, double binds are experienced personally as tensions in our identity as we occupy our professional/institutional roles and also seek to empathize with the experiences of our students and empower them to contribute to the design of their education. As a community, we need a language for talking about these personally experienced tensions, enabling us to share and compare such moments.

It is important to clarify here, though, that double binds are present across human interactions. Indeed, the original identification of double binds emerged from psychology-based assessments of family relationships. Subsequently, double binds have been identified in multiple forms of interpersonal communication and in broader communicative contexts. We might reasonably anticipate that when we as designers open our processes to input from users and are truly committed to integrating such input into our design choices, double binds will proliferate. Following this process as instructor-designers who maintain professional commitments to our host institutions as well as conventional knowledge gained from lore handed down in our profession and our own wisdom developed from prior teaching experiences, we should expect to inevitably and repeatedly encounter double-bind dilemmas when we seek out and attempt to use input from our students.

Double binds are not something that we should expect to always be able to design our way around—even as we have a language for naming them as they occur. Double binds are manifestations of competing value systems as we bring our students into potentially transformative contact with the design of the classes they inhabit. As we open ourselves to interactions around the artful choices we make about our classes, those interactions will necessarily involve a range of dimensions, including the political, economic, social, and personal that will compete for priority in our design choices. Such competitions will be experienced as mild annoyances and as career-altering dilemmas. We should expect double binds to be part of the essence of our work, not something that can be resolved for all time with a single, clever design decision

My purpose here is not to solve these three forms of double binds (or the many others that we face). Instead, I want to provide a framework that facilitates naming and discussing a phenomenon that we experience as instructor-designers who want to embrace the values of UX and attend to the needs and desires of learners.

■ Conclusion

This chapter identifies three types of double binds that an instructor may encounter when attempting to teach from a user experience perspective. Other experiences from this class as well as other classes I have offered would provide countless other examples of double binds. Inherent in our commitment to follow the priorities of UX when designing our courses is the experience of double binds. Such double binds are not signs that our course designs are flawed—that we have somehow come up short in our understanding of our students and some set of readily identified design requirements. Instead, I would advocate, double binds are an inherent part of the experience of being a committed instructor-designer. Indeed, if we go too long without experiencing a double bind, we might begin to question if we are truly hearing the students we are seeking to understand. As a broad community of instructors, I think we might begin to routinely exchange stories about the double binds we have experienced. We might begin to share mutual wonder and perhaps a few laughs about these experiences in our dispersed educational settings. In essence, we might normalize talk about double binds in our collective experience as instructor-designers.

■ References

Bateson, G., Jackson, D. D., Haley, J. & Weakland, J. H. (1963). A note on the double bind—1962. *Family Process, 2*(1), 154–161.

Béguin, P. (2003). Design as a mutual learning process between users and designers. *Interacting with Computers, 15*(5), 709–730.

Ford, J. D. (2018). Going rogue: How I became a communication specialist in an engineering department. *Technical Communication Quarterly, 27*(4), 336-342.

Ford, J. D. & Teare, S. (2006). The right answer is communication when capstone engineering courses drive the questions. *Journal of STEM Education, 7*(3), 5-12.

Gist, C. D. (2017). Voices of aspiring teachers of color: Unraveling the double bind in teacher education. *Urban Education, 52*(8), 927–956.

Khovanskaya, V., Baumer, E. & Sengers, P. (2015). Double binds and double blinds: Evaluation tactics in critically oriented HCI. In *Proceedings of The Fifth Decennial Aarhus Conference on Critical Alternatives* (CA '15) (pp. 53–64). Aarhus University Press. https://doi.org/10.7146/aahcc.v1i1.21266.

Tannen, D. (1983, April 15-17). *Cross-cultural communication* [Paper presentation]. State Meeting of the California Association of Teachers of English to Speakers of Other Languages, Los Angeles, CA, United States. https://files.eric.ed.gov/fulltext/ED253061.pdf.

Van Dijck, J. (2009). Users like you? Theorizing agency in user-generated content. *Media, Culture & Society, 31*(1), 41–58.

Wendt, R. F. (1998). The sound of one hand clapping: Counterintuitive lessons extracted from paradoxes and double binds in participative organizations. *Management Communication Quarterly, 11*(3), 323–371.

Zachry, M. & Spyridakis, J. H. (2016). Human-centered design and the field of technical communication. *Journal of Technical Writing and Communication, 46*(4), 392–401.

12. User Experience in the Professional and Technical Writing Major: Pedagogical Approaches and Student Perspectives

Jennifer Bay, Margaret Becker, Ashlie Clark, Emily Mast, Brendan Robb, and Korbyn Torres
PURDUE UNIVERSITY

Abstract: User experience can serve as a framework for introducing students to the field of professional and technical writing by having them engage in user experience research with current students and alumni of their academic program. Students not only learn to perform this research but also to analyze and assess user experience in light of the broader field's research agenda, as well as reflect on their own relationship to the research. We present a case study of an undergraduate research methods class that asked students to assess user experiences in our professional writing major. We present the pedagogical approach we took to user experience and show how students approached the projects, the challenges and successes of their approaches, what they learned about their major, and finally, how those insights changed the way they approached their education and future careers. A key takeaway is learning about a flexible pedagogical approach to user experience that combines program assessment, introduction of students to the major, development and donor relations, as well as critical reflection on students as users. Perhaps most importantly, this article includes the voices of undergraduates in the professional writing major, both in their roles as users and as user experience researchers.

Keywords: user experience, usability, students as users, curricular revision

Key Takeaways:

- User experience can serve as a robust framework for understanding how programmatic experiences can facilitate student engagement with/in a field of study.
- Undergraduate student perspectives have much to teach us about user experience in professional and technical communication curricula and programs.
- Flexible pedagogical approaches to user experience that combine program assessment, introduction of students to the major, development and donor relations, as well as critical reflection on students as users, can help us assess programs successfully.

This chapter explores a central research question for educators of professional and technical writing majors: *How can a program best prepare students for future career opportunities and the skills needed to succeed in those careers?* We argue for user experience as a pedagogical approach for educating students about one university's professional writing major. User experience is often conflated with "usability" in technical communication courses and textbooks; that is, undergraduate students are taught how to assess the usability of a document or project or how to conduct basic research on users or potential users of a product (Lauer & Brumberger, 2016). Much of this pedagogical work at the undergraduate level is accomplished through traditional textbook explanations of methodology or via academic assignments, and it is often presented more simplistically due to the nature of undergraduate education (Chong, 2016; Rose & Tenenberg, 2017).

As Claire Lauer and Eva Brumberger (2016) remind us, "*Usability* focuses on evaluating how well a user can navigate through a variety of tasks that an end product was designed to facilitate" (p. 249). This definition seems to mimic traditional assessment practices in education where students are evaluated on how well they perform a set of tasks which they have been taught how to do (McGovern, 2007). Missing from this model are the interactions and interplay between various factors across a student's experience with a program or major. Usability as a pedagogical application, then, is limited in its ability to capture the entire environment and its influences on student experiences. Likewise, considering usability as a pedagogical approach can seem utilitarian and consumer-driven; students and instructors, in such a model, value the classroom as a place where they can easily extract the appropriate information or skill set to demonstrate success, which translates into a job.

Instead, we argue that user experience (UX) can serve as a more robust framework for understanding how a programmatic experience can facilitate student engagement with/in a field of study. *User experience*, as a concept, attempts to capture all of the aspects embedded in one's experience with an outside entity or situation. As Lauer and Brumberger (2016) remind us, "UX suggests designing for interconnectedness, where tasks and texts no longer exist individually or in a silo, but instead connect across a broad and complex landscape of interfaces and environments" (p. 249). They point out that UX better allows for the possibility that users might react or use information processes and products in unanticipated ways. In this model, UX emphasizes the interactivity of experience across multiple levels, users, processes, and deliverables. UX also incorporates the notion of time, offering a model in which interactivity might happen across and be affected by temporality. Rather than user testing one experience with a product, service, or situation, UX allows for the more complex and dynamic interplay of multiple elements which shapes the user's experience across time and space.

In the model we present here, students engage in UX research with current students and alumni of their own program. Students not only learn to perform this research but also to analyze and assess user experience in light of the broader field's research agenda, as well as reflect on their own relationship to the research. As this article demonstrates, undergraduate student perspectives have much to teach us about user experience in the professional and technical communication curriculum.

We present a case study of an undergraduate research methods class that asked students to assess user experiences in the professional and technical writing major at Purdue. In teams, we surveyed, interviewed, and visually mapped our large network of alumni, with particular attention to location and job position, as well as surveying current students in the major. We framed much of this work around data visualization methods (Wolfe, 2015), especially in mapping our program's alumni, in order to contextualize the ways in which user experience can also function as "big data" (McNely et al., 2015). We went into the project with the following research question: *How effective is our professional writing curriculum for alumni and students?* As we proceeded through the projects, we nuanced that question of "effectiveness" in terms of various factors, including preparation for jobs and internships, confidence, and connections between curricula and job skills. We produced research reports that assessed and evaluated the data, as well as posters based on our research, and presented them to major stakeholders of the program.

Our chapter outlines the pedagogical approach we took to user experience and then proceeds to show how students approached their projects, the challenges and successes of their approaches, what they learned about their major, and finally, how those insights changed the way they approached their education and future careers. We conclude with plans for how we can use the information for curricular (re)design, and suggest ways for how we might continue having students and faculty collaborate in classrooms on user experience research to continue to both educate students and develop curricula. A key takeaway for readers is learning about a flexible pedagogical approach to user experience that combines program assessment, introduction of students to the major, development and donor relations, as well as critical reflection on students as users. Perhaps most importantly, this article is co-written by undergraduates in the professional and technical writing major, demonstrating their roles as users and as user experience researchers.

■ User-Centered Research and the Undergraduate Major

As this volume and prior research illuminates, there is no one consensus on how we are to approach the concept of "user experience" in professional and technical writing (Lallemand et al., 2015). Building from traditional usability testing that seeks to make products usable and user-friendly (Nielsen, 1994), as well as user-centered design, which centralizes the user in a product development cycle (Still & Crane, 2017), user experience encompasses the entire exploration of motivations, experiences, needs, and affordances of users (Pucillo & Cascini, 2014). As Liza Potts (2015) has noted, UX can also extend to what she calls experience architecture:

> an emerging practice, one that draws together issues of information design, information architecture, interaction design,

and usability studies to assess and build products, services, and processes. The outcomes of a well-architected system include systems, interfaces, and policies that support participation, growth, and sustainability—in other words, building experiences that are focused on human experience. (p. 256)

When we develop a major or concentration, we are creating an experience for students. We want students to proceed through a program and not only learn concepts, theories, and approaches, but also to develop a sense of themselves as future professionals entering a community of practice. These students will also be "products" of a program and its approaches, much like we see doctoral students as products of a particular program, with particular strengths and ways of seeing the world. They will be part of the larger community of practitioners, but also part of an alumni network. Thus, it is not just a matter of teaching students professional and technical writing theories, approaches, and genres, but constructing a program as experience is also about teaching students to inhabit an identity that distinguishes them as alumni of its program, as well as part of a larger community of practice that is the field.

Engineering an experience for students that cultivates membership in academic, alumni, and practitioner communities requires attention to students as users of and in the academic program. There has been extensive research on user-centered design, usability, and the user experience in professional and technical writing, but we have found less attention to how we are to understand students as "users" in an undergraduate major. Beth Hewett and Christa Ehmann Powers (2007) argue for seeing students as users in order to develop strong online instruction. Other scholars have followed to consider the "student as user" perspective in online educational environments (Bartolotta et al., 2017; Blythe, 2001). Felicia Chong (2016) uses the lenses of usability and user-centered design to consider technical communication textbooks and syllabi. More recently, Joseph Bartolotta et al.'s (2018) special issue of *Computers & Composition* on user-centered design and usability in the composition classroom embraces and complicates the idea of seeing students as users in writing classrooms. Natasha Jones (2018) argues for seeing students as expert end users of pedagogical products such as syllabi, and that, as such, we need to consider their needs in composing classroom charter documents. Dawn Opel and Jacqueline Rhodes (2018), though, caution us in adopting the language of efficiency and expediency inherent to some UX work, which can posit education as an ecology of currency and exchange rather than one of learning. Perhaps as mediators between these two positions, Shivers-McNair et al. (2018) describe an instructor and students' case study of how they used user-centered design in the classroom. Such a collaboration demonstrates how students are both learners and users simultaneously; as such, students can occupy multiple different positions and perspectives as they move throughout a program or curriculum.

One approach we might take is thinking about specific sites or courses as micro-testing grounds to gauge the experiences of a program's students and/or alumni. In a sense, this approach relies on what we might term *"programmatic UX,"* or taking the temperature of users at a specific moment and in a particular context. Programmatic UX could be one way to iteratively research, test, and refine particular aspects of a program's user experience. In what follows, we present a case study of one attempt to test the user experience of an academic program as it is defined by the students in the major. Because students are both users and experts in a program, they occupy an important space in which they can reflect on how useful the program is currently to them, as well as be able to investigate its use by other stakeholders. At the same time, they are still learning and so need to learn methods of assessing usability and user experience. This case study demonstrates how students learned user experience research methods while they simultaneously functioned as users of a program, providing a unique snapshot of their reflections as user-learners in the program. In what follows, each co-author discusses contributions and experiences in the class as co-constructors and co-authors of the research. This project was approved as exempt by Purdue's Institutional Review Board under number IRB 2019-2011.

▪ A Case Study on Curricular User Experience

One of the key courses in our professional and technical writing major is English 203: Introduction to Research for Professional Writers. It is a methods course that introduces students to key approaches to conducting and analyzing research in the field, such as literature reviews, interviews, focus groups, surveys, and usability testing, as well as newer approaches such as photovoice, data visualization, and storytelling methods. Jenny teaches this course regularly on a yearly basis and generally uses service-learning pedagogy to organize the course projects. However, she has observed that based on graduating senior perspectives in capstone courses, recent graduates of the major possess less knowledge of career trajectories and larger trends in the field. Part of this issue may result from institutional constraints that have affected course offerings and staffing. In recent years, full-time faculty positions have not been re-advertised when faculty have left, leaving the program down faculty. Likewise, many faculty are tasked with administrative appointments that leave less time for teaching in the major, resulting in more graduate students teaching major courses. Often those instructors will only teach a course once before turning it over to another graduate student to teach. While these graduate students are excellent teachers and scholars, they have little experience in or knowledge of the major and the needs of students. Most of their prior teaching experiences have been in business and technical writing service courses. And graduate students often do not have the institutional history or longevity to make a sustained impact on the program.

The turnover in instructors for our core courses, as well as the lack of faculty teaching the major, resulted in students who were not quite knowledgeable about their career possibilities, the affordances of the major, and the kinds of work they may want to pursue post-graduation. But also compounding this issue was a lack of institutional research on our alumni, such as where they are located, the kinds of positions they pursued, and the connection between degree and career. Unlike programs such as engineering or computer science, the professional and technical writing program at our university does not have dedicated staff to collect and maintain data on our alumni (in fact, as a humorous aside, when Jenny requested data on our professional writing alumni from the university development office, she received a list of alumni from the creative writing major instead). She realized that without understanding the prior experiences of alumni, it would be difficult to design a better experience for current students.

Based on these exigencies, Jenny decided to take a user-centered approach to the course and have students investigate the varied experiences of professional and technical writers, including those of alumni, current students, and even writers who did not graduate from the program. Students in the course would help design their own learning by conducting research based on their own questions, needs, and understandings. Taking this user-centered approach required that we also learn about core competencies in the broader field of professional and technical writing, how those competencies have evolved over time, and emerging competencies that alumni might be expected to learn. Jenny constructed a series of readings, assignments, and projects that allowed students in the course to see themselves as "users" of the major's knowledge, courses, and professional development, but also to conduct research on alumni and peers as "users." In short, the assignments and projects asked the students to analyze various user experiences of the major over time.

As the instructor and developer of this approach, Jenny wondered how well this would work since, in one sense, she was having users work with other users. That is, these various stakeholders, while all users in one sense, occupied different vantage points and perspectives. Jenny hoped that they would each learn from each other to answer questions such as the following: What would it mean to see students as "users" of the major? Were they users of knowledge learned from the major? Users of theories from courses? Or users of their degree from Purdue? What were the experiences of students in the major, both during their coursework and looking back as alumni? In short, what were the parameters of user experience as defined by students and alumni?

∎ UX Research Projects

Jenny developed a scaffolded approach where assignments were integrated with and dependent on one another to enhance student learning. Students would have a subject matter experts project that was ongoing throughout the semester, a few traditional secondary research projects that would provide them with background research and understandings, and larger, more complex projects that engaged with the user experience of the program at multiple levels.

Background Research Projects

Students read key articles that both enacted the research methods we would discuss and also reported on research outlining core competencies and emerging areas in professional and technical writing. Students would produce two different short reports: one highlighting a core competency in a specific career position or subfield and a second on an emerging area in professional and technical writing. These two assignments were very traditional in the sense that formal, researched reports would be a standard, expected genre in many research methods courses. The difference in this case is that the two areas—core competencies and emerging areas—would serve as background theories for the remaining work for the course.

Research Training

As part of their preparation for this project, students completed CITI training that would prepare them to interact with human participants and data in ethical ways. While none of the work students completed could be considered true research contributing to general knowledge, all survey instruments were anonymous, and in collecting data on alumni, students only relied on publicly available information online. Similarly, the information collected is being used programmatically and internally to help shape curricula and student user experiences. Thus, while we present some of the results here, we emphasize more of the process and learning about the various user experiences of our program.

Subject Matter Experts Project

An ongoing project for the course was the subject matter experts project. Throughout the semester, students conducted informational interviews with alumni from our program either in person or via Skype. The assumption behind this assignment is that one of the best ways to discover information about a profession, career, or field of study is via an informational interview with a subject matter expert in that field. An *informational interview* is an interview with a professional in order to discover information about their field of work or study (Decarie, 2010; Mulvaney, 2003) and is often conducted with an employee of a company, agency, or organization. The informational interviewer is not seeking a job but is seeking to discover more information about how that person became a professional in that field of work.

Jenny approached this project from a user-centered perspective: rather than pre-selecting alumni for the students to interview, students were allowed to vote on five alumni from the program's LinkedIn alumni group. Students in the course joined the LinkedIn alumni group, which brought them into a community of practice and situated them along with other alumni as users in the program; they then reviewed member profiles to find professionals with interesting profiles or backgrounds. Jenny asked students to select one of those alumni to serve as a subject matter expert who would be interviewed by the class. Students had to consider the potential speaker's background, career trajectory, experiences, field of study, positions held, educational background, etc. Students also provided possible questions which were used to collaboratively develop a list of questions to ask each speaker. After choosing alumni, Jenny created a Google survey to allow students to vote on their choice of subject matter experts to invite to class, and Jenny invited the top five alumni.

One programmatic illumination from this project was that the LinkedIn alumni group is a self-selected group, meaning that members were not necessarily alumni of our specific professional writing program. Almost all of the members were alumni from Purdue, but they may have earned different degrees and were working as professional or technical writers. Thus, some of these users were not necessarily users of the program but were users in the field, which provided a rich set of perspectives. For instance, one subject matter expert (SME) was an alumnus of a graduate program in the College of Agriculture but worked as a technical writer in Silicon Valley to support his family. He had no knowledge of technical writing before taking the job, so his user experience was in the field. What the diversity of group members showed was that members identified themselves in terms of their careers first and their majors/education second. They saw professional and technical writing less as a field of study and more as a career trajectory that was not necessarily connected to an academic program. In thinking of program assessment, then, career preparation as a category of assessment might need to be more nuanced.

Also of note is that the instructor, Jenny, did not vote on the subject matter experts, which allowed students in the class to really pursue their own interests, agendas, and backgrounds. These choices provided the instructor with interesting perspectives on student user interests. At times, Jenny was unsure whether these alumni were really the "best" choices, but what became apparent is that taking a user-centered approach requires respecting those user choices and decisions as valid ones. As Lauer and Brumberger (2016) note, UX allows for unexpected understandings and uses of information products. It may be that students in the course wanted a more well-rounded approach to the major than just a specific educational or academic path. After each interview, students were asked to write up a short report on the interview and their thoughts and observations. Margaret noted, for instance, that the importance of being a lifelong learner seemed to be a theme throughout the SME speakers, as they all touched on it at some level in their talks. The idea of continuous learning is probably one of the biggest takeaways she had because it has been brought up again and again. After hearing one of the speakers who did freelance work, Brendan wondered how many technical writers are freelancers and if this is a viable career option for someone who has worked in the industry for about ten years. Emily also observed that most of the speakers had taken time to work or gain another experience before going back to graduate school. She had never met anyone who had done this before the interviews with the speakers for this class, and is considering this option for herself.

As students reflected, they recognized that college students often have difficulty identifying exactly what career they want to have. In fact, this is a source of stress for many during their entire college careers. The subject matter experts who came to talk to our class were more than helpful, setting students' minds at ease. The experts may have had different careers, but they each assured students that they would have a multitude of options for when they graduate from college. The main advice that each expert gave was clear: no employer expects a new employee to be perfect. The speakers reiterated that it is not necessary to know exactly what to do the first day on the job, and no employer should expect that from them. Asking questions and actively looking for information is encouraged in order to show an employer how eager new employees are to learn. New experiences and opportunities are daunting; however, being open to these experiences will be beneficial at a new job. The experts assured students that a new job should not be something that frightens them. No matter what career they would end up pursuing, the environment and work should never be something that scares students. The variety of careers the speakers discussed led students to feel that they could be open and versatile in the current job market.

Another important takeaway from the subject matter experts' experiences was that it is crucial to form connections. Many speakers discussed the processes that they had undergone while applying for their jobs and how the connections they had formed led them to their current position. Finally, Margaret noted specifically that by allowing students to choose the alumni they wanted to hear from, our professor was encouraging the class to take an active role in the formation of the course outcomes. Margaret noted that she gained more from the course due to this active involvement in comparison to courses where the course outcomes were prescribed.

As you can see, students were able to use these interviews to enhance and nuance their alumni projects by better understanding perspectives they had not previously considered and incorporating that data into their other projects in the course. Moreover, they developed more confidence in how they might be able to approach the larger projects, as well as their work in the major. Assessment in this context might take into account more than the ability to get a job in the field and consider lifelong skills of learning and adaptation as what allows individuals to achieve success.

Alumni Project

Halfway through the semester, students were tasked with creating a proposal for a research project that asked students to discover more about alumni who had graduated from the undergraduate program. The outcome of this project was multifold: to discover career pathways and possible life trajectories, to learn more about how alumni specifically used their degrees or the knowledge they gained from the program, and to develop a stronger alumni network that students could leverage and learn from as they progressed in the program. Moreover, Jenny hoped to use this information to redesign or adjust the program, if needed. Students were asked to make multiple decisions for this project: to propose who to survey and why; to identify how to contact them or find their data; to choose and design the format of the survey; to determine what questions to ask, how to encourage responses, how to collect and analyze the data, and how to display the data; and, finally, to decide what conclusions to draw. Each team submitted a proposal on what or who should be surveyed, why that population, how to access the population, what questions would be asked, what roles and responsibilities students would have on the team, and what timeline would be followed to complete the work. Later, each team submitted a data collection instrument that would be used, along with any other documentation needed. Finally, students completed a final report on the results of their research.

Students brainstormed possible projects in class and divided into groups based on different research interests. Three groups were formed, each with a different focus relating to the program itself. One group decided to create a database of alumni with information such as email addresses, current locations, job titles, and current employers. A second group wanted to create and distribute a survey to current students in the program since they were key stakeholders in the program. The third group authored a survey sent out to recent alumni on the LinkedIn alumni group. Of interest was the second group's work with current students, which was a bit outside of the boundaries of the project; they saw the need to start collecting information and networking with current students *before* they become alumni. This approach clearly came from the user experiences of the students themselves, who may have wanted to feel more connected to the program earlier in the major.

After students worked on their research and analysis, they had a chance to present their results to faculty members within the major. Students prepared posters that outlined their research methods and results, and presented them to members of the professional writing program, as well as other stakeholders such as alumni relations. The key outcome of this project was for students to discover innovative ways to present data visually to non-users of the program.

The following sections contain more details from students on how they conceived, executed, and learned from these projects. Results from two of the three projects are represented here, as the authors were directly involved in them. What we hope comes through is how these students learned by researching the user experience of their own major rather than just traditional pedagogies of research methods.

■ Understanding the User Experience of Current Students

The work students did as a team to interpret feedback from current professional writing students was eye-opening. Brendan, Emily, Korbyn, and Ashlie's project was focused on obtaining more information about current students in the major and using the feedback provided in order to understand how to make the program more functional and worthwhile for students. The research these students performed was also beneficial to them as students of the program since the information they collected increased the awareness of the students around them. They felt that it was strange that there was no prior research into the students in the professional writing program because they assumed that the program would know everything about the students and alumni. The team decided to send out a survey in order to obtain the answers to their questions. That process in itself was something with which the group had little previous experience. The time and planning that went into creating the survey was something that they hadn't considered to be difficult, but turned out to be quite demanding. To understand how to create an effective survey, the team researched and spent time attempting to gather as much data as possible. They needed to create a survey which was unbiased, yet still asked specific questions to collect the desired feedback. The trouble was related to leading questions, as the team did not want to affect the responses they received with the framing of the prompts. Part of this issue might have been because the students themselves belonged to the population being studied. Appendix A shows the final survey questions the team developed, some of which were prompted by the articles read for class and the SME interviews. Appendix B outlines some of the results of the survey that the team articulated in their final report.

The team presented the results of their survey to the program faculty, both orally and visually (see Figure 12.1). The presentation occurred during an interactive poster session with stakeholders of the program, including faculty, development officers, and undergraduate and graduate students. It allowed the team to provide information about current students and their expectations for the program from students themselves. It also enabled staff and faculty to consider what it was that current students wanted to receive from courses related to professional writing. Since no other data had been collected about student wants and needs, it was not hard to identify where the program could improve in the eyes of the students. Most notably from the presentation, students did not feel as prepared for after graduation as they would have liked, which reinforces what emerged from the SME project: students may need a more explicit focus on self-efficacy and adaptation.

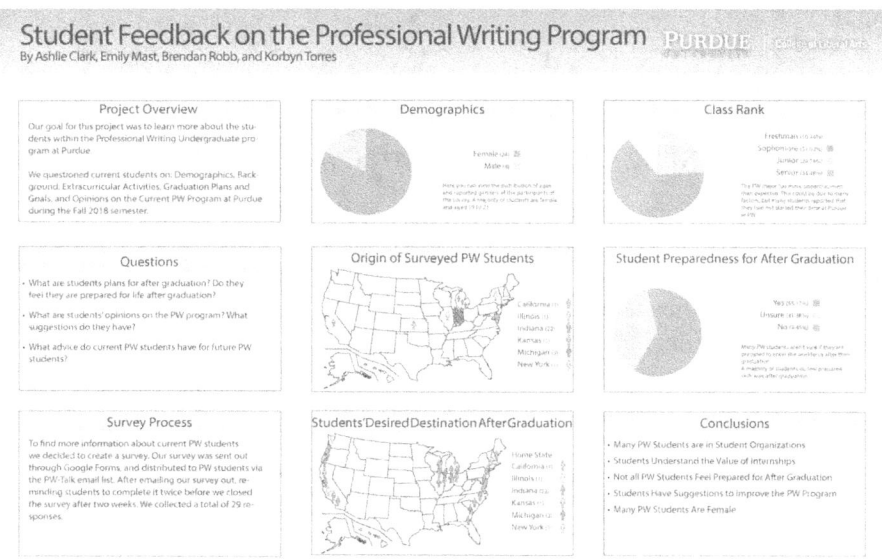

Figure 12.1. Current student research project poster.

Alumni Data Visualization Project

For this project, Margaret's team compiled existing data points on the program's alumni into a single database. The purpose of the project was to create a database that could be updated periodically to produce graphs and charts on professional writing program students and alumni. For example, one of the graphics that was produced from this database is a map of the geographical locations of our alumni which shows the diversity of their job locations (see Figure 12.2).

Figure 12.2. Google map of professional writing alumni locations.

The method used to collect this data unfolded as the team worked on the project since it was difficult to collect data from scratch. Data on alumni of the professional writing program was collected through multiple outlets and was stored in a Google Sheets file. First, data was gathered from the Purdue Professional Writing Group on LinkedIn by sorting through the group members for graduates of the program. Many members of the group were not professional writing alumni and thus were not added to the database. The team looked at connections to our faculty in the program, as well as other alumni for more names to add to the database. A final data source was the PW-Talk email list, which is a listserv for current students and alumni of the program. In all, students collected data for over 300 program alumni.

For each alum added to the database, the following information was obtained: name, job title, location, graduation year, and whether or not they attended graduate school. The team decided on these categories based on some of the SME speakers and the fact that some alumni had continued on in the graduate program at Purdue. If any of the information was not available, the field was marked with "n/a." In order to discover some of this information, the team had to do the difficult work of googling the names of these alumni to see who they could find. One challenge was finding information for alumni who graduated before 2000, as many of these alumni had no online presence or had changed career trajectories, making them difficult to find.

The resulting data set was used to create visual graphics, including a word cloud graphic of job titles (see Figure 12.3), as well as pie charts and graphs displayed in a poster for the final presentation to stakeholders. The most valuable aspect of this project for Margaret was creating something that would be used for purposes beyond turning it in for a grade. Beyond creating the poster displaying the results of the project to members of the English department, the team was able to share the database with the administration of the professional writing program for them to use for their own purposes. For Margaret, this type of "service learning" is the most beneficial because it combines the learning process with applications outside of the classroom. Throughout the project development, Margaret reported more enthusiasm for this project in comparison to others completed in the past because the end product would be used to inform others rather than simply to be turned in for a final grade.

■ Conclusions

Several common threads of the user experience emerge from these project reflections, which we didn't realize until writing this chapter. The first is that user experience in the professional writing major includes more than just academic or career preparation; rather, it also includes life preparation. As Ashlie notes, the UX approach of the class led her to become more aware and understanding of other human beings with whom she interacts. Likewise, there was a consensus that the subject matter experts reinforced that everyone is human; we all make mistakes and are still learning while on the job. There was an awareness of work-life balance and that one's career may take them to unexpected places, both geographically and careerwise, which is reflected in the mapping of our alumni.

Another interesting learning moment on the part of students was that large institutions do not always practice good data collection and management. That is, in contrast to companies, universities do not always track their "users" or assess their user experiences in holistic ways. Some of this is due to privacy concerns and educational rights, but it might also be due to the lack of a culture of user experience assessment throughout a degree program or major. Thus, the UX approach of the class meant compiling information not only for student projects and grades, but for the program as a whole. Students believed that the program administrators could use the information gleaned from the survey to help structure the program and its curriculum to something that the students could be proud of by the time they graduate.

A final conclusion is that this particular UX approach treats users as value co-creators of the program. Keshab Acharya (2017) notes that to understand how value is created, we need to "look at the interactive relationships between the product, the designer, and the end-user" (p. 30). *User value*, then, is a result of a dialogue or interaction between multiple elements. In this sense, the UX approach of the class engaged students as value co-creators of the program. By better understanding the program, its stakeholders, and its position in the larger field of work and study, students, as users, helped create value in the program, for themselves, as well as the stakeholders engaging in their projects.

Figure 12.3. Word cloud of alumni job titles.

These conclusions led us to see how programmatic assessment does not necessarily need to occur from the outside looking in; rather, perhaps students can be the most lucid assessors of our programs. Students, as users, can provide rich reflections on the value of a program and where that program can be strengthened. What we learned from this experience was that assessing a program needs to take into consideration the metrics and voices of those most impacted: students and alumni.

Future Directions

Based on the results of this approach, it's clear that the user experience research conducted by these students will create better ways to assess student experiences of the major as well as track alumni. One of the first steps is meeting individually with all of the students in the major to get a better sense of their experiences, needs, and career plans. While university academic advisors can meet with students, these advisors are not in the program and do not have backgrounds in professional writing. Using a modified version of the survey will also provide consistency across the program. Meeting individually with students will help build the foundations for networking needed to sustain strong programmatic user experiences.

After completing these meetings with students, some sort of method for assessing the program when students graduate will be developed, along with a follow-up for students after graduation. Jenny plans to engage current students and classes to continue participating in this evaluation of user experience so there can be a reciprocal and iterative process for understanding the user experiences of the program, as well as continue to teach students how to research and respond to user experience as a methodological approach. We also plan to collect information from students in our capstone courses and encourage them to connect to faculty and other students via social networking tools like LinkedIn. Finally, the program just updated its plan of study for the major to make the requirements more explicit to students. What we realized from this holistic assessment of understanding user experience is that current students and alumni did not always understand the program and its possible trajectories. Updating the plan of study allows us to make the possible tracks in the major more explicit in the hopes that it can guide students toward possible futures. We hope that such pedagogical approaches to researching user experience in the major can continue to strengthen our network of alumni, the program, and its plan of study, as well as the learning capacity and humanity of our students.

References

Acharya, K. R. (2017). User value and usability in technical communication: A value-proposition design model. *Communication Design Quarterly Review*, *4*(3), 26–34.

Bartolotta, J., Bourelle, T. & Newmark, J. (2017). Revising the online classroom: Usability testing for training online technical communication instructors. *Technical Communication Quarterly*, *26*(3), 287–299. https://doi.org/10.1080/10572252.2017.1339495.

Blythe, S. (2001). Designing online courses: User-centered practices. *Computers and Composition, 18*(4), 329–346. https://doi.org/10.1016/S8755-4615(01)00066-4.

Chong, F. (2016). The pedagogy of usability: An analysis of technical communication textbooks, anthologies, and course syllabi and descriptions. *Technical Communication Quarterly, 25*(1), 12–28. https://doi.org/10.1080/10572252.2016.1113073.

Decarie, C. (2010). Literacy and informational interviews. *Business Communication Quarterly, 73*(3), 306–317.

Hewett, B. & Powers, C. E. (2007). Guest editors' introduction. Online teaching and learning: Preparation, development, and organizational communication. *Technical Communication Quarterly, 16*(1), 1–13. https://doi.org/10.1207/s15427625tcq1601_1.

Jones, N. N. (2018). Human centered syllabus design: Positioning our students as expert end-users. *Computers and Composition, 49*, 25–35.

Lallemand, C., Gronier, G. & Koenig, V. (2015). User experience: A concept without consensus? Exploring practitioners' perspective through an international survey. *Computers in Human Behavior, 43*, 35–48.

Lauer, C. & Brumberger, E. (2016). Technical communication as user experience in a broadening industry landscape. *Technical Communication, 63*(3), 248–264.

McGovern, H. (2007). Training teachers and serving students: Applying usability testing in writing programs. *Journal of Technical Writing and Communication, 37*(3), 323–346.

McNely, B., Spinuzzi, C. & Teston, C. (2015). Contemporary research methodologies in technical communication. *Technical Communication Quarterly, 24*(1), 1–13.

Mulvaney, M. K. (2003). The information interview: Bridging college and beyond. *Business Communication Quarterly, 66*(3), 66–70.

Nielsen, J. (1994). *Usability engineering*. Academic Press.

Opel, D. S. & Rhodes, J. (2018). Beyond student as user: Rhetoric, multimodality, and user-centered design. *Computers and Composition, 49*, 71–81.

Potts, L. (2015). Archive experiences: A vision for user-centered design in the digital humanities. In J. Rodolfo & W. Hart-Davidson (Eds.), *Rhetoric and the digital humanities* (pp. 255–263). University of Chicago Press.

Pucillo, F. & Cascini, G. (2014). A framework for user experience, needs and affordances. *Design Studies, 35*(2), 160–179.

Rose, E. & Tenenberg, J. (2017). Making practice-level struggles visible: Researching UX practice to inform pedagogy. *Communication Design Quarterly Review, 5*(1), 89–97.

Shivers-McNair, A., Phillips, J., Campbell, A., Mai, H. H., Yan, A., Macy, J. F., Wenlock, J., Fry, S. & Guan, Y. (2018). User-centered design in and beyond the classroom: Toward an accountable practice. *Computers and Composition, 49*, 36–47.

Still, B. & Crane, K. (2017). *Fundamentals of user-centered design: A practical approach*. CRC Press.

Wolfe, J. (2015). Teaching students to focus on the data in data visualization. *Journal of Business and Technical Communication, 29*(3), 344–359.

Appendix A: Survey to Current Professional Writing Students

Hello! Purdue undergraduate students in English 203, Introduction to Research for Professional Writers, are conducting an informal survey of the current Professional Writing students to learn more about the backgrounds and career goals of students in the major and minor. This survey will take between 5–10 minutes. You are not required to complete this survey. If you have any questions feel free to contact us. Thank you for participating in this survey.

* Required

1. What is/are you major(s)? *
2. What is/are your minor(s)? *
3. What is your class rank (by credits)? *
   - ○ Freshman
   - ○ Sophomore
   - ○ Junior
   - ○ Senior
   - ○ Other:
4. Please enter your expected year and semester of graduation *
5. Are you a transfer student? *
   - ○ Yes
   - ○ No
6. Did you start Purdue as a Professional Writing major? *
   - ○ Yes
   - ○ No
7. Why did you choose Professional Writing at Purdue?
8. Are you involved in any student organizations? *
   - ○ Yes
   - ○ No
9. If so, what are they?
10. Do you currently have an internship? *
    - ○ Yes
    - ○ No
11. Do you plan on applying for any internships? *
    - ○ Yes
    - ○ No
    - ○ Maybe
12. If you have participated in an internship, what advice would you to give someone pursuing internships?
13. What is your goal for after graduation?
14. Do you feel your degree is preparing you for the path you want to pursue? *
    - ○ Yes
    - ○ No
    - ○ Unsure
15. List three skills you think are going to be the most valuable to you after graduation.

16. Do you have any job prospects/graduate school admission offers lined up? *
    - Yes
    - No
    - N/A
17. What area of the country/world are you hoping to live/work in after graduation?
18. Do you have any recommendations for students to be successful in the program?
19. If you could make any suggestions for the Purdue Professional Writing program, what would they be?
20. Age
21. Gender
22. What is/are your racial/ethnic background(s)?
23. Where are you from? (State/Country)

■ Appendix B: Survey Results

We asked a total of 23 questions in our survey on current students within the undergraduate major and received 29 responses. Within our questions, 11 were required, while 12 were voluntary-response. We began by having participants provide their major(s) and minor(s). All respondents were professional writing majors, except for one student who was an aeronautical engineering technology major with a professional writing minor. Seven of the 29 respondents had double majors. Students minored in a variety of topics, and in total, there were 24 different minors reported. Of the 29 respondents 16 had more than one minor. Overall, there were limited amounts of like minors between students. Communication minors were the most frequently reported as there were six students with this minor. There were three students minoring in Spanish, film/video studies, history, or creative writing. There were two students who were professional writing minors.

Next, participants selected their class rank. The majority of respondents were seniors, with sophomores being the next most populated group. The dominance of seniors and sophomores in the major was reflected when participants provided their expected semester of graduation. The majority of participants were expecting to graduate in either Spring 2019 or Spring 2021.

Participants reported whether they were transfer students and whether they began their time at Purdue as a professional writing major. Three of the respondents indicated that they were transfer students, and more than half of participants responded that they did not start at Purdue as a professional writing major.

The first non-required fill-in-the-blank question, "Why did you choose Professional Writing at Purdue?" resulted in 27 responses. Overall, participants explained that professional writing was a practical degree for their future plans. Many participants expressed their interest in English and writing, believing that professional writing is a major that allows them to continue on their career path while still being marketable.

Overall, 21 of the respondents were involved in student organizations. Everyone who answered "yes" to being involved in a student organization provided the organization(s) they were a part of in the following question. Many of the organizations did not overlap, but five students reported their involvement with the PWA, a student organization specific to professional writing majors.

Out of all the respondents, 23 did not currently have internships, but when asked if they planned on applying, 18 responded positively. Although only six participants had an internship at the time, we received 13 responses when asked what advice they'd give to someone pursuing an internship. Overall, participants advised to apply to both a large variety of different internships as well as looking broadly. One notable response was:

> Apply early. Give yourself grace. It is okay to be frustrated— sometimes people and organizations take on interns that they don't really know what to do with. It's frustrating but embrace it and try to continue making content.

Each person who provided their goal after graduation had their own unique plan. Of all the respondents, 23 hope to obtain a job and six intend to go on to graduate school. For those that hope to enter the job market, some notable careers include publishing, editing, technical writing, or something purely technical. Still others simply hope to obtain a job after graduation.

Only one participant did not believe that their degree was preparing them for their future career. Overall, participants were confident that they were being successfully trained for their goals, but 12 respondents were unsure if their schooling would actually provide the tools they need for their future careers. Every participant except one provided three skills they perceived to be most valuable after graduation. Skills in writing and communication were the most frequently reported skills with 12 and 11 responses respectively. Design skills was said seven times, editing and research both six times, and teamwork five.

Although many participants were seniors, only four of ten had job prospects lined up for after they graduate. All 28 respondents to this question were drawn to working somewhere in the United States. Most responses were either places on the east or west coasts. However, five respondents wish to stay in the Midwest.

Twenty-one participants gave recommendations to their fellow professional writing majors. One student urged others to

> Participate. This is an English degree, and nothing is harder than trying to have a conversation about a reading and no one wants to participate. You'll learn so much more from a discussion than

> the professor telling you what something means. Your ideas are valid.

Some explained that hard work is beneficial, while others urged others to pursue classes outside the English department.

When asked if they had any suggestions for the program, 19 participants responded with some advice. Many suggested a change to the curriculum to teach what they called "hard skills." They feared the degree focused more on abstracts than technical skills. Others wanted to see the department advertised more.

Lastly, we asked for age, gender, racial/ethnic background, and origin. Of the respondents, females dominated the major. Only five males in total responded to the survey. A vast majority of respondents identify as Caucasian, four reported they identified as Hispanic and two identified as Native American. The age of professional writing majors ranges from 16 to 23. Ten participants were 19. When prompted with their home state, 22 respondents said they were from Indiana.

13. Program as Product: UX and Writing Program Design in Technical and Professional Communication

Christine Masters-Wheeler
FRANCIS MARION UNIVERSITY

Gracemarie Mike Fillenwarth
ROWAN UNIVERSITY

Abstract: This chapter discusses the value that user experience (UX) can bring to programmatic assessment and design. After exploring previous work on assessment, we turn to UX as a methodology that can help expand the scope of assessment practices to cover not just learning outcomes and curricula, but the entire range of programmatic work. We next discuss the implications of this shift, particularly in viewing our programs as products and students as users. Through this discussion, we show the relevance of various UX methods for programmatic research, with a particular focus on Guo's breakdown of four UX fundamentals: value, usability, adoptability, and desirability. We conclude by describing interface mapping as a UX method applicable to programmatic research and discussing how further UX methods could be deployed.

Keywords: program assessment, UX and program design, interface mapping, UX and higher education

Key Takeaways:

- Faculty and administrators can use a UX lens for programmatic design, assessment, and redesign, framing the program as the product and the student as the user.
- To enact this lens, faculty and administrators can study a program's interfaces: the various ways that students interact with a program's representatives, spaces, activities, and artifacts.
- When assessing a program, we can ask questions about four aspects of UX: value, usability, adoptability, and desirability.
- Multiple UX approaches can be combined depending on program needs—surveys, focus groups, journey maps, and participatory design—but initial approaches, such as student and alumni surveys, can provide simple but effective feedback on a program's value, usability, adoptability, and desirability.

As undergraduate technical and professional communication (TPC) programs have continued to proliferate (Melonçon & Henschel, 2013), discussions of approaches to program design, redesign, and assessment have also continued. As TPC administrators consider the range of available approaches to building and improving programs, we argue that user experience (UX) methods can provide an innovative approach to program redevelopment. In this chapter, we explore how UX approaches to program redesign differ from existing approaches, and we forward the idea of program as "product" and students as "users" to theoretically ground this shift to UX-based research methods. Next, we offer a preliminary study that explores student interaction with program "interfaces" at two universities: a public liberal arts university in the southeast United States with an established TPC program and a public research university in the northeast United States with a young TPC program. Through this research, we demonstrate the value that UX-grounded research brings to program redesign, and we offer suggestions for initial and extended programmatic research based on the idea of students as users of programs.

▌ Approaches to Program Redesign

Numerous scholars have addressed assessment both as a required element of university-level programs and as an opportunity to redesign TPC programs. Tammy Rice-Bailey (2016) points out that, at its core, assessment at the programmatic level is concerned with "assessing student learning outcomes against program learning objectives" (p.1), and much of the literature on assessment in TPC programs demonstrates this focus. Researchers have taken a theoretical approach to this task (Gulbrandsen, 2012), used evidence-based approaches (Allen, 2010; Hundleby & Allen, 2010; Thomas & McShane, 2007), and emphasized the value of portfolio assessment (Cargile Cook & Zachry, 2010; Rice-Bailey 2016). While much research on assessment has focused on learning outcomes and objectives and corresponding curricular elements, some scholars have branched out to consider additional program elements and approaches to assessment (Coppola et al., 2016; Lam et al., 2016). Yet traditional learning outcome-centered program assessment models remain typical. As Joanna Schreiber and Lisa Melonçon (2019) acknowledge, however, traditional assessment methods typically do not address larger programmatic issues. Focusing on whether or not learning outcomes have been met does not allow opportunities to reflect on the complexities of writing programs, for example, those related to staffing, faculty development, marketing, and internship programs. Schreiber and Melonçon (2019) as well as Meredith Johnson et al. (2017) propose integrating continuous improvement (CI) practices into program administration.

While applying continuous improvement paradigms to program design can be beneficial and productive, we argue that program design could be enhanced further through the application of UX models. (See Kelli Cargile Cook's chapter in this collection for more on CI.) CI models resemble UX models in that they work towards the systemic improvement of processes and designs. As Schreiber and Melonçon (2019) note, "Continuous improvement, because it treats the workplace like a system of relations, can help uncover, credit, and situate a range of work processes that are often invisible and overlooked" (p. 8). Similarly, UX has the potential to illuminate the invisible or overlooked experiences of the users of an organization's product or service. Many programs include alumni when gathering feedback on program design processes, yet only including alumni in these processes may cause programs to miss out on gathering current or future students' perspectives. Feedback from alumni, who may have forgotten what it was like to be a student or may only recall program elements relevant to their current work, does not necessarily illuminate the full range of student experience as a continuous journey through an educational program from beginning to end. (Indeed, such surveys are susceptible to recall bias—a well-documented phenomenon especially in retrospective medical studies.) Michael Salvo and Jingfang Ren's (2007) positioning of students as valued stakeholders in a continuous improvement process and Jeffrey Jablonski and Ed Nagelhout's (2010) stakeholder focus that relies on the "complex use of assessment strategies" (p. 173) stand as strong examples of our larger vision for incorporating UX into programmatic assessment and revision.

UX methods can be applied to systems as well as to specific products, not only in profit-driven businesses, but also in non-profit organizations and governmental agencies. Nonprofits, hospitals, municipal offices, and other public entities have implemented UX methods to improve the experiences of the people they serve. Emma Rose et al. (2017) use UX strategies in working with a nonprofit organization, improving immigrant populations' access to health insurance. Lacey Kruger (2014) specifically argues that nonprofits should borrow UX strategies from for-profits by tailoring messages to donors as website users with the goal of convincing them to make online donations. In such a scenario, the website content on nonprofits' websites may be geared primarily toward donors, but the main "products" are the services that the organizations provide. In another hypothetical example, a soup kitchen's products would be the free meals that they serve to the public. Improving the user experience of people who receive the free meals would involve making sure that clients' needs are valued and met. UX researchers could gather information on areas such as how clients perceive the quality of food to how they are treated by staff and volunteers. The organization's primary mission may be to offer free meals, but how those meals are delivered and experienced by clients impacts how clients as well as donors perceive value in the organization. From these examples, we can see how nonprofit organizations of all kinds can use UX to improve stakeholder experiences of their products, whether those products are informational materials, goods, or services.

In higher education, our *products* are the programs that we offer to students. In this setting, an approach towards students as customers often carries through to student services personnel who arrange housing; offer tutoring, advising, and counseling; organize first-year-experience programs; and provide a range of other programs that are designed to guarantee student satisfaction and success. These student services programs help to keep retention rates high. However, the emphasis on improving "student experience" per se usually stops before it gets to the level of academic programs. Here, and rightly so, faculty members as well as program administrators relate to students primarily as learners, not consumers. At the classroom level, the idea of regarding students as consumers seems ridiculous and out of place; the two identities of learner and consumer seem to inherently conflict. We argue, however, that applying UX to academic program design can respect students' roles as learners while also acknowledging their roles as "users" of educational products. The programs we shape and develop as educational experiences are products with perceived value from a student's perspective.

■ Why "Product"?

Should educational programs really be framed as products? Understandably, faculty members may feel strongly that consumerist attitudes do not belong in higher education. We are committed to providing students with rich learning environments. We expect that programs of study will challenge students to grow as human beings, to develop their capacities for critical thought, and to experience broad cultural ideas in addition to subject-area knowledge. A high-quality educational experience cannot be neatly packaged because it consists of many variables, including the variety of electives offered and the unique perspectives that individual faculty members share with students. A degree program is not a product in the sense that it can or should be manufactured or standardized. However, looking at a specific program as a product can help to identify what it offers students apart from other academic programs and from the larger university. While a program exists within a larger university system, it is a distinct entity with its own appeal and has its own specific kinds of students. Focusing on programs as products could help us to identify areas of student-user experience that we are able to influence and change as program administrators. For our purposes, a program-product could be viewed as a type of designed experience that has a structure, a brand identity, and a number of associated artifacts. Students encounter the idea of the TPC program-product and perceive it as having a certain worth or value.

Programs are products associated with university brands, and they are marketed to prospective students who have many choices about where to enroll. It may be a question of semantics, as Eric Stoller (2014) argues, yet "calling ourselves anything but a business seems unfair and untrue. Students pay a great deal for the product that is higher education" (n.p.). Almost all students and/or their families contribute at least some of their own funds towards their higher education. Students pay for opportunities to take classes and earn degrees, and they *should* understand that there is no guarantee as to whether they will pass, fail, or get a job just because they paid for an educational experience. However, because they invest financially in these educational experiences, students are more than clients or the recipients of services; they assume roles as consumers, to a certain extent, in addition to their roles as learners. As program administrators, if we focus exclusively on students in their roles as learners, we may miss opportunities to enhance our programs in ways that could improve students' user experience of our products.

Emphasizing students' roles as consumers, university administrations often employ many of the same strategies used in businesses. Kevin Elliot and Margaret Healy (2001) found "student-centeredness" or "the extent to which students feel welcome and valued" as the most important factor in student satisfaction (p. 7). Studies like this one, while not explicitly framed as part of a user experience initiative, could represent a type of UX methods application in higher ed. Similarly, Bridget Burns (2016) has called for more institutions to adopt the practice of "process mapping" to improve student experiences. She makes the point that "[a]s consumers, we expect that retailers or service providers have designed the experience around the customer. We become frustrated when things are counterintuitive, bureaucratic, slow, difficult or painful. So why should we tolerate flawed processes that frustrate our students?" (n.p.). She gives examples of process mapping initiatives conducted by Georgia State University and Michigan State University that assisted students, especially first-generation students who lacked external support, with navigating university processes such as those surrounding admissions and financial aid.

Despite the apparent realities of higher education as a type of business, framing students as users for program development purposes does not mean that we should encourage students to identify primarily as consumers. Louise Bunce et al. (2017) found that students who identify as consumers tend to have "passive, instrumental attitudes to learning," "may have little interest in what is actually being taught," and "show reduced responsibility for producing their own knowledge" (p. 1959). However, the researchers also speculate that "students with a lower learner identity may develop a consumer orientation because they do not identify strongly as learners, and not because they necessarily come to university with a pre-existing higher consumer orientation" (p. 1970). Also, the researchers determined that more mature students and those who were involved in extracurricular or volunteer activities identify less strongly as consumers. As experienced teachers recognize, students' willingness to engage in active learning or see themselves as learners greatly depends on their own orientations, abilities, and access to the resources that they need. Improving student experiences could help them to identify as learners instead of as consumers and thereby improve learning outcomes.

Student experiences with an academic program may be influenced by a range of issues that are not apparently related to learning outcomes but that nonetheless may impact them indirectly. For example, the way we deliver specific program information in the course catalog, in the student portal, and in various materials circulated by departments can impact how students understand program requirements and electives, how they understand what will be covered in individual classes, and whether they will enroll in our courses. Students may be affected by other concerns; for example, when joining a program or declaring a major or minor, they may not know where to go for advising. Student satisfaction also can be greatly impacted by access to extracurricular offerings within the major, such as workshops and clubs. Yet, while program administrators may be able to influence some of these concerns, larger institutional systems and processes are also in play.

Viewing student experience as user experience forces us to view programs from a new angle. Adding UX to our continuous improvement practices can challenge underlying assumptions about what education means—in a beneficial way. Framing students as users can be a disruptive and innovative program design practice (Johnson et al., 2017). UX in program design positions students as active learners who already possess valuable knowledge sets, even as they seek more skills and knowledge from an educational program.

■ Users and Interfaces

Students are the users of our *products*—the educational experiences facilitated by our programs. Yet, our unspoken assumptions may resemble the reverse scenario—we may tend to regard students as the products of our programs. However, programs cannot take all of the credit for creating professionals; rather, students take what they learn in courses, internships, and other related experiences and then determine their own career paths. By framing the program as the product and the student as the user, we are highlighting students' roles and responsibilities in their own learning. Program mission statements define our products, which are specific educational experiences designed for specific users. The continuous improvement and UX processes that we apply in program design can increase the quality of these educational experiences, but students ultimately determine how they interact with the product and how they use it in their lives and careers. Because students obviously enroll in academic programs to learn what they do not already know, it is easy to overlook areas where they do have expertise. Traditional assessment strategies that measure learning outcomes do not necessarily acknowledge what students already know outside of the program's content. UX research can reveal valuable insights that students have on topics such as how courses are being taught (not just what is being taught), whether accommodations for student needs are being addressed and met, whether advising practices are effective, how the program approaches the practicum or internship process, and how the program is marketed. Program design, ideally, would include researching how current and even future students view a wide range of issues related to their educational experiences at the program level.

Many students are already expert users of educational systems, and their orientations toward any aspect of a learning environment are based on what they already know from their extensive careers as learners—from pre-K through their initial years of college. In this vein of valuing what students already know, Natasha Jones (2018) acknowledges that students are, in fact, "expert end-users" of course syllabi, and she discusses ways that syllabus design can impact student success in a composition program. Jones underscores how a human-centered approach could possibly reveal "concerns about accessibility, cultural and linguistic diversity, and varied learning styles," and she also emphasizes that human-centered design (HCD) is not necessarily a "magic bullet to be instituted without critical reflection, genuine collaboration, and careful implementation in an iterative and ongoing manner" (p. 34). A human-centered methodological approach is especially suited to doing UX design in professional and technical communication programs because it allows us to practice what we preach and apply the UX, HCD, and usability concepts that we teach in our courses.

As a first step in applying UX principles to program redesign, we now turn to our study of the various ways that students interact with a program's representatives, spaces, activities, and artifacts. These sites of interaction may be viewed as *interfaces*. Identifying these allows us to create a map of all the sites where students encounter the *idea* of an individual TPC program. These interfaces may fall into some of the "programmatic landscapes" as defined by Schreiber and Melonçon (2019); however, the focus for a UX methodology will be on how students experience these areas, which will be completely different from how a program administrator experiences them. Because we are, in fact, program administrators, we expect that this preliminary map of interfaces will be iterative; it may continue to change as we gather information from students about their actual experiences through methods such as surveys, focus groups, and interviews. Mapping out interfaces is important because the process identifies potential sites where students encounter *anything* program related. For example, students may encounter the idea of our programs through *artifacts* (such as promotional materials, web portals, or course catalogs), through talking with *programmatic administrators* (advisors and faculty), and through *experiences* (such as award ceremonies or student club events). With this understanding, we can then look more deeply at how individual students interact with and perceive various aspects of a program.

■ Employing UX Research Methods: A Preliminary Study

As explored in earlier chapters, professionals and academics have many models and frameworks available for thinking through user experience. In our preliminary study, we focus on an extremely simple and practical UX framework that can be applied to program development. This simple framework was created by industry expert Frank Guo (2012), who conceptualizes the four fundamental elements of UX as "value, usability, adoptability, and desirability." While Guo's approach is geared towards business products, these four elements of UX may also be applied to the design of any system. Guo simplifies the purpose behind each element with a question:

- **Value**—Is it useful?
- **Usability**—Is it easy to use?
- **Adoptability**—Is it easy to start using?
- **Desirability**—Is it fun and engaging?

While Guo's examples usually involve actual consumer products like iPhones, his elements and their associated question can help us think about improving program design from a UX perspective. Our preliminary study, therefore, examines user (student) experience with our programs by asking the following questions:

- Through which interfaces do students encounter our programs?
- What are students' experiences with our programs and program interfaces like in terms of value, usability, adoptability, and desirability?
- To answer these questions, we employed surveys of current students and alumni; this data will assist in identifying what specific interfaces need to be redesigned and in what way. In this section, we explain our methodology for creating the survey questions, and we report our results in the next section. Our research protocol was reviewed by the Institutional Review Board (IRB) at Francis Marion University and declared as exempt under the federal human subjects protection regulations (reference number Masters-08-12-2019-001). These initial survey findings will direct us to refine more detailed questions for future focus groups and interviews.

To explore Guo's four UX elements in our programs' interfaces, we have developed and administered a survey to current students and alumni at our respective programs that have some similarities and many differences. Gracemarie's program at an R2 university (formerly a regional comprehensive university only three years prior) has recently developed a minor, certificate (for non-writing arts majors), and concentration (for writing arts majors) in technical and professional writing. These programs came in response to calls for increased marketability and improved writing skills in students as well as new faculty expertise. Despite this growth in the program and the addition of new courses such as Scientific Writing and Rhetoric, Medical Writing and Rhetoric, and Writing for Nonprofits, it remains largely under enrolled, especially when compared to creative writing courses in the writing arts department, which are nearly always at capacity. Increasing student awareness of these programs is a major concern of faculty, so we focused the survey to collect data about students' interactions with artifacts, people, and experiences that helped them learn about the program and choose to enroll. Surveys targeted writing arts majors, non-writing arts majors who enroll in technical and professional writing courses, and program alumni.

Christine's program, in contrast, is situated at a regional comprehensive university and has a well-established major and minor in professional writing.

Enrollments have remained fairly constant over the last 15 to 20 years. Currently, the program advisory committee is in the process of evaluating course offerings, deciding whether adding more electives would be welcomed by students, and considering whether these course additions would be feasible and sustainable. The program would like to investigate how current students experience the program as well as gather alumni opinions about the program.

Absent a baseline model for this type of survey, we combined elements of other types of surveys used in our programs and in academia more broadly. Our survey is different from the type of "alumni relations" surveys that Schreiber and Melonçon (2019) describe, not only because its target audience is both alumni and current students, but because the questions center on perceptions of the program on a broad level rather than seeking specifically to gather opinions about course content or about the workplace importance of specific skills and knowledge that are taught in the program.

Similar to the work of Salvo and Ren (2007), our survey elicits student feedback as a valuable source of information about the program, rather than relying only on "expert" feedback common in more traditional approaches to programmatic assessment. Like Salvo and Ren's survey, our survey questions determine basic information about participants' progress through programs. Our survey diverges from this model, however, in the focus and scope of our questions. While Salvo and Ren focus on students' individual experiences with technologies, genres, and skills developed in specific classes and student approaches to learning, our survey takes a more open-ended approach that invites participants to share the program experiences that they found to be most and least valuable, practical, and useful. As a result, our survey focuses far less on curriculum and more on the overall interaction a student has with a program.

Through this survey, we seek to identify the multimodality of student interactions. Some interfaces are concrete artifacts, while some interfaces are immaterial—they involve exchanging ideas about the program by talking to people and participating (voluntarily or involuntarily) in experiences. We must also keep in mind that the interfaces through which students encounter our programs actually involve varying degrees of programmatic involvement (and therefore control). For example, some interfaces may be experienced in a non-university environment (such as a brochure distributed at a college fair) or a non-program sanctioned encounter (such as students talking in a lounge about the easiest courses to take in a program). While we may not have the ability (or desire) to control each of these interfaces, the experience of mapping an individual program's interfaces is an essential step in moving toward a robust analysis of user experience.

Questions About Participant Identity

The first set of survey questions asks students four questions about their institution, major or minor area of study, and how far they have progressed in their program. In our analysis of survey results, we evaluate significant differences in the answers of current students versus alumni across both institutions. Responses from current students and alumni of each institution's technical / professional writing program are considered valid. A complete list of questions for each section may be found in Appendix A.

Questions About Value

Of course, we want our students to perceive value in our programs as well as in our institutions. High school graduates interested in going to college have many choices for where they will enroll and what they will study. Therefore, the perceived value of a program is important to prospective students as well as current students and alumni. Keshab Acharya (2016) argues that users should define a product's *value* by participating in the design process. As current users of a program, current students can become co-creators of value in an educational setting when they give feedback. This section of the survey includes five questions that center on value in terms of how useful students perceive the program to be. It is similar to marketing surveys that assess brand loyalty and perception of value by asking whether or not customers would recommend the product to others. Here, we purposely stay away from leading questions about course content, the evaluation of specific courses, or the assessment of specific learning outcomes. However, there's nothing preventing our respondents from mentioning those topics in their open-ended answers. This UX survey focuses on general attitudes about the program's worth or usefulness, but the primary focus is not on evaluation of program content. Survey questions about perceived value from students' perspectives should complement, not replace, alumni and employer surveys that help determine which TPC curriculum areas are valuable in professional settings.

Questions About Usability or Use

The term *usability* can refer to a product's usefulness as well as to the research methods that measure user experience at specific points in time. Guo chooses the term usability to refer to the stage of user experience after the adoption of a product when users become engaged in active, regular use of the product. In other words, this category refers to experiences that users have while they are interacting with the product. We adopt Guo's "usability" category because we want to measure how easy it is for students to "use" our programs without encountering practical or logistical problems. This category is separated from user perceptions of value and desirability, although somewhat arbitrarily—user perceptions about value and desirability cannot be completely divided from the more practical aspects of use. With a physical product such as an iPhone interface, users could have difficulties if they did not recognize an icon or know where to press on the screen. However, their inability to navigate an interface will also affect their perceptions of the product's value and desirability. With our programs, students could have difficulties, for example, if they could not find and understand the program requirements. UX methods that focus on "usability," understood as students' "use" of a program, can help us to identify and remove any barriers that may hinder students' progress through these requirements. Our survey asks five questions concerning usability that focus on how easily students progress through the program. In contrast to the adoptability section, which deals with how easy it is for students to learn about and enter the program, this section focuses on students' progression as program users. In order for the program to be "usable," students should easily be able to find information about how to complete the program and then make effective progress toward completing the program.

Questions About Adoptability

Questions around the idea of *adoptability* center on whether students have access to information that allows them to know that the program exists and then to easily understand what they can expect to learn in it. This section asks five questions that help to establish how students perceive what we have called the program interfaces—the sites where the *idea* of the program surfaces for students. Becoming aware of the program and what it entails allows student to evaluate whether it suits their needs. This section of the survey also measures how easy students thought it was for them to join the program by declaring it as their major/minor (or certificate, if applicable). The first question in this section helps us to identify where students interface with the idea of the program. Respondents are given a list of sites that they can check off to indicate where they have heard about the program. In the survey, this list appears as continuous, but we have identified the answers as possibly belonging to three distinct groupings: artifacts, people, and events or activities (see Appendix A for a complete list of options). Respondents also may write in their own answers in the "other" response.

Questions About Desirability

The element of *desirability* involves students' satisfaction with the program. Education is not entertainment—it is not supposed to be "fun." Nonetheless, as we address in our discussion of UX methods, there may be ways to evaluate whether students are engaged and satisfied that go beyond data usually gathered through traditional course evaluations, which come with their own controversies about gender bias, racial bias, and general ineffectiveness in evaluating personnel. The four questions in this section assess student attitudes about general program characteristics, including program names, course titles, related activities, and logistical or other aspects of the program. Desirability questions specifically allow us to gather data on student attitudes towards potential program changes that may be in the very early brainstorming stages. As with the other survey sections, the data gathered from these questions should be used in combination with other expert and professional sources when considering program improvements. The survey concludes with an open-ended question asking for additional comments or ideas regarding program improvement. Although the responses may touch on any of the areas discussed previously, we include this question in the desirability section.

■ Survey Results

After receiving IRB approval, we distributed our survey link via email to student and alumni lists, department Facebook groups, and LinkedIn messages in late August and early September of 2019. Based on student and alumni lists that we compiled as program administrators, we attempted to directly email or message 40 of the approximately 140 current and former professional writing students from Francis Marion University. However, others may have found the survey link on social media, even though we did not message them directly because we had no current contact information. At Rowan University, we directly contacted 22 students and alumni of the estimated 27 individuals who are either program alumni or current students. After keeping the survey open for approximately three weeks, we received a total of 39 responses. Of these 39, we discarded three; one was a duplicate made by a software error, and two were from students not in the program who answered only questions about their major and minor before abandoning the survey. The total 36 valid responses gave us a response rate of 58 percent across both programs from the 62 individuals to whom we directly reached out and a response rate of 22 percent out of the estimated total current students and alumni across both programs. In the next sections, we report the survey results following the participant identity, value, adoptability, use, and desirability groupings.

Participant Identity

Francis Marion University students and alumni comprised 58 percent (21) of the total responses, and 42 percent (15) of the total responses were from Rowan University. Of the 36 responses, 44 percent (16) reported that they graduated prior to Fall 2019. The earliest graduation year reported was 2003, and the most recent graduate earned a degree in August of 2019. Fifty-six percent (20) of the participants reported that they are current students, and of these, three expect to graduate in the current semester (Fall 2019), 12 expect to graduate in 2020, and four expect to graduate between 2021 and 2023. Of the current students, five indicated that they needed one to two more classes to graduate, three needed three to five more classes, five needed six to nine more classes, and one needed ten or more classes. Two responded that they have finished all of their classes, 12 responded that they are not current students, and eight (all Rowan students) indicated that they were not sure how many classes they needed to graduate. Of the program graduates, five were from Rowan and 11 were from Francis Marion. Of the current students, ten attend Francis Marion and ten attend Rowan.

Survey participants represent a range of writing majors and minors. Francis Marion professional writing majors numbered 17 and were the largest group of respondents; Rowan writing arts majors submitted eight responses. Eleven "other" majors participated in the survey (four from Francis Marion and seven from Rowan). A total of eight writing minors, collaterals, concentrations, or undergraduate certificate students participated—four from Francis Marion and four from Rowan. Four students reported that they currently were not pursuing a declared major, minor, or certificate in writing (all from Rowan). We considered these responses as valid because the students had attended classes in the program, had knowledge of the program, and potentially could still declare the program in their plan of study.

Value

Feedback on the value of both programs was positive. Sixty-nine percent (25) of participants said that they would recommend "Technical / Professional Writing as an area of study," and 28 percent (10) said "maybe-it depends." One respondent (3%) left the question blank. None of the participants indicated that they would *not* recommend Technical / Professional Writing as an area of study. When asked to explain the reasons for their answers, 11 respondents (31%) explicitly commented on the value of the program in preparing them for future careers; a number of others talked more vaguely about "skills" that their programs provide.

When asked "What could be changed to make the Technical / Professional Writing program more practical, useful, or valuable to students?" responses were largely class-centered, with multiple students suggesting the following:

- adding more classes that speak to specific skills needed for technical and professional communication, such as graphic design, typography, Darwin Information Typing Architecture (DITA), resume writing, and grammar
- providing more experiential learning opportunities, including service learning or client projects
- providing more opportunities for cross-disciplinary study
- removing required courses, such as creative writing and literature, that felt irrelevant to technical and professional writers
- allowing more flexibility in classes for students to apply their own interests

Beyond courses, respondents offered four additional suggestions. One participant requested help with internship placement, one requested help with job placement, and one sought help with developing a broader understanding of what the field of technical and professional writing encompasses. A final comment suggested running more classes in the summer.

The most valuable qualities of the programs reported by multiple respondents included both course-related and broader aspects of the program. In terms of course-related feedback, respondents appreciated client projects that gave the opportunity for real-world writing experiences and the variety of classes available (one respondent in particular noted the value of literature and creative writing classes for their current jobs). More generally, students noted the value of having "good" professors; the benefits of developing real-world skills, such as document design, workplace communication, HTML, professionalism, and grammar/punctuation; the breadth and applicability of these skills; and the family-like feeling the program had.

In regard to our question about least valuable qualities of the programs, we received far less data, with 67 percent (24) of respondents either not responding or stating that everything they learned was valuable. The only common response among respondents who provided commentary on the least valuable aspects was required coursework in creative writing and literature.

Use

One of the primary ways students "use" our programs is through classes, so it is critical to understand how students learn about what courses are available during a given semester. A healthy majority of 43 percent (15) of the 35 respondents who answered the question indicated that they consulted their advisors first when figuring out which classes to take. The remaining respondents consulted course catalogs (31%, 11), an online student portal (11%, 4), the semester schedule (9%, 3), and a department website or advising sheet (6%, 2).

Most students reported that it was easy to progress through their courses and understand course requirements. Of the 35 responses to the question "How easy or difficult was it to progress through your Technical/Professional Writing courses?" 40 percent (14) responded "5" on a scale of 1 to 5 (with 5 indicating highest level of ease), 26 percent of participants (9) answered "4," 29 percent (10) answered "3," and 6 percent (2) answered "2." When asked how understandable they found the program's course requirements, 43 percent (15) of students answered "5" on a scale of 1 to 5 (with 5 indicating the highest level of ease), 34 percent (12) answered "4," 20 percent (7) answered "3," and 3 percent (1) answered "1." Notable obstacles to progressing through the program or understanding course requirements included the limited availability of course offerings and course times, particularly for respondents who noted they were working in addition to attending school full time.

In response to the question "How could we make the Technical/Professional Writing program requirements clearer?" there were ten meaningful responses (i.e., responses other than "everything is clear" or "N/A"). Out of these, eight requested that clearer documentation about plans of study be provided, particularly by advisors or online. Several students noted that they found the course catalog complicated, and they requested simplified documents with more clearly stated requirements.

Adoptability

For a program to be adoptable, students must first hear about it, become interested, and decide to declare its offered credential within their plan of study. Our survey found that students heard about the program from a range of sources, and we consider these sources as interfaces for the *idea* of the program—the sites where students see or hear the program mentioned by people, through artifacts, or at events. When asked the question "At any time in the past or present, where do you remember hearing about the Technical/Professional Writing program?" students most often mentioned "professors" (17). The second most common way students heard about the program was through sources that list courses offered, including catalogs, schedules, and student portal sites (16; see Table 13.1). None of the participants indicated that they had heard about the program from student showcases, high school counselors, or high school teachers. Overall, when grouped into the categories of artifacts, people, and events, students most commonly heard about the program through artifacts (55), followed by people (41) and events (7).

Table 13.1. Number of Times Students Heard about Programs from Artifacts, People, and Events

Interface	Artifacts	People	Events	Grand Total
Professors		17		17
Catalog, schedules, or student portal	16			16
Department or program website	14			14
University website list of degrees and programs	13			13
University staff		8		8
Advisors		8		8
Brochures, flyers, or marketing handouts	7			7
Current students		5		5
Department or program social media pages	4			4
Alumni		3		3
Student clubs and activities			2	2
Open houses or orientations			2	2
Department workshops or events			2	2
Major requirements sheet	1			1
College fairs			1	1
Grand Total	55	41	7	103

Sixteen out of the 36 participants indicated that they *first* heard about the program from a faculty or staff member (15) or another student (1). Twelve respondents reported that they first heard about the program from an artifact such as a catalog (5), website (5), email (1), or flyer (1). The other eight respondents gave vague or non-applicable answers, or they left the question blank. When asked who or what was the biggest influence on their decision to study technical/professional writing, survey respondents reported advisors as having the biggest influence (33%, 12). The second biggest factor was a desire for skills or opportunities (22%, 8), followed by a passion for writing (11%, 4) and practicality of the program and its requirements (8%, 3). Just one respondent named "interesting classes" as a top factor, and another student named "other students." The remaining respondents left the question blank.

In terms of ease of declaring technical/professional writing, students rated their experience on a scale of 1–5, with 1 being "Difficult" and 5 being "Easy." An overwhelming majority of participants, or 24 out of 36 (67%), rated their experience as a 5. Another 22 percent (8) were split evenly between a 4 and a 3. Only two respondents (6%) selected 1, believing the process to be difficult. Interestingly, most students responded to the question "What made declaring Technical / Professional Writing as an area of study easy or difficult?" by describing their personal reasons for choosing technical and professional writing as an area of study, rather than describing the physical process of formally declaring the program through the university.

Desirability

Gauging desirability is important for helping program administrators build programs that appeal to students. In responding to the question "Do you prefer an open plan of study (with many course options) or a well-defined plan of study (with fewer course options)?" of the 32 respondents who did not leave the question blank, most prefer a balance between an open plan of study and a well-defined plan of study (61%, 20). Approximately 15 percent (5) favored an open course plan, and 12 percent (4) favored a more rigid plan of study. One respondent, an alum, noted their opinion that the course plan itself ultimately wasn't that important: "What's most important, I think, is that students are able to connect the dots between course trajectory and future job prospects."

The courses that sounded the most interesting or engaging to survey participants were Editing, Writing for Nonprofits, and Writing for the Workplace, with 67 percent of respondents (24) rating themselves as being "very interested" in these courses. Twelve of the remaining courses listed received "very interested" ratings from 50 to 59 percent of respondents, and nine additional courses received "very interested" ratings from 33–47 percent of respondents. Three remaining classes—Video Production for Tech Comm, Writing for Engineering, and DITA/Structured Content Authoring—received "very interested" ratings from just 25 to 28 percent of students. (See Appendix B for more detailed information on rankings.) Ratings for most classes were approximately proportional to the number of respondents from both programs, with a few notable exceptions. The Rhetoric of New Media "very interested" ratings were broken down into 21 percent from Rowan and 79 percent from Francis Marion. User Experience Design had a similar distribution, with 25 percent of "very interested" ratings coming from Rowan and 75 percent from Francis Marion. The most striking difference in ratings, however, was for Advanced Business Communication, which received "very interested" ratings from seven percent of students from Rowan and 93 percent of students from Francis Marion.

Turning to major names that piqued student interest, the major that participants perceived as most interesting was Professional and Technical Writing, which earned "very interesting" ratings from 75 percent (27) of participants. Technical and Professional Writing received the next highest rating of 61 percent (22). The remaining categories received "very interesting" ratings from approximately 50 to 58 percent of students, with the exception of the three lowest-rated major names: Creative Writing (47%, 17), Rhetoric and Writing Studies (42%, 15), and Digital Writing and Rhetoric (39%, 14). (See Appendix C for additional information on these ratings.)

In addition to opinions on naming, participants gave feedback on changes that would make a technical/professional writing program more interesting and engaging to students. Out of the choices we provided, participants most often answered that adding more career preparation workshops would make the program more interesting and engaging to students (72%, 26). The next highest-rated options, both at 47 percent (17), were "Offer a greater variety of electives" and "Offer a wider variety of class times" (which could also fall into the Use category). Garnering fewer, but still substantial responses were "Teach a wider range of software and technology" and "Allow students more choices for projects" (both at 44%, 16). Thirty-one percent of respondents (11) thought that existing course content should be updated, and the same percentage thought that more social activities should be provided for students. Only eight percent of participants (3) responded "Nothing—keep everything the same."

At the end of the survey, we provided a space for respondents to comment regarding ideas for program improvements. The 15 non-blank responses were widely varied. In terms of overlapping responses, two respondents requested that the program name be changed from "Professional Writing" or "Professional Communication" to "Technical Communication" to clarify to employers the type of writing students were learning. Three respondents also expressed interest in taking a medical writing course.

■ Discussion

In reflecting upon this data, we can garner a number of insights from each of the four fundamentals of UX that can be used as a starting point for additional research. In this section, we discuss the most significant of these for our programs, modeling how a UX-based survey can provide helpful input for technical and professional writing program administrators. Though this analysis is particular to our own programs, we hope that our discussion of our findings will help faculty and administrators gain insight into the iterative process of UX methodologies (Nielsen, 1993), with each iteration helping to enhance the user experience. Understanding this approach is helpful as administrators map out their own plans for engaging in program (re)design.

One of the consistent findings of our survey was the importance of people—particularly professors and advisors—and artifacts as program interfaces. Professors were mentioned, often by name, in questions surrounding program value, and advisors were cited as an essential component of ease of use. Professors also played a large role in adoptability by introducing students to available programs, and advisors contributed through their assistance in helping students go through the steps of formally adopting their program. At Francis Marion, where faculty members function as student advisors, a professor and advisor may be the same person. At Rowan, however, faculty advisors have been recently replaced by professional advisors. The significant role played by both groups highlights the importance of understanding when and how students interact with professors and advisors through their journeys in our programs, and it speaks to the critical need for both groups to be well informed about their programs. To further study the role that non-technical and professional writing faculty and advisors can play in helping students shape their programs of study, we envision also interviewing a few students individually. These interviews could build on survey questions and result in *journey mapping* (a tool to visualize a user's process accomplishing a goal) that could pinpoint key opportunities where we could introduce more students to our programs.

Artifacts also played a large role in respondents' experiences in their programs, particularly in the areas of adoptability and ease of use. Though students' first exposure to the program was typically through a person, artifacts more commonly provided information throughout students' experience in a program. As artifacts also came up as a highly requested way to clarify program requirements for questions regarding ease of use, we need to seriously consider the role of documents in helping students understand and navigate our programs. Learning what specific artifacts were most impactful would be an aim of additional research; follow-up interviews and focus groups should certainly focus on students' experiences with encountering and using various program documents to determine how specifically artifacts impact students. Questions regarding content, design, and access to these artifacts would all be relevant. Participatory design projects, as described by Salvo and Ren (2007), could follow, perhaps assigned as course projects where students would develop engaging and useful program artifacts. Depending on administrators' expertise and available resources (including time), methods such as eye-tracking of web-based artifacts, participatory design (in which participants actually help create their ideal experience), card sorting (in which participants organize topics according to categories), or tree tests (in which participants demonstrate how they would work through a site map) could also be implemented. Whichever methods are chosen, the priority should remain on understanding users' experiences and taking their feedback to heart during the redesign process.

In sum, artifacts play an important role in advertising and helping students move through programs; however, our survey results underscore that people are often the first site of encounter, or interface, for potential enrollees in our programs. Our field acknowledges and discusses methods to improve the user experience of artifacts such as websites and documents; however, we think it is important to also acknowledge how people serve as sites of encounter with our programs. As program administrators, we would like to strategize how to better equip professors inside and outside of our departments, as well as university staff and advisors, with more knowledge about and familiarity with what we have to offer students. Implementing UX tools such as interviews, focus groups, or observations would be a starting point for additional research to help us learn more about student-faculty/advisor interactions. Methods such as think-aloud testing could also be implemented with faculty and advisors to help improve the usability of the documents from which they draw their knowledge.

In considering the value of our programs, respondents often mentioned career readiness and specific skills for use on the job, indicating, perhaps unsurprisingly, the connection most participants felt regarding the value of studying technical and professional writing. Along these lines, it is also unsurprising that participants would express negative views toward literature and creative writing, which have less explicit applicability to most workplaces. This emphasis on jobs is also useful in thinking about how Rowan, with its goal of expanding student enrollment, might better convey the value of its program. In the next stage of research, we can use this data to develop journey maps of program users and their experiences, delving into exactly when in their experience as students job preparation becomes a priority.

In reflecting on the ease of use of our programs, the results of our survey indicate a conflict between respondents' reports. On one hand, most respondents reported that progressing through a program is relatively easy; on the other hand, it is remarkable that 8 of the 20 students who participated in the survey didn't know how many classes they needed to finish their programs. This data further points to the importance of pinpointing how students access information about our programs and providing resources—whether through people, artifacts, or experiences—that help them confidently navigate through their course of study. As a next phase of research, *task analysis*, which examines the actions users take as they work toward completing a task, would be a particularly helpful research tool to implement. In the case of our programs in particular, task analysis relating to advising and course selection would provide helpful insights into the ways that various people, artifacts, and experiences come into play as students navigate the course registration process.

In terms of desirability, we see interesting similarities and differences in how Rowan and Francis Marion students favored courses. Editing, one of the top three courses students expressed interest in, had not been offered at Francis Marion prior to 2020, and it is a new course at Rowan that was first offered in Fall 2020. While we could speculate about student interest in this course as perhaps being connected to perceived workplace usefulness or a reflection of participants' acknowledgement of editing as an area in which they lack expertise, there is no way from our survey to draw these conclusions. Instead, further research should be done to understand how an editing course fits into what students desire from a technical and professional writing program. Similarly, participants' slight preference for the major name "Professional and Technical Writing" over "Technical and Professional Writing" is noteworthy, especially given a few participants' beliefs that the degree title "Professional Writing" was unhelpful for job seeking. While we could again speculate about students' reasoning for preferring one variation over the other, additional research could more productively illuminate students' perceptions regarding this distinction. Interviews or focus groups could be particularly helpful for learning more about major and course preferences.

▌ Next Steps

As indicated through our discussion in the previous section, UX methodologies are best enacted as an iterative process. The survey discussed here is an example of what an initial step in applying a UX perspective to programmatic design might look like. Keeping in mind the iterative nature of UX design, after this initial round of user data collection, the next stage is to employ additional UX research methods that will be helpful in more deeply investigating the key areas illuminated through survey responses. Our plan moving forward, and our advice to other programs who choose to conduct a survey as the first step in a UX research and design process, is to identify one to three insights from the survey for additional research.

Yet, we also want to emphasize that reflecting on insights and deciding on how to proceed takes time—these processes cannot happen all at once. Administering programs while teaching and advising students is a challenge in itself, and over the past several months as the COVID-19 pandemic has hit, this challenge has intensified. After completing the work of compiling and analyzing survey data, we found it challenging to take time to reflect on the results and ask ourselves exactly what we wanted our follow-up research questions and methods to be.

For both programs, a shared follow-up question was "Which artifacts are valued most by students and which artifacts could be improved?" This question was posed in a focus group at Francis Marion after the initial survey was conducted. When asked which artifacts made an impact on students, one student mentioned that she remembered being struck by a small, quarter-page handout that she found on a professor's door. The handout listed jobs for professional writing majors. Seeing these potential career paths helped to convince the student to major in professional writing. The handout was not one of the official program materials—the professor independently provided it. So, while the program's website lists potential careers as a way to advertise the major, students actually may pay more attention to other types of artifacts, especially when they are presented by professors (even when just on their office doors). In the focus group, students indicated that they are influenced more by offline materials than by online materials. This response leads us to question whether faculty members and administrators may be overestimating the impact of websites and social media pages on students' decision-making processes. A next step would be to work with students to develop more appealing offline materials and figure out how to distribute them in ways that will have a personal impact.

While we believe that UX methods have the potential to transform programmatic assessment redesign, we recognize that this approach also comes with its own challenges. One of the most obvious is the commitment of time and resources that is required when including users in the assessment process. Especially given the layered nature of UX methods and the breadth of user interfaces, a single initial user survey can end up spiraling into dozens of distinct projects. While it may be possible to incorporate this work into existing demands for assessment or even use these areas of investigation as class research topics, it is also likely that administrators will need to prioritize what can be studied and what must wait for future work. We hope that other programs might improve upon our survey questions if they decide to use this method as a first step in an ongoing UX program design process. However, programs could also gather valuable feedback from students by skipping a survey and holding interviews or focus groups as their initial UX-based research method.

In designing both the initial and follow-up portions of usability-based programmatic research, it is vitally important to be attentive to the ethical dimensions of our research methods. Given its focus on people and their experience, user-based research provides the opportunity for radical inclusivity as we seek to learn about the range of user experiences with our programs. Nevertheless, we must take care to ensure our research designs do in fact allow us to engage with the diversity of program users, taking care both to *not exclude* as well as *purposely include*. For example, holding a focus group in the evening hours may prohibit students who are parents or students with jobs from participating; choosing to run a focus group during a class period instead would ensure that students with diverse backgrounds, life circumstances, and experiences could contribute. Similarly, we must intentionally seek out perspectives of minority or marginalized students (as well as faculty or administrative collaborators) as we incorporate user experience methods, not only to ensure a representative research sample, but to ensure we have the information needed to build welcoming, inclusive programs.

In a similar vein, we must keep in mind that UX methods for programmatic (re)design are not a "one and done" approach. Just as program (re)development is a continuous process (Schreiber & Melonçon, 2019), UX research is a continuous process. As our students, institutions, and worlds change, so too will student needs and experiences with our programs. For example, in a pre-COVID-19 world, Christine's focus group finding leads us to reassess the value of physical artifacts. In the world in the midst of a pandemic (as of this writing), however, when students may not be physically on campus, such physical artifacts will obviously shift in importance in students' experience. As we move to a post-pandemic world, there will surely be lasting changes on institutions and departments that make it necessary to reconsider students' experience in our programs. All of this is not to discourage user research in the present moment or to demand incessant research that never allows us to make changes, but simply to encourage faculty and administrators using UX-based approaches to programs to adopt an attitude of continual curiosity toward user experience, as advocated by Schreiber and Melonçon, and to be attentive to context and time in planning and analyzing data.

Finally, we want to emphasize that UX shouldn't be seen exclusively as a problem-solving or trouble-shooting methodology. While it is natural to begin our programmatic work with consideration of known trouble spots in our programs, we view user involvement as a method that can truly transform what we conceive program administration and assessment to be. The involvement of students as co-producers of our programs is the ideal to strive toward, even if not immediately practical.

■ References

Acharya, K. R. (2016). User value and usability in technical communication: A value-proposition design model. *Communication Design Quarterly*, *4*(3), 26–34.

Allen, J. (2010). Mapping institutional values and the Technical Communication curriculum: A strategy for grounding assessment. In M. N. Hundleby & J. Allen (Eds.), *Assessment in technical and professional communication* (pp. 39–56). Routledge. https://doi.org/10.4324/9781315225098-4.

Bunce, L., Baird, A. & Jones, S. E. (2017). The student-as-consumer approach in higher education and its effects on academic performance. *Studies in Higher Education*, *42*(11), 1958–1978. https://doi.org/10.1080/03075079.2015.1127908.

Burns, B. (2016, September 27). Reverse engineering the student experience. *Inside Higher Ed*. https://www.insidehighered.com/views/2016/09/27/redesigning-college-processes-student-mind-essay.

Cargile Cook, K. & Zachry, M. (2010). Politics, programmatic self-assessment, and the challenge of cultural change. In M. N. Hundleby & J. Allen (Eds.), *Assessment in technical and professional communication* (pp. 65–79). Routledge. https://doi.org/10.4324/9781315225098-6.

Coppola, N. W., Elliot, N., Newsham, F. & Klobucar, A. (2016). Programmatic research: An interpretive framework for writing program assessment. *Programmatic Perspectives*, *8*(2), 4–46.

Elliott, K. M. & Healy, M. A. (2001). Key factors influencing student satisfaction related to recruitment and retention. *Journal of Marketing for Higher Education, 10*(4), 1–11. https://doi.org/10.1300/J050v10n04_01.

Gulbrandsen, K. (2012). Revising the technical communication service course. *Programmatic Perspectives, 4*(2), 243–254.

Guo, F. (2012, April 24). More than usability: The four elements of user experience, Part I. *UXmatters.* https://www.uxmatters.com/mt/archives/2012/04/more-than-usability-the-four-elements-of-user-experience-part-i.php.

Hundleby, M. N. & Allen, J. (Eds.). (2010). *Assessment in technical and professional communication.* Routledge. https://doi.org/10.4324/9781315225098.

Jablonski, J. & Nagelhout, E. (2010). Assessing professional writing programs using technology as a site of praxis. In M. N. Hundleby & J. Allen (Eds.), *Assessment in technical and professional communication* (pp. 171–187). Routledge. https://doi.org/10.4324/9781315225098-13.

Johnson, M. A., Simmons, W. M. & Sullivan, P. (2017). *Lean technical communication: Toward sustainable program innovation.* Routledge; Taylor & Francis Group.

Jones, N. N. (2018). Human centered syllabus design: Positioning our students as expert end-users. *Computers and Composition, 49*, 25–35. https://doi.org/10.1016/j.compcom.2018.05.002.

Kruger, L. (2014). Designing nonprofit experiences: Building a UX toolkit. *User Experience Magazine, 14*(2). https://uxpamagazine.org/designing-nonprofit-experiences/.

Lam, C., Hannah, M. A. & Friess, E. (2016). Connecting programmatic research with social media: Using data from Twitter to inform programmatic decisions. *Programmatic Perspectives, 8*(2), 47–71.

Melonçon, L. & Henschel, S. (2013). Current state of U.S. undergraduate degree programs in technical and professional communication. *Technical Communication, 60*(1), 45–64.

Nielsen, J. (1993). Iterative user-interface design. *Computer, 26*(11), 32–41.

Rice-Bailey, T. (2016). *TC program assessment* [White paper]. Council for Programs in Technical and Scientific Communication.

Rose, E. J., Racadio, R., Wong, K., Nguyen, S., Kim, J. & Zahler, A. (2017). Community-based user experience: Evaluating the usability of health insurance information with immigrant patients. *SIAS Faculty Publications, 756.* https://digitalcommons.tacoma.uw.edu/ias_pub/756.

Salvo, M. J. & Ren, J. (2007). Participatory assessment: Negotiating engagement in a technical communication program. *Technical Communication, 54*(4), 424–439.

Schreiber, J. & Melonçon, L. (2019). Creating a continuous improvement model for sustaining programs in technical and professional communication. *Journal of Technical Writing and Communication, 49*(3), 252–278. https://doi.org/10.1177/0047281618759916.

Stoller, E. (2014, June 5). The business of higher education. *Inside Higher Ed.* https://www.insidehighered.com/blogs/student-affairs-and-technology/business-higher-education.

Thomas, S. & McShane, B. J. (2007). Skills and literacies for the 21st century: Assessing an undergraduate professional and technical writing program. *Technical Communication, 54*(4), 412–423. JSTOR. https://www.jstor.org/stable/43090954.

Appendix A: Survey Form

Student and Alumni Survey

You have been asked to participate in a research project conducted by Christine Masters from Francis Marion University, in the Department of English and Gracemarie Fillenwarth from Rowan University, in the Department of Writing Arts.

The purpose of the project is to gain an understanding of student and alumni experiences with our Technical and Professional Writing Programs.

Read the information below and ask questions about anything you do not understand before deciding whether or not to participate.

• Your participation in this research is voluntary. You have the right not to answer any question and to stop participating at any time for any reason. Answering the questions will take about 20 minutes depending upon the depth of your responses.

• You will not be compensated for your participation.

• All of the information you provide will be confidential and stored in a secure place. However, the researcher cannot guarantee the security of the computer you use or the security of data transfer between that computer and data collection point. Please consider this carefully when responding to these questions.

• If this is a written or online survey, only the researchers will have access to your responses. Your responses, made anonymous, may be quoted or referenced within future academic work.

• I understand that I am ONLY eligible to participate if I am over the age of 18.

Please contact the following investigators with any questions or concerns: Christine Masters cmasters@fmarion.edu, 843-661-1806; Gracemarie Fillenwarth, fillenwarth@rowan.edu, 570-301-7075. If you feel you have been treated unfairly, or you have questions regarding your rights as a research participant, you may contact Teresa Herzog, Chair of the Institutional Review Board at the Francis Marion University, therzog@fmarion.edu; Phone: 843-661-1562.

* Required

1. **Informed Consent** *
   Mark only one oval.

   ◯ I am over 18 and consent to participate in this survey.
   ◯ I am under 18 or do not wish to participate in this survey.   *Stop filling out this form.*

Note to participants

We use the phrase "Technical / Professional Writing program" throughout the survey to refer to both the Technical and Professional Writing program at Rowan University and the Professional Writing program at Francis Marion University.

2. **Which school do you/did you attend?**
   Mark only one oval.

   ◯ Francis Marion University
   ◯ Rowan University
   ◯ Other: _____   *After the last question in this section, stop filling out this form.*

3. **What is (or was) your undergraduate major?**

4. **What is (or was) your undergraduate minor?**
   For FMU students with collaterals, please list both collaterals.

5. **In which month and year do you expect to graduate, or when did you graduate?**

6. If you are a current student, approximately how many more classes do you need to finish your Technical / Professional Writing major, minor, or concentration/CUGS?
Mark only one oval.

   ○ 10 or more classes
   ○ 6 to 9 classes
   ○ 3 to 5 classes
   ○ 1 to 2 classes
   ○ I'm not a current student.
   ○ I'm not sure.
   ○ Other: _____

7. At any time in the past or present, where do you remember hearing about the Technical / Professional Writing program?
Check all that apply.
Check all that apply.

   ☐ Brochures, flyers, or marketing handouts
   ☐ University catalog
   ☐ Semester schedules
   ☐ Student portal
   ☐ University website list of degrees and programs
   ☐ Department or program website
   ☐ Department or program social media pages
   ☐ High school counselors
   ☐ High school teachers
   ☐ University advisors (student services)
   ☐ Departmental or program advisors
   ☐ Current students
   ☐ Alumni
   ☐ University staff
   ☐ University professors
   ☐ College fairs
   ☐ Open houses
   ☐ Orientations
   ☐ Graduation or award ceremonies
   ☐ Student clubs and activities
   ☐ Student showcases
   ☐ Department or workshops or events
   ☐ Other: _____

8. Where did you FIRST hear about the Technical / Professional Writing program?

   _____

9. Who or what was the biggest influence on your decision to study Technical / Professional Writing?

   _____
   _____
   _____
   _____

10. **How easy or difficult was it to declare your Technical / Professional Writing major, minor, or concentration/CUGS?**
    Mark only one oval.

	1	2	3	4	5	
Difficult	○	○	○	○	○	Easy

11. **What made declaring your Technical / Professional Writing major, minor, or concentration/CUGS easy or difficult?**

    _____
    _____
    _____
    _____
    _____

12. **How easy or difficult was it to progress through your Technical / Professional Writing courses? If you are a current student, rate your experience so far.**
    Mark only one oval.

	1	2	3	4	5	
Difficult	○	○	○	○	○	Easy

13. **Please describe any obstacles that you encounter(ed) as a Technical / Professional Writing student.**

    _____
    _____
    _____
    _____
    _____

14. **How understandable are the Technical / Professional Writing program's course requirements?**
    Mark only one oval.

	1	2	3	4	5	
Confusing	○	○	○	○	○	Clear

15. **How could we make the Technical / Professional Writing program requirements clearer?**

    _____
    _____
    _____
    _____
    _____

16. **At registration time, where would you typically go FIRST to figure out which Technical / Professional Writing classes to sign up for?**
    Mark only one oval.
    - ○ Advisor
    - ○ Course Catalog
    - ○ Semester Schedules
    - ○ Student Portal
    - ○ Other:

17. **Would you recommend Technical / Professional Writing as an area of study?**
    Mark only one oval.
    ◯ Yes
    ◯ Maybe - it depends
    ◯ No
    ◯ Other: _____

18. **Please explain your reasons for recommending or for not recommending Technical / Professional Writing to others.**

    _____
    _____
    _____
    _____

19. **What could be changed to make the Technical / Professional Writing program more practical, useful, or valuable to students?**

    _____
    _____
    _____
    _____

20. **What qualities of the Technical / Professional Writing program are most valuable to you?**

    _____
    _____
    _____
    _____

21. **What qualities of the Technical / Professional Writing program are least valuable to you?**

    _____
    _____
    _____
    _____

22. **Do you prefer an open plan of study (with many course options) or a well-defined plan of study (with fewer course options)?**
    Mark only one oval.
    ◯ An open study plan with many course options
    ◯ A balance between freedom and structure
    ◯ Well-defined study plan with fewer course options
    ◯ No opinion
    ◯ Other: _____

23. If you could take any combination of courses for your Technical / Professional Writing major or minor, which of these courses sound interesting or engaging to you? For alumni, check the courses that you would find interesting or useful based on your current preferences, experience, or professional knowledge.
Mark only one oval per row.

	Not interested	Somewhat interested	Very interested	Neutral - no opinion
Editing	○	○	○	○
Digital Content Development	○	○	○	○
Web Design	○	○	○	○
Copyediting	○	○	○	○
Intercultural Communication	○	○	○	○
Video Production for Technical Communicators	○	○	○	○
Foundations of Professional Writing	○	○	○	○
Technical Communication	○	○	○	○
Business Writing	○	○	○	○
The Rhetoric of New Media	○	○	○	○
Multimedia Writing	○	○	○	○
Writing for the Health Professions	○	○	○	○
Scientific Writing and Rhetoric	○	○	○	○
Medical Writing and Rhetoric	○	○	○	○
Writing for Engineering Professions	○	○	○	○
Writing for Nonprofits	○	○	○	○
Grant Writing	○	○	○	○
User Experience Design	○	○	○	○
DITA / Structured Content Authoring	○	○	○	○
Writing, Research, and Technology	○	○	○	○
Writing for the Workplace	○	○	○	○
Magazine Article Writing	○	○	○	○
Publication Layout and Design	○	○	○	○
Professions in Writing Arts	○	○	○	○
Creative Writing – any type	○	○	○	○
Literature – any period / type	○	○	○	○

24. How interesting or engaging do the following majors seem to you, based on the name alone?
Mark only one oval per row.

	Not interesting	Somewhat interesting	Very interesting	Neutral - no opinion
Technical Communication	○	○	○	○
Digital Writing and Rhetoric	○	○	○	○
Creative Writing	○	○	○	○
Writing and Publication Studies	○	○	○	○
Writing Arts	○	○	○	○
Rhetoric and Writing Studies	○	○	○	○
Professional and Technical Writing	○	○	○	○
Technical and Professional Writing	○	○	○	○
Professional Writing	○	○	○	○
Publishing and Writing for the Public	○	○	○	○

Appendix B: Course Names Table

Course Name	Existing @?	"Very Interested" as % of Total	Very Interested	Somewhat Interested	Not Interested	Neutral	Blank	Rowan "Very"	% of "Very"	FMU "Very"	% of "Very"	Alumni "Very"	% of "Very"
Editing	Rowan*	67%	24	9	1	0	2	8	33%	16	67%	9	75%
Writing for the Workplace	Rowan	67%	24	8	1	1	2	8	33%	16	67%	9	75%
Writing for Nonprofits	Both	67%	24	7	2	0	3	9	38%	15	63%	8	67%
Foundations of PW	FMU	58%	21	10	3	1	1	7	33%	14	67%	6	50%
Technical Communication	Both	58%	21	9	2	1	3	5	24%	16	76%	10	83%
Business Writing	FMU	58%	21	8	4	2	1	5	24%	16	76%	8	67%
Advanced Tech Comm	FMU	56%	20	10	3	0	3	5	25%	15	75%	9	75%
Grant Writing	Neither	56%	20	8	7	0	1	8	40%	12	60%	7	58%
Multimedia Writing	Neither	56%	20	8	3	1	4	8	40%	12	80%	7	58%
Digital Content Development	Neither	53%	19	11	4	1	1	6	32%	13	68%	8	67%
The Rhetoric of New Media	Both**	53%	19	8	6	1	2	4	21%	15	79%	8	67%
Creative Writing	Both	53%	19	7	8	0	2	7	37%	12	63%	4	33%
Publication Layout & Design	Rowan	50%	18	12	4	0	2	6	33%	12	67%	6	50%
Copyediting	Neither	50%	18	10	3	1	4	4	22%	14	78%	7	58%
Web Design	Neither	50%	18	9	6	1	2	5	28%	13	72%	7	58%
Writing, Research, Technology	Rowan	50%	18	9	6	1	2	5	28%	13	72%	8	67%
Magazine Article Writing	Rowan	47%	17	10	5	1	3	8	47%	9	53%	4	33%
Professions in Writing Arts	Rowan	47%	17	6	8	1	4	8	47%	9	53%	5	42%
Writing for the Health Professions	FMU	44%	16	7	10	1	2	7	44%	9	56%	5	42%
Advanced Business Communication	FMU	42%	15	11	6	2	2	1	7%	14	93%	7	58%
Intercultural Communication	Neither	42%	15	8	8	2	3	5	33%	10	67%	7	58%
Medical Writing & Rhetoric	Rowan	42%	15	5	10	2	4	5	33%	10	67%	7	58%
Scientific Writing & Rhetoric	Rowan	36%	13	10	7	3	3	8	62%	5	38%	5	42%
Literature	Both	33%	12	11	10	0	3	6	50%	6	50%	5	42%
User Experience Design	Neither	33%	12	10	10	1	3	3	25%	9	75%	6	50%
Video Production for Tech Comm	Neither	28%	10	10	11	1	4	3	30%	7	70%	4	33%
Writing for Engineering	Neither	25%	9	9	12	2	4	3	33%	6	67%	4	33%
DITA/Structured Content Authoring	Neither	25%	9	6	12	5	4	1	11%	8	89%	5	42%

*Rowan has two editing courses, "Editing for Publication" and "Editing the Literary Journal"
**Rowan's New Media class is called "Introduction to New Media"

Appendix C: Majors Table

Program / Major Name	Existing @?	"Very Interesting" as % of Total	Very Interesting	Somewhat Interesting	Not Interesting	Neutral	Blanks	Rowan "Very"	% of "Very"	FMU "Very"	% of "Very"	Alumni "Very"	% of "Very"
Professional and Technical Writing	Neither	75%	27	6	2	0	1	8	30%	19	70%	11	92%
Technical and Professional Writing	Rowan	61%	22	10	2	0	2	6	27%	16	73%	8	67%
Professional Writing	FMU	58%	21	12	1	1	1	6	29%	15	71%	7	58%
Professional and Digital Writing	Neither	56%	20	11	3	1	1	5	25%	15	75%	8	67%
Writing & Publication Studies	Neither	53%	19	11	4	1	1	9	47%	10	53%	5	42%
Publishing & Writing for the Public	Neither	53%	19	11	4	1	1	7	37%	12	63%	6	50%
Technical Communication	Neither	50%	18	12	5	0	1	6	33%	12	67%	6	50%
Writing Arts	Rowan	50%	18	8	8	1	1	7	39%	11	61%	3	25%
Creative Writing	Both	47%	17	9	8	1	1	6	35%	11	65%	4	33%
Rhetoric & Writing Studies	Neither	42%	15	12	7	1	1	6	40%	9	60%	5	42%
Digital Writing & Rhetoric	Neither	39%	14	12	6	1	3	3	21%	11	79%	6	50%

Note. *The green shading indicates the highest-rated responses from each program.*

Contributors

Traci Austin is Associate Professor of Business Administration at Sam Houston State University (SHSU). In the College of Business Administration at SHSU, she teaches undergraduate business communication as well as managerial communication for its MBA program. She earned a doctorate in English with specialization in composition and rhetoric from the University of Nebraska-Lincoln. She holds master's degrees in instructional systems design and technology from SHSU and in linguistics from The Ohio State University. She came to university teaching after a career in higher education fundraising and resource development. She is a member of SHSU's Engaging Spaces committee, an initiative aimed at encouraging active learning on campus. The committee provides the funding, support, and motivation for faculty members to integrate evidence-based active-learning practices in their classrooms. With Lindsay Clark, she co-directs the College of Business Administration's communication lab, a space where students can, with faculty input, design, troubleshoot, and practice professional presentations and other oral communication activities. For the past two years, she has served as a Gallup-Certified Strengths Coach and has used the CliftonStrengths assessment in her undergraduate and graduate courses to assist students in career readiness and professional development. Her research interests include communication pedagogy, applied communication, communication technology, and multimodal and visual communication.

Jennifer Bay is the director of the professional writing program and Associate Professor of English at Purdue University, where she teaches undergraduate courses in the professional and technical writing major and graduate courses in professional writing, community engagement, and rhetorical theory. Her research focuses on community engagement and experiential learning, digital rhetorics, feminist rhetorics, and rhetorical theory. Her work has appeared in journals such as the *Journal of Business and Technical Communication*, *Rhetoric Society Quarterly*, *Technical Communication Quarterly*, *Computers & Composition*, *College English*, and *Programmatic Perspectives*, as well as in edited collections.

Margaret Becker received her B.S. in psychological sciences and B.A. in professional writing from Purdue University in May 2020. She works as the Strategy & Research Lead at ExpiWell, a Purdue-founded software company.

Lee-Ann Kastman Breuch is Professor and chair of the Department of Writing Studies at the University of Minnesota. Her research investigates rhetoric and digital writing in a variety of settings such as classrooms, professional organizations, websites, and social media, and she has published in journals including *Computers and Composition*, *Journal of Advanced Composition*, *Technical Communication*, *Journal of Business and Technical Communication*, and *Technical Communication Quarterly*. Her most recent book, *Involving the Audience: A Rhetorical Perspective of Using Social Media to Improve Websites* (ATTW Book Series with

Routledge), explores social media comments as a form of usability. Her previous books address issues of digital writing and online instruction, including *Virtual Peer Review: Teaching and Learning About Writing in Online Environments* (SUNY 2004). She is a graduate faculty member in the rhetoric and scientific and technical communication program, the literacy and rhetorical studies program, and the human factors and ergonomics program at University of Minnesota. She is a recipient of the Distinguished Teaching Award at University of Minnesota (2002) and teaches courses in technical communication, writing pedagogy, digital writing, research methods, and usability. With Ann Hill Duin, she is co-director of the Technical Communication Advisory Board[1] in the Department of Writing Studies, a group of working professionals who advise curriculum and experiential learning opportunities for writing studies students. She is past president of the national organization Council for Programs in Technical and Scientific Communication[2] (2016–2018) and current member of the Executive Board.

Kelli Cargile Cook is Professor and founding chair of the Professional Communication Department at Texas Tech University. Prior to this appointment, she served as Professor and director of technical communication and rhetoric at Texas Tech and as Associate Professor at Utah State University. Her scholarship focuses on online education, online training, program development and assessment, and user experience design. She co-edited two collections on online education in technical communication: *Online Education 2.0: Evolving, Adapting, and Reinventing Online Technical Communication* (2013) and *Online Education: Global Questions, Local Answers* (2005). She is a past president of the Association of Teachers of Technical Writing and of the Council for Programs in Technical and Scientific Communication.

Ashlie Clark is a 2020 graduate of Purdue University with a bachelor's degree in professional writing. She lives in Lafayette, Indiana, with her two cats and works at Ivy Tech's Crawfordsville site.

Lindsay Clark is Assistant Professor of Business Administration at Sam Houston State University (SHSU), where she teaches business communication courses at the undergraduate and graduate levels, including managerial communication and business ethics. She earned her Ph.D. in rhetoric and professional writing from Oklahoma State University while teaching technical writing, environmental writing, and multimodal composition courses. As the co-chair of the University Writing in the Disciplines Committee at SHSU, she works with faculty to develop and integrate writing assignments into discipline-based courses and to assess writing-enhanced courses across campus. To support students' communication and leadership development, she serves as a Gallup-Certified Strengths Coach and uses the CliftonStrengths assessment to mentor undergraduate

---

1. https://cla.umn.edu/writing-studies/alumni-friends/technical-communication-advisory-board.
2. https://cptsc.org/.

business majors and MBA students on career readiness and professional development. She also co-directs the College of Business Administration's communication lab, assisting students with conducting research, preparing for interviews, and designing and practicing professional presentations. She is a member of the Association for Writing Across Curriculum Mentoring Committee and serves as the secretary/treasurer for the Association for Business Communication, Southwest Region. Her research includes visual and multimodal communication, genre theory and pedagogy, and teaching writing in the disciplines.

Kate Crane is Associate Professor of English specializing in technical communication, rhetoric, and writing studies at Eastern Washington University (EWU). She currently serves as director of the M.A. in English with emphasis in rhetoric and technical communication and as director of the B.A. in English Studies. Her current research focuses on the user experience of curricular and programmatic design, and she has used this area of knowledge to help revamp programs at EWU. In addition to this work, she has worked on user-centered design and usability projects for EyeGuide and the University of North Texas Libraries' Portal to Texas History. She is the co-author, with Brian Still, of *Fundamentals of User-Centered Design: A Practical Approach* and has published in the *Journal of Technical Writing and Communication* and *Communication Design Quarterly*.

Ann Hill Duin is Professor of Writing Studies and Graduate-Professional Distinguished Teaching Professor at the University of Minnesota, receiving the 2021 Ronald S. Blicq Award for Distinction in Technical Communication from the IEEE Professional Communication Society and the 2021 J. R. Gould Award for Excellence in Teaching from the Society for Technical Communication. Her research and teaching focus on the impact of emerging technologies on technical communication, digital literacy, analytics, collaboration, and writing futures. She served 15 years in administrative roles including vice provost and associate vice president for information technology, where her commitment to shared leadership resulted in collective vision and action: a virtual university, a new college, business intelligence/academic analytics initiatives, and inter-institutional partnerships. She is published in many academic journals including *Computers and Composition*, *IEEE Transactions on Professional Communication*, *Technical Communication Quarterly*, and *Communication Design Quarterly*, and edited collections focused on user experience in augmented reality, workplace writing, and innovative teaching in technical communication. Her 2021 book, co-authored with Isabel Pedersen, *Writing Futures: Collaborative, Algorithmic, Autonomous*, prepares scholars and practitioners to investigate and plan for the social, digital literacy, and civic implications arising from emerging technologies. Her international collaboration includes research leadership in the Digital Life Institute at Ontario Tech University and mentorship of global virtual teams as part of Trans-Atlantic Pacific Partnership initiatives.

Gracemarie Mike Fillenwarth is Assistant Professor in the Department of Writing Arts at Rowan University, where she teaches courses in technical and professional writing and administers the department's internship program. She also serves as interim WAC coordinator. Her work, which focuses on writing program administration and pedagogy across a range of contexts, has been published in *Rhetoric Review*, *IEEE Transactions on Professional Communication*, and *Connexions*, as well as a number of edited collections. She is currently working on a book examining the administrative infrastructure of the Young Women's Christian Association's early 20th-century International Institute movement for immigrant women.

Laura Gonzales is Assistant Professor of Digital Writing and Cultural Rhetorics in the Department of English at the University of Florida. Her work threads together language diversity, community engagement, and technology design. She is the author of *Sites of Translation: What Multilinguals Can Teach Us About Digital Writing and Rhetoric*, which was awarded the 2016 Digital Rhetoric Collaborative Book Prize and the 2020 CCCC Advancement of Knowledge Award. She is the current chair of the Diversity Committee for the Council of Programs in Technical and Scientific Communication.

Emily Gresbrink earned her Masters of Science in Scientific and Technical Communication from the University of Minnesota–Twin Cities, with a minor in health informatics. She earned her Bachelors of Arts in Journalism from the University of Wisconsin–Eau Claire. Her research interests encompass technical communication, risk communication, public health crises, and the rhetoric of health and medicine. Her writing has been published in Programmatic Perspectives, and the Association for Computing Machinery. In addition to piloting the Technical Communication Advisory Board Mentoring Board at the University of Minnesota, she helped establish the graduate student professionalization subcommittee in the Council for Programs in Technical and Scientific Communication, and works closely with the mentoring and resources subcommittee and for the Online Writing Centers Association.

Tharon W. Howard served for more than a decade as the graduate program director of the Master of Arts in professional communication program at Clemson University. He also helped create and teaches in the rhetorics, communication, and information design doctoral program. He is a recipient of the Society for Technical Communication's (STC) J. R. Gould Award for Excellence in Teaching Technical Communication and the STC's Rainey Award for Excellence in Research. As director of the Clemson University Usability Testing Facility, he conducts sponsored research aimed at improving and creating new software interfaces, online document designs, and information architectures for clients including Pearson Higher Education, IBM, NCR Corp., and AT&T. For his work promoting the importance of usability in both industry and technical communication, Howard was awarded the Usability Professionals Association's Extraordinary Service Award. Howard is the series editor for the Routledge-ATTW Series on Technical and Professional Communication, and he created Clemson's Center for Electronic and Digital Publishing. He also designed and directed Clemson's Multimedia Authoring Teaching and Research Facility, where faculty and graduate students develop interactive, stand-alone multimodal productions and experiment with emerging instructional technologies, augmented reality devices, and interface designs. Howard is the author of *Design to Thrive: Creating Online Communities and Social Networks That Last* and *A Rhetoric of Electronic Communities*, co-author of *Visual Communication: A Writer's Guide*, and co-editor of *Electronic Networks: Crossing Boundaries and Creating Communities*. Howard received his doctoral degree in rhetoric and composition from Purdue University in 1992.

Sarah Martin is a faculty instructor in the Department of Professional Communication at Texas Tech University. She teaches business communication courses and is an experienced researcher and consultant with diverse expertise in government and Fortune 500 environments. Her research interests include business and technical communication, user experience (UX), and user-centered design (UCD). She holds a Ph.D. in technical communication and rhetoric from Texas Tech University and an MBA from the Naval Postgraduate School.

Emily Mast graduated from Purdue University with a B.A. in professional writing, a minor in business economics, and an Honors College diploma in December 2020.

Christine Masters-Wheeler is Assistant Professor in the Department of English, Modern Languages, and Philosophy at Francis Marion University, where she coordinates the professional writing program, supervises internships, teaches undergraduate writing courses, and facilitates an honors service symposium. Her work has appeared in the edited collection *Excellence, Innovation and Ingenuity in Honors Education* and in *Ada: A Journal of Gender, New Media, and Technology*.

Beau Pihlaja is Assistant Professor at Texas Tech University in the technical communication and rhetoric program in the Department of English. His research focuses on intercultural technical and professional communication, digitally mediated rhetoric, and the materiality of everyday rhetorics. His recent work has appeared in *Written Communication* and *Technical Communication Quarterly*. He regularly teaches courses on global technical communication, research methods, and everyday rhetorics/technical communication.

Brendan Robb, from Northern Michigan, is a graduate of Purdue University's professional writing program.

Luke Thominet is Assistant Professor of Writing and Rhetoric at Florida International University, where he teaches courses in technical communication, rhetorical theory, document design, and academic writing, among other topics. His research interests include technical communication, user experience, design thinking, and academic institutional discourse. His recent projects have examined community participation in user experience design during video game development, the rhetorical construction of academic job market correspondence, team-based learning in technical communication courses, and the voice of community members on institutional review boards. His work has appeared in the edited collection *Effective Teaching of Technical Communication*, and in several journals, including *The Journal of Business and Technical Communication, Communication Design Quarterly*, and *Technical Communication Quarterly*.

Korbyn Torres is a 2020 Purdue University graduate with a degree in English. She is currently pursuing work opportunities in editing/publishing or digital communications.

Josephine Walwema is a teaching professor at the University of Washington, Seattle. Her research focuses on rhetoric, global technical communication, and business and professional communication, and has been published in *Technical Communication Quarterly, Technical Communication, Connexions*, and *IEEE Transactions on Professional Communication*.

Mark Zachry is Professor of Human-Centered Design and Engineering at the University of Washington (UW). In addition to teaching the capstone course for undergraduates in his department, he teaches courses in user research techniques, user-centered design, and theoretical foundations of human-centered design. At UW, he directs the Communicative Practices in Virtual Workspaces Lab. He is a Fellow of the Association of Teachers of Technical Writing (ATTW) and an Associate Fellow of the Society for Technical Communication (STC). At UW, he is director of the individual interdisciplinary Ph.D. program.

www.ingramcontent.com/pod-product-compliance
Lightning Source LLC
Chambersburg PA
CBHW071229070526
44583CB00017B/2112